TOP
10
OF FILM
RUSSELL ASH

DK

DK

LONDON, NEW YORK,
MUNICH, MELBOURNE, DELHI

DK LONDON

SENIOR EDITOR Neil Lockley
SENIOR ART EDITOR Kevin Ryan
DTP DESIGNER Rajen Shah
PRODUCTION CONTROLLER
Heather Hughes
MANAGING EDITORS Adèle Hayward,
Sharon Lucas
MANAGING ART EDITORS Marianne Markham,
Karen Self
CATEGORY PUBLISHER Stephanie Jackson

DK DELHI

PROJECT EDITOR Ranjana Saklani
PROJECT ART EDITOR Shefali Upadhyay
DTP DESIGNERS Rajesh Chibber,
Balwant Singh
MANAGING ART EDITOR Aparna Sharma

Published in Great Britain in 2003 by Dorling Kindersley,
80 Strand, London WC2R ORL

A Penguin Ccompany

2 4 6 8 10 9 7 5 3 1
Copyright © 2003 Dorling Kindersley Limited
Text copyright © 2003 Russell Ash

A CIP catalogue record of this book is available
from the British Library.

ISBN 14053 00507

Reproduction by Media Development Printing Ltd., UK
Printed and Bound by Neografia, Slovakia

See our complete catalogue at
www.dk.com

CONTENTS

Along with other books of lists, I have been compiling *The Top 10 of Everything* annually for 15 years, and am here developing one of its most popular sections into an entirely new book. I should clarify that this is not strictly a book of "10 Bests". Unless stated otherwise, the lists are ranked by films' income, and so are a measure of public taste as reflected by the numbers of people who bought tickets to see them. Critical opinion – of professional critics, industry specialists, and public polls – is represented by Top 10s of award winners.

MEASURES OF SUCCESS

For the years prior to the 1960s, the Top 10 lists that present the commercial success of various films are based on the then standard of US rental income – the amount paid by cinemas to distributors. From then onwards, actual US box office receipts increasingly became the measure of relative success. Since about 1986, data on non-US income too has been used to arrive at the overall rankings – which may then differ from those based, say, exclusively on US revenue. Most of a film's income is earned in the early weeks of its release – hence the great importance attached to its opening weekend. Certain films, such as the *Harry Potter* and *Lord of the Rings* franchises, are released late in the year, but continue to earn well into the next year and even beyond, with per-film totals cumulative over time. These do not generally include subsidiary income, such as from TV broadcasts, merchandising, video and DVD release.

FACTS AND FIGURES

Rather than swamp every list with a sea of figures, the precise total income – which varies continuously – is included only in those instances where it provides a meaningful annexe to the ranking. Figures are usually given in US dollars – the virtual *lingua franca* of the movie business – but for certain country-specific lists, local currencies are given. It's worth noting that not all countries report box office figures, and many provide only admission numbers.

There are arguments as to whether two further factors should be included in arriving at these rankings, but which in most instances are not. The first is inflation:

Silent Success
The original silent version of *Ben-Hur* (1925), with Ramon Novarro in the title role, had a then record budget of $3.9 million and made $9 million at the US box office.

but any index linking would have to assume that a film earned 100 per cent of its total in the same place at the same time, which would be a false premise, since inflation varies over time and from country to country, as do ticket prices. The second would be to take account of budgets: except where otherwise noted, I follow the industry's standard and base comparative rankings on actual income, irrespective of profitability, but indicate notable "flops", as film terminology goes.

REACHING FOR THE STARS

I have tried to cover many of the most popular and iconic stars, along with the names of the characters they played (though cameo and voice-only roles are generally excluded), as well as multifarious genres and sub-genres, and award winners. I have also explored such quirky byways as the worst disasters at cinemas (those that burned down, rather than showed bad films), or films with the most extras. However, in an attempt to span the entire history of cinema from the silent era to the present, I apologize if your favourite films, actors, or directors are not featured – there are thousands of potential candidates who could not be squeezed into this debut volume.

Deadlines are as much a bugbear of those who write about films as those who make them. In most instances, my cut-off point had to be early 2003 – hence the latest *Matrix* films and other summer blockbusters regrettably could not be included, but will be next time around, for which your suggestions and corrections will be welcomed. Please write to me c/o the publishers, or e-mail me direct at: ash@pavilion.co.uk

Worldwide Web
Based on a 1962 comic book, *Spider-Man* (2002) was made with a $139-million budget but earned over $800 million worldwide.

Invented just over 100 years ago – at about the same time as the car, and just before the aeroplane – cinema has had a global impact of similar magnitude. The studios, from the great names of the past to the independents of the modern era, are components of an international business that employs countless people, generates vast incomes, and provides the content of a high proportion of the world's TV programmes, video, and DVD releases. Despite the rise of alternative media, regular cinema-going remains a significant cultural activity for a large segment of the planet's population – 1.64 billion cinema tickets were sold in the US in 2002 – while the language of cinema has become a world language, and its stars among the most recognized, revered – and occasionally reviled – of all celebrities. As the Top 10 lists show, there's no business like show business.

Film – Mightier Than the Sword
Arnold Schwarzenegger as *Conan the Barbarian* (1982). The fantasy ingredient of such films is just one of the factors that have enabled the cinema to prosper as a universally popular medium.

TOP 10 FILM-PRODUCING COUNTRIES (PER MILLION PEOPLE)

	COUNTRY	FILMS PRODUCED IN 2000
1	Hong Kong *	27.78
2	Iceland	21.21
3	Luxembourg	6.81
4	Ireland	5.80
5	Denmark	4.47
6	Switzerland	4.33
7	Norway	3.13
8	Austria	2.92
9	France	2.88
10	USA	2.76

Source: *Screen Digest*

* Hong Kong no longer has the status of a country, but for some statistical purposes it is still considered as such, not least because its commercial importance, especially as a leading film producer, sets it apart from mainland China, of which it is now a part.

Duel Role

James K. Hackett took the parts of both Rudolf Rassendyll and King Rudolf of Ruritania in the earliest of six film versions of *The Prisoner of Zenda*, based on Anthony Hope's bestselling novel.

Did you know?

The first feature film made in India was the 4-reel *Raja Harishchandra*, directed by Dadasaheb (Dhundiraj Govind) Phalke, which opened on 3 May 1913 at the Coronation Cinematograph, Bombay.

TOP 10 COUNTRIES SPENDING THE MOST PER FILM PRODUCED

	COUNTRY	AVERAGE INVESTMENT PER FILM IN 2000 ($)
1	USA	13,630,000
2	UK	9,430,000
3	Australia	4,410,000
4	France	4,340,000
5	Japan	4,270,000
6	Ireland	4,260,000
7	Germany	4,250,000
8	New Zealand	4,000,000
9	Argentina	3,300,000
10	Netherlands	3,220,000

Source: *Screen Digest*

TOP 10 FILM-PRODUCING COUNTRIES

	COUNTRY	FILMS PRODUCED IN 2000
1	India	855
2	USA	762
3	Japan	282
4	Hong Kong	185
5	France	171
6 =	Italy	103
=	Philippines	103
8	Bangladesh	100
9	Spain	98
10 =	Germany	90
=	UK	90

Source: *Screen Digest*

THE 10 FIRST FEATURE FILMS IN THE US

	FILM	REELS	US RELEASE
1	Oliver Twist	5	20 May 1912
2	Richard III	5	15 Oct 1912
3	From the Manger to the Cross	5	17 Oct 1912
4	Cleopatra	6	13 Nov 1912
5	The Adventures of Lieutenant Petrosino *	4	Nov 1912
6	One Hundred Years of Mormonism	5	3 Feb 1913
7	The Prisoner of Zenda	4	18 Feb 1913
8	Hiawatha *	4	Mar 1913
9	The Battle of Gettysburg	5	1 Jun 1913
10	The Seed of the Fathers	6	10 Jul 1913

* Precise release dates unknown

A feature film either has a running time of more than an hour or comprises more than 3,000 ft (914 m) of film. In the pioneer era, a reel of 35-mm film contained about 1,000 ft (305 m), run at around 60 ft (18 m) per minute, hence a four-reel film had a running time of just over an hour. Cecil B. DeMille's *The Squaw Man* (6 reels, 15 February 1914) was the first feature made in Hollywood while *The Story of the Kelly Gang* (Australia, 26 December 1906) is considered the world's first feature.

THE 10 FIRST FEATURE FILMS IN THE UK

	FILM	REELS	UK RELEASE*
1	Oliver Twist	4	Aug 1912
2	Lorna Doone	5	Dec 1912
3	East Lynne	6	May 1913
4 =	The Battle of Waterloo	5	Jul 1913
=	Ivanhoe	6	Jul 1913
=	A Message from Mars	4	Jul 1913
7	David Copperfield	8	Aug 1913
8 =	A Cigarette-Maker's Romance	4	Sep 1913
=	The House of Temperley	5	Sep 1913
=	King Charles	4	Sep 1913

* Precise release dates unknown

The first feature film released in the UK was coincidentally adapted from the same Charles Dickens novel as the first in the US. Directed by Thomas Bentley, it eccentrically cast an actress, Ivy Millais, as Oliver Twist. Many pioneer feature films were also adaptations of stage productions: *A Message from Mars* was taken from a play by Richard Ganthony, and *The House of Temperley* from a play by Sherlock Holmes author Sir Arthur Conan Doyle – which he in turn had adapted from his own novel, *Rodney Stone*.

TOP 10 OVERSEAS SETTINGS FOR HOLLYWOOD FILMS

	COUNTRY	FILMS*
1	UK	900
2	France	830
3	Canada	418
4	Mexico	259
5	Italy	199
6	Germany	170
7	Russia	156
8	China	128
9	Spain	115
10	India	96

* 1912–99
Source: Patrick Robertson, *Film Facts* (2001)

These are the foremost of 129 individual countries depicted in a total of 4,805 feature films surveyed in the period 1912–99. In the early years of Hollywood, overseas shooting was comparatively rare, so many settings were studio replicas rather than actual locations.

TOP 10 YEARS FOR THE MOST US FEATURE FILM RELEASES

	YEAR	FILMS RELEASED
1	1921	854
2	1918	841
3	1928	820
4	1920	797
5	1937	778
6	1938	769
7	1935	766
8	1939	761
9	1922	748
10	1927	743

The greatest output of feature films occurred in the 1920s and 1930s, often regarded as Hollywood's "Golden Years". The highest post-War year was 1951, with 654 releases, and 1978 the lowest, with 354. Few recent years have seen production exceed 500, with 2002's total reaching 467.

TOP 10 DISTRIBUTORS BY BOX OFFICE REVENUE

	STUDIO	FILMS	GROSS IN 2002 ($)
1	Sony	27	1,453,412,930
2	Buena Vista	28	1,179,299,915
3	Warner Bros.	32	1,050,049,624
4	Fox	22	917,506,553
5	Universal	19	864,833,008
6	New Line	12	839,457,765
7	Paramount	40	687,962,410
8	Dreamworks	7	464,424,230
9	MGM/ United Artists	23	360,248,650
10	Miramax	37	336,191,859

In 2002, the revenue of all US distributors was $9,519,600,000, of which the Top 10 made $8,153,386,944, equivalent to 86 per cent of the total and an average gross of $33 million per film.

Vietnam, England
Despite being set in Vietnam, the actual shooting of Stanley Kubrick's *Full Metal Jacket* (1987) took place in studios and on location in England.

10 TOP CINEMAS & AUDIENCES

TOP 10 YEARS FOR CINEMA ADMISSIONS IN THE US *

	YEAR	FILMS	BOX OFFICE GROSS ($)	ADMISSIONS
1	1946	400	1,692,000,000	4,067,300,000
2	1947	426	1,594,000,000	3,664,400,000
3	1948	444	1,506,000,000	3,422,700,000
4	1949	490	1,448,000,000	3,168,500,000
5	1950	483	1,379,000,000	3,017,500,000
6	1951	433	1,332,000,000	2,840,100,000
7	1952	389	1,325,000,000	2,777,700,000
8	1953	404	1,339,000,000	2,630,600,000
9	1954	369	1,251,000,000	2,270,400,000
10	1955	319	1,204,000,000	2,072,300,000

* 1946–present

Source: Motion Picture Association of America

The year 1955 was the last on record when US movie attendance was greater than two billion. From 1956, admissions continued to decline (until 1963, when there was a slight increase), in 1971 reaching a low of 820,300,000. Since 1991, admissions have increased each year, in 2002 hitting 1,639,300,000 – a figure last exceeded in 1957.

TOP 10 YEARS FOR CINEMA ADMISSIONS IN THE UK

	YEAR	ADMISSIONS
1	1946	1,635,000,000
2	1945	1,585,000,000
3	1944	1,575,000,000
4	1943	1,541,000,000
5	1948	1,514,000,000
6	1942	1,494,000,000
7	1947	1,462,000,000
8	1949	1,430,000,000
9	1950	1,395.800,000
10	1951	1,365,000,000

When they were first recorded in 1933, there were 903 million cinema admissions in the UK. The first post-War year, 1946, retains the record for the highest number of cinema admissions of all time. Even allowing for present day access to television, video, and other alternatives, these figures are especially remarkable, since the population in 1946 was estimated at 48,016,000 or 80 per cent that in 2002 (59,987,000), but was equivalent to 34 annual visits per person, compared with fewer than three today.

TOP 10 COUNTRIES WITH THE MOST CINEMA ADMISSIONS

	COUNTRY	ADMISSIONS IN 2002
1	India *	2,800,000,000
2	USA	1,639,300,000
3	France	185,100,000
4	UK	176,000,000
5	Germany	163,900,000
6	Japan	160,800,000
7	Mexico	154,000,000
8	Spain	134,700,000
9	Canada *	119,620,000
10	South Korea	107,000,000

* 2001

Source: Screen International/Screen Digest

TOP 10 COUNTRIES BY BOX OFFICE REVENUE

	COUNTRY	ESTIMATED GROSS IN 2002 ($)
1	USA	9,519,600,000
2	Japan	1,700,000,000
3	UK	1,300,000,000
4	France	1,040,000,000
5	Germany	1,000,000,000
6	Spain	663,000,000
7	Italy	564,600,000
8	South Korea	530,000,000
9	Australia	499,900,000
10	Mexico	483,000,000

Source: Screen International

TOP 10 COUNTRIES WITH THE MOST EXPENSIVE CINEMA TICKETS

	COUNTRY	AVERAGE TICKET ($)
1	Japan	10.08
2	Switzerland	8.13
3	Taiwan	7.84
4	Iceland	6.99
5	Sweden	6.86
6	UK	6.64
7	Denmark	6.51
8	Norway	6.14
9	Finland	5.98
10	Israel	5.70

Source: *Screen Digest*
The USA falls just outside this list, at number 11, with an average ticket price of $5.66.

TOP 10 COUNTRIES WITH THE CHEAPEST CINEMA TICKETS

	COUNTRY	AVERAGE TICKET ($)
1	India	0.21
2	Romania	0.44
3	Philippines	0.69
4	Egypt	0.74
5	Colombia	1.18
6	Russia	1.37
7	Slovakia	1.46
8	Lithuania	1.70
9	South Africa	1.82
10	Bulgaria	1.83

Source: *Screen Digest*
These comparatively low prices (India's represents just two per cent of those in Japan) explain why, despite often high attendance figures, certain countries have relatively little impact on the overseas income of major movies.

TOP 10 COUNTRIES WITH THE MOST CINEMA SCREENS

	COUNTRY	SCREENS IN 2001
1	China	65,500
2	USA	36,764
3	India	11,962
4	France	5,236
5	Germany	4,792
6	Spain	3,770
7	UK	3,248
8	Italy	3,050
9	Canada	2,900
10	Japan	2,585

Source: *Screen Digest*

TOP 10 CINEMA-GOING COUNTRIES

	COUNTRY	AVERAGE ADMISSIONS PER CAPITA*
1	USA	5.58
2	Iceland	5.54
3	Australia	5.05
4	Singapore	4.72
5	Ireland	4.36
6	New Zealand †	4.23
7	Canada	3.99
8	Spain	3.74
9	Luxembourg	3.35
10	Hong Kong #	3.30

* 2001
† 2000
# Overall China figure 0.09 (2000)
India and UK follow with admission figures of 2.93 and 2.67 respectively.
Source: *Screen Digest*

THE 10 WORST CINEMA DISASTERS

	LOCATION/DATE	INCIDENT	NO. KILLED
1	Yili, Xinjiang, China/18 Feb 1977	Cinema fire	694
2	Dandong (formerly Antung) Liaoning, China/13 Feb 1937	Cinema fire	658
3	Abadan, Iran/22 Aug 1978	Cinema fire (arson by extremists during screening of *Gavaznha* (*The Deer*; 1976)	422
4	Karamay, China/8 Dec 1994	Cinema fire; dead include 288 children	324
5	Amude, Syria/13 Nov 1960	Cinema fire and stampede caused by blazing film	152
6 =	San Juan, Puerto Rico/20 Jun 1919	Cinema fire/panic in the Mayaguez Theater	150
=	Igolkino, Russia/12 Mar 1929	Cinema fire caused by ignition of film *The Wind*	150
8	Jilin (formerly Kirin), China/ 20 Mar 1930	Cinema fire	130
9	Seoul, South Korea/10 Mar 1930	Cinema fire and panic	104
10	Izmir (formerly Smyrna), Turkey/ 21 Sep 1924	Cinema fire	104

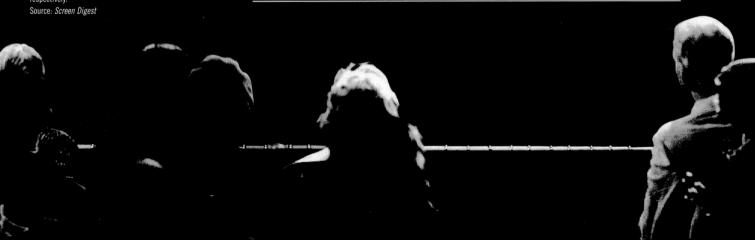

TOP 10 ARTISAN FILMS

	FILM*	YEAR
1	The Blair Witch Project	1999
2	The Ninth Gate	1999
3	Book of Shadows: Blair Witch 2	2000
4	National Lampoon's Van Wilder	2002
5	Stir of Echoes	1999
6	Jonah: A VeggieTales Movie *	2002
7	Dr. T & the Women	2000
8	Buena Vista Social Club †	1999
9	Black Mask	1996
10	Boat Trip	1998

* Animated
† Documentary

Under the Hollywood studio system, a small group of studios controlled the movie industry; they owned all production facilities and acted as producers, distributors, and exhibitors. Although some of the original studios no longer exist, as a result of mergers and takeovers most of the leading names are now components of large global media conglomerates, while there are also some newer independent studios. Today the studios are mainly financial and distribution organizations, with the actual production undertaken under their aegis by independent production companies. The films listed here represent the Top 10 productions distributed by each of the major studios (based on worldwide revenue), irrespective of production company(ies).

I'll be Back

Made by Carolco Pictures and distributed by TriStar/Columbia, *Terminator 2: Judgment Day* – the sequel to an Orion film – typifies the complex nature of today's studio structure.

TOP 10 DIMENSION FILMS

	FILM	YEAR
1	Scary Movie	2000
2	Scream	1996
3	Scream 2	1997
4	Scream 3	2000
5	Spy Kids	2001
6	Scary Movie 2	2001
7	Spy Kids 2: The Island of Lost Dreams	2002
8	Halloween H20: 20 Years Later	1998
9	The Faculty	1998
10	From Dusk Till Dawn	1996

Dimension, the "genre" subsidiary of Miramax, has been making mainly sci-fi and horror films since about 1993.

TOP 10 BUENA VISTA FILMS

	FILM*	YEAR
1	The Sixth Sense	1999
2	Armageddon	1998
3	Pretty Woman	1990
4	Pearl Harbor	2001
5	Signs	2002
6	Who Framed Roger Rabbit	1988
7	The Rock	1996
8	Ransom	1996
9	Unbreakable	2000
10	Enemy of the State	1998

* Excluding animated Disney features

Following Walt Disney's death in 1966, a new management team launched the company in novel directions, establishing Touchstone Pictures, a production company concentrating on films aimed at a more adult audience, such as the highly successful *Pretty Woman* (1990), with Buena Vista the distributor for these and for Disney's animated films.

TOP 10 COLUMBIA FILMS*

	FILM	YEAR
1	Spider-Man	2002
2	Men in Black	1997
3	Terminator 2: Judgment Day	1991
4	Men in Black II	2002
5	Godzilla	1998
6	Basic Instinct	1992
7	Close Encounters of the Third Kind	1977
8	Air Force One	1997
9	As Good as It Gets	1997
10	Hook	1991

* Including Sony and TriStar

Founded in 1924 by Harry Cohn and his brother Jack, Columbia was built up into a studio to rival the established giants MGM and Paramount. In 1934, Frank Capra's *It Happened One Night* swept the board, unprecedentedly winning "Best Picture", "Best Director", "Best Actor", and "Best Actress" Oscars. In subsequent years, stars of the box office appeal of Rita Hayworth and films ranging from successful major productions such as *Lost Horizon* (1937) and *The Jolson Story* (1946) to serials including *Batman*, consolidated Columbia's commercial success. In the 1950s – the decade in which both Cohn brothers died – Columbia's award-winning and successful films included *The Bridge on the River Kwai* (1957), *On the Waterfront* (1954), and *From Here to Eternity* (1953). The 1960s brought such classics as *Lawrence of Arabia* (1962) and *A Man For All Seasons* (1966), and the hugely profitable Columbia-distributed *Easy Rider* (1969). After an uneasy period in the 1970s, Columbia was taken over by Coca-Cola, and during the 1980s produced many hits, including *Ghostbusters* (1984). Following a two-year stint under the control of English producer David Puttnam, Columbia took over TriStar Pictures before itself being acquired by the Sony Corporation. Every one of the films in this Top 10 earned more than $300 million worldwide.

	FILM	YEAR
1	Rain Man	1988
2	Die Another Day	2002
3	Gone With the Wind	1939
4	The World Is Not Enough	1999
5	GoldenEye	1995
6	Hannibal	2001
7	Tomorrow Never Dies	1997
8	Rocky IV	1985
9	Stargate	1994
10	The Birdcage	1996

Metro Goldwyn Mayer, founded in 1924, established its pre-eminence in the 1930s and 1940s with the success of *Gone With the Wind* and *The Wizard of Oz* (both 1939), contracts with stars such as Greta Garbo, Spencer Tracy, and Clark Gable (the studio's motto was "more stars than there are in heaven"), and productions that ranged from the *Tarzan* series to Tom and Jerry cartoons. After the 1951 departure of its head, Louis B. Mayer, MGM experienced mixed fortunes, with only occasional hits – such as *Ben-Hur* (1959) and *Doctor Zhivago* (1965). After the 1969 acquisition of the company by airline tycoon Kirk Kerkorian, its film-making activities were temporarily abandoned until 1981, when it acquired United Artists and was relaunched, with the *James Bond* films the studio's principal money-makers.

	FILM*	YEAR
1	Shakespeare in Love	1998
2	Bridget Jones's Diary	2001
3	Chicago	2002
4	The English Patient	1996
5	Life Is Beautiful (La Vita è bella)	1998
6	Good Will Hunting	1997
7	Pulp Fiction	1994
8	Gangs of New York	2002
9	Chocolat	2000
10	Amélie	2001

* Excluding Dimension films

Founded in 1979 by brothers Harvey and Bob Weinstein, and named after their parents Miriam and Max, Miramax is a production and distribution company that has been part of the Walt Disney Company since 1993. It continues to operate as a major force in achieving both critical acclaim and commercial success for releases that might otherwise have been disregarded as "art" films. Its unrivalled place among independents has won Miramax 194 Oscar nominations in all categories, with 48 wins, including three "Best Pictures".

	FILM	YEAR
1	Lord of the Rings: The Two Towers	2002
2	Lord of the Rings: The Fellowship of the Ring	2001
3	Se7en	1995
4	Rush Hour 2	2001
5	The Mask	1994
6	Austin Powers: The Spy Who Shagged Me	1999
7	Austin Powers in Goldmember	2002
8	Rush Hour	1998
9	Dumb & Dumber	1994
10	Teenage Mutant Ninja Turtles	1990

Bridget's Big Earner

Bridget Jones's Diary is one of Miramax's highest-earning films, having grossed a total of over $280 million at the worldwide box office.

TOP 10 ORION FILMS

	FILM	YEAR
1	Dances With Wolves	1990
2	The Silence of the Lambs	1991
3	The Addams Family	1991
4	Platoon	1986
5	Arthur	1981
6	Back to School	1986
7	The Terminator	1984
8	10	1979
9	Addams Family Values	1993
10	Throw Momma From the Train	1987

Orion Pictures Corporation was founded in 1978 by a group of executives who broke away from United Artists (represented in its logo, which depicts the five stars in the constellation of Orion). The company was sold to MGM in 1997.

Did you know?

Universal Studios opened on 15 March 1915 on a former chicken farm. The world's largest studio, it was also the first to open to the public – until the arrival of talkies made it impossible to admit chattering visitors to the sets.

TOP 10 SONY CLASSICS FILMS

	FILM	YEAR
1	Crouching Tiger, Hidden Dragon	2000
2	Talk to Her	2002
3	Across the Sea of Time *	1995
4	Howards End	1992
5	Wings of Courage	1995
6	Thrill Ride: The Science of Fun *	1997
7	Cirque du Soleil – Journey of Man *	2000
8	All About My Mother	1999
9	Central Station	1998
10	Lone Star	1996

* Documentary

Founded in 1992, Sony Pictures Classics is an autonomous company within Sony Picture Entertainment that acquires, produces, and distributes independent films from the US and around the world. Although often regarded as "art" films, in contrast to more commercial releases, *Crouching Tiger, Hidden Dragon* made more than $200 million globally and won the "Best Foreign Language" Oscar.

TOP 10 PARAMOUNT FILMS

	FILM	YEAR
1	Titanic	1997
2	Forrest Gump	1994
3	Mission: Impossible 2	2000
4	Ghost	1990
5	Indiana Jones and the Last Crusade	1989
6	Mission: Impossible	1996
7	Raiders of the Lost Ark	1981
8	Grease	1978
9	What Women Want	2000
10	Deep Impact	1998

Paramount Pictures, which owes its origin in 1912 to Adolph Zukor's Famous Players Film Company, emerged following a series of mergers in the 1920s. With names such as Mae West, Bing Crosby and Bob Hope, and Cecil B. DeMille, it entered a golden age in the 1930s and 1940s. *The Godfather* relaunched the studio's fortunes in the 1970s, with *Grease*, *Saturday Night Fever*, Eddie Murphy films, and the *Star Trek* and *Indiana Jones* series reinforcing its position.

TOP 10 20th CENTURY-FOX FILMS

	FILM	YEAR
1	Star Wars: Episode I – The Phantom Menace	1999
2	Independence Day	1996
3	Star Wars: Episode IV – A New Hope	1977
4	Star Wars: Episode II – Attack of the Clones	2002
5	Star Wars: Episode VI – Return of the Jedi	1983
6	Home Alone	1990
7	Star Wars: Episode V – The Empire Strikes Back	1980
8	Cast Away	2000
9	Mrs. Doubtfire	1993
10	Ice Age *	2002

* Animated

William Fox, a New York nickelodeon owner, founded a film production company in 1912, and at his California studios created a number of popular films. With the coming of sound he pioneered its use, especially through the medium of Fox Movietone newsreels. The company was merged with 20th Century Pictures in 1935, and under the control of Darryl F. Zanuck and Joseph M. Schenck achieved some of its greatest successes in the 1940s, especially a series of musicals starring Betty Grable. The 1950s and 1960s were less lucrative, however, and despite the box office success of *The Sound of Music* (1965), the studio suffered a number of setbacks, including the failure of the colossally expensive *Cleopatra* (1963). Its return to prosperity began in the 1970s with *The French Connection* (1971) and was consolidated by the outstanding achievement of *Star Wars* (1977) and its successors. In 1985, 20th Century-Fox was acquired by Rupert Murdoch, thereby permitting Fox television stations to show the company's productions. With the end of the 20th century, the studio became known simply as Fox. Such is the success of its recent blockbusters that each of its Top 10 has made in excess of $350 million.

TOP 10 RKO FILMS

	FILM	YEAR
1	Bambi *	1942
2	Snow White and the Seven Dwarfs *	1937
3	Cinderella *	1950
4	Song of the South *	1946
5	The Best Years of Our Lives	1946
6	The Bells of St. Mary's	1945
7	The Conqueror	1956
8	Hans Christian Andersen	1952
9	The Bachelor and the Bobby-Soxer	1947
10	Notorious	1946

* Original distributor prior to Disney

Following a series of company mergers in the early years of cinema, RKO (Radio-Keith-Orpheum) emerged in 1928. It became famous for such films as *King Kong* (1933) and *Citizen Kane* (1941) and for its Fred Astaire and Ginger Rogers musicals. RKO was acquired by eccentric millionaire Howard Hughes 20 years later, but after he sold it, the company abandoned making films in favour of television broadcasting.

TOP 10 UNITED ARTISTS FILMS

	FILM*	YEAR
1	Moonraker	1979
2	The Spy Who Loved Me	1977
3	Thunderball	1965
4	Live and Let Die	1973
5	Goldfinger	1964
6	Rocky	1976
7	Diamonds Are Forever	1971
8	One Flew Over the Cuckoo's Nest	1975
9	You Only Live Twice	1967
10	The Man With the Golden Gun	1974

* Excluding films made since MGM merger
United Artists was formed in 1919 by actors including Charlie Chaplin and Douglas Fairbanks and director D.W. Griffith to provide an independent means of producing and distributing their films. It never actually owned a studio, but rented production facilities. After many vicissitudes, and a successful run in the 1970s with the consistently successful *James Bond* films, the global earnings of which ensure they dominate in this list, it was merged with MGM in 1981.

TOP 10 UNIVERSAL FILMS

	FILM	YEAR
1	Jurassic Park	1993
2	E.T. the Extra-Terrestrial	1982
3	The Lost World: Jurassic Park	1997
4	Jaws	1975
5	The Mummy Returns	2001
6	The Mummy	1999
7	Jurassic Park III	2001
8	Notting Hill	1999
9	The Flintstones	1994
10	Apollo 13	1995

Universal Pictures, founded in 1912 by Carl Laemmle, went through a precarious period in the 1930s, its few commercial hits coming from W.C. Fields and Abbott and Costello comedies, the *Flash Gordon* serial, and *Woody Woodpecker* cartoons. The company changed hands in 1936 and again 1952, when it was acquired by Decca Records. In 1962 it was sold to MCA, which developed its strengths as a TV production company and inaugurated the organized studio tours that became a major tourist attraction in the USA. Films from artists such as Alfred Hitchcock and Clint Eastwood were followed by the mega-successful *Jaws* and its successors. Steven Spielberg and George Lucas have provided the studio with some all-time blockbusters – all those in the Top 10 have earned upwards of $350 million worldwide.

TOP 10 WARNER BROS. FILMS

	FILM	YEAR
1	Harry Potter and the Sorcerer's Stone	2001
2	Harry Potter and the Chamber of Secrets	2002
3	Twister	1996
4	Ocean's Eleven	2001
5	The Matrix	1999
6	Batman	1989
7	The Bodyguard	1992
8	Robin Hood: Prince of Thieves	1991
9	The Fugitive	1993
10	Batman Forever	1995

It was the coming of sound that launched the newly formed Warner Bros. into its place in cinema history with *The Jazz Singer* (1927), its best-known early production. In the 1940s it was a major force in the field of animation with *Bugs Bunny* and other cartoons. In the 1960s it focused on TV production, and in the 1970s, following a series of takeovers, it embarked on an era of notable success that began with *The Exorcist* (1973). At the time that *Batman* became the then eighth highest-earning film ever, the company merged with Time, Inc. to become a component of the media empire AOL Time Warner. All films in the Top 10 have earned $330 million or more.

Jaws of Victory
Once the highest-earning film of all time, Universal Pictures' *Jaws* heralded the era of the blockbuster movie and launched the directing career of Steven Spielberg.

TOP 10 BESTSELLING DVDs IN THE US

	FILM	YEAR*	SALES IN RELEASE YEAR ($)
1	The Lord of the Rings: The Fellowship of the Ring	2002	257,300,000
2	Spider-Man	2002	215,300,000
3	Monsters, Inc.	2002	202,000,000
4	Harry Potter and the Sorcerer's Stone	2002	166,700,000
5	Shrek	2001	157,000,000
6	Star Wars: Episode II – Attack of the Clones	2002	144,800,000
7	Pearl Harbor	2001	144,000,000
8	The Fast and the Furious	2002	132,000,000
9	Ice Age	2002	124,800,000
10	Lilo & Stitch	2002	116,100,000

* Of DVD release

The surge of DVD sales in 2002 far eclipsed those of most earlier years: *Gladiator* was the bestselling DVD of 2000 with sales of $63.1 million, which would only just have merited a place in the Top 20 of 2002.

TOP 10 FILMS THAT BECAME LIVE-ACTION TV SERIES

	FILM/TV SERIES (IF DIFFERENT)	FILM YEAR	TV SERIES YEAR
1	My Big Fat Greek Wedding (My Big Fat Greek Life)	2002	2003
2	Look Who's Talking (Baby Talk)	1989	1991
3	Stargate (Stargate SG-1)	1994	1997
4	Dangerous Minds	1995	1996
5	Animal House (Delta House)	1978	1979
6	9 to 5	1980	1982
7	M*A*S*H	1970	1972
8	Clueless	1995	1996
9	Working Girl	1988	1990
10	The Odd Couple	1968	1970

Many successful films have given rise to live-action TV series, with these the highest-earning originals, the top 6 having made over $100 million each worldwide. Several animated films have extended into TV series, among them *Aladdin* and *Buzz Lightyear of Star Command* (from *Toy Story*), while a number of live-action films have generated animated TV series, among them *Spider-Man*, *The Mummy*, and *The Mask*.

TOP 10 BESTSELLING VIDEOS IN THE US

	FILM	YEAR*
1	Star Wars: Episode I – The Phantom Menace	2000
2	Pearl Harbor	2001
3	The Lord of the Rings: The Fellowship of the Ring	2002
4	Remember the Titans	2001
5	Spider-Man	2002
6	The Princess Diaries	2001
7	Miss Congeniality	2002
8	The Mummy Returns	2001
9	Jurassic Park III	2001
10	X-Men	2000

* Of video in US

TOP 10 MOST-RENTED DVDs IN THE US*

	FILM	RENTAL REVENUE ($)†
1	Ocean's Eleven	33,900,000
2	Training Day	30,320,000
3	Don't Say a Word	28,540,000
4	Mr. Deeds	26,970,000
5	The Others	25,350,000
6	Spy Game	24,910,000
7	Insomnia	24,600,000
8	John Q.	24,100,000
9	Panic Room	24,010,000
10	The Sum of All Fears	23,860,000

* DVD came of age to such an extent in 2002 that all the films in this Top 10 belong to that year.

† In release year

Freeze Frame

Having earned over $430 million worldwide, *The Matrix* went on to repeat its success in the DVD market.

TOP 10 BESTSELLING DVDs IN THE UK*

	FILM	YEAR†
1	The Lord of the Rings: The Fellowship of the Ring	2001
2	Gladiator	2000
3	Harry Potter and the Philosopher's Stone	2001
4	The Matrix	1999
5	Star Wars: Episode 2 – Attack of the Clones	2002
6	Shrek	2001
7	The Mummy	1999
8	Monsters, Inc.	2001
9	Bridget Jones's Diary	2001
10	The Mummy Returns	2001

* To 1 January 2003
† Of original film release
Source: British Video Association

TOP 10 MOST-RENTED DVDs IN THE UK*

	FILM	YEAR†
1	The Others	2001
2	Minority Report	2002
3	Swordfish	2001
4	About a Boy	2002
5	The 51st State (aka Formula 51)	2001
6	Panic Room	2002
7	Shallow Hal	2001
8	Black Hawk Down	2001
9	American Pie 2	2001
10	The Fast and the Furious	2001

* To 1 January 20003
† Of original film release
Source: MRIB

TOP 10 BESTSELLING VIDEOS IN THE UK*

	FILM	YEAR†
1	The Jungle Book	1967
2	Titanic	1997
3	Snow White and the Seven Dwarfs	1937
4	The Lord of the Rings: The Fellowship of the Ring	2001
5	Toy Story	1995
6	The Lion King	1994
7	Shrek	2001
8	Gladiator	2000
9	Harry Potter and the Philosopher's Stone	2001
10	Beauty and the Beast	1991

* To 1 January 2003
† Of original film release
Source: British Video Association/Official UK Charts

Did you know?

In the US in 2002, DVD and VHS rentals and sales were worth $20.3 billion, more than double the revenue generated by domestic film releases.

TOP 10 MOST-RENTED VIDEOS IN THE UK*

	FILM	YEAR†
1	Four Weddings and a Funeral	1994
2	Dirty Dancing	1987
3	Basic Instinct	1992
4	Crocodile Dundee	1986
5	Gladiator	1992
6	Sister Act	1992
7	Forrest Gump	1994
8	The Sixth Sense	1999
9	Home Alone	1990
10	Ghost	1990

* To 1 January 2003
† Of original film release
Source: MRIB

TOP 10 COUNTRIES FOR VIDEO PIRACY

	COUNTRY	MARKET %*	LOSS IN 2000 ($)
1	Russia	80	250,000,000
2	China	91	168,000,000
3	Brazil	35	120,000,000
4	India	60	75,000,000
5	Taiwan	44	42,000,000
6	Ukraine	90	40,000,000
7 =	Argentina	45	30,000,000
=	Israel	50	30,000,000
=	Philippines	80	30,000,000
=	South Africa	30	30,000,000

* Percentage of market pirated
Source: International Intellectual Property Alliance

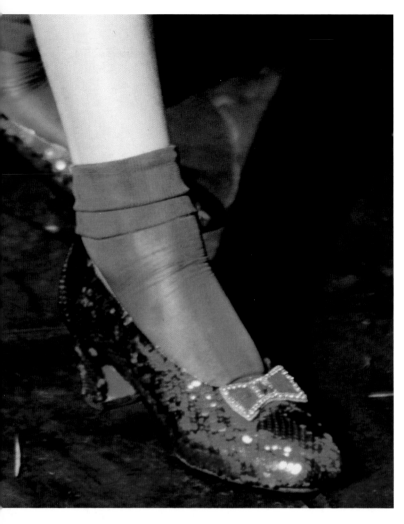

TOP 10 ITEMS OF FILM MEMORABILIA SOLD AT AUCTION*

	ITEM/AUCTION	PRICE ($)
1	David O. Selznick's Oscar for *Gone With the Wind*: Sotheby's, New York, 12 Jun 1999 (bought by Michael Jackson)	1,542,500
2	Judy Garland's ruby slippers from *The Wizard of Oz*: Christie's, New York, 26 May 2000	666,000
3	Clark Gable's Oscar for *It Happened One Night*: Christie's, Los Angeles, 15 Dec 1996	607,500
4	Bette Davis's Oscar for *Jezebel*: Christie's, New York, 19 Jul 2001 (bought by Steven Spielberg)	578,000
5	Vivien Leigh's Oscar for *Gone With the Wind*: Sotheby's, New York, 15 Dec 1993	562,500
6	Statue of the falcon from *The Maltese Falcon*: Christie's Rockefeller, New York, 5 Dec 1994	398,500
7	James Bond's Aston Martin DB5 from *Goldfinger*: Sotheby's, New York, 28 Jun 1986	275,000
8 =	Victor Fleming's Oscar for *Gone With the Wind*: Christie's Rockefeller, New York, 6 Dec 1994	244,500
=	Clark Gable's personal script for *Gone With the Wind*: Christie's, Los Angeles, 15 Dec 1996	244,500
10	"Rosebud" sled from *Citizen Kane*: Christie's, Los Angeles, 15 Dec 1996	233,500

* Excluding posters and animation cels

A Price Above Rubies

The ruby slippers worn by Judy Garland as Dorothy Gale in *The Wizard of Oz* were silver until it was decided that red would be more striking in this early Technicolor film. The iconic footwear — one of seven pairs that were made — fetched $666,000 at auction.

TOP 10 FILMS WITH THE MOST EXTRAS

	FILM	COUNTRY	YEAR	EXTRAS
1	Gandhi	UK	1982	294,560
2	Kolberg	Germany	1945	187,000
3	Monster Wangmagwi	South Korea	1967	157,000
4	War and Peace	USSR	1968	120,000
5	Ilya Muromets (The Sword and the Dragon)	USSR	1956	106,000
6	Dun-Huang (aka Ton ko)	Japan	1988	100,000
7	Razboiul independentei (The War of Independence)	Romania	1912	80,000
8	Around the World in 80 Days	US	1956	68,894
9 =	Intolerance	US	1916	60,000
=	Dny Zrady (Days of Betrayal)	Czechoslovakia	1973	60,000

Some 200,000 of the extras in *Gandhi* were volunteers, with a further 94,560 paid a fee. They appeared in the funeral sequence, filmed on 31 January 1981 (the 33rd anniversary of Gandhi's actual funeral). After editing, the scene lasted just 2 minutes 5 seconds. *Kolberg* used actual German troops diverted from the German front during the closing stages of World War II. The extras in *War and Peace* were accompanied by some 11,000 horses, but *Around the World in 80 Days* secured the services of the most diverse menagerie of animal extras, a total of 8,552, including 3,800 sheep, 2,448 buffalos, 950 donkeys, 800 horses, 512 monkeys, 17 bulls, 15 elephants, 6 skunks, and 4 ostriches. Recent films such as *The Lord of the Rings: The Two Towers* (2002) feature huge computer-generated crowd scenes, suggesting that the days of the "cast of thousands" of human extras may be over.

TOP 10 HIGHEST-EARNING MOVIE PEOPLE*

	NAME	PROFESSION	INCOME, 2003 ($)
1	George Lucas	Director/producer/writer	200,000,000
2	Steven Spielberg	Director/producer	100,000,000
3	Stephen King	Novelist/screenwriter	52,400,000
4	Tom Clancy	Novelist/screenwriter	47,800,000
5	Brian Grazer and Ron Howard	Producers	45,000,000
6	Dean Koontz	Writer/producer	44,200,000
7	Mary Higgins Clark	Writer	43,600,000
8	J.K. Rowling	Novelist	41,800,000
9	Jerry Bruckheimer	Producer	40,000,000
10	Michael Bay	Director	36,000,000

* Excluding actors and actresses
Source: *Forbes* magazine

Several of these movie millionaires combine various roles, while Stephen King and J.K. Rowling, for example, are bestselling novelists whose books have generated some of the most successful films of the recent years, including, respectively, *The Green Mile* and the *Harry Potter* series.

TOP 10 LONGEST FILMS EVER SCREENED

	FILM	DIRECTOR/COUNTRY	YEAR	DURATION
1	The Cure for Insomnia	John Henry Timmis IV, USA	1987	87 hr
2	The Longest and Most Meaningless Movie in the World	Vincent Patouillard, UK	1970	48 hr
3	The Burning of the Red Lotus Temple	Star Film Company, China	1931	27 hr
4	Die Zweite Heimat	Edgar Reitz, West Germany	1992	25 hr 32 m
5	**** (aka Four Stars)	Andy Warhol, USA	1967	25 hr
6	Heimat – Eine deutsche Chronik	Edgar Reitz, West Germany	1984	15 hr 40 m
7	Berlin Alexanderplatz	Rainer Werner Fassbinder, West Germany/Italy	1980	15 hr 21 m
8	Resan (The Journey)	Peter Watkins, Sweden	1987	14 hr 33 m
9	Comment Yukong déplaça les montagnes (How Yukong Moved the Mountains)	Joris Ivens and Marceline Lorigan, France	1976	12 h 43 m
10	Out 1: Noli me Tangere	Jacques Rivette and Suzanne Schiffman, France	1971	12 hr 9 m

The list includes commercially screened films, although *The Cure for Insomnia*, which depicts L.D. Groban reciting a 4,080-page poem, was shown only once, in Chicago, from 31 January to 3 February 1987. *The Longest and Most Meaningless Movie in the World* was later cut to a more manageable 1 hour 30 minutes, but remained just as meaningless. *The Burning of the Red Lotus Temple* was shown in its entirety, but later broken up into separate episodes, while the two *Heimat* films and *Berlin Alexanderplatz* have been screened in full, but are more commonly shown as a TV mini- (or, perhaps, maxi-) series.

TOP 10 PRICES FOR FILM POSTERS AT AUCTION

	POSTER*/AUCTION	PRICE ($)
1	The Mummy, 1932: Sotheby's, New York, 1 Mar 1997	453,500
2	Metropolis, 1926: Sotheby's, New York, 28 Oct 2000	357,750
3	King Kong, 1933: Sotheby's, New York, 16 Apr 1999	244,500
4	Frankenstein, 1931: Odyssey Auctions, Los Angeles, 11 Oct 1993	198,000
5	Men in Black, 1934: Sotheby's, New York, 4 Apr 1998	109,750
6 =	Play Ball, 1929: Sotheby's, New York, 16 Apr 1999	96,000
=	Three Little Pigskins, 1934: Sotheby's, New York, 16 Apr 1999	96,000
8	Casablanca, 1942: Christie's, London, 27 Mar 2000	86,608 (sold at £54,000)
9	Flying Down to Rio, 1933: Christie's, Los Angeles, 15 Dec 1996	82,800
10	Touchdown Mickey, 1932: Butterfield Auctions, Los Angeles, 14 Oct 2000	79,800

* Highest priced example of each – other film posters, for instance *King Kong* posters, have also achieved very high prices.

THE 10 FIRST TECHNICOLOR FEATURE FILMS

	FILM	US RELEASE
1	Becky Sharp	13 Jun 1935
2	Captain Blue Blood	31 Dec 1935
3	The Trail of the Lonesome Pine	13 Mar 1936
4	Dancing Pirate	22 May 1936
5	Ramona	25 Sep 1936
6	The Garden of Allah	19 Nov 1936
7	God's Country and the Woman	10 Jan 1937
8	Wings of the Morning	11 Mar 1937
9	A Star Is Born	20 Apr 1937
10	Vogues of 1938	2 Aug 1937

Although there were numerous earlier colour processes, the coming of Technicolor revolutionized the film industry. A short film, *La Cucaracha*, was released in 1934, but *Becky Sharp* was the first feature-length Technicolor film – although critics of the process claimed that the colour was so unrealistic that the skin colour of the cast resembled "boiled salmon dipped in mayonnaise". These pioneering films were followed by such classics as the animated *Snow White and the Seven Dwarfs* (21 December 1937) and *Gone With the Wind* (15 December 1939), the first colour film to win a "Best Picture" Oscar.

True Colours

Becky Sharp, the pioneering Technicolor film, was the story of a social climber, based on W.M. Thackeray's *Vanity Fair*. It heralded a major shift in filmmaking from monochrome to colour.

BOX OFFICE HITS & MISSES

Once a rare phenomenon, the multi-million-dollar budget film is now commonplace, with the average production cost of a Hollywood feature film today approaching $60 million. The blockbuster film that earns $100 million or more is also no longer unusual – indeed, the $100-million opening weekend has now been breached – while total US box office revenue has almost trebled in the past two decades. The top films of each decade from 1920 to the present and the Top 10 films of each year for the past half-century provide a fascinating summary of the hits and misses of past generations. We also explore some of the largest budgets, fastest- and highest-earning, and most profitable films, as well as the biggest flops, the top opening weekends, and other records, including those achieved by remakes and sequels, and the global blockbusters from Hollywood to Bollywood, and countries in between.

In the Lead
Made with an unprecedented $15 million budget, *Ben-Hur* (1959) won a record 11 Oscars as well as earning more than $70 million at the US box office.

TOP 10 ALL-TIME MONEY MAKERS

TOP 10 HIGHEST-GROSSING FILMS OF ALL TIME WORLDWIDE

	FILM	YEAR	USA ($)	OVERSEAS ($)	WORLD TOTAL ($)
1	Titanic *	1997	600,800,000	1,234,600,000	1,835,400,000
2	Harry Potter and the Sorcerer's Stone	2001	317,600,000	649,400,000	967,000,000
3	Star Wars: Episode I – The Phantom Menace	1999	431,100,000	492,000,000	923,100,000
4	Jurassic Park	1993	357,100,000	563,000,000	920,100,000
5	The Lord of the Rings: The Two Towers	2002	334,800,000	547,000,000	881,800,000
6	Harry Potter and the Chamber of Secrets	2002	261,700,000	604,000,000	865,700,000
7	The Lord of the Rings: The Fellowship of the Ring	2001	313,400,000	547,200,000	860,600,000
8	Independence Day	1996	306,300,000	505,000,000	811,200,000
9	Spider-Man	2002	403,700,000	402,000,000	805,700,000
10	Star Wars †	1977	461,000,000	337,000,000	798,000,000

* "Best Picture" Academy Award
† Retitled *Star Wars: Episode IV – A New Hope* on its 10 April 1981 re-release
Star Wars was the first film ever to gross over $500 worldwide, an achievement that just 25 films have emulated in the past 25 years.
Titanic broke all records, becoming the first – and to date the only – film ever to earn more than $500 million (and went on to make over $600 million) in the US alone. In March 2003, *Harry Potter and the Chamber of Secrets* became only the third film ever (after *Titanic* and *Harry Potter and the Sorcerer's Stone*) to earn more than $600 million outside the US.

TOP 10 HIGHEST-GROSSING FILMS OF ALL TIME IN THE US ADJUSTED FOR INFLATION

	FILM	YEAR	ACTUAL GROSS ($)	ADJUSTED ($)*
1	Gone With the Wind	1939	198,700,000	2,616,800,000
2	Snow White and the Seven Dwarfs †	1937	187,700,000	2,386,300,000
3	Star Wars	1977	461,000,000	1,392,900,000
4	Bambi †	1942	102,800,000	1,154,700,000
5	Pinocchio †	1940	84,300,000	1,102,500,000
6	Fantasia †	1940	76,400,000	999,200,000
7	The Sound of Music	1965	163,200,000	948,700,000
8	Jaws	1975	260,000,000	884,900,000
9	One Hundred and One Dalmatians †	1961	144,000,000	881,800,000
10	The Exorcist	1973	204,600,000	843,900,000

* As at 31 March 2003
† Animated
Unless inflation is factored in, the escalating price of cinema tickets – and hence the total income that films generate – makes the list of all-time blockbusters biased toward recent releases: box office income of $1 million earned 50 years ago (1953), for example, would be worth almost $7 million today. However, any inflation-indexing inevitably assumes that the bulk of a film's income was earned in its release year, which is clearly not the case, since the total gross of any film is cumulative often over many years from its release (and, with re-releases, may even increase decades later). The ranking indicated by this list must therefore be taken only as a guide and an impressionistic answer to the question, "If the box office income of film X had been earned today, how much would it be worth?", rather than a precise reflection of the inflation-adjusted earning of every dollar ever earned by each film.

Did you know?

Made with an unprecedented budget of $1,488,000, Disney's classic animated film *Snow White and the Seven Dwarfs* (1937) is the earliest film to earn over $100 million at the US box office.

TOP 10 BLACK & WHITE FEATURE FILMS

	FILM	YEAR
1	Young Frankenstein	1974
2	Manhattan	1979
3	Psycho	1960
4	Mom and Dad	1944
5	Paper Moon	1973
6	From Here to Eternity	1953
7	Some Like It Hot	1959
8	The Best Years of Our Lives *	1946
9	Lenny	1974
10	The Last Picture Show	1971

* "Best Picture" Academy Award

Since the mid-1950s, the majority of films have been made in colour, but a handful of films produced before the colour era and some released since then, where the director opted for black and white rather than colour for aesthetic reasons, have earned upwards of $20 million. The films in this list are exclusively monochrome, rather than combination black and white and colour films (monochrome films with colour sequences, or vice versa).

TOP 10 HIGHEST-GROSSING FILMS OF ALL TIME OUTSIDE THE US

	FILM	YEAR	NON-US INCOME ($)
1	Titanic *	1997	1,234,600,000
2	Harry Potter and the Sorcerer's Stone	2001	649,400,000
3	Harry Potter and the Chamber of Secrets	2002	604,000,000
4	Jurassic Park	1993	563,000,000
5	The Lord of the Rings: The Fellowship of the Ring	2001	547,200,000
6	The Lord of the Rings: The Two Towers	2002	547,000,000
7	Independence Day	1996	505,000,000
8	Star Wars: Episode I – The Phantom Menace	1999	492,000,000
9	The Lion King †	1994	459,000,000
10	Spider-Man	2002	402,000,000

* "Best Picture" Academy Award
† Animated

Lady of the Lake

Cate Blanchett as Elf Queen Galadriel in world blockbuster *The Lord of the Rings: The Fellowship of the Ring*. She quipped that she took the part because "I've always wanted to have pointy ears!"

House of Horror

Psycho was filmed in black and white because director Alfred Hitchcock believed the story would be too gory if presented in colour. The home of murderer Norman Bates, played by Anthony Perkins, was based on a gothic-style house in Santa Cruz, California, and is now preserved at Universal Studios, Hollywood.

TOP 10 HIGHEST-GROSSING FILMS OF ALL TIME IN THE US

	FILM	YEAR	US GROSS($)
1	Titanic *	1997	600,800,000
2	Star Wars †	1977	461,000,000
3	E.T. the Extra-Terrestrial	1982	435,000,000
4	Star Wars: Episode I – The Phantom Menace	1999	431,100,000
5	Spider-Man	2002	403,700,000
6	Jurassic Park	1993	357,100,000
7	The Lord of the Rings: The Two Towers	2002	334,800,000
8	Forrest Gump *	1994	329,700,000
9	Harry Potter and the Sorcerer's Stone	2001	317,600,000
10	The Lord of the Rings: The Fellowship of the Ring	2001	313,400,000

* "Best Picture" Academy Award
† Later retitled *Star Wars: Episode IV – A New Hope*

TOP 10 HIGHEST-GROSSING FILMS OF ALL TIME IN THE UK

	FILM	YEAR*	UK GROSS (£)
1	Titanic	1998	69,000,000
2	Harry Potter and the Sorcerer's Stone	2001	66,000,000
3	The Lord of the Rings: The Fellowship of the Ring	2001	62,800,000
4	The Lord of the Rings: The Two Towers	2002	57,100,000
5	Harry Potter and the Chamber of Secrets	2002	54,000,000
6	The Full Monty	1997	52,232,058
7	Star Wars: Episode I – The Phantom Menace	1999	51,063,811
8	Jurassic Park	1993	47,886,423
9	Toy Story 2 †	2000	44,306,070
10	Bridget Jones's Diary	2001	42,007,008

* Of release in UK
† Animated

Inevitably, bearing inflation in mind, the top-grossing films of all time are releases from recent years, although it is also true that UK cinema admissions rose sharply in recent years – from 97,370,000 in 1990 to 175,902,533 in 2002. From the nadir of the late 1960s and 1970s, today's films are both more widely viewed (even excluding video) than those of 15 to 25 years ago, as well as grossing considerably more at the box office.

Titanic Success

All-time blockbuster *Titanic* remains unrivalled as the all-time top-earning film in almost every country in the world, confounding critics who claimed that films about the disaster were as doomed as the vessel itself.

TOP 10 HIGHEST-EARNING REMAKES OF HOLLYWOOD FILMS

	FILM	ORIGINAL	REMAKE
1	Ocean's Eleven	1960	2001
2	Batman	1966	1989
3	Planet of the Apes	1968	2001
4	Meet the Parents	1992	2000
5	Doctor Dolittle	1967	1998
6	The Nutty Professor	1963	1996
7	Cape Fear	1962	1991
8	The Haunting	1963	1999
9	The Thomas Crown Affair	1968	1999
10	Sabrina	1954	1995

This Top 10 includes only remakes with the identical title; retitled remakes such as *Dracula/Bram Stoker's Dracula* (1931/1992) are ineligible, as are live-action versions of animated films such as *One Hundred and One Dalmatians/101 Dalmatians* (1961/1991). The "original" film is the previous significant Hollywood version of a film, but many subjects – such as *The Three Musketeers* and *Hamlet* – have been remade often while many others have been remade under different titles. All remakes in this list have earned $100 million-plus worldwide but not all remakes are successful, with recent examples, such as *Psycho* (1960/1998) and *Rollerball* (1975/2002), earning less than their celebrated predecessors.

TOP 10 HIGHEST-GROSSING FILM FRANCHISES OF ALL TIME

	FRANCHISE	FILMS	YEARS	WORLD GROSS ($)*
1	James Bond	20	1963–2002	3,630,600,000
2	Star Wars	5	1977–2002	3,471,600,000
3	Jurassic Park	3	1993–2001	1,901,000,000
4	Harry Potter	2	2001–2002	1,832,700,000
5	The Lord of the Rings	2	2001–2002	1,742,400,000
6	Batman	4	1989–1997	1,268,400,000
7	Indiana Jones	3	1981–1989	1,211,700,000
8	Star Trek	10	1979–2002	1,053,700,000
9	Men in Black	2	1997–2002	1,013,400,000
10	Mission: Impossible	2	1996–2000	1,012,400,000

* Cumulative global earnings of the original film and all its sequels to 31 Mar 2003

Certain films series have become recognizable "brands" that are effectively marketed as franchised products, along with associated merchandise. Once established with a powerful recognition factor, they attract a loyal audience for subsequent releases, which has enabled the Top 10 to accrue cumulative $1 billion-plus revenues.

Spanish Eyes
Najwa Nimri in *Abre Los Ojos* (*Open Your Eyes*), which was remade by Hollywood as *Vanilla Sky*. Unusually, one star, Penelope Cruz, appeared in both versions.

TOP 10 HIGHEST-EARNING REMAKES OF FOREIGN FILMS*

	REMAKE	YEAR	ORIGINAL	COUNTRY	YEAR
1	Godzilla	1998	Gojira	Japan	1954
2	True Lies	1994	La Totale!	France	1991
3	Vanilla Sky	2001	Abre Los Ojos	Spain	1997
4	City of Angels	1998	Wings of Desire	Germany	1988
5	The Birdcage	1996	La Cage aux Folles	France	1978
6	The Ring	2002	Ringu	Japan	1998
7	Three Men and a Baby	1987	Trois Hommes et un Couffin	France	1985
8	Twelve Monkeys	1995	La Jetée	France	1965
9	Nine Months	1995	Neuf Mois	France	1993
10	Insomnia	2002	Insomnia	Norway	1997

* Ranked by the relative international success of the Hollywood remake
Hollywood has made something of a habit of taking foreign — especially French — films and remaking them for the Anglophone market, with Japan proving a fertile source of such inspiration: *The Magnificent Seven* (1960), for example, is a remake of Akira Kurosawa's *The Seven Samurai* (1954), while Clint Eastwood's first "spaghetti Western", *A Fistful of Dollars* (1964), and *Last Man Standing* (1996), starring Bruce Willis, are both remakes of Kurosawa's *Yojombo the Bodyguard* (1961). The Top 10 represents the most successful results of this route to the US and international screen, the first nine of which have each earned in excess of $100 million worldwide.

TOP 10 FILM SEQUELS THAT MOST OUTEARNED THE ORIGINAL*

	HIGHEST-EARNING SEQUEL	YEAR	ORIGINAL	YEAR
1	Terminator 2: Judgment Day	1991	The Terminator	1984
2	Lethal Weapon 3	1992	Lethal Weapon	1987
3	Rambo: First Blood Part II	1985	First Blood	1982
4	Austin Powers: The Spy Who Shagged Me	1999	Austin Powers: International Man of Mystery	1997
5	Die Hard: With a Vengeance	1995	Die Hard	1988
6	Rocky IV	1985	Rocky	1976
7	Toy Story 2	1999	Toy Story	1995
8	Star Wars: Episode I – The Phantom Menace	1999	Star Wars †	1977
9	Indiana Jones and the Last Crusade	1989	Raiders of the Lost Ark	1981
10	Ace Ventura: When Nature Calls	1995	Ace Ventura: Pet Detective	1994

* Ranked by differential between original and highest-earning sequel (by total global gross)
† Later retitled *Star Wars: Episode IV – A New Hope*

TOP 10 MOST PROFITABLE FILMS OF ALL TIME*

	FILM/YEAR	BUDGET (M$)	GROSS ($)	PROFIT RATIO
1	The Blair Witch Project (1999)	0.035	248,662,839	7,104.65
2	American Graffiti (1973)	0.75	115,000,000	153.33
3	Snow White and the Seven Dwarfs (1937) †	1.488	187,670,866	126.12
4	The Rocky Horror (Picture) Show (1975)	1.2	139,876,417	116.56
5	Rocky (1976) #	1.1	117,235,147	106.58
6	Gone With the Wind (1939) #	3.9	390,555,278	100.14
7	The Full Monty (1997)	3.5	256,950,122	73.41
8	Star Wars (1977) ‡	11.0	797,998,007	72.55
9	E.T. the Extra-Terrestrial (1982)	10.5	756,774,579	72.07
10	My Big Fat Greek Wedding (2002)	5.0	353,927,695	70.79

* Minimum entry $100 million world gross
† Animated
# Academy Award for "Best Picture"
‡ Later retitled *Star Wars: Episode IV – A New Hope*

This Top 10 embodies the filmmaker's ambition to make a modest-budget film and earn a colossal sum at the global box office. While all have earned more than $100 million worldwide, there are others that were nearly as successful without achieving such a total gross, ranging from *Dr. No* (1963), made on a $950,000 budget and earning almost $60 million (a ratio of 62.74), to *El Mariachi* (1993), a $7,000-budget film that earned more than $2 million (ratio 291.56). It should be noted that this budget and that for No.1 film *The Blair Witch Project* represent only the costs of making the films: further post-production costs, for example to enhance the sound quality, were incurred prior to theatrical release. For comparison, all-time blockbuster *Titanic* (1997) had a budget of $200 million and earned $1,835,388,188, a ratio of 9.18.

TOP 10 MOST SEEN FILMS OF ALL TIME IN THE US BY ADMISSIONS*

	FILM	YEAR	ADMISSIONS
1	Gone With the Wind	1939	202,044,569
2	Star Wars	1977	178,119,595
3	The Sound of Music	1965	142,415,376
4	E.T. the Extra-Terrestrial	1982	141,925,359
5	The Ten Commandments	1956	131,000,000
6	Titanic	1997	129,201,761
7	Jaws	1975	128,078,818
8	Snow White and the Seven Dwarfs *	1937	109,000,000
9	One Hundred and One Dalmatians *	1961	99,917,251
10	The Empire Strikes Back	1980	98,106,044

* Animated
Source: Exhibitor Relations Co., Inc.

This list is based on the actual number of people purchasing tickets at the US box office. Since it takes account of the relatively greater numbers of tickets sold to children and other discounted sales (such as matinées for popular films), it differs from lists that present total box office receipts which, as ticket prices increase, tend to give prominence to more recent films. Precise totals for certain films are unreliable, while non-US attendance figures have become a contentious issue, especially in those countries where season tickets enable cinemagoers to attend without purchasing tickets for specific films.

Did you know?

Robert Rodriguez, the director of the highly profitable *El Mariachi* (1993), earned $3,000 of the film's $7,000 budget by acting as a human guinea pig for a cholesterol-busting drug. He wrote the script while quarantined in the laboratory.

TOP 10 FASTEST FILMS TO REACH $100 MILLION IN THE US

	FILM	US RELEASE	DAYS
1	Spider-Man	3 May 2002	3
2	Star Wars: Episode II – Attack of the Clones	16 May 2002	4
3 =	Star Wars: Episode I – The Phantom Menace	19 May 1999	5
=	Harry Potter and the Sorcerer's Stone	16 Nov 2001	5
=	The Lord of the Rings: The Two Towers	18 Dec 2002	5
6 =	The Lost World: Jurassic Park	23 May 1997	6
=	Austin Powers in Goldmember	26 July 2002	6
=	Harry Potter and the Chamber of Secrets	15 Nov 2002	6
9 =	Independence Day	3 Jul 1996	7
=	Rush Hour 2	3 Aug 2001	7

Like the 0–60 mph acceleration of a car, the performance speed of a film – especially the time taken to reach million dollar increments – is increasingly taken as a measure of its commercial success, with these standing out as the Ferraris of the movie world. Back in 1983, *Return of the Jedi* (aka *Star Wars: Episode VI – Return of the Jedi*) was hailed for its achievement in breaking the $100 million barrier in just 19 days, since when some 60 films have bettered this record.

TOP 10 FASTEST FILMS TO REACH $200 MILLION IN THE US

	FILM	US RELEASE	DAYS
1	Spider-Man	3 May 2002	9
2	Star Wars: Episode II – Attack of the Clones	16 May 2002	12
=	The Lord of the Rings: The Two Towers	18 Dec 2002	12
4	Star Wars: Episode I – The Phantom Menace	19 May 1999	13
5	Harry Potter and the Sorcerer's Stone	16 Nov 2001	15
6	Harry Potter and the Chamber of Secrets	15 Nov 2002	17
7	The Lord of the Rings: The Fellowship of the Ring	19 Dec 2001	19
8	Independence Day	3 Jul 1996	20
9	Jurassic Park	11 Jun 1993	22
10	Titanic	19 Dec 1997	25

Having rocketed to $100 million in record time, *Spider-Man* continued to weave its spell by topping $200 million during only its second weekend on release, going on to score an unequalled four consecutive weekends with takings more than $35 million. In fact, fewer than 50 films have ever passed the $200 million milestone during the entire span of their US release, so these 10 represent a particularly special group.

TOP 10 FASTEST FILMS TO REACH $300 MILLION IN THE US

	FILM	US RELEASE	DAYS
1	Spider-Man	3 May 2002	22
2	Star Wars: Episode I – The Phantom Menace	19 May 1999	28
3	The Lord of the Rings: The Two Towers	18 Dec 2002	34
4	Titanic	19 Dec 1997	44
5	Harry Potter and the Sorcerer's Stone	16 Nov 2001	52
6	Jurassic Park	11 Jun 1993	67
7	The Lord of the Rings: The Fellowship of the Ring	19 Dec 2001	102
8	Star Wars: Episode II – Attack of the Clones	16 May 2002	104
9	Independence Day	3 Jul 1996	116
10	The Lion King *	15 Jun 1994	150

* Animated

Two other films, *E.T. the Extra-Terrestrial* (1982) and *Forrest Gump* (1994), also eventually made over $300 million, while *Star Wars* and *Return of the Jedi* attained this cumulative total only after their re-releases in 1982 and 1997 respectively. The first five in the list are the only releases ever to power on through the $400 million barrier.

Frankly, My Dear …

As the budget escalated to almost $4 million, the producers of *Gone With the Wind* realized they would have to sell an unprecedented $10 million worth of tickets to break even. In fact, it made $14 million in its first year, and went on to set an unbeaten record for admissions.

TOP 10 BIGGEST FLOPS OF ALL TIME*

	FILM	YEAR	BUDGET	ESTIMATED LOSS ($)
1	The Adventures of Pluto Nash	2002	100,000,000	95,600,000
2	Town & Country	2001	90,000,000	81,500,000
3	Cutthroat Island	1995	92,000,000	79,700,000
4	Monkeybone	2001	75,000,000	68,400,000
5	Final Fantasy: The Spirits Within	2001	137,000,000	62,600,000
6	Osmosis Jones	2001	75,000,000	61,100,000
7	The Postman	1997	80,000,000	59,600,000
8	Soldier	1998	75,000,000	57,700,000
9	The Four Feathers	2002	80,000,000	57,600,000
10	Ballistic: Ecks vs. Sever	2002	70,000,000	54,600,000

* This list only includes films that are not on release any longer, as of 31 March 2003, otherwise *The Core* (2003) with a budget of $85,000,000 and an estimated loss of $69,800,000 would be at No. 4. The figures shown here are based on earnings balanced against the production cost. In most instances, the bulk of the relatively low earnings each managed to achieve came from North America — after their initial homeland failure, some were never released overseas, or were, but succeeded in recouping only small sums. Notable flops of yesteryear have also been progressively overtaken by the stinkers of the 1990s and 2000s, so that highly publicized 1980s losses such as the $34.2 million of *Heaven's Gate* (1980) have faded into the mists of time. Produced in the same year, British-made *Raise the Titanic* lost some $33 million, prompting producer (Lord) Lew Grade to comment, "It would have been cheaper to lower the Atlantic!"

British Victory
Despite being both a British film and shown on a limited number of screens, *The Full Monty* triumphed at the US box office.

TOP 10 BIGGEST BUDGETS

	FILM	YEAR	BUDGET ($)
1	Titanic	1997	200,000,000
2 =	Waterworld	1995	175,000,000
=	Wild, Wild West	1999	175,000,000
4	Terminator 3: Rise of the Machines	2003	170,000,000
5	Tarzan *	1999	145,000,000
6	Die Another Day	2002	142,000,000
7 =	Armageddon	1998	140,000,000
=	Lethal Weapon 4	1998	140,000,000
=	Men in Black II	2002	140,000,000
=	Pearl Harbor	2001	140,000,000
=	Treasure Planet *	2002	140,000,000

* Animated

The two most expensive films ever made are water-based, large-scale marine special effects being a major factor in escalating budgets.

TOP 10 FILMS EARNING THE MOST AT FEWEST CINEMAS IN THE US

	FILM	YEAR	CINEMAS	US GROSS ($)
1	The Rocky Horror Picture Show	1975	200	139,876,417
2	Boyz N the Hood	1991	917	57,504,069
3	The Royal Tenenbaums	2001	999	52,364,010
4	New Jack City	1991	905	47,624,253
5	The Full Monty	1997	783	45,950,122
6	O Brother, Where Art Thou?	2000	847	45,512,588
7	Gosford Park	2001	918	41,308,615
8	The Piano	1993	671	40,157,856
9	The Doctor	1991	958	38,120,905
10	Dead Again	1991	940	38,016,380

While major US releases are shown at upwards of 3,000 screens, these films all managed to earn substantial grosses despite being restricted to fewer than 1,000 screens.

TOP 10 FILMS SHOWN AT MOST SCREENS IN THE US

	FILM	US RELEASE	SCREENS
1	Harry Potter and the Chamber of Secrets	15 Nov 2002	3,682
2	Harry Potter and the Sorcerer's Stone	16 Nov 2001	3,672
3	Mission: Impossible 2	24 May 2000	3,653
4	The Lord of the Rings: The Two Towers	18 Dec 2002	3,622
5	Spider-Man	3 May 2002	3,615
6	Austin Powers in Goldmember	26 Jul 2002	3,613
7	Shrek	18 May 2001	3,587
8	Men in Black II	3 Jul 2002	3,557
9	Planet of the Apes	27 Jul 2001	3,500
10	Daredevil	14 Feb 2003	3,474

THE 10 FIRST FILMS TO MAKE $100 MILLION AT THE US BOX OFFICE

	FILM	US RELEASE
1	Snow White and the Seven Dwarfs	21 Dec 1937
2	Gone With the Wind	15 Dec 1939
3	Bambi *	13 Aug 1942
4	One Hundred and One Dalmatians *	25 Jan 1961
5	Mary Poppins	26 Aug 1964
6	The Sound of Music	9 Dec 1965
7	Doctor Zhivago	22 Dec 1965
8	The Jungle Book *	18 Oct 1967
9	The Graduate	21 Dec 1967
10	Butch Cassidy and the Sundance Kid	24 Oct 1969

* Animated

Although it took several years for some of these films to hit the magic $100 million at the US box office, they are outstanding for having attained that level at a time when relatively few films generated more than $10 million. It is also of interest that four of these early blockbusters were animated features, precursors of the even higher-earning animated films of recent years, evidence that the enduring commercial success of such timeless classics – often through multiple re-releases – transcends the changing tastes of the audiences for live-action films.

THE 10 FIRST FILMS TO MAKE $200 MILLION AT THE US BOX OFFICE

	FILM	US RELEASE
1	The Exorcist	26 Dec 1973
2	Jaws	20 Jun 1975
3	Star Wars: Episode IV – A New Hope *	25 May 1977
4	Star Wars: Episode V – The Empire Strikes Back *	21 May 1980
5	Raiders of the Lost Ark	12 Jun 1981
6	E.T. the Extra-Terrestrial	11 Jun 1982
7	Star Wars: Episode VI – Return of the Jedi *	25 May 1983
8	Ghostbusters	7 Jun 1984
9	Beverly Hills Cop	5 Dec 1984
10	Back to the Future	3 Jul 1985

* As later retitled

It took over 30 years for 10 films to make $100 million at the US box office, but only 12 for 10 to attain the $200 million milestone. *The Exorcist* achieved this level despite – or perhaps as a result of – being described as "The Scariest Movie of All Time", and receiving an "R" rating in the US, thus restricting its audiences by excluding unaccompanied under-17s. Taking inflation into account, it is the highest-earning R-rated film ever.

Extra-Ordinary

With total earnings just short of $435 million at the US box office, *E.T. the Extra-Terrestrial* is the third highest-earning film ever.

THE 10 FIRST FILMS TO MAKE $300 MILLION AT THE US BOX OFFICE

	FILM	US RELEASE
1	Star Wars: Episode IV – A New Hope *	25 May 1977
2	E.T. the Extra-Terrestrial	11 Jun 1982
3	Star Wars: Episode VI – Return of the Jedi *	25 May 1983
4	Jurassic Park	11 Jun 1993
5	The Lion King †	15 Jun 1994
6	Forrest Gump	6 Jul 1994
7	Independence Day	3 Jul 1996
8	Titanic	19 Dec 1997
9	Star Wars: Episode I – The Phantom Menace	19 May 1999
10	Harry Potter and the Sorcerer's Stone	16 Nov 2001

* As later retitled
† Animated

The first two *The Lord of the Rings* films, *Spider-Man*, and *Star Wars: Episode II – Attack of the Clones* are the only other films to date to have broken through the $300 million barrier, while *Star Wars: Episode V – The Empire Strikes Back* and *Harry Potter and the Chamber of Secrets* fell short of this total.

TOP 10 OPENING DAYS OF ALL TIME IN THE US

	FILM	US RELEASE	SCREENS	OPENING DAY ($)
1	Spider-Man	3 May 2002	3,615	39,406,872
2	Harry Potter and the Sorcerer's Stone	16 Nov 2001	3,682	32,333,203
3	Star Wars: Episode II – Attack of the Clones	16 May 2002	3,161	30,141,417
4	Harry Potter and the Chamber of Secrets	15 Nov 2002	3,682	29,631,453
5	Star Wars: Episode I – The Phantom Menace	19 May 1999	2,970	28,542,349
6	Austin Powers in Goldmember	26 Jul 2002	3,613	26,452,351
7	The Lord of the Rings: The Two Towers	18 Dec 2002	3,622	26,159,972
8	Planet of the Apes	27 Jul 2001	3,500	24,612,000
9	The Mummy Returns	4 May 2001	3,401	23,382,000
10	Rush Hour 2	3 Aug 2001	3,118	23,108,000

Creep Show
Like many of the most successful films released on Labor Day, *Jeepers Creepers*, directed by master of the macabre Victor Salva and starring Jonathan Breck as the eponymous Creeper, was an R-rated horror film.

TOP 10 MEMORIAL DAY OPENING WEEKENDS IN THE US

	FILM	US RELEASE	SCREENS	WEEKEND ($)
1	The Lost World: Jurassic Park	23 May 1997	3,281	90,161,880
2	Pearl Harbor	25 May 2001	3,214	75,177,654
3	Mission: Impossible 2	24 May 2000	3,653	70,816,215
4	Mission: Impossible	22 May 1996	3,012	56,811,602
5	Godzilla	20 May 1998	3,310	55,726,951
6	The Flintstones	27 May 1994	2,498	37,182,745
7	Indiana Jones and the Last Crusade	24 May 1989	2,327	37,031,573
8	Indiana Jones and the Temple of Doom	23 May 1984	1,687	33,936,113
9	Beverly Hills Cop II	20 May 1987	2,326	33,014,153
10	Return of the Jedi *	25 May 1984	1,002	30,490,619

* Later retitled *Star Wars: Episode VI – Return of the Jedi*
These are mostly films that opened on the Friday preceding Memorial Day (which is celebrated on the last Monday in May), but some, including both *Mission: Impossible* films, gained a couple of extra days' income by opening on the previous Wednesday.

TOP 10 FOURTH OF JULY OPENING WEEKENDS IN THE US

	FILM	US RELEASE	SCREENS	WEEKEND ($)
1	Men in Black II	3 Jul 2002	3,557	52,148,751
2	Men in Black	2 Jul 1997	3,020	51,068,455
3	Independence Day	3 Jul 1996	2,882	50,228,264
4	The Perfect Storm	30 Jun 2000	3,407	41,325,042
5	Armageddon	1 Jul 1998	3,127	36,089,972
6	Terminator 2: Judgment Day	3 Jul 1991	2,274	31,765,506
7	Wild Wild West	30 Jun 1999	3,342	27,687,484
8	The Firm	30 Jun 1993	2,393	25,400,000
9	Apollo 13	30 Jun 1995	2,197	25,353,380
10	The Patriot	28 Jun 2000	3,061	22,413,710

It is perhaps no coincidence that several of these films, all of which opened in the week before Independence Day, contain a strong element of heroism and patriotism, often in the face of hostile alien invaders.

TOP 10 LABOR DAY OPENING WEEKENDS IN THE US*

	FILM	US RELEASE	SCREENS	WEEKEND ($)
1	Jeepers Creepers	31 Aug 2001	2,944	15,831,700
2	The Crow: City of Angels	30 Aug 1996	2,423	9,785,111
3	First Kid	30 Aug 1996	1,878	8,434,651
4	Hoodlum	29 Aug 1997	2,020	8,162,768
5	The Prophecy	1 Sep 1995	1,663	7,510,332
6	FearDotCom	30 Aug 2002	2,550	7,087,457
7	"O"	31 Aug 2001	1,434	6,916,625
8	Excess Baggage	29 Aug 1997	2,211	6,309,583
9	Highlander: Endgame	1 Sep 2000	1,543	6,223,330
10	Milk Money	2 Sep 1994	1,361	5,846,533

* The first Monday in September is observed as Labor day in the US

High Flyer

Pearl Harbor achieved an impressive Memorial Day Weekend opening despite competition from *Shrek* (2001) which had been released the previous week.

TOP 10 HALLOWEEN OPENING WEEKENDS IN THE US*

	FILM	US RELEASE	SCREENS	WEEKEND ($)
1	Jackass: The Movie	25 Oct 2002	2,509	22,763,437
2	K-PAX	26 Oct 2001	2,541	17,215,275
3	Stargate	28 Oct 1994	2,033	16,651,018
4	House on Haunted Hill	29 Oct 1999	2,710	15,946,032
5	Thir13en Ghosts	26 Oct 2001	2,781	15,165,355
6	Book of Shadows: Blair Witch 2	27 Oct 2000	3,317	13,223,887
7	Ghost Ship	25 Oct 2002	2,787	11,503,423
8	(John Carpenter's) Vampire$	30 Oct 1998	1,793	9,106,497
9	Halloween II	30 Oct 1981	1,211	7,446,508
10	Red Corner	31 Oct 1997	2,244	7,403,362

* Halloween falls on 31 October

TOP 10 THANKSGIVING OPENING WEEKENDS IN THE US*

	FILM	DATE	SCREENS	WEEKEND ($)*
1	Toy Story 2 †	24 Nov 1999	3,236	80,102,784
2	Unbreakable	22 Nov 2000	2,708	46,010,629
3	A Bug's Life †	25 Nov 1998	2,686	45,820,335
4	101 Dalmatians	27 Nov 1996	2,794	45,073,479
5	Back to the Future Part II	22 Nov 1989	1,865	43,016,225
6	Toy Story †	22 Nov 1995	2,457	39,071,176
7	Flubber	26 Nov 1997	2,641	35,892,031
8	Rocky IV	27 Nov 1985	1,325	31,770,105
9	End of Days	24 Nov 1999	2,593	31,509,775
10	Spy Game	21 Nov 2001	2,770	30,566,960

* Thanksgiving is celebrated on the fourth Thursday in November. Many Americans use this opportunity to take an extended break and films are often released in this period to take advantage of the 5-day weekend.
† Animated

TOP 10 CHRISTMAS OPENING WEEKENDS IN THE US*

	FILM	US RELEASE	SCREENS	WEEKEND ($)
1	The Lord of the Rings: The Fellowship of the Ring	19 Dec 2001	3,359	66,114,741
2	The Lord of the Rings: The Two Towers	18 Dec 2002	3,622	62,007,528
3	Cast Away	22 Dec 2000	2,767	39,852,075
4	Catch Me If You Can	25 Dec 2002	3,156	30,082,000
5	Titanic	19 Dec 1997	2,674	28,638,131
6	Patch Adams	25 Dec 1998	2,712	25,262,280
7	Tomorrow Never Dies	19 Dec 1997	2,807	25,143,007
8	Beavis and Butt-head Do America †	20 Dec 1996	2,190	20,114,233
9	Stepmom	25 Dec 1998	2,358	19,142,440
10	You've Got M@il	18 Dec 1998	2,691	18,426,749

* Films released up to one week before 25 December
† Animated

TOP 10 R-RATED OPENING WEEKENDS IN THE US

	FILM	US RELEASE	SCREENS	WEEKEND ($)
1	Hannibal	9 Feb 2001	3,230	58,003,121
2	8 Mile	8 Nov 2002	2,470	51,240,555
3	American Pie 2	10 Aug 2001	3,063	45,117,985
4	Scary Movie	7 Jul 2000	2,912	42,346,669
5	Air Force One	25 Jul 1997	2,919	37,132,505
6	Red Dragon	4 Oct 2002	3,357	36,540,945
7	Interview with the Vampire	11 Nov 1994	2,604	36,389,705
8	Gladiator	5 May 2000	2,938	34,819,017
9	Scream 3	4 Feb 2000	3,467	34,713,342
10	Ransom	8 Nov 1996	2,676	34,216,088

The rating system of the Motion Picture Association of America dictates that R-Rated films may be viewed by persons under the age of 17 only if accompanied by a parent or adult guardian. While this clearly identifies the nature of films that are so-rated, it also restricts the audience by excluding families who do not wish to expose their children to "unsuitable" material, hence films that achieved a successful opening weekend in spite of this limitation are especially noteworthy.

TOP 10 OPENING WEEKENDS IN THE US

	FILM	US RELEASE	SCREENS	WEEKEND ($)
1	Spider-Man	3 May 2002	3,615	114,844,116
2	Harry Potter and the Sorcerer's Stone	16 Nov 2001	3,672	90,294,621
3	Harry Potter and the Chamber of Secrets	15 Nov 2002	3,682	88,357,488
4	Star Wars: Episode II – Attack of the Clones	17 May 2002	3,161	80,027,814
5	Austin Powers in Goldmember	26 Jul 2002	3,613	73,071,188
6	The Lost World: Jurassic Park	23 May 1997	3,281	72,132,785
7	Planet of the Apes	27 Jul 2001	3,500	68,532,960
8	The Mummy Returns	4 May 2001	3,401	68,139,035
9	Rush Hour 2	3 Aug 2001	3,118	67,408,222
10	Star Wars: Episode I – The Phantom Menace	21 May 1999	2,970	64,810,970

TOP 10 OPENING WEEKENDS IN THE UK

	FILM	UK RELEASE	SCREENS	WEEKEND (£)
1	Harry Potter and the Chamber of Secrets	15 Nov 2002	524	18,871,829
2	Harry Potter and the Sorcerer's Stone	16 Nov 2001	507	16,335,627
3	The Lord of the Rings: The Two Towers	20 Dec 2002	501	13,063,560
4	Star Wars: Episode II – Attack of the Clones	17 May 2002	467	11,386,209
5	The Lord of the Rings: The Fellowship of the Ring	21 Dec 2001	470	11,058,045
6	Star Wars: Episode I – The Phantom Menace	16 Jul 1999	460	9,512,295
7	Spider-Man	14 Jun 2002	509	9,426,969
8	Monsters, Inc. *	25 Jan 2002	503	9,200,257
9	Die Another Day	11 Nov 2002	430	9,122,344
10	Toy Story 2 *	11 Feb 2000	496	7,971,539

* Animated

TOP 10 OPENING WEEKENDS IN AUSTRALIA

	FILM	AUSTRALIAN RELEASE	WEEKEND ($AUS)
1	The Lord of the Rings: The Two Towers	26 Dec 2002	14,115,394
2	Star Wars: Episode II – Attack of the Clones	16 May 2002	11,967,380
3	Harry Potter and the Chamber of Secrets	28 Nov 2002	10,640,941
4	Spider-Man	6 Jun 2002	10,563,980
5	The Lord of the Rings: The Fellowship of The Ring	26 Dec 2001	9,749,937
6	Harry Potter and the Sorcerer's Stone	29 Nov 2001	9,249,505
7	Star Wars: Episode I – The Phantom Menace	3 Jun 1999	9,139,628
8	Independence Day	29 Aug 1996	7,707,634
9	Mission: Impossible 2	1 Jun 2000	6,395,638
10	Men in Black	11 Sep 1997	6,227,000

Light Fantastic

The first three *Star Wars* films were released in 1977–83. Their eagerly awaited prequel, *Star Wars: Episode I – The Phantom Menace*, starring Ewan McGregor as the young Jedi Obi-Wan Kenobi, opened to huge audiences worldwide.

TOP 10 OPENING WEEKENDS OF COMEDY FILMS IN THE US*

	FILM	US RELEASE	WEEKEND ($)
1	Austin Powers in Goldmember	26 Jul 2002	73,071,188
2	Dr. Seuss's How the Grinch Stole Christmas	17 Nov 2000	55,820,330
3	Austin Powers: The Spy Who Shagged Me	11 Jun 1999	54,917,604
4	Scooby-Doo	14 Jun 2002	54,155,312
5	American Pie 2	10 Aug 2001	45,117,985
6	Nutty Professor II: The Klumps	28 Jul 2000	42,518,830
7	Scary Movie	7 Jul 2000	42,346,669
8	Big Daddy	25 Jun 1999	41,536,370
9	Ace Ventura: When Nature Calls	10 Nov 1995	37,804,076
10	Mr. Deeds	28 Jun 2002	37,162,787

* Excluding animated films

Half this Top 10 are sequels to films whose originals had established a solid audience base. The personal appeal of certain stars is also evident in the multiple appearances of Mike Myers (both Austin Powers films), Jim Carrey (*Dr. Seuss's How the Grinch Stole Christmas* and *Ace Ventura: When Nature Calls*), and Adam Sandler (*Big Daddy* and *Mr. Deeds*).

TOP 10 OPENING WEEKENDS OF SCIENCE-FICTION FILMS IN THE US

	FILM	US RELEASE	WEEKEND ($)
1	Spider-Man	3 May 2002	114,844,116
2	Star Wars: Episode II – Attack of the Clones	17 May 2002	80,027,814
3	The Lost World: Jurassic Park	23 May 1997	72,132,785
4	Planet of the Apes	27 Jul 2001	68,532,960
5	Star Wars: Episode I – The Phantom Menace	21 May 1999	64,810,970
6	Signs	2 Aug 2002	60,117,080
7	X-Men	14 Jul 2000	54,471,475
8	Men in Black II	5 Jul 2002	52,148,751
9	Men in Black	4 Jul 1997	51,068,455
10	Jurassic Park III	20 Jul 2001	50,771,645

Monkey Business

Helena Bonham Carter as Ari in Tim Burton's *Planet of the Apes*. The original film (1968) had a budget of $5.8 million and made $26 million at the US box office, while the remake cost $100 million but made more than twice as much in its first weekend as its forerunner had during its entire release period.

TOP 10 OPENING WEEKENDS OF ANIMATED FILMS IN THE US

	FILM	US RELEASE	WEEKEND ($)
1	Monsters, Inc.	2 Nov 2001	62,577,067
2	Toy Story 2 *	26 Nov 1999	57,388,839
3	Ice Age	15 Mar 2002	46,312,454
4	Shrek	18 May 2001	42,347,760
5	The Lion King	24 Jun 1994	40,888,194
6	Dinosaur	19 May 2000	38,854,851
7	Lilo & Stitch	21 Jun 2002	35,260,212
8	Tarzan	18 Jun 1999	34,221,968
9	A Bug's Life *	28 Nov 1998	33,258,052
10	Pokémon: The First Movie	12 Nov 1999	31,036,678

* Second weekend; opening weekend release in limited number of cinemas only

TOP 10 OPENING WEEKENDS OF ANIMATED FILMS IN THE UK

	FILM	UK RELEASE	WEEKEND (£)
1	Monsters, Inc.	8 Feb 2002	9,200,257
2	Toy Story 2	11 Feb 2000	7,971,539
3	Shrek	29 Jun 2001	4,686,210
4	A Bug's Life	5 Feb 1999	4,204,067
5	Chicken Run	30 Jun 2000	3,488,755
6	Toy Story	22 Mar 1996	3,387,160
7	Tarzan	22 Oct 1999	3,055,218
8	Ice Age	22 Mar 2002	3,029,738
9	Pokémon: The First Movie	14 Apr 2000	2,833,721
10	Dinosaur	13 Oct 2000	2,128,218

Monster Movie

Jurassic Park (1993) opened with a roar, achieving the then highest-ever opening weekend. It went on to become the all-time worldwide top earner, a position it held until 1997, when it was eclipsed by *Titanic*.

TOP 10 OPENING WEEKENDS OF 1993 IN THE US

	FILM	WEEKEND ($)
1	Jurassic Park	47,059,460
2	The Firm	24,900,000
3	The Fugitive	23,758,855
4	Mrs. Doubtfire	20,468,847
5	Cliffhanger	20,458,022
6	Indecent Proposal	18,387,632
7	Sleepless in Seattle	17,253,733
8	The Pelican Brief	16,600,000
9	In the Line of Fire	15,269,388
10	Rising Sun	15,195,941

Schindler's List also opened in 1993. Despite taking only $3 million on its first weekend, it went on to make almost $100 million in the US and more than $300 million worldwide, and won the "Best Picture" Oscar.

TOP 10 OPENING WEEKENDS OF 1994 IN THE US

	FILM	WEEKEND ($)
1	The Lion King	40,888,194
2	The Flintstones *	37,182,745
3	Interview with the Vampire	36,389,705
4	True Lies	25,869,770
5	Forrest Gump	24,450,602
6	The Mask	23,117,068
7	Star Trek: Generations	23,116,394
8	Clear and Present Danger	20,348,017
9	The Santa Clause	19,321,992
10	Wolf	17,911,366

* Released Memorial Day weekend (27 May), a four-day holiday

TOP 10 OPENING WEEKENDS OF 1995 IN THE US

	FILM	WEEKEND ($)
1	Batman Forever	52,784,433
2	Ace Ventura: When Nature Calls	37,804,076
3	Pocahontas	29,531,619
4	Toy Story	29,140,617
5	GoldenEye	26,205,007
6	Apollo 13	25,353,380
7	Congo	24,642,539
8	Mortal Kombat	23,283,887
9	Die Hard: With a Vengeance	22,162,245
10	Casper	22,091,975

TOP 10 OPENING WEEKENDS OF 1996 IN THE US

	FILM	WEEKEND ($)
1	Independence Day	50,228,264
2	Mission: Impossible	45,436,830
3	Twister	41,059,405
4	Ransom	34,216,088
5	101 Dalmatians	33,504,025
6	Star Trek: First Contact	30,716,131
7	Space Jam	27,528,529
8	The Nutty Professor	25,411,725
9	The Rock	25,069,525
10	Eraser	24,566,446

TOP 10 OPENING WEEKENDS OF 1997 IN THE US

	FILM	WEEKEND ($)
1	The Lost World: Jurassic Park	72,132,785
2	Men in Black	51,068,455
3	Batman and Robin	42,872,606
4	Air Force One	37,135,505
5	Star Wars *	35,906,661
6	Scream 2	32,926,342
7	Liar Liar	31,423,025
8	Titanic	28,638,131
9	Flubber	26,725,207
10	Tomorrow Never Dies	25,143,007

* Special Edition re-release of 1977 film

TOP 10 OPENING WEEKENDS OF 1998 IN THE US

	FILM	WEEKEND ($)
1	Godzilla	44,047,541
2	Deep Impact	41,152,375
3	The Waterboy	39,414,071
4	Armageddon	36,089,972
5	Lethal Weapon 4	34,048,124
6	A Bug's Life	33,258,052
7	Rush Hour	33,001,803
8	The Truman Show	31,542,121
9	Saving Private Ryan	30,576,104
10	The X-Files	30,138,758

You wait years for a film about comet or asteroid impact, then two come along at once: *Deep Impact* and *Armageddon* were released within two months of each other, but both did well at the box office, with global totals of $350 million and $555 million respectively.

TOP 10 OPENING WEEKENDS OF 1999 IN THE US

	FILM	WEEKEND ($)
1	Star Wars: Episode I – The Phantom Menace	64,820,970
2	Toy Story 2	57,388,839
3	Austin Powers: The Spy Who Shagged Me	54,917,604
4	The Mummy	43,369,635
5	Big Daddy	41,536,370
6	The World is Not Enough	35,519,007
7	Runaway Bride	35,055,556
8	Tarzan	34,221,968
9	The Haunting	33,435,140
10	Pokémon: The First Movie	31,036,678

TOP 10 OPENING WEEKENDS OF 2000 IN THE US

	FILM	WEEKEND ($)
1	Mission: Impossible 2	57,845,297
2	How the Grinch Stole Christmas	55,082,330
3	X-Men	54,471,475
4	Nutty Professor II: The Klumps	42,518,830
5	Scary Movie	42,346,669
6	The Perfect Storm	41,325,042
7	Charlie's Angels	40,128,550
8	Dinosaur	38,854,851
9	Gladiator	34,819,017
10	Scream 3	34,713,342

Cast Away just failed to make the Top 10 – but went on to outearn almost all its rivals, with a world total of over $400 million.

TOP 10 OPENING WEEKENDS OF 2001 IN THE US

	FILM	WEEKEND ($)
1	Harry Potter and the Sorcerer's Stone	90,294,621
2	Planet of the Apes	68,532,960
3	The Mummy Returns	68,139,035
4	Rush Hour 2	67,408,222
5	Monsters, Inc.	62,577,067
6	Pearl Harbor	59,078,912
7	Hannibal	58,003,121
8	Jurassic Park III	50,771,645
9	Lara Croft: Tomb Raider	47,735,743
10	The Lord of the Rings: The Fellowship of the Ring	47,211,490

TOP 10 OPENING WEEKENDS OF 2002 IN THE US

	FILM	WEEKEND ($)
1	Spider-Man	114,844,116
2	Harry Potter and the Chamber of Secrets	88,357,488
3	Star Wars: Episode II – Attack of the Clones	80,027,814
4	Austin Powers in Goldmember	73,071,188
5	The Lord of the Rings: The Two Towers	62,007,528
6	Signs	60,117,080
7	Scooby-Doo	54,155,312
8	Men in Black II	52,148,751
9	8 Mile	51,240,555
10	Die Another Day	47,072,040

Along came a Spider ...

Spider-Man (2002) became the highest-earning film in a weekend and the fastest ever to reach $100M, $200M, and $300M in the US. It has now earned more than $800M worldwide.

TOP 10 FILMS OF THE 1920s

	FILM	YEAR
1	The Big Parade	1925
2	The Four Horsemen of the Apocalypse	192
3	Ben-Hur	1926
4	The Ten Commandments	1923
5	What Price Glory?	1926
6	The Covered Wagon	1923
7	Way Down East	192
8	The Singing Fool	1928
9	Wings	192
10	The Gold Rush	1925

Earnings data for early films is unreliable, but if this list were extended back to the first decade of the 20th century, *The Birth of a Nation* (1915) would be a contender as the highest-earning film of the silent era.

TOP 10 FILMS OF THE 1930s

	FILM	YEAR
1	Gone With the Wind *	1939
2	Snow White and the Seven Dwarfs †	1937
3	The Wizard of Oz	1939
4	Frankenstein	193
5	King Kong	1933
6	San Francisco	1936
7 =	Hell's Angels	1930
=	Lost Horizon	1937
=	Mr. Smith Goes to Washington	1939

* "Best Picture" Academy Award
† Animated

TOP 10 FILMS OF THE 1940s

	FILM	YEAR
1	Bambi *	1942
2	Pinocchio *	1940
3	Fantasia *	1940
4	Song of the South †	1946
5	Mom and Dad	1944
6	Samson and Delilah	1949
7	The Best Years of Our Lives #	1946
8	The Bells of St. Mary's	1945
9	Duel in the Sun	1946
10	This is the Army	1943

* Animated
† Part animated/part live-action
# "Best Picture" Academy Award

The top four were classic Disney cartoons, appealing in this era as colourful escapism during and after the austerity of the war years.

Apocalypse Then
Rudolph Valentino as tango expert Julio Desnoyers in *The Four Horsemen of the Apocalypse* (1921), a silent saga that is reputed to have earned a then remarkable $9 million.

	FILM	YEAR
1	Lady and the Tramp *	1955
2	Peter Pan *	1953
3	Cinderella *	1950
4	The Ten Commandments	1956
5	Ben-Hur †	1959
6	Sleeping Beauty *	1959
7	Around the World in 80 Days †	1956
8	This is Cinerama	1952
9	South Pacific	1958
10	The Robe	1953

* Animated
† "Best Picture" Academy Award

	FILM	YEAR
1	One Hundred and One Dalmatians *	1961
2	The Jungle Book *	1967
3	The Sound of Music †	1965
4	Thunderball	1965
5	Goldfinger	1964
6	Doctor Zhivago	1965
7	You Only Live Twice	1967
8	The Graduate	1968
9	Butch Cassidy and the Sundance Kid	1969
10	Mary Poppins	1964

* Animated
† "Best Picture" Academy Award

	FILM	YEAR
1	Star Wars *	197
2	Jaws	1975
3	Grease	1978
4	Close Encounters of the Third Kind	197
5	The Exorcist	197
6	Superman	1978
7	Saturday Night Fever	197
8	Jaws 2	1978
9	Moonraker	197
10	The Spy Who Loved Me	197

* Later retitled *Star Wars: Episode IV – A New Hope*
In the 1970s, the arrival of the two prodigies, Steven Spielberg and George Lucas, set the scene for the high adventure blockbusters, the domination of which has continued ever since. Lucas wrote and directed *Star Wars*, while Spielberg directed *Jaws* and wrote and directed *Close Encounters of the Third Kind*.

You'll Believe a Man Can Fly
One of the highest-earning films of the 1970s, topping $300 million worldwide, *Superman* won an Oscar for its spectacular special effects.

TOP 10 FILMS OF THE 1980s

	FILM	YEAR
1	E.T. the Extra-Terrestrial	1982
2	Return of the Jedi *	1983
3	The Empire Strikes Back †	1980
4	Indiana Jones and the Last Crusade	1989
5	Rain Man #	1988
6	Raiders of the Lost Ark	1981
7	Batman	1989
8	Back to the Future	1985
9	Who Framed Roger Rabbit	1988
10	Top Gun	1986

* Later retitled *Star Wars: Episode VI – Return of The Jedi*
† Later retitled *Star Wars: Episode V – The Empire Strikes Back*
# "Best Picture" Academy Award
The 1980s was the decade of the adventure film, with George Lucas and Steven Spielberg continuing to assert their control of Hollywood, as directors, writers, or producers of no fewer than

TOP 10 FILMS OF THE 1990s

	FILM	YEAR
1	Titanic *	1997
2	Star Wars: Episode I – The Phantom Menace	1999
3	Jurassic Park	1993
4	Independence Day	1996
5	The Lion King †	1994
6	Forrest Gump *	1994
7	The Sixth Sense	1999
8	The Lost World: Jurassic Park	1997
9	Men in Black	1997
10	Armageddon	1998

* "Best Picture" Academy Award
† Animated
Each of the Top 10 films of the 1990s has earned more than $550 million around the world, making a total of more than $8.4 billion between them.

TOP 10 FILMS OF THE 2000s*

	FILM	YEAR
1	Harry Potter and the Sorcerer's Stone	200
2	The Lord of the Rings: The Two Towers	2002
3	Harry Potter and the Chamber of Secrets	2002
4	The Lord of the Rings: The Fellowship of the Ring	200
5	Spider-Man	200
6	Star Wars: Episode II – Attack of the Clones	2002
7	Mission: Impossible 2	2000
8	Monsters, Inc. †	200
9	Shrek †	200
10	Gladiator #	2000

* As at 31 March 2003

TOP 10 FILMS OF 1953

	FILM
1	Peter Pan *
2	The Robe
3	From Here to Eternity †
4	The House of Wax
5	Shane
6	How to Marry a Millionaire
7	Niagara
8	Gentlemen Prefer Blondes
9	Knights of the Round Table
10	Salome

* Animated
† "Best Picture" Academy Award

TOP 10 FILMS OF 1954

	FILM
1	White Christmas
2	20,000 Leagues Under the Sea
3	Rear Window
4	The Caine Mutiny
5	The Glenn Miller Story
6	The Country Girl
7	Seven Brides for Seven Brothers
8 =	The High and the Mighty
=	A Star is Born
10	Magnificent Obsession

TOP 10 FILMS OF 1955

	FILM
1	Lady and the Tramp *
2	Cinerama Holiday
3	Mister Roberts
4	Battle Cry
5	Oklahoma!
6	Guys and Dolls
7	Picnic
8	Not as a Stranger
9	I'll Cry Tomorrow
10 =	The Sea Chase
=	The Seven Year Itch
=	Strategic Air Command

* Animated

TOP 10 FILMS OF 1956

	FILM
1	The Ten Commandments
2	Around the World in 80 Days *
3	Giant
4	Seven Wonders of the World
5	The King and I
6	Trapeze
7	War and Peace
8	High Society
9	Teahouse of the August Moon
10	The Eddy Duchin Story

* "Best Picture" Academy Award

TOP 10 FILMS OF 1957

	FILM
1	The Bridge on the River Kwai *
2	Peyton Place
3	Sayonara
4	Old Yeller
5	Bayou (Poor White Trash)
6	Raintree County
7 =	A Farewell to Arms
=	Island in the Sun
9 =	Gunfight at the OK Corral
=	Pal Joey

* "Best Picture" Academy Award

TOP 10 FILMS OF 1958

	FILM
1	South Pacific
2	Auntie Mame
3	Cat on a Hot Tin Roof
4	No Time for Sergeants
5	Gigi *
6	The Seventh Voyage of Sinbad
7	The Vikings
8	Vertigo
9	The Young Lions
10	Some Came Running

* "Best Picture" Academy Award

TOP 10 FILMS OF 1959

	FILM
1	Ben-Hur *
2	Sleeping Beauty †
3	The Shaggy Dog
4	Operation Petticoat
5	Darby O'Gill and the Little People
6	Some Like It Hot
7	Pillow Talk
8	North by Northwest
9	Imitation of Life
10	Suddenly Last Summer

* "Best Picture" Academy Award
† Animated

TOP 10 FILMS OF 1960

	FILM
1	Swiss Family Robinson
2	Psycho
3	Spartacus
4	Exodus
5	La Dolce Vita
6	The Alamo
7	Butterfield 8
8	The World of Suzie Wong
9	The Apartment *
10	Ocean's Eleven

* "Best Picture" Academy Award

Racing Ahead

Made with a then huge $15-million budget, *Ben-Hur* was the last and one of the most successful epics of the 1950s, scooping 11 Academy Awards, a record it held until equalled by *Titanic*.

TOP 10 FILMS OF 1961

	FILM
1	One Hundred and One Dalmatians *
2	West Side Story †
3	The Guns of Navarone
4	El Cid
5	The Absent-Minded Professor
6	The Parent Trap
7	Lover Come Back
8	King of Kings
9	Come September
10	Flower Drum Song

* Animated
† "Best Picture" Academy Award

TOP 10 FILMS OF 1962

	FILM
1	How the West Was Won
2	The Longest Day
3	Lawrence of Arabia *
4	In Search of the Castaways
5	The Music Man
6	That Touch of Mink
7	Mutiny on the Bounty
8	Hatari
9	To Kill a Mockingbird
10	Gypsy

* "Best Picture" Academy Award

TOP 10 FILMS OF 1963

	FILM
1	Cleopatra
2	It's a Mad, Mad, Mad, Mad World
3	Tom Jones *
4	Irma la Douce
5	The Sword in the Stone
6	Son of Flubber
7	Dr. No
8	Charade
9	Bye Bye Birdie
10	Come Blow Your Horn

* "Best Picture" Academy Award

TOP 10 FILMS OF 1964

	FILM
1	Mary Poppins
2	My Fair Lady *
3	Goldfinger
4	The Carpetbaggers
5	From Russia With Love
6	A Shot in the Dark
7	A Hard Day's Night
8	The Unsinkable Molly Brown
9	The Pink Panther
10	Father Goose

* "Best Picture" Academy Award

TOP 10 FILMS OF 1965

	FILM
1	The Sound of Music *
2	Doctor Zhivago
3	Thunderball
4	Those Magnificent Men in their Flying Machines
5	That Darn Cat
6	The Great Race
7	Cat Ballou
8	What's New Pussycat?
9	Shenandoah
10	Von Ryan's Express

* "Best Picture" Academy Award

TOP 10 FILMS OF 1966

	FILM
1	The Bible ... In the Beginning
2	Hawaii
3	Who's Afraid of Virginia Woolf?
4	A Man for All Seasons *
5	Lt. Robin Crusoe, U.S.N.
6	The Russians Are Coming, the Russians Are Coming
7	Grand Prix
8	The Professionals
9	Alfie
10	Georgy Girl

* "Best Picture" Academy Award

TOP 10 FILMS OF 1967

	FILM
1	The Jungle Book *
2	Bonnie and Clyde
3	The Dirty Dozen
4	Valley of the Dolls
5	You Only Live Twice
6	To Sir, With Love
7	The Born Losers
8	Thoroughly Modern Millie
9	Camelot
10	The Sand Pebbles †

* Animated
† Released in the US on 20 Dec 1966, but earned most of its income in 1967

What the Doctor Ordered

Although beaten as "Best Picture" by *The Sound of Music*, *Doctor Zhivago* nevertheless went on to earn over $100 million in the US alone.

Bob and Harry

Paul Newman as Butch Cassidy (Robert Leroy Parker) and Robert Redford as The Sundance Kid (Harry Longbaugh) co-starred in the top earning film of 1969. Director Roy George Hill had originally cast them in the opposite roles.

TOP 10 FILMS OF 1968

	FILM
1	The Graduate †
2	Funny Girl
3	2001: A Space Odyssey
4	Guess Who's Coming to Dinner
5	The Odd Couple
6	Bullitt
7	Romeo and Juliet
8	Oliver! *
9	Rosemary's Baby
10	Planet of the Apes

† Released in the US on 21 December 1967, but became the most successful film of 1968, earning more than $100 million at the box office.
* "Best Picture" Academy Award

TOP 10 FILMS OF 1969

	FILM
1	Butch Cassidy and the Sundance Kid
2	The Love Bug
3	Midnight Cowboy *
4	Easy Rider
5	Hello, Dolly!
6	Bob and Carol and Ted and Alice
7	Paint Your Wagon
8	True Grit
9	Cactus Flower
10	Goodbye, Columbus

* "Best Picture" Academy Award

TOP 10 FILMS OF 1970

	FILM
1	Love Story
2	Airport
3	M*A*S*H
4	Patton *
5	The Aristocats †
6	Woodstock
7	Little Big Man
8	Ryan's Daughter
9	Tora! Tora! Tora!
10	Catch-22

* "Best Picture" Academy Award
† Animated

TOP 10 FILMS OF 1971

	FILM
1	Billy Jack
2	Fiddler on the Roof
3	Diamonds Are Forever
4	The French Connection *
5	Summer of '42
6	Carnal Knowledge
7	Dirty Harry
8	A Clockwork Orange
9	The Last Picture Show
10	Bedknobs and Broomsticks

* "Best Picture" Academy Award

TOP 10 FILMS OF 1972

	FILM
1	The Godfather *
2	The Poseidon Adventure
3	What's Up, Doc?
4	Deliverance
5	Jeremiah Johnson
6	Cabaret
7	The Getaway
8	Lady Sings the Blues
9	Everything You Always Wanted to Know About Sex …
10	The Valachi Papers

* "Best Picture" Academy Award
Made with a budget of $6 million, *The Godfather* earned $135 million at the US box office.

TOP 10 FILMS OF 1973

	FILM
1	The Exorcist
2	The Sting *
3	American Graffiti
4	Papillon
5	The Way We Were
6	Magnum Force
7	Last Tango in Paris
8	Live and Let Die
9	Robin Hood †
10	Paper Moon

* "Best Picture" Academy Award
† Animated

TOP 10 FILMS OF 1974

	FILM
1	Blazing Saddles
2	The Trial of Billy Jack
3	Earthquake
4	The Godfather, Part II *
5	Airport 1975
6	The Longest Yard
7	Benji
8	Murder on the Orient Express
9	Herbie Rides Again
10	The Texas Chain Saw Massacre

* "Best Picture" Academy Award

TOP 10 FILMS OF 1975

	FILM
1	Jaws
2	The Rocky Horror Picture Show
3	The Towering Inferno
4	One Flew Over the Cuckoo's Nest *
5	Young Frankenstein
6	Shampoo
7	Dog Day Afternoon
8	The Life and Times of Grizzly Adams
9	The Return of the Pink Panther
10	Three Days of the Condor

* "Best Picture" Academy Award

TOP 10 FILMS OF 1976

	FILM
1	Rocky *
2	A Star is Born
3	All the President's Men
4	The Omen
5	King Kong
6	Silver Streak
7	The Enforcer
8	The Bad News Bears
9	Silent Movie
10	The Pink Panther Strikes Again

* "Best Picture" Academy Award

TOP 10 FILMS OF 1977

	FILM
1	Star Wars *
2	Close Encounters of the Third Kind
3	Saturday Night Fever
4	Smokey and the Bandit
5	The Goodbye Girl
6	Oh, God!
7	A Bridge too Far
8	The Deep
9	The Spy Who Loved Me
10	Annie Hall †

* Later retitled *Star Wars: Episode IV – A New Hope*
† "Best Picture" Academy Award

TOP 10 FILMS OF 1978

	FILM
1	Grease
2	National Lampoon's Animal House
3	Superman
4	Every Which Way But Loose
5	Jaws 2
6	Heaven Can Wait
7	The Deer Hunter *
8	Hooper
9	Revenge of the Pink Panther
10	Halloween

* "Best Picture" Academy Award

TOP 10 FILMS OF 1979

	FILM
1	The Amityville Horror
2	Star Trek: The Motion Picture
3	Alien
4	Apocalypse Now
5	The Muppet Movie
6	10
7	The Jerk
8	Rocky II
9	Moonraker
10	Manhattan

TOP 10 FILMS OF 1980

	FILM
1	The Empire Strikes Back *
2	9 to 5
3	Stir Crazy
4	Kramer vs. Kramer †
5	Airplane
6	Coal Miner's Daughter
7	Any Which Way You Can
8	Private Benjamin
9	Smokey and the Bandit II
10	The Blues Brothers

* Later retitled *Star Wars: Episode V – The Empire Strikes Back*
† "Best Picture" Academy Award; released in the US on 19 December 1979, earning most of its income during 1980.

TOP 10 FILMS OF 1981

	FILM
1	Raiders of the Lost Ark
2	Superman II
3	Arthur
4	Stripes
5	The Cannonball Run
6	Chariots of Fire *
7	For Your Eyes Only
8	The Four Seasons
9	Time Bandits
10	Clash of the Titans

* "Best Picture" Academy Award

TOP 10 FILMS OF 1982

	FILM
1	E.T. the Extra-Terrestrial
2	Tootsie
3	An Officer and a Gentleman
4	Rocky III
5	On Golden Pond *
6	Porky's
7	Star Trek II: The Wrath of Khan
8	48 Hrs.
9	Poltergeist
10	The Best Little Whorehouse in Texas

* Released in a limited number of cinemas in December 1981, but widely in January 1982.

TOP 10 FILMS OF 1983

	FILM
1	Return of the Jedi *
2	Terms of Endearment †
3	Flashdance
4	Trading Places
5	WarGames
8	Octopussy
6	Sudden Impact
9	Staying Alive
7	Mr. Mom
10	Risky Business

* Later retitled *Star Wars: Episode VI – Return of the Jedi*
† "Best Picture" Academy Award

TOP 10 FILMS OF 1984

	FILM
1	Ghostbusters
2	Beverly Hills Cop
3	Indiana Jones and the Temple of Doom
4	Gremlins
5	The Karate Kid
6	Police Academy
7	Footloose
9	Romancing the Stone
8	Star Trek III: The Search for Spock
10	Splash!

TOP 10 FILMS OF 1985

	FILM
1	Back to the Future
2	Rambo: First Blood Part II
3	Rocky IV
4	The Color Purple
5	Out of Africa *
6	Cocoon
7	The Jewel of the Nile
8	Witness
9	The Goonies
10	Spies Like Us

* "Best Picture" Academy Award

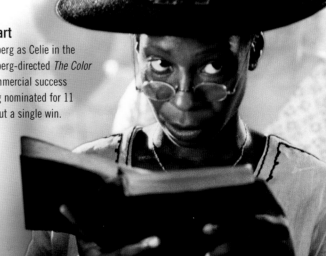

Purple Heart
Whoopi Goldberg as Celie in the Steven Spielberg-directed *The Color Purple*, a commercial success despite being nominated for 11 Oscars without a single win.

TOP 10 FILMS OF 1986

FILM

1 Top Gun
2 Crocodile Dundee
3 Platoon *
4 The Karate Kid Part II
5 Star Trek IV: The Voyage Home
6 Back to School
7 The Golden Child
8 Ruthless People
9 Aliens
10 Ferris Bueller's Day Off

* "Best Picture" Academy Award

TOP 10 FILMS OF 1987

FILM

1 Fatal Attraction
2 Beverly Hills Cop II
3 The Living Daylights
4 The Untouchables
5 Three Men and a Baby
6 Dirty Dancing
7 Good Morning, Vietnam
8 Moonstruck
9 Stakeout
10 The Secret of My Succe$s

TOP 10 FILMS OF 1988

FILM

1 Rain Man *
2 Who Framed Roger Rabbit
3 Coming to America
4 Twins
5 A Fish Called Wanda
6 Rambo III
7 Die Hard
8 Crocodile Dundee II
9 Big
10 The Naked Gun

* "Best Picture" Academy Award

TOP 10 FILMS OF 1989

FILM

1 Indiana Jones and the Last Crusade
2 Batman
3 Back to the Future, Part II
4 Look Who's Talking
5 Dead Poets Society
6 Lethal Weapon 2
7 Honey, I Shrunk the Kids
8 Ghostbusters II
9 The Little Mermaid *
10 Born on the Fourth of July

* Animated

TOP 10 FILMS OF 1990

FILM

1 Home Alone
2 Ghost
3 Pretty Woman
4 Dances With Wolves *
5 Total Recall
6 Back to the Future, Part III
7 Die Hard 2: Die Harder
8 Presumed Innocent
9 Teenage Mutant Ninja Turtles
10 Kindergarten Cop

* "Best Picture" Academy Award

TOP 10 FILMS OF 1991

FILM

1 Terminator 2: Judgment Day
2 Robin Hood: Prince of Thieves
3 Beauty and the Beast *
4 Hook
5 The Silence of the Lambs †
6 JFK
7 The Addams Family
8 Cape Fear
9 City Slickers
10 Hot Shots!

* Animated
† "Best Picture" Academy Award

TOP 10 FILMS OF 1992

FILM

1 Aladdin *
2 The Bodyguard
3 Basic Instinct
4 Lethal Wespon 3
5 Batman Returns
6 Home Alone 2: Lost in New York
7 A Few Good Men
8 Sister Act
9 Bram Stoker's Dracula
10 Wayne's World

* Animated

TOP 10 FILMS OF 1993

FILM

1 Jurassic Park
2 Mrs. Doubtfire
3 The Fugitive
4 Indecent Proposal
5 Schindler's List *
6 The Firm
7 Cliffhanger
8 Sleepless in Seattle
9 Philadelphia
10 The Pelican Brief

* "Best Picture" Academy Award

TOP 10 FILMS OF 1994

FILM

1 The Lion King *
2 Forrest Gump †
3 True Lies
4 The Flintstones
5 The Mask
6 Speed
7 Dumb & Dumber
8 Four Weddings and a Funeral
9 Interview With the Vampire: The Vampire Chronicles
10 Disclosure

* Animated
† "Best Picture" Academy Award

Home Economics

Top film of 1990, *Home Alone* earned some $286 million in the US and $248 million in the rest of the world.

TOP 10 FILMS OF 1995

FILM

1 Die Hard: With a Vengeance
2 Toy Story *
3 GoldenEye
4 Pocahontas *
5 Batman Forever
6 Se7en
7 Casper †
8 Jumanji
9 Waterworld
10 Apollo 13

* Animated
† Part animated, part live-action

TOP 10 FILMS OF 1996

FILM

1 Independence Day
2 Twister
3 Mission: Impossible
4 The Rock
5 The Hunchback of Notre Dame *
6 101 Dalmatians
7 Ransom
8 The Nutty Professor
9 Jerry Maguire
10 Eraser

* Animated

TOP 10 FILMS OF 1997

FILM

1 Titanic *
2 The Lost World: Jurassic Park
3 Men in Black
4 Tomorrow Never Dies
5 Air Force One
6 As Good As It Gets
7 Liar Liar
8 My Best Friend's Wedding
9 The Fifth Element
10 The Full Monty

* "Best Picture" Academy Award

TOP 10 FILMS OF 1998

FILM

1 Armageddon
2 Saving Private Ryan
3 Godzilla
4 A Bug's Life *
5 There's Something About Mary
6 Deep Impact
7 Mulan *
8 Doctor Dolittle
9 Shakespeare in Love
10 Lethal Weapon 4

* Animated

TOP 10 FILMS OF 1999

FILM

1 Star Wars: Episode I – The Phantom Menace
2 The Sixth Sense
3 Toy Story 2 *
4 Tarzan *
5 The Matrix
6 The Mummy
7 Notting Hill
8 The World is Not Enough
9 American Beauty
10 Austin Powers: The Spy Who Shagged Me

* Animated

TOP 10 FILMS OF 2000

FILM

1 Mission: Impossible 2
2 Gladiator *
3 Cast Away
4 What Women Want
5 Dinosaur †
6 Dr. Seuss's How the Grinch Stole Christmas
7 Meet the Parents
8 The Perfect Storm
9 X-Men
10 What Lies Beneath

* "Best Picture" Academy Award
† Animated

TOP 10 FILMS OF 2001

FILM

1 Harry Potter and the Sorcerer's Stone
2 The Lord of the Rings: The Fellowship of the Ring
3 Monsters, Inc.*
4 Shrek *
5 Pearl Harbor
6 Ocean's Eleven
7 The Mummy Returns
8 Jurassic Park III
9 Planet of the Apes
10 Hannibal

* Animated

TOP 10 FILMS OF 2002

FILM

1 The Lord of the Rings: The Two Towers
2 Harry Potter and the Chamber of Secrets
3 Spider-Man
4 Star Wars: Episode II – Attack of the Clones
5 Men in Black II
6 Signs
7 Die Another Day
8 Ice Age *
9 My Big Fat Greek Wedding
10 Minority Report

* Animated

Sailing into History

The record worldwide gross of *Titanic* is double that of the second highest-earning film, *Harry Potter and the Sorcerer's Stone* (2001).

	FILM	YEAR	LANGUAGE*	TOTAL (US$)
1	Crouching Tiger, Hidden Dragon	2000	Mandarin	128,078,872
2	Life Is Beautiful	1998	Italian	57,600,759
3	Amélie	2001	French	33,225,499
4	The Gods Must Be Crazy	1984	Afrikaans	30,031,783
5	Il Postino	1995	Italian	21,845,977
6	Like Water for Chocolate	1993	Spanish	21,665,468
7	La Dolce Vita	1966	Italian	19,500,000
8	Brotherhood of the Wolf	2002	French	18,828,863
9	I am Curious (Yellow)	1969	Swedish	18,570,318
10	La Cage aux Folles	1979	French	17,921,489

* Some dubbed into English, other subtitled

TOP 10 FILMS OF ALL TIME IN JAPAN

	FILM/COUNTRY*	YEAR	TOTAL (US$)
1	Sen to Chihiro no Kamikakushi (Japan) †	2001	228,612,367
2	Harry Potter and the Sorcerer's Stone	2001	127,687,138
3	Harry Potter and the Chamber of Secrets	2002	123,639,707
4	Titanic	1997	101,800,644
5	The Lord of the Rings: The Two Towers	2002	59,156,943
6	Star Wars: Episode I – The Phantom Menace	1999	50,812,345
7	Mononoke Hime (Japan) †	1997	49,959,609
8	Kindaichi Shonen no Jikenbo (Japan) †	1997	47,637,131
9	Armageddon	1998	45,533,387
10	Independence Day	1996	44,239,833

* USA unless otherwise stated
† Animated

TOP 10 FILMS OF ALL TIME IN AUSTRALIA

	FILM/COUNTRY	YEAR	TOTAL (AUS$)
1	Titanic	1997	57,642,943
2	Crocodile Dundee	1986	47,707,045
3	The Lord of the Rings: The Fellowship of The Ring	2001	46,725,000
4	The Lord of the Rings: The Two Towers	2002	45,183,872
5	Harry Potter and the Sorcerer's Stone	2001	42,302,657
6	Star Wars: Episode I – The Phantom Menace	1999	38,828,310
7	Harry Potter and the Chamber of Secrets	2002	37,009,842
8	Babe	1995	36,776,544
9	Star Wars: Episode II – Attack of the Clones	2002	33,432,227
10	Jurassic Park	1993	33,002,776

Life Is Beautiful, 1998
Oscar-winning *Life Is Beautiful* (*La Vita è bela*) has made some $230 million worldwide and topped an American Film Institute survey of favourite foreign films in the US.

Did you know?

Actor-director Roberto Benigni came across the title of his film, *Life Is Beautiful*, in a 1940 letter by communist leader Leon Trotsky, written despite being aware that he was under imminent threat of assassination.

TOP 10 FILMS OF ALL TIME IN GERMANY

	FILM/COUNTRY*	YEAR	TOTAL (EUROS)
1	Titanic	1998	118,195,600
2	The Lord of the Rings: The Fellowship of The Ring	2001	78,751,699
3	Harry Potter and the Sorcerer's Stone	2001	76,250,269
4	The Lord of the Rings: The Two Towers	2002	72,910,575
5	Der Schuh des Manitu (Germany)	2001	64,885,845
6	Harry Potter and the Chamber of Secrets	2002	59,299,013
7	Independence Day	1996	54,979,727
8	Star Wars: Episode I – The Phantom Menace	1999	51,057,368
9	The Lion King	1994	50,359,247
10	Jurassic Park	1993	47,085,387

* USA unless otherwise stated

TOP 10 FILMS OF ALL TIME IN FRANCE

	FILM/COUNTRY*	YEAR	TOTAL (US$)
1	Titanic	1998	138,928,349
2	Astérix & Obélix: Mission Cleopatra (France)	2002	75,846,048
3	Taxi 2 (France)	2000	63,703,757
4	Astérix & Obélix contre César (France)	1999	59,154,242
5	Star Wars: Episode I – The Phantom Menace	1999	55,825,511
6	The Fifth Element	1997	54,080,230
7	Les visiteurs II: Les couloirs du temps (France)	1998	53,898,537
8	Harry Potter and the Chamber of Secrets	2002	53,257,276
9	Le dîner de cons (France)	1999	53,155,025
10	Harry Potter and the Sorcerer's Stone	2001	48,745,200

* USA unless otherwise stated

Tiger Economy
Taiwanese director Ang Lee's martial arts drama *Crouching Tiger, Hidden Dragon* has earned more than $200 million globally, in addition to winning an Oscar for "Best Picture in a Foreign Language".

TOP 10 FILMS OF ALL TIME IN THE NETHERLANDS *

	FILM/COUNTRY†	YEAR	TOTAL (EUROS)
1	Titanic	1998	23,570,666
2	Harry Potter and the Sorcerer's Stone	2001	15,357,620
3	Lord of the Rings: The Fellowship of the Ring	2001	14,145,857
4	The Lion King	1994	13,350,497
5	Jurassic Park	1993	10,133,641
6	Harry Potter and the Chamber of Secrets	2002	10,025,115
7	Flodder in Amerika (The Netherlands)	1992	8,305,214
8	Schindler's List	1994	7,747,636
9	Sixth Sense	2000	7,615,010
10	Basic Instinct	1992	6,989,800

* From 1992 to 1 January 2003
† USA unless otherwise stated

TOP 10 FILMS OF ALL TIME IN SPAIN

	FILM/COUNTRY*	YEAR	TOTAL (US$)
1	Titanic	1997	43,672,525
2	The Lord of the Rings: The Two Towers	2002	33,032,495
3	The Lord of the Rings: The Fellowship of the Ring	2001	28,925,390
4	The Sixth Sense	1999	27,305,275
5	Harry Potter and the Chamber of Secrets	2002	25,890,767
6	Star Wars: Episode I – The Phantom Menace	1999	25,808,403
7	Harry Potter and the Sorcerer's Stone	2001	24,685,592
8	The Others	2001	24,599,316
9	Mortadelo y Filemón (Spain)	2003	24,102,774
10	Spider-Man	2002	22,074,731

* USA unless otherwise stated

TOP 10 FILMS OF ALL TIME IN BRAZIL

	FILM	YEAR*	TOTAL (US$)
1	Titanic	1998	67,072,763
2	The Sixth Sense	1999	25,635,945
3	Spider-Man	2002	15,917,016
4	Independence Day	1996	15,189,740
5	The Lost World: Jurassic Park	1997	12,726,530
6	Insomnia	2002	12,321,136
7	Conspiracy Theory	1997	10,756,200
8	Mission: Impossible 2	2000	10,543,442
9	The Lord of the Rings: The Fellowship of the Ring	2002	10,223,268
10	Harry Potter and the Sorcerer's Stone	2001	9,883,339

* Of release in Brazil; 1995–2003 only

Titanic is not only the highest-earning film of all time in Brazil, but also the film attracting the most admissions, a total of 16,374,377 in its release year alone.

TOP 10 FILMS OF ALL TIME IN SOUTH AFRICA

	FILM/COUNTRY*	YEAR†	TOTAL (US$)
1	Titanic	1998	6,791,489
2	Panic Mechanic (South Africa)	1996	3,403,550
3	Mr. Bones (South Africa)	2002	2,863,287
4	Men in Black	1997	2,420,676
5	Die Another Day	2002	2,409,898
6	The Lord of the Rings: The Two Towers	2002	2,330,478
7	Sweet Home Alabama	2003	2,272,854
8	The Lost World: Jurassic Park	1997	2,263,596
9	Notting Hill	1999	2,201,023
10	Spider-Man	2002	2,099,494

* USA unless otherwise stated
† Of release in South Africa; 1995–2003 only

A Lot of Sense

The Sixth Sense proved a world blockbuster, often through word-of-mouth. In Brazil it earned just $219,260 in its opening week, but such was its popularity that it went on to claim second place among the country's highest earners.

TOP 10 FILMS OF ALL TIME IN NORWAY

	FILM/COUNTRY*	YEAR	ADMISSIONS
1	Titanic	1998	1,360,505
2	The Lord of the Rings: The Fellowship of the Ring	2001	984,593
3	The Lord of the Rings: The Two Towers	2002	964 545
4	Elling (Norway)	2001	769,923
5	Harry Potter and the Sorcerer's Stone	2001	849,826
6	Solan, Ludvig og Gurin med reverompa (Gurin with the Foxtail) (Norway)	1998	674,926
7	Tomorrow Never Dies	1998	619,038
8	Notting Hill	1999	585,981
9	Bridget Jones's Diary	2001	577,827
10	Heftig og begeistret (Cool and Crazy) (Norway/Sweden)	2001	556,200

* USA unless otherwise stated

Elling is a graphic example of how films that are popular in the country in which they were made often do not travel: despite being the most watched Norwegian film, and nominated for an Academy Award, it was shown in a maximum of 19 cinemas in the USA, and in the 19 weeks of its release made a total of just $313,436.

TOP 10 FILMS OF ALL TIME IN DENMARK

	FILM/COUNTRY*	YEAR†	ADMISSIONS
1	Titanic	1998	1,362,510
2	The Lord of the Rings: The Fellowship of the Ring	2002	1,300,000
3	Olsen Banden Ser Rødt (The Olsen Gang Sees Red (Denmark)	1976	1,201,145
4	One Flew Over the Cuckoo's Nest	1976	1,119,769
5	Olsen Banden Deruda (The Olsen Gang Outta Sight) (Denmark)	1977	1,044,772
6	E.T. the Extra-Terrestrial	1982	1,018,707
7	Grease	1978	1,006,102
8	Olsen Banden går i krug (The Olsen Gang Goes to War) (Denmark)	1978	1,005,753
9	Out of Africa (Denmark)	1986	998,909
10	Walter og Carlo – op på fars hat (Denmark)	1985	953,743

* USA unless otherwise stated
† Of release in Denmark

National releases feature prominently in Denmark's Top 10 by admissions, with Academy Award "Best Picture" winner *Out of Africa* – which portrays the life story of Danish author Karen Blixen – also making a strong showing.

TOP 10 COUNTRIES: LORD OF THE RINGS VS HARRY POTTER

	COUNTRY	THE LORD OF THE RINGS (1)*	HARRY POTTER (1)†	THE LORD OF THE RINGS (2)#	HARRY POTTER (2)‡	TOTAL ($)
1	USA	313,364,114	317,575,550	338,457,054	261,970,615	1,231,367,333
2	Japan	68,100,000	163,000,000	61,353,133	142,786,414	435,239,547
3	UK	90,594,754	94,332,297	91,532,943	96,615,756	373,075,750
4	Germany	72,958,930	69,527,477	76,610,552	65,159,415	284,256,374
5	France	35,100,000	48,745,200	39,919,459	53,257,276	177,021,935
6	Spain	28,925,390	24,685,997	33,032,495	25,890,767	112,534,649
7	Australia	23,774,327	22,065,721	27,339,152	22,311,914	95,491,114
8	South Korea	20,800,000	21,500,000	29,678,185	25,361,777	97,339,962
9	Italy	21,210,584	29,000,000	21,570,303	21,497,815	93,278,702
10	Mexico	15,590,373	17,061,008	16,028,285	17,159,598	65,839,264
	Total of Top 10 countries	690,418,472	807,493,250	735,521,561	732,011,347	2,965,444,630

* *The Lord of the Rings: The Fellowship of the Ring* (2001)
† *Harry Potter and the Sorcerer's Stone* (2001)
# *The Lord of the Rings: The Two Towers* (2002)
‡ *Harry Potter and the Chamber of Secrets* (2002)

Gaps of several years often separate the release of a blockbuster and its follow-up, and it is remarkable that both the *Harry Potter* and *Lord of the Rings* films were not only colossal hits on their release, but that they were followed a year later by equally successful sequels, all four films gaining places in the Top 10 top highest-earning films of all time.

Taking Off

Harry Potter and the Sorcerer's (or *Philosopher's*) *Stone* is second only to *Titanic* (1998) among the biggest box office hits in cinema history.

TOP 10 TITANIC COUNTRIES

	COUNTRY	TOTAL ($)
1	USA	600,788,188
2	Germany	141,822,168
3	France	138,928,349
4	UK	119,168,117
5	Japan	101,800,644
6	Brazil	67,072,763
7	Italy	47,955,658
8	Canada	46,836,305
9	Spain	43,672,525
10	Australia	34,829,051

All-time blockbuster *Titanic* (1998) has earned a total of $1,835,388,188 worldwide, of which the Top 10 countries have contributed $1,342,873,768 or 73 per cent. Total US admissions are reported to be 128,099,826.

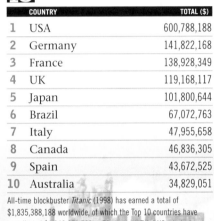

TOP 10 FILMS IN INDIA (ADJUSTED FOR INFLATION)

	FILM	YEAR	TOTAL (RS.)	ADJUSTED (RS.)
1	Sholay	1975	290,000,000	1,913,500,000
2	Hum Aapke Hai Kaun	1994	600,000,000	1,081,730,819
3	Mother India	1957	35,000,000	1,063,595,000
4	Roti Kapada aur Makaan	1974	115,000,000	922,459,846
5	Mughal-e-Azam	1960	35,000,000	873,306,450
6	Upkaar	1967	54,000,000	818,181,862
7	Muqaddar Ka Sikandar	1978	105,000,000	795,454,588
8	Aradhana	1969	55,000,000	785,714,278
9	Dilwale Dulhaniya Le Jayenge	1995	500,000,000	776,525,642
10	Amar Akbar Anthony	1977	95,000,000	738,341,978

While India has a thriving film industry in many languages, and practitioners such as Satyajit Ray (Bengali film director and winner of the Lifetime Achievement Oscar) who have garnered much critical acclaim, it is the Bombay- (now Mumbai-) based "Bollywood" films, made in Hindi, that dominate both in India and in the fast-growing international market, mainly created by Indians settled abroad.

TOP 10 FILMS IN INDIA

	FILM	YEAR	TOTAL (RS.)
1	Gadar	2001	650,000,000
2	Hum Aapke Hai Kaun	1994	600,000,000
3	Dilwale Dulhaniya Le Jayenge	1995	500,000,000
4	Raja Hindustani	1996	450,000,000
5	Kuch Kuch Hota Hai	1998	425,000,000
6	Kabhi Khushi Kabhi Gham	2001	380,500,000
7	Kaho Na Pyaar Hai	2000	350,000,000
8	Karan Arjun	1995	320,000,000
9 =	Border	1997	300,000,000
=	Lagaan	2001	300,000,000

TOP 10 ACTORS

	ACTOR	MAJOR FILMS	BIGGEST BLOCKBUSTER	TOTAL OF ALL FILMS (RS.)
1	Amitabh Bachchan	60	Sholay	22,112,243,425
2	Dharmendra	43	Sholay	16,246,140,935
3	Rajesh Khanna	28	Aradhana	10,017,060,327
4	Dilip Kumar	25	Mughal-e-Azam	9,983,598,131
5	Dev Anand	19	Johnny Mera Naam	7,307,125,969
6	Raj Kapoor	16	Sangam	6,860,832,506
7	Manoj Kumar	16	Roti Kapada aur Makaan	6,830,472,577
8	Jeetendra	27	Dharam Veer	6,504,148,116
9	Ashok Kumar	26	Kismet	5,957,893,395
10	Shashi Kapoor	21	Roti Kapada aur Makaan	5,333,733,749

Referred to as a one-man industry in his heydey, Amitabh Bachchan – who starred in three of the Top 10 Indian films (adjusted for inflation), seven of the Top 10 films of 1970s, and four of the Top 10 of 1980s – made a "comeback" as TV presenter of the Indian version of *Who Wants to Be a Millionaire* in July 2000. Today, at 61, his films continue to find a place in the top films of the 2000s (four films, including a voice-over narration for Oscar-nominated *Lagaan*). He is the only Bollywood star with a waxworks figure in Madame Tussauds.

TOP 10 ACTRESSES

	ACTRESS	MAJOR FILMS	BIGGEST BLOCKBUSTER	TOTAL OF ALL FILMS (RS.)
1	Hema Malini	40	Sholay	6,675,645,563
2	Madhuri Dixit	12	Hum Aapke Hai Kaun	3,509,110,923
3	Sridevi	17	Himmatwala	3,340,220,604
4	Vyjayantimala	12	Sangam	3,253,377,889
5	Nargis	12	Mother India	3,195,823,141
6	Asha Parekh	19	Upkaar	3,066,818,867
7	Zeenat Aman	20	Roti Kapada aur Makaan	3,038,853,164
8	Sadhana	12	Waqt	2,996,539,953
9	Mumtaz	19	Do Raaste	2,910,940,259
10	Waheeda Rehman	20	Ram aur Shyam	2,794,801,615

TOP 10 INDIAN FILMS IN THE US

	FILM	YEAR	US TOTAL ($)
1	Monsoon Wedding	2001	8,398,377
2	Kabhi Khushi Kabhi Gham	2001	2,705,000
3	Hum Aapke Hai Kaun	1994	2,500,000
4	Kuch Kuch Hota Hai	1998	2,100,000
5	Hum Saath Saath Hain	1999	2,005,094
6	Taal	1999	1,980,000
7	Dilwale Dulhaniya Le Jayenge	1995	1,600,000
8	Kaho Na Pyaar Hai	2000	1,500,000
=	Mohabbatein	2000	1,500,000
10	Hum Dil De Chuke Sanam	1999	1,250,000

Made on a budget of Rs.7 million, *Monsoon Wedding*, a joyous but critical examination of North Indian familial traditions and culture, made at least $22 million worldwide, but only approximately 5 per cent of its revenue was generated in India.

TOP 10 INDIAN FILMS IN THE UK

	FILM	YEAR	UK TOTAL (£)
1	Kabhi Khushi Kabhi Gham	2001	2,222,898
2	Monsoon Wedding	2001	2,104,439
3	Devdas	2002	1,663,692
4	Hum Aapke Hai Kaun	1994	1,530,000
5	Dilwale Dulhaniya Le Jayenge	1995	1,490,000
6	Kuch Kuch Hota Hai	1998	1,441,000
7	Mohabbatein	2000	1,100,000
8	Lagaan	2001	681,521
9	Hum Tumhare Hain Sanam	2002	663,778
10	Mujhse Dosti Karoge	2002	611,164

Kabhi Khushi Kabhi Gham, in which the main characters settle in the UK, made an unprecedented 40 per cent-plus of its gross in the overseas market.

Making a Song and Dance

Madhuri Dixit, the second most successful Indian actress, in BAFTA-nominated *Devdas* (2002), which had the then biggest-ever Indian film budget of Rs. 550 million. The film sought to unabashedly celebrate the traditions of music, dance, colour, and opulent sets for which Bollywood is famous.

Curry Eastern

India's first "Spaghetti Western", and its first 70-mm film, *Sholay* is still considered a benchmark for commercial success: it ran for a continuous 5 years at the Minerva cinema in Bombay (now Mumbai).

TOP 10 ACTOR/ACTRESS PAIRINGS

	ACTOR/ACTRESS	FILMS	TOTAL (RS.)
1	Dharmendra/Hema Malini	15	7,170,010,809
2	Raj Kapoor/Nargis	9	3,873,617,182
3	Amitabh Bachchan/Rekha	6	3,198,198,477
4	Amitabh Bachchan/Jaya Bachchan	4	3,185,606,886
5	Amitabh Bachchan/Parveen Babi	8	3,080,495,372
6	Amitabh Bachchan/Raakhee	7	3,012,213,177
7	Rajesh Khanna/Mumtaz	6	2,812,069,266
8	Shahrukh Khan/Kajol	5	2,450,172,966
9	Amitabh Bachchan/Hema Malini	6	2,363,429,601
10	Dharmendra/Zeenat Aman	6	2,311,291,730

TOP 10 DIRECTORS

	DIRECTOR	FILMS	MOST SUCCESSFUL	TOTAL (RS.)
1	Manmohan Desai	14	Amar Akbar Anthony	6,714,885,031
2	Raj Kapoor	8	Sangam	4,343,015,113
3	Yash Chopra	10	Trishul	4,033,634,180
4	Raj Khosla	10	Do Raaste	3,950,324,266
5	Prakash Mehra	9	Muqaddar Ka Sikandar	3,919,021,684
6	Ramesh Sippy	6	Sholay	3,778,661,747
7	Shakti Samanta	10	Aradhana	3,684,678,414
8	Subhash Ghai	11	Vidhaata	3,506,208,674
9	Vijay Anand	8	Johnny Mera Naam	3,258,436,436
10	Manoj Kumar	5	Roti Kapada aur Makaan	3,179,553,578

TOP 10 BOLLYWOOD FILMS OF THE 1950s

	FILM	YEAR	EARNINGS (RS)
1	Mother India	1957	35,000,000
2 =	Madhumati	1958	20,000,000
=	Naya Daur	1957	20,000,000
4 =	Pyaasa	1957	18,000,000
=	Shri 420	1955	18,000,000
6 =	Anari	1959	15,000,000
=	Awaara	1951	15,000,000
=	Azaad	1955	15,000,000
=	Chalti ka Naam Gaadi	1958	15,000,000
=	Devdas	1955	15,000,000
=	Tumsa Nahi Dekha	1957	15,000,000

The first decade after India's independence from colonial rule saw a host of films that addressed the hopes and despairs of a new nation. *Naya Daur, Pyaasa, Shri 420, Anari,* and *Awaara,* all showed dispossessed heroes struggling against unemployment, corrupt businessmen/industrialists, or black-marketeers, with moments of optimism provided by warm-hearted, hard-working, idealistic poor folk.

TOP 10 BOLLYWOOD FILMS OF THE 1960s

	FILM	YEAR	EARNINGS (RS)
1	Aradhana	1969	55,000,000
2	Upkaar	1967	54,000,000
3	Do Raaste	1969	50,000,000
4 =	Aankhen	1968	40,000,000
=	Ram aur Shyam	1967	40,000,000
6 =	Ek Phool Do Mali	1969	37,500,000
=	Sangam	1964	37,500,000
8 =	Jewel Thief	1967	35,000,000
=	Mughal-e-Azam	1960	35,000,000
=	Phool aur Pathar	1966	32,000,000
=	Waqt	1965	32,000,000

While colour films started in India with *Aan* (1952), the technology was slow to pick up. Even in the 1960s, one film, the historical epic *Mughal-e-Azam*, was primarily in black and white, with only one climactic song sequence in colour. *Sangam* was the first Indian film to be shot in European locations.

TOP 10 BOLLYWOOD FILMS OF THE 1970s

	FILM	YEAR	EARNINGS (RS)
1	Sholay	1975	290,000,000
2	Roti Kapada aur Makaan	1974	115,000,000
3	Muqaddar Ka Sikandar	1978	105,000,000
4	Amar Akbar Anthony	1977	95,000,000
5	Dharam Veer	1977	85,000,000
6	Trishul	1978	77,000,000
7 =	Don	1978	75,000,000
=	Hum Kisi Se Kum Nahin	1977	75,000,000
=	Mr. Natwarlal	1979	75,000,000
10	Suhaag	1979	72,000,000

Anger against social injustice and inequality characterised many of the films during the 1970s, even as settings shifted increasingly from rural to urban. Amitabh Bachchan, who acted in 7 of the films listed here, made a career of playing the "angry young man".

TOP 10 BOLLYWOOD FILMS OF THE 1980s

	FILM	YEAR	EARNINGS (RS)
1	Maine Pyar Kiya	1989	150,000,000
2	Ram Teri Ganga Maili	1985	125,000,000
3 =	Coolie	1983	110,000,000
=	Ram Lakhan	1989	110,000,000
=	Tezaab	1988	110,000,000
6 =	Betaab	1983	100,000,000
=	Naseeb	1981	100,000,000
8	Tridev	1989	95,000,000
9	Himmatwala	1983	93,000,000
10 =	Andhaa Kanoon	1983	90,000,000
=	Karma	1986	90,000,000
=	Mard	1985	90,000,000

Mother Courage

Oscar-nominated *Mother India* foregrounded the iconic figure of an Indian peasant woman who stood by her moral values in the face of all adversity, and eventually proved her integrity by killing her own wayward son.

	FILM	YEAR	EARNINGS (RS)
1	Hum Aapke Hai Kaun	1994	600,000,000
2	Dilwale Dulhaniya Le Jayenge	1995	500,000,000
3	Raja Hindustani	1996	450,000,000
4	Kuch Kuch Hota Hai	1998	425,000,000
5	Karan Arjun	1995	320,000,000
6	Border	1997	300,000,000
7	Dil To Pagal Hai	1997	280,000,000
8	Biwi No. 1	1999	210,000,000
9	Ishq	1997	205,000,000
10	Hum Saath Saath Hain	1999	190,000,000

The 1990s witnessed the beginning of India's transition from a protected, highly state-controlled economy to a globalized one. Parallel changes in the film industry saw a heavy increase in the rate of investments, production costs, and stars' remuneration, as well as first-time multiplexes and theatre sound technologies that promised audiences a novel experience. Indian cinema's sibling industry – music – evolved from being dominated by just a couple of companies that had ruled for decades to a mushrooming of different music labels. Most significantly, Bollywood discovered the vast non-resident Indian (NRI) market and started making films that catered to the sentiments of expatriate Indians.

	FILM	YEAR	EARNINGS (RS)
1	Gadar	2001	650,000,000
2	Kabhi Khushi Kabhi Gham	2001	380,500,000
3	Kaho Na Pyaar Hai	2000	350,000,000
=	Lagaan	2001	350,000,000
5	Devdas	2002	292,400,000
6	Mohabbatein	2000	250,000,000
7	The Hero	2003	225,700,000
8	Kaante	2002	212,600,000
9	Raaz	2002	211,400,000
10	Indian	2001	200,000,000

Many blockbusters in the 1990s and 2000s were made featuring NRI characters, albeit with a nostalgia-evoking invocation of "Indian" values and culture (*Dilwale Dulhaniya Le Jayenge, Kuch Kuch Hota Hai, Kabhi Khushi Kabhi Gham, Kaho Na Pyaar Hai, Mohabbatein*). Patriotism is a staple that works within the Indian market, with heroes in *Gadar, The Hero*, and *Indian* saving the country and its values from external enemies. Interestingly, while budgets and revenues seem to be climbing with every passing year, in terms of budget/profit ratio these films still can not compare with all-time blockbuster *Sholay* (budget Rs.20 million/gross Rs.290 million) as opposed to *Gadar* (budget Rs.180 million/gross Rs.650 million).

Did you know?

Lagaan was shot in Bhuj district in Gujarat, an area that was destroyed by an earthquake in January 2001, just after the film was completed. The producers provided relief aid to the villages of the region.

Perfect Pitch

Lagaan, set in 1890s in colonial India, tells the story of villagers who take on the challenge of playing a cricket match against a British garrison, thrown at them by a whimsical officer. If they win, the drought-stricken villagers need not pay their taxes – a matter of life and death for them. The film was nominated for the "Best Foreign Language Picture" Oscar.

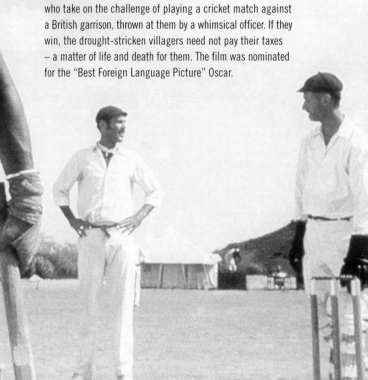

In this star-gazing selection, the lists of the Top 10 Stars of the Year since 1950 are based on an annual poll of major cinemas and provide a series of time capsules of the biggest draws and most magnetic actors and actresses of the past half century, while the Top 10 Stars of Tomorrow lists present a fascinating range of authoritative predictions, many of which came true, while others failed to materialize. The biggest-earners, those appearing in the most $100 million-plus films, the most prolific, and other stars' Top 10s are accompanied by lists featuring the Top 10 films (by earning) of some 75 actors and 60 actresses, presenting a concise summary of the careers of current stars and some of the great names from the past, from Ben Affleck to Bruce Willis, Julie Andrews to Catherine Zeta-Jones.

Blonde Ambition
Marilyn Monroe summed up her own desire, and perhaps that of many other performers, remarking "I want to be a big star more than anything. It's something precious."

TOP 10 STARS OF 1950*

	STAR
1	John Wayne
2	Bob Hope
3	Bing Crosby
4	Betty Grable
5	James Stewart
6	Abbott and Costello
7	Clifton Webb
8	Esther Williams
9	Spencer Tracy
10	Randolph Scott

Since 1933, the *International Motion Picture Almanac* has conducted an annual poll of cinemas to assess which stars they considered the top box office draws of each year. Appearances in the list frequently coincide with the release of a notable film, or with a star's success at the Academy Awards that year. This was the second of 25 years in which John Wayne had appeared in the list, and the first of four in which he topped it.

TOP 10 STARS OF 1951

	STAR
1	John Wayne
2	Dean Martin/Jerry Lewis
3	Betty Grable
4	Abbott and Costello
5	Bing Crosby
6	Bob Hope
7	Randolph Scott
8	Gary Cooper
9	Doris Day
10	Spencer Tracy

World War II pin-up (and once the highest-paid woman in the USA) Betty Grable was included for her 10th consecutive year in the 1951 Stars of the Year list, having topped it in 1943.

TOP 10 STARS OF 1952

	STAR
1	Dean Martin/Jerry Lewis
2	Gary Cooper
3	John Wayne
4	Bing Crosby
5	Bob Hope
6	James Stewart
7	Doris Day
8	Gregory Peck
9	Susan Hayward
10	Randolph Scott

Dean Martin and Jerry Lewis are the only screen partnership, other than Fred Astaire and Ginger Rogers and Abbott and Costello, to figure in the Stars of the Year lists. They made their duo debut in 1949 in *My Friend Irma*, and a total of 16 films up to 1956.

Audiences Prefer Blondes

Marilyn Monroe first appeared in the Stars of the Year Top 10 in 1953, the year in which she appeared in three films, *Niagara*, *Gentlemen Prefer Blondes*, and *How to Marry a Millionaire*.

TOP 10 STARS OF 1953

	STAR
1	Gary Cooper
2	Dean Martin/Jerry Lewis
3	John Wayne
4	Alan Ladd
5	Bing Crosby
6	Marilyn Monroe
7	James Stewart
8	Bob Hope
9	Susan Hayward
10	Randolph Scott

Gary Cooper had featured among the Stars of the Year since 1936, and the previous year had starred in the Western classic *High Noon*.

TOP 10 STARS OF 1954

	STAR
1	John Wayne
2	Dean Martin/Jerry Lewis
3	Gary Cooper
4	James Stewart
5	Marilyn Monroe
6	Alan Ladd
7	William Holden
8	Bing Crosby
9	Jane Wyman
10	Marlon Brando

White Christmas, the film that earned Bing Crosby a place in this year's list, contained the title song previously heard in his *Holiday Inn* (1942), going on to become the bestselling song of all time.

TOP 10 STARS OF 1955

	STAR
1	James Stewart
2	Grace Kelly
3	John Wayne
4	William Holden
5	Gary Cooper
6	Marlon Brando
7	Dean Martin/Jerry Lewis
8	Humphrey Bogart
9	June Allyson
10	Clark Gable

List-leaders James Stewart and Grace Kelly had appeared together the previous year in Alfred Hitchcock's Oscar-nominated thriller *Rear Window*.

TOP 10 STARS OF 1956

	STAR
1	William Holden
2	John Wayne
3	James Stewart
4	Burt Lancaster
5	Glenn Ford
6	Dean Martin/Jerry Lewis
7	Gary Cooper
8	Marilyn Monroe
9	Kim Novak
10	Frank Sinatra

This was the last year in which Dean Martin and Jerry Lewis appeared together in the list. After making their final film together, *Hollywood or Bust* (1956), they pursued solo careers.

TOP 10 STARS OF 1957

	STAR
1	Rock Hudson
2	John Wayne
3	Pat Boone
4	Elvis Presley
5	Frank Sinatra
6	Gary Cooper
7	William Holden
8	James Stewart
9	Jerry Lewis
10	Yul Brynner

Already known as a popular singer, Pat Boone, whose *Love Letters in the Sand* was the biggest-selling US single of 1957, made his acting debut this year with films including *April Love*, the title track of which was also a chart hit.

TOP 10 STARS OF 1958

	STAR
1	Glenn Ford
2	Elizabeth Taylor
3	Jerry Lewis
4	Marlon Brando
5	Rock Hudson
6	William Holden
7	Brigitte Bardot
8	Yul Brynner
9	James Stewart
10	Frank Sinatra

Elizabeth Taylor had been making films since 1942, but this was the year in which she received her first Oscar nomination, for her role in *Raintree Country* (1957), and was to gain her second for *Cat on a Hot Tin Roof* (1958).

Did you know?

John Wayne's appearance in the Stars of the Year list of 1956 coincided with the release of *The Conqueror*, in which he starred incongruously as Genghis Khan. Filmed downwind of a nuclear test site, many of the cast and crew died after succumbing to radiation-linked cancer.

Star Quality

Having already been nominated for a "Best Actor" Oscar on three occasions, Marlon Brando won on the fourth, for his performance in *On the Waterfront*, released in 1954 – the year in which he made his first appearance in the Stars of the Year list.

10 TOP STARS OF THE YEAR 1959–1971

TOP 10 STARS OF 1959

	STAR
1	Rock Hudson
2	Cary Grant
3	James Stewart
4	Doris Day
5	Debbie Reynolds
6	Glenn Ford
7	Frank Sinatra
8	John Wayne
9	Jerry Lewis
10	Susan Hayward

Susan Hayward, one of three actresses in this year's Stars of the Year list, was awarded her sole "Best Actress" Oscar this year – her fifth nomination – for her role in *I Want to Live!* (1958).

TOP 10 STARS OF 1960

	STAR
1	Doris Day
2	Rock Hudson
3	Cary Grant
4	Elizabeth Taylor
5	Debbie Reynolds
6	Tony Curtis
7	Sandra Dee
8	Frank Sinatra
9	Jack Lemmon
10	John Wayne

Doris Day appeared in the Stars of the Year list more frequently than any other actress, 10 times from 1951 to 1966, topping it on four occasions. She received her sole Oscar nomination this year for *Pillow Talk* (1959).

TOP 10 STARS OF 1961

	STAR
1	Elizabeth Taylor
2	Rock Hudson
3	Doris Day
4	John Wayne
5	Cary Grant
6	Sandra Dee
7	Jerry Lewis
8	William Holden
9	Tony Curtis
10	Elvis Presley

Sandra Dee had just married teen heartthrob singer Bobby Darin, starring with him and Rock Hudson this year in *Come September* – one of the first films to be screened as an in-flight movie.

TOP 10 STARS OF 1962

	STAR
1	Doris Day
2	Rock Hudson
3	Cary Grant
4	John Wayne
5	Elvis Presley
6	Elizabeth Taylor
7	Jerry Lewis
8	Frank Sinatra
9	Sandra Dee
10	Burt Lancaster

Burt Lancaster had previously won a "Best Actor" Oscar for his role in *Elmer Gantry* (1960), and was nominated this year for his title role in *Birdman of Alcatraz* (1962).

TOP 10 STARS OF 1963

	STAR
1	Doris Day
2	John Wayne
3	Rock Hudson
4	Jack Lemmon
5	Cary Grant
6	Elizabeth Taylor
7	Elvis Presley
8	Sandra Dee
9	Paul Newman
10	Jerry Lewis

Making the first of his 14 appearances among the Stars of the Year, Paul Newman received his third Oscar nomination in 1963 for his role in *Hud*. He did not win an acting award until his eighth nomination, for *The Color of Money* (1986).

TOP 10 STARS OF 1964

	STAR
1	Doris Day
2	Jack Lemmon
3	Rock Hudson
4	John Wayne
5	Cary Grant
6	Elvis Presley
7	Shirley MacLaine
8	Ann-Margret
9	Paul Newman
10	Jerry Lewis

Known by a diminutive of her full name, Swedish born Ann-Margret (Olsson) appeared this year alongside Elvis Presley in *Love in Las Vegas*.

Sixties Star

Cary Grant (born Archibald Alexander Leach) was almost 60 – 25 years older than co-star Audrey Hepburn – when he made *Charade* (1963). He appeared in the annual Stars of the Year list 11 times from 1944 to 1966, when he made his last film.

TOP 10 STARS OF 1965

	STAR
1	Sean Connery
2	John Wayne
3	Doris Day
4	Julie Andrews
5	Jack Lemmon
6	Elvis Presley
7	Cary Grant
8	James Stewart
9	Elizabeth Taylor
10	Richard Burton

Sean Connery had been making films for 10 years, but with this year's release of *Thunderball*, his fourth in the James Bond role, he was a natural choice as the No. 1 box office draw.

TOP 10 STARS OF 1966

	STAR
1	Julie Andrews
2	Sean Connery
3	Elizabeth Taylor
4	Jack Lemmon
5	Richard Burton
6	Cary Grant
7	John Wayne
8	Doris Day
9	Paul Newman
10	Elvis Presley

Julie Andrew was an obvious lead candidate for this year's Stars of the Year, having won the "Best Actress" Oscar for her title role in *Mary Poppins* the previous year, and starring in this year's "Best Picture", *The Sound of Music*, .

TOP 10 STARS OF 1967

	STAR
1	Julie Andrews
2	Lee Marvin
3	Paul Newman
4	Dean Martin
5	Sean Connery
6	Elizabeth Taylor
7	Sidney Poitier
8	John Wayne
9	Richard Burton
10	Steve McQueen

One of the greatest actors never to win an Oscar, Richard Burton received the fifth of seven nominations this year for his role in *Who's Afraid of Virginia Woolf?* (1966).

TOP 10 STARS OF 1968

	STAR
1	Sidney Poitier
2	Paul Newman
3	Julie Andrews
4	John Wayne
5	Clint Eastwood
6	Dean Martin
7	Steve McQueen
8	Jack Lemmon
9	Lee Marvin
10	Elizabeth Taylor

Clint Eastwood made the first of 21 entries in the Stars of the Year list this year, placing him second only to John Wayne for overall appearances.

TOP 10 STARS OF 1969

	STAR
1	Paul Newman
2	John Wayne
3	Steve McQueen
4	Dustin Hoffman
5	Clint Eastwood
6	Sidney Poitier
7	Lee Marvin
8	Jack Lemmon
9	Katharine Hepburn
10	Barbra Streisand

Katharine Hepburn won back-to-back "Best Actress" Oscars for *Guess Who's Coming to Dinner* (1967) and *The Lion in Winter* (1968).

TOP 10 STARS OF 1970

	STAR
1	Paul Newman
2	Clint Eastwood
3	Steve McQueen
4	John Wayne
5	Elliott Gould
6	Dustin Hoffman
7	Lee Marvin
8	Jack Lemmon
9	Barbra Streisand
10	Walter Matthau

Elliott Gould had received his only Oscar nomination for *Bob & Carol & Ted & Alice* (1969), and in 1970 starred in *M*A*S*H*.

Queen Elizabeth

Included nine times among the Stars of the Year between 1958 and 1968, Elizabeth Taylor took the title role of the Egyptian queen in *Cleopatra* (1963). If linked for inflation, the $44 million budget of this epic flop would be equivalent to more than $263 million today.

TOP 10 STARS OF 1971

	STAR
1	John Wayne
2	Clint Eastwood
3	Paul Newman
4	Steve McQueen
5	George C. Scott
6	Dustin Hoffman
7	Walter Matthau
8	Ali MacGraw
9	Sean Connery
10	Lee Marvin

George C. Scott had won the "Best Actor" Oscar in 1970 for his title role in *Patton*, relased the same year – achieving notoriety for his refusal to accept the award.

TOP 10 STARS OF 1972

	STAR
1	Clint Eastwood
2	George C. Scott
3	Gene Hackman
4	John Wayne
5	Barbra Streisand
6	Marlon Brando
7	Paul Newman
8	Steve McQueen
9	Dustin Hoffman
10	Goldie Hawn

Gene Hackman had entered his second decade of filmmaking by winning a "Best Actor" Oscar for his role in "Best Picture"-winning *The French Connection* (1971).

TOP 10 STARS OF 1973

	STAR
1	Clint Eastwood
2	Ryan O'Neal
3	Steve McQueen
4	Burt Reynolds
5	Robert Redford
6	Barbra Streisand
7	Paul Newman
8	Charles Bronson
9	John Wayne
10	Marlon Brando

This was Burt Reynolds's first of 12 appearances in the Stars of the Year list, which he topped on five occasions. He had appeared in the Oscar-nominated *Deliverance* the previous year.

TOP 10 STARS OF 1974

	STAR
1	Robert Redford
2	Clint Eastwood
3	Paul Newman
4	Barbra Streisand
5	Steve McQueen
6	Burt Reynolds
7	Charles Bronson
8	Jack Nicholson
9	Al Pacino
10	John Wayne

Jack Nicholson made the first of four appearances in the Stars of the Year in 1974, when he was nominated for a "Best Actor" Oscar for his role in *Chinatown*, released the same year.

TOP 10 STARS OF 1975

	STAR
1	Robert Redford
2	Barbra Streisand
3	Al Pacino
4	Charles Bronson
5	Paul Newman
6	Clint Eastwood
7	Burt Reynolds
8	Woody Allen
9	Steve McQueen
10	Gene Hackman

The was the last of nine occasions on which Steve McQueen appeared as one of the Stars of the Year, and the first of Woody Allen's five consecutive appearances.

TOP 10 STARS OF 1976

	STAR
1	Robert Redford
2	Jack Nicholson
3	Dustin Hoffman
4	Clint Eastwood
5	Mel Brooks
6	Burt Reynolds
7	Al Pacino
8	Tatum O'Neal
9	Woody Allen
10	Charles Bronson

Mel Brooks made the first of his three appearances among the Stars of the Year following the success of films such as his *Blazing Saddles* (1974) and *Silent Movie* (1976).

TOP 10 STARS OF 1977

	STAR
1	Sylvester Stallone
2	Barbra Streisand
3	Clint Eastwood
4	Burt Reynolds
5	Robert Redford
6	Woody Allen
7	Mel Brooks
8	Al Pacino
9	Diane Keaton
10	Robert De Niro

Diane Keaton's place in the list this year relates particularly to her "Best Actress" Oscar win for *Annie Hall* – which also won "Best Picture" and "Best Director" for Woody Allen.

TOP 10 STARS OF 1978

	STAR
1	Burt Reynolds
2	John Travolta
3	Richard Dreyfuss
4	Warren Beatty
5	Clint Eastwood
6	Woody Allen
7	Diane Keaton
8	Jane Fonda
9	Peter Sellers
10	Barbra Streisand

Having risen to prominence with his Oscar-nominated role in *Saturday Night Fever* (1977), John Travolta secured his place among the Stars of the Year in 1978 with *Grease*.

TOP 10 STARS OF 1979

	STAR
1	Burt Reynolds
2	Clint Eastwood
3	Jane Fonda
4	Woody Allen
5	Barbra Streisand
6	Sylvester Stallone
7	John Travolta
8	Jill Clayburgh
9	Roger Moore
10	Mel Brooks

Jill Clayburgh received "Best Actress" Oscar nominations in two consecutive years, in 1978 for *An Unmarried Woman* and 1979 for *Starting Over*.

Great Scott!

Robert Redford topped the Stars of the Year list in 1974 – the second of seven appearances – following his title role in the adaptation of F. Scott Fitzgerald's *The Great Gatsby*.

TOP 10 STARS OF 1980

	STAR
1	Burt Reynolds
2	Robert Redford
3	Clint Eastwood
4	Jane Fonda
5	Dustin Hoffman
6	John Travolta
7	Sally Field
8	Sissy Spacek
9	Barbra Streisand
10	Steve Martin

Sissy Spacek's only appearance in the Stars of the Year list coincided with her sole "Best Actress" Oscar, for *Coal Miner's Daughter* (1980).

TOP 10 STARS OF 1981

	STAR
1	Burt Reynolds
2	Clint Eastwood
3	Dudley Moore
4	Dolly Parton
5	Jane Fonda
6	Harrison Ford
7	Alan Alda
8	Bo Derek
9	Goldie Hawn
10	Bill Murray

Along with the release of *Raiders of the Lost Ark*, this year saw the first of Harrison Ford's 12 appearances spanning three decades (1981–2000) of the Stars of the Year.

TOP 10 STARS OF 1982

	STAR
1	Burt Reynolds
2	Clint Eastwood
3	Sylvester Stallone
4	Dudley Moore
5	Richard Pryor
6	Dolly Parton
7	Jane Fonda
8	Richard Gere
9	Paul Newman
10	Harrison Ford

Richard Gere gained the first of his three entries in the Stars of the Year list this year after the success of *An Officer and a Gentleman* (1982).

TOP 10 STARS OF 1983

	STAR
1	Clint Eastwood
2	Eddie Murphy
3	Sylvester Stallone
4	Burt Reynolds
5	John Travolta
6	Dustin Hoffman
7	Harrison Ford
8	Richard Gere
9	Chevy Chase
10	Tom Cruise

Eddie Murphy established himself with the first of seven consecutive appearances, and a total nine in all, after this year's release of *Trading Places*.

Take Five
Jane Fonda in *9 to 5* (1980), in which she co-starred with Lily Tomlin and Dolly Parton. She earned a place in the Stars of the Year lists in five consecutive years (1978–82), winning the "Best Actress" Oscar in this period for *Coming Home* (1978).

TOP 10 STARS OF 1984

	STAR
1	Clint Eastwood
2	Bill Murray
3	Harrison Ford
4	Eddie Murphy
5	Sally Field
6	Burt Reynolds
7	Robert Redford
8	Prince
9	Dan Aykroyd
10	Meryl Streep

Bill Murray's prominence in the list relates to his appearance in *Ghostbusters*, released this year, while Prince achieved his one-off presence on the strength of *Purple Rain*, also released this year.

TOP 10 STARS OF 1985

	STAR
1	Sylvester Stallone
2	Eddie Murphy
3	Clint Eastwood
4	Michael J. Fox
5	Chevy Chase
6	Arnold Schwarzenegger
7	Chuck Norris
8	Harrison Ford
9	Michael Douglas
10	Meryl Streep

The first of Michael J. Fox's three appearances in the Stars of the Year is linked to the release of *Back to the Future* (1985), the first of his *Back to the Future* trilogy.

TOP 10 STARS OF 1986

	STAR
1	Tom Cruise
2	Eddie Murphy
3	Paul Hogan
4	Rodney Dangerfield
5	Bette Midler
6	Sylvester Stallone
7	Clint Eastwood
8	Whoopi Goldberg
9	Kathleen Turner
10	Paul Newman

Tom Cruise had made the first of his 13 appearances in the Stars of the Year in 1983, but rocketed to head the list with the release of both *Top Gun* and *The Color of Money* in this year.

TOP 10 STARS OF 1987

	STAR
1	Eddie Murphy
2	Michael Douglas
3	Michael J. Fox
4	Arnold Schwarzenegger
5	Paul Hogan
6	Tom Cruise
7	Glenn Close
8	Sylvester Stallone
9	Cher
10	Mel Gibson

Paul Hogan's three consecutive years in the list (1986–88) neatly bracket the releases of *Crocodile Dundee* and *Crocodile Dundee II*.

Pretty Woman

Julia Roberts made her first appearance as a Star of the Year in 1990. She had already received an Oscar nomination for *Steel Magnolias* (1989) and this year gained a second for her role in *Pretty Woman*. Her sixth film, it remains her most successful to date.

TOP 10 STARS OF 1988

	STAR
1	Tom Cruise
2	Eddie Murphy
3	Tom Hanks
4	Arnold Schwarzenegger
5	Paul Hogan
6	Danny DeVito
7	Bette Midler
8	Robin Williams
9	Tom Selleck
10	Dustin Hoffman

Tom Hanks secured the first of eight appearances as a Star of the Year with the 1988 release of *Big*.

TOP 10 STARS OF 1989

	STAR
1	Jack Nicholson
2	Tom Cruise
3	Robin Williams
4	Michael Douglas
5	Tom Hanks
6	Michael J. Fox
7	Eddie Murphy
8	Mel Gibson
9	Sean Connery
10	Kathleen Turner

Two entries from this year, Michael Douglas and Kathleen Turner, co-starred in *The War of the Roses*.

TOP 10 STARS OF 1990

	STAR
1	Arnold Schwarzenegger
2	Julia Roberts
3	Bruce Willis
4	Tom Cruise
5	Mel Gibson
6	Kevin Costner
7	Patrick Swayze
8	Sean Connery
9	Harrison Ford
10	Richard Gere

Kevin Costner gained the first of six placings in the Stars of the Year with "Best Picture" Oscar-winning *Dances With Wolves*. He also won "Best Director", but lost out to Jeremy Irons for "Best Actor".

TOP 10 STARS OF 1991

	STAR
1	Kevin Costner
2	Arnold Schwarzenegger
3	Robin Williams
4	Julia Roberts
5	Macaulay Culkin
6	Jodie Foster
7	Billy Crystal
8	Dustin Hoffman
9	Robert De Niro
10	Mel Gibson

Following his success with *Total Recall* (1990), *Terminator 2: Judgment Day*, the highest-earning film of the year, enabled Arnold Schwarzenegger to maintain his high place in the chart.

TOP 10 STARS OF 1992

	STAR
1	Tom Cruise
2	Mel Gibson
3	Kevin Costner
4	Jack Nicholson
5	Macaulay Culkin
6	Whoopi Goldberg
7	Michael Douglas
8	Clint Eastwood
9	Steven Seagal
10	Robin Williams

The exceptional box office success of *Home Alone* (1990) and *Home Alone 2: Lost in New York* (1992) guaranteed Macaulay Culkin a place in the list.

TOP 10 STARS OF 1993

	STAR
1	Clint Eastwood
2	Tom Cruise
3	Robin Williams
4	Kevin Costner
5	Harrison Ford
6	Julia Roberts
7	Tom Hanks
8	Mel Gibson
9	Whoopi Goldberg
10	Sylvester Stallone

Clint Eastwood had appeared in the list before, but earned his place at the top after the release of "Best Picture" Oscar-winning *Unforgiven*, which also won him the "Best Director" award.

TOP 10 STARS OF 1994

	STAR
1	Tom Hanks
2	Jim Carrey
3	Arnold Schwarzenegger
4	Tom Cruise
5	Harrison Ford
6	Tim Allen
7	Mel Gibson
8	Jodie Foster
9	Michael Douglas
10	Tommy Lee Jones

Although Jim Carrey had made earlier films, his meteoric rise to stardom began with *Ace Ventura: Pet Detective*, *The Mask*, and *Dumb & Dumber*, all of which date from this year.

TOP 10 STARS OF 1995

	STAR
1	Tom Hanks
2	Jim Carrey
3	Brad Pitt
4	Harrison Ford
5	Robin Williams
6	Sandra Bullock
7	Mel Gibson
8	Demi Moore
9	John Travolta
10 =	Kevin Costner
=	Michael Douglas

After the success of *Interview with the Vampire: The Vampire Chronicles*, Brad Pitt reinforced his claim to fame this year with *Se7en* and *Twelve Monkeys*.

TOP 10 STARS OF 1996

	STAR
1 =	Tom Cruise
=	Mel Gibson
3	John Travolta
4	Arnold Schwarzenegger
5	Sandra Bullock
6	Robin Williams
7	Sean Connery
8	Harrison Ford
9	Kevin Costner
10	Michelle Pfeiffer

After the success of *Pulp Fiction* (1994), John Travolta continued his run at the box office with films including *Broken Arrow*, *Phenomenon*, and *Michael*, all released in 1996.

TOP 10 STARS OF 1997

	STAR
1	Harrison Ford
2	Julia Roberts
3	Leonardo DiCaprio
4	Will Smith
5	Tom Cruise
6	Jack Nicholson
7	Jim Carrey
8	John Travolta
9	Robin Williams
10	Tommy Lee Jones

It would be hard to imagine Leonardo DiCaprio's not making an appearance in this year's list, given the phenomenal success of *Titanic*, but he was nonetheless relegated into third place by Harrison Ford (*Air Force One*) and Julia Roberts (*My Best Friend's Wedding*).

TOP 10 STARS OF 1998

	STAR
1	Tom Hanks
2	Jim Carrey
3	Leonardo DiCaprio
4	Robin Williams
5	Meg Ryan
6	Mel Gibson
7	Adam Sandler
8	Eddie Murphy
9	Cameron Diaz
10	Julia Roberts

The success of Adam Sandler's *The Waterboy* and *The Wedding Singer* ensured him a place in the Stars of the Year for 1998 – with *Big Daddy* providing a repeat appearance the following year.

TOP 10 STARS OF 1999

	STAR
1	Julia Roberts
2	Tom Hanks
3	Adam Sandler
4	Bruce Willis
5	Mike Myers
6	Tom Cruise
7	Will Smith
8	Mel Gibson
9	Meg Ryan
10	Sandra Bullock

Mike Myers' second outing for the *Austin Powers* franchise considerably outearned the first, assuring him a place in the list for this year.

TOP 10 STARS OF 2000

	STAR
1	Tom Cruise
2	Julia Roberts
3	George Clooney
4	Eddie Murphy
5	Russell Crowe
6	Mel Gibson
7	Martin Lawrence
8	Tom Hanks
9	Jim Carrey
10	Harrison Ford

The box office success of such films as *Mission: Impossible 2*, *Erin Brockovich*, *A Perfect Storm*, *Nutty Professor II: The Klumps*, and *Gladiator* placed the first five actors at the top of this year's ladder.

Hanks' Thanks

Topping the Stars of the Year list three times in the 1990s, Tom Hanks had roles in *Saving Private Ryan* (shown here) and other films, including *Forrest Gump* (1994) and *Apollo 13* (1995), that stood out among the highest earning of the decade.

TOP 10 STARS TO APPEAR MOST OFTEN IN THE "STARS OF THE YEAR" LISTS*

	NAME	YEAR	APPEARANCES
1	John Wayne	1949–74	25
2	Clint Eastwood	1968–93	21
3	Gary Cooper	1936–57	18
4 =	Clark Gable	1933–55	15
=	Bing Crosby	1934–54	15
6	Paul Newman	1963–86	14
7 =	Bob Hope	1941–53	13
=	Jerry Lewis	1951–64	13
=	Harrison Ford	1981–2000	13
=	Tom Cruise	1983–2000	13
10	Burt Reynolds	1973–84	12

* Since their inception in 1933 to 2000

TOP 10 STARS OF TOMORROW – 1950

	STAR
1	Dean Martin and Jerry Lewis (double act)
2	William Holden
3	Arlene Dahl
4	Ruth Roman
5	Vera-Ellen
6	John Lund
7	William Lundigan
8	Dean Jagger
9	Joanne Dru
10	James Whitmore

Starting in 1941, the Quigley Publishing Company, publishers of the *International Motion Picture Almanac*, have polled film exhibitors across the USA annually to identify the individuals who they consider "the players most likely to achieve major stardom". The results represent a fascinating year-by-year evaluation that ranges from sometimes astonishingly prescient predictions at the genesis of the careers of now-famous stars, while inevitably also identifying numerous actors and actresses who failed to realize the success that had been foretold for them.

TOP 10 STARS OF TOMORROW – 1951

	STAR
1	Howard Keel
2	Thelma Ritter
3	Shelley Winters
4	Frank Lovejoy
5	Debra Paget
6	David Brian
7	Piper Laurie
8	Gene Nelson
9	Dale Robertson
10	Corinne Calvet

Both Thelma Ritter and Shelley Winters were nominated for Oscars for films of this year.

TOP 10 STARS OF TOMORROW – 1952

	STAR
1	Marilyn Monroe
2	Debbie Reynolds
3	Marge and Gower Champion
4	Mitzi Gaynor
5	Kim Hunter
6	Rock Hudson
7	Audie Murphy
8	David Wayne
9	Forrest Tucker
10	Danny Thomas

Marge, wife and dancing partner of Gower Champion, was the cartoonist's model for Snow White in *Snow White and the Seven Dwarfs* (1937).

Into the Sunset

William Holden appeared in 25 films before achieving his Oscar-nominated breakthrough as Joe Gillis in *Sunset Boulevard* (1950).

TOP 10 STARS OF TOMORROW – 1953

	STAR
1	Janet Leigh
2	Gloria Grahame
3	Tony Curtis
4	Terry Moore
5	Rosemary Clooney
6	Julie Adams
7	Robert Wagner
8	Scott Brady
9	Pier Angeli
10	Jack Palance

Gloria Grahame won a "Best Supporting Actress" Oscar this year for *The Bad and the Beautiful* (1952) while Julie Adams celebrated her place in this list by appearing in the B-Movie masterpiece *Creature from the Black Lagoon* (1954).

TOP 10 STARS OF TOMORROW – 1954

	STAR
1	Audrey Hepburn
2	Maggie McNamara
3	Grace Kelly
4	Richard Burton
5	Pat Crowley
6	Guy Madison
7	Suzan Ball
8	Elaine Stewart
9	Aldo Ray
10	Cameron Mitchell

Audrey Hepburn was an obvious first choice, having won a "Best Actress" Oscar for her debut nomination in *Roman Holiday*. Also, this was the year in which Grace Kelly appeared in the Hitchcock classics *Dial M for Murder* and *Rear Window*.

TOP 10 STARS OF TOMORROW – 1955

	STAR
1	Jack Lemmon
2	Tab Hunter
3	Dorothy Malone
4	Kim Novak
5	Ernest Borgnine
6	James Dean
7	Anne Francis
8	Richard Egan
9	Eve Marie Saint
10	Russ Tamblyn

Although he had earlier TV appearances, Jack Lemmon's first film roles date from this year, launching a long and hugely successful career.

TOP 10 STARS OF TOMORROW – 1956

	STAR
1	Rod Steiger
2	Jeffrey Hunter
3	Natalie Wood
4	Dana Wynter
5	Tim Hovey
6	Yul Brynner
7	George Nader
8	Joan Collins
9	Sheree North
10	Sal Mineo

Yul Brynner's inclusion was hardly a surprise: he won the "Best Actor" Oscar for *The King and I* this year.

TOP 10 STARS OF TOMORROW – 1957

	STAR
1	Anthony Perkins
2	Sophia Loren
3	Jayne Mansfield
4	Don Murray
5	Carroll Baker
6	Martha Hyer
7	Elvis Presley
8	Anita Eckberg
9	Paul Newman
10	John Kerr

Elvis Presley had only just started his career, but had already made three films, including, this year, the legendary *Jailhouse Rock*.

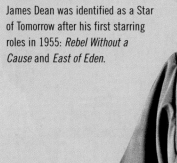

Did you know?

William Holden was best man at the 1952 wedding of future US President Ronald Reagan to Nancy Davis. Reagan was himself a Star of Tomorrow in its very first year, 1941.

Cause Célèbre

James Dean was identified as a Star of Tomorrow after his first starring roles in 1955: *Rebel Without a Cause* and *East of Eden*.

Lara's Theme
Julie Christie's as Lara in *Doctor Zhivago* (1965).
Her star status was confirmed the following year
when she won the "Best Actress" Oscar for her
role in *Darling*.

TOP 10 STARS OF TOMORROW – 1958

	STAR
1	Joanne Woodward
2	Red Buttons
3	Diane Varsi
4	Andy Griffith
5	Anthony Franciosa
6	Hope Lange
7	Brigitte Bardot
8	Burl Ives
9	Mickey Shaughnessy
10	Russ Tamblyn

Brigitte Bardot had recently moved from French
popularity to international stardom with *And God
Created Woman* (1956).

TOP 10 STARS OF TOMORROW – 1959

	STAR
1	Sandra Dee
2	Ricky Nelson
3	James Garner
4	Curt Jurgens
5	Lee Remick
6	John Saxon
7	Sidney Poitier
8	Ernie Kovacs
9	Kathryn Grant
10	Carolyn Jones

Former child star and singer Ricky Nelson had
topped the US chart with *Poor Little Fool* in 1958
and starred in *Rio Bravo* this year.

TOP 10 STARS OF TOMORROW – 1960

	STAR
1	Jane Fonda
2	Stephen Boyd
3	John Gavin
4	Susan Kohner
5	Troy Donahue
6	Angie Dickinson
7	Tuesday Weld
8	Fabian
9	James Darren
10	George Hamilton

Jane Fonda had appeared in her debut film
Tall Story when she hit the top of the Stars
of Tomorrow list.

TOP 10 STARS OF TOMORROW – 1961

	STAR
1	Hayley Mills
2	Nancy Kwan
3	Horst Buchholz
4	Carol Lynley
5	Delores Hart
6	Paula Prentiss
7	James Hutton
8	Juliet Prowse
9	Connie Stevens
10	Warren Beatty

Hayley Mills, the daughter of British actor John
Mills, won the last ever Juvenile Oscar for
Polyanna, and starred in *The Parent Trap*
this year.

TOP 10 STARS OF TOMORROW – 1962

	STAR
1	Bobby Darin
2	Ann-Margret
3	Richard Beymer
4	Suzanne Pleshette
5	Capucine
6	George Peppard
7	James MacArthur
8	Peter Falk
9	Michael Callan
10	Yvette Mimieux

Leading actor and actress of the year, Bobby
Darin and Ann-Margret, had appeared together
in *State Fair*.

TOP 10 STARS OF TOMORROW – 1963

	STAR
1	George Chakiris
2	Peter Fonda
3	Stella Stevens
4	Diane McBain
5	Pamela Tiffin
6	Pay Wayne
7	Dorothy Provine
8	Barnara Eden
9	Ursula Andress
10	Tony Bill

Like his sister Jane, Peter Fonda entered the list
in his debut film year, when he starred in *Tammy
and the Doctors*.

TOP 10 STARS OF TOMORROW – 1964

	STAR
1	Elke Sommer
2	Annette Funicello
3	Susannah York
4	Elizabeth Ashley
5	Stefanie Powers
6	Harve Presnell
7	Dean Jones
8	Keir Dullea
9	Nancy Sinatra
10	Joey Heatherton

This was Harve Presnell's debut year in film. He
was later to appear in such blockbusters as
Saving Private Ryan (1998).

TOP 10 STARS OF TOMORROW – 1965

	STAR
1	Rosemary Forsyth
2	Michael Anderson, Jr.
3	Michael Caine
4	Michael Parks
5	Mary Ann Mobley
6	Jocelyn Lane
7	Mia Farrow
8	Julie Christie
9	Richard Johnson
10	Senta Berger

Michael Caine had made *The Ipcress File* this
year, the first of his Harry Palmer secret agent
films based on Len Deighton's novels.

TOP 10 STARS OF TOMORROW – 1966

	STAR
1	Elizabeth Hartman
2	George Segal
3	Alan Arkin
4	Raquel Welch
5	Geraldine Chaplin
6	Guy Stockwell
7	Robert Redford
8	Beverly Adams
9	Sandy Dennis
10	Chad Everett

George Segal and Sandy Dennis, along with Elizabeth Taylor and Richard Burton, comprised the entire cast of this year's *Who's Afraid of Virginia Woolf?*, all of whom were nominated for Oscars, with Taylor and Dennis winning.

TOP 10 STARS OF TOMORROW – 1967

	STAR
1	Lynn Redgrave
2	Faye Dunaway
3	James Caan
4	John Phillip Law
5	Michele Lee
6	Michael Sarazin
7	Sharon Tate
8	Michael York
9	Hywel Bennett
10	David Hemmings

Another British star's daughter headed the list this year: Lynn Redgrave, daughter of Michael Redgrave and star of *Georgy Girl*.

TOP 10 STARS OF TOMORROW – 1968

	STAR
1	Dustin Hoffman
2	Katharine Ross
3	Katharine Houghton
4	Estelle Parsons
5	Judy Geeson
6	Robert Drivas
7	Robert Blake
8	Jim Brown
9	Gayle Hunnicut
10	Carol White

Katherine Ross appeared alongside Dustin Hoffman in *The Graduate*, for which both were nominated for Oscars.

TOP 10 STARS OF TOMORROW – 1969

	STAR
1	Jon Voight
2	Kim Darby
3	Glenn Campbell
4	Richard Benjamin
5	Mark Lester
6	Olivia Hussey
7	Leonard Whiting
8	Ali McGraw
9	Barbara Hershey
10	Alan Alda

Jon Voight, co-starred with Dustin Hoffman this year in *Midnight Cowboy*, his first major film.

TOP 10 STARS OF TOMORROW – 1970

	STAR
1	Donald Sutherland
2	Liza Minnelli
3	Goldie Hawn
4	Jack Nicholson
5	Genevieve Bujold
6	Dyan Cannon
7	Marlo Thomas
8	Beau Bridges
9	Sharon Farrell
10	Peter Boyle

Jack Nicholson had been appearing in films for over a decade, but in 1970 was acclaimed for his role in multi-Oscar nominated *Five Easy Pieces*.

TOP 10 STARS OF TOMORROW – 1971

	STAR
1	Jennifer O'Neill
2	Karen Black
3	Gary Grimes
4	Sally Kellerman
5	Arthur Garfunkel
6	Bruce Davison
7	Richard Roundtree
8	Deborah Winters
9	Jane Alexander
10	Rosalind Cash

Karen Black had appeared alongside Jack Nicholson in *Five Easy Pieces*, and in 1971 appeared in *Drive He Said*, which Nicholson directed.

Post-*Graduate*

Dustin Hoffman, who headed the Stars of Tomorrow list in 1968, had made his debut the previous year with *The Graduate*, for which he was nominated for a "Best Actor" Oscar.

TOP 10 STARS OF TOMORROW – 1972

	STAR
1	Al Pacino
2	Edward Albert
3	Jeff Bridges
4	Joel Grey
5	Sandy Duncan
6	Timothy Bottoms
7	Madeline Kahn
8	Cybill Shepherd
9	Malcolm McDowell
10	Ron O'Neal

Al Pacino topped this year's list when his third film, *The Godfather*, was released – and won the "Best Picture" Oscar.

STARS OF TOMORROW – 1973

STAR
Diana Ross
Michael Moriarty
Marsha Mason
Joe Don Baker
Jeannie Berlin
Candy Clark
Robert De Niro
Jan-Michael Vincent
Roy Scheider
Tatum O'Neal

Ross had just made the transfer from her ... career, originally with the Supremes and ...lo, to acting, receiving an Oscar nomination ... role as Billie Holiday in *Lady Sings the* ... 1972).

Did you know?

Richard Gere, who appears with John Travolta in the Stars of the Year for 1977, became a star with *Days of Heaven* (1978), *American Gigolo* (1980), and *An Officer and a Gentleman* (1982), after Travolta had turned them down.

TOP 10 STARS OF TOMORROW – 1974

	STAR
1	Valerie Perrine
2	Richard Dreyfuss
3	Randy Quaid
4	Deborah Raffin
5	Joseph Bottoms
6	Ron Howard
7	Sam Waterston
8	Linda Blair
9	Keith Carradine
10	Steven Warner

Ron Howard, who had appeared in *American Graffiti* (1973), continued to act but also went to direct such blockbusters as *Dr. Seuss's How ... Grinch Stole Christmas* (2000), winning the "Be... Director" Oscar for *A Beautiful Mind* (2001).

Fever Pitch

John Travolta takes to the dance floor as disco king Tony Manero in his breakthrough third film, *Saturday Night Fever* (1977).

TOP 10 STARS OF TOMORROW – 1975

	STAR
1	Stockard Channing
2	Bo Svenson
3	Susan Blakely
4	William Atherton
5	Brad Dourif
6	Perry King
7	Bo Hopkins
8	Conny Van Dyke
9	Ronee Blakely
10	Paul Le Mat

The Stars of Tomorrow lists are inevitably subject to unpredictable events: the year that Conny Van Dyke was included in the list, she abandoned her film career and moved into television.

TOP 10 STARS OF TOMORROW – 1976

	STAR
1	Sylvester Stallone
2	Talia Shire
3	Jessica Lange
4	Sissy Spacek
5	Robby Benson
6	Sam Elliott
7	Margaux Hemingway
8	Susan Sarandon
9	Ellen Greene
10	Lenny Baker

Sylvester Stallone had only minor acting parts, such as "Subway Thug" in Woody Allen's *Bananas* (1971), until 1976 when he wrote and took the title role in *Rocky*, the year's highest-earning film.

TOP 10 STARS OF TOMORROW – 1977

	STAR
1	John Travolta
2	Karen Lynn Gorney
3	Michael Ontkean
4	Mark Hamill
5	Harrison Ford
6	Carrie Fisher
7	Kathleen Quinlan
8	Peter Firth
9	Richard Gere
10	Melinda Dillon

Mark Hamill, Harrison Ford, and Carrie Fisher all starred in *Star Wars*, the film of the year – and the highest-earning in the USA for the next 20 years.

TOP 10 STARS OF TOMORROW – 1978

	STAR
1	Christopher Reeve
2	John Belushi
3	Brad Davis
4	Amy Irving
5	John Savage
6	Brooke Adams
7	Gary Busey
8	Brooke Shields
9	Harry Hamlin
10	Tim Matheson

Christopher Reeve headed the list of Stars of Tomorrow after taking the title role in *Superman*, after *Grease*, the highest-earning film of the year.

Top 10
Bo Derek topped the Stars of Tomorrow list in 1979 after shooting to stardom with her second film, *10,* in which she co-starred with Dudley Moore.

TOP 10 STARS OF TOMORROW – 1979

	STAR
1	Bo Derek
2	Dennis Christopher
3	Treat Williams
4	Michael O'Keefe
5	Lisa Eichhorn
6	Sigourney Weaver
7	Chris Makepeace
8	Ricky Schroder
9	Karen Allen
10	Mary Steenburgen

Sigourney Weaver had appeared in uncredited bit parts until becoming an overnight sensation this year for her role in *Alien*.

TOP 10 STARS OF TOMORROW – 1980

	STAR
1	Timothy Hutton
2	Debra Winger
3	Cathy Moriarty
4	Dennis Quaid
5	Diana Scarwid
6	William Hurt
7	Michael Biehn
8	Miles O'Keefe
9	Peter Gallagher
10	Martin Hewitt

Debra Winger beat 200 aspiring actresses to appear opposite John Travolta in *Urban Cowboy* this year, which led in turn to her starring role in *An Officer and a Gentleman* (1982).

TOP 10 STARS OF TOMORROW – 1981

	STAR
1	Matt Dillon
2	Rachel Ward
3	Griffin O'Neal
4	Henry Thomas
5	Kathleen Turner
6	Eric Roberts
7	Mel Gibson
8	Molly Ringwald
9	Sean Young
10	Elizabeth McGovern

Kathleen Turner entered the list after making just one film, *Body Heat* (1981), while Mel Gibson, who had appeared this year in Australian-made *Gallipoli*, had yet to appear in a Hollywood film.

TOP 10 STARS OF TOMORROW – 1982

	STAR
1	Tom Cruise
2	Sean Penn
3	Matthew Broderick
4	Jennifer Beals
5	Ally Sheedy
6	Cynthia Rhodes
7	Kevin Kline
8	Rosanna Arquette
9	Andrew McCarthy
10	Deborah Foreman

Although leading the Stars of Tomorrow list – the last to be published – Tom Cruise had appeared in only two films, *Endless Love* and *Taps* (both 1981) but before the decade was out he was starring in

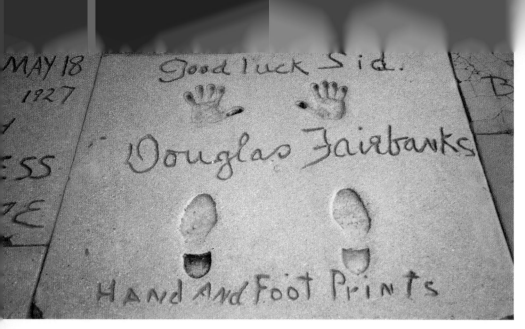

Good luck Sid.

MAY 18 1927

Douglas Fairbanks

Hand And Foot Prints

Signs of the Times

Mary Pickford and Douglas Fairbanks, part-owners of Grauman's Chinese Theatre, inaugurated the tradition of stars "signing" the forecourt.

THE 10 FIRST STAR IMPRINTS AT GRAUMAN'S CHINESE THEATRE

	STAR(S)	DATE
1	Mary Pickford and Douglas Fairbanks	30 Apr 1927
2	Norma Talmadge	18 May 1927
3	Norma Shearer	1 Aug 1927
4	Harold Lloyd	21 Nov 1927
5	William S. Hart	28 Nov 1927
6	Tom Mix and Tony (his horse)	12 Dec 1927
7	Colleen Moore	19 Dec 1927
8	Gloria Swanson	1927 *
9	Constance Talmadge	1927 *
10	Charles Chaplin	c. Jan 1928 *

* Date unknown

Since 1927, when Sid Grauman opened his Chinese Theatre in Hollywood, movie stars have been placing their handprints, footprints, and signatures in the concrete of the forecourt. Today they represent a catalogue of Hollywood greats and are among its most popular tourist attractions. Stars who have added their imprints in the 21st century include Anthony Hopkins, Nicolas Cage, and Morgan Freeman.

TOP 10 ACTORS BY TOTAL US BOX OFFICE GROSS

	ACTOR	FILMS	US GROSS ($)
1	Harrison Ford	31	3,191,831,016
2	Samuel L. Jackson	56	2,850,696,263
3	Tom Hanks	30	2,807,539,290
4	Tom Cruise	26	2,437,140,228
5	James Earl Jones	36	2,326,924,965
6	Eddie Murphy	27	2,300,000,784
7	Mel Gibson	33	2,299,636,698
8	Robin Williams	41	2,230,226,135
9	Jim Cummings	25	2,222,385,022
10	Rance Howard	38	2,190,913,090

TOP 10 ACTRESSES BY TOTAL US BOX OFFICE GROSS

	ACTRESS	FILMS	US GROSS ($)
1	Julia Roberts	27	1,889,883,547
2	Carrie Fisher	25	1,760,869,785
3	Whoopi Goldberg	41	1,683,352,258
4	Kathy Bates	31	1,451,827,177
5	Drew Barrymore	27	1,303,932,619
6	Cameron Diaz	21	1,291,842,748
7	Maggie Smith	20	1,286,654,699
8	Bonnie Hunt	16	1,270,837,762
9	Sally Field	20	1,237,398,519
10	Glenn Close	28	1,237,198,134

TOP 10 MOST PROLIFIC ACTORS WORLDWIDE

	ACTOR	CAREER*	FILMS†
1	Mel Blanc	1937–2002	898
2	Adoor Bhasi	1961–87	549
4	Tom London	1915–66	529
3	Bud Osborne	1912–66	525
5	Edmund Cobb	1915–66	509
6	Lee Phelps	1917–66	496
7	Prem Nazir	1952–89	487
8	Oliver Hardy	1914–86	441
9	Lee Moran	1912–36	437
10	Irving Bacon	1923–58	432

* Including TV movies, films featuring archive footage, posthumous releases, etc
† Based on number of entries in The Internet Movie Database (http://us.imdb.com/)
The 10 actors listed here performed in a total of 5,278 films between them, although a number were "shorts" made during the silent film era, including numerous cowboy films starring Tom London and Edmund Cobb. Mel Blanc, who heads this list, is actually a borderline case, since he provided the voice of such perennial animated films characters as Bugs Bunny and Daffy Duck. If he is excluded from the list, the 10th place would be Frank Ellis (career 1920–66), with a tally of 425 films.

TOP 10 MOST PROLIFIC ACTRESSES WORLDWIDE

	ACTOR	CAREER*	FILMS†
1	Bess Flowers	1923–64	481
2	Mae Questel	1930–99	328
3	Lalita Pawar	1928–97	321
4	Sharada	1961–98	305
5	Florence Lawrence	1906–36	292
6	Mary Pickford	1908–2002	276
7	Mary Gordon	1925–50	259
8	Sridevi	1967–2003	258
9	Ann Doran	1922–86	251
10	Claire McDowell	1910–45	232

* Including TV movies, films featuring archive footage, posthumous releases, etc
† Based on number of entries in The Internet Movie Database (http://us.imdb.com/)
Most of the Hollywood actresses featured here appeared in silent movies that were frequently very short. Also, since the performers had no dialogue to learn and production techniques were rudimentary, such films could be made in a matter of days. The careers of some spanned very long periods, from child star to elderly character actress, and include voice-only parts, such as Mae Questel's roles as cartoon characters Betty Boop and Olive Oyl.

TOP 10 STARS OF THE MOST $100 MILLION-PLUS FILMS

	STAR	$100M+ FILMS
1	Tom Hanks	13
2	Harrison Ford	11
3 =	Tom Cruise	10
=	Mel Gibson	10
5 =	Eddie Murphy	9
=	Julia Roberts	9
7 =	Samuel L. Jackson	8
=	Robin Williams	8
9 =	Jim Carrey	7
=	John Travolta	7

The members of this élite group of stars have each appeared in many high-earning films, but are especially notable for having roles (or supplying the voices for animated and other films) in the greatest number that have made more than $100 million at the US box office. For each star (excluding John Travolta), the total revenue of his or her $100 million-plus films alone is more than $1 billion, and over $2 billion in the case of Tom Hanks and Harrison Ford. However, there are several other actors who have made fewer $100 million-plus films, but have achieved comparable totals, among them Bill Paxton and Tommy Lee Jones.

LEGENDS (FEMALE) CHOSEN BY THE AMERICAN FILM INSTITUTE

	ACTRESS
1	Katharine Hepburn
2	Bette Davis
3	Audrey Hepburn
4	Ingrid Bergman
5	Greta Garbo
6	Marilyn Monroe
7	Elizabeth Taylor
8	Judy Garland
9	Marlene Dietrich
10	Joan Crawford

Source: American Film Institute
This, and the adjacent list, is drawn from the Top 10 of the American Film Institute's list of the "50 Greatest American Screen Legends", which comprises the top 25 male and top 25 female legends selected by more than 1,800 prominent individuals in the film community from a list of 500.

TOP 10 LEGENDS (MALE) CHOSEN BY THE AMERICAN FILM INSTITUTE

	ACTOR
1	Humphrey Bogart
2	Cary Grant
3	James Stewart
4	Marlon Brando
5	Fred Astaire
6	Henry Fonda
7	Clark Gable
8	James Cagney
9	Spencer Tracy
10	Charlie Chaplin

Source: American Film Institute

Beating All

Fred Astaire, the only musical star in the American Film Institute's Top 10 Screen Legends, in *Ziegfeld Follies* (1946). Gene Kelly, who appeared in the same film was ranked at No. 15.

TOP 10 HIGHEST-EARNING ACTORS

·	ACTOR	ESTIMATED INCOME($), 2002
1	Adam Sandler	47,000,000
2	Bruce Willis	46,000,000
3	Tom Hanks	45,000,000
4 =	Ben Affleck	40,000,000
=	Cameron Diaz	40,000,000
=	Mel Gibson	40,000,000
=	Robert DeNiro	40,000,000
8	Arnold Schwarzenegger	35,000,000
9	Samuel L. Jackson	34,000,000
10 =	Sandra Bullock	30,000,000
=	Harrison Ford	30,000,000
=	Keanu Reeves	30,000,000

Source: *Forbes* magazine
This list excludes actresses who are primarily singers but who have also appeared in films, such as Madonna, Britney Spears, and Jennifer Lopez. Actors with the audience magnetism of Bruce Willis can today routinely command $20,000,000 or more per movie, while percentage earnings can add further sums, although their actual estimated annual income fluctuates according to whether they have appeared in a recent successful film.

TOP 10 LONGEST CAREERS

	ACTOR/ACTRESS*	CAREER†	YEARS
1	Mickey Rooney	1926–2003	77
2	John Gielgud	1924–2000	76
3	Lillian Gish	1912–87	75
4	Sylvia Sidney	1927–96	69
5 =	Bessie Love	1915–83	68
=	Gloria Stuart	1932–2000	68
7 =	George Burns	1929–94	65
=	Louise Rainer	1932–97	65
9	Marlene Dietrich	1919–79	60
10	Don Ameche	1935–94	59

* Minimum qualification: one Oscar nomination
† First to last release, excluding TV roles, documentaries, appearances in archive footage, etc

Did you know?

Arnold Schwarzenegger received a record salary of $30 million of his role in *Terminator 3: The Rise of the Machines* (2003).

TOP 10 BEN AFFLECK FILMS

	FILM	ROLE	YEAR
1	Armageddon	A.J. Frost	1998
2	Pearl Harbor	Capt. McCawley	2001
3	Shakespeare in Love	Ned Alleyn	1998
4	Good Will Hunting	Chuckie Sullivan	1997
5	The Sum of All Fears	Jack Ryan	2002
6	Daredevil	Matt Murdock/ Daredevil	2003
7	Forces of Nature	Ben Holmes	1999
8	Changing Lanes	Gavin Banek	2002
9	Dogma	Bartleby	1999
10	Bounce	Buddy Amaral	2000

Behind the Mask

Antonio Banderas appeared in Spanish films from 1982 to 1992, when he starred in his first Hollywood production, *The Mambo Kings*. His top-earning film to date, *The Mask of Zorro*, made more than $250 million worldwide.

TOP 10 KEVIN BACON FILMS

	FILM	ROLE	YEAR
1	Apollo 13	Jack Swigert	1995
2	A Few Good Men	Capt. Jack Ross	1992
3	JFK	Willie O'Keefe	1991
4	Hollow Man	Sebastian Caine	2000
5	Sleepers	Sean Nokes	1996
6	National Lampoon's Animal House	Chip Diller	1978
7	The River Wild	Wade	1994
8	Footloose	Ren MacCormack	1984
9	Flatliners	David Labraccio	1990
10	Wild Things	Sgt. Ray Duquette	1998

Kevin Bacon inspired a game called "Six Degrees of Kevin Bacon", whereby he is considered the centre of the entertainment universe and any actor can be linked to him in no more than six steps, for example, Marilyn Monroe was in *Niagara* (1953) with George Ives, who was in *Stir of Echoes* (1999) with Kevin Bacon — hence two degrees of separation, or a "Bacon number" of two. One source has estimated that more than 570,000 actors can be linked to him within six or fewer Bacon numbers!

TOP 10 WOODY ALLEN FILMS

	FILM	ROLE	YEAR
1	Manhattan	Isaac Davis *†#	1979
2	Hannah and Her Sisters	Mickey Sachs *†#	1986
3	Annie Hall	Alvy Singer *†#	1977
4	Small Time Crooks	Ray Winkler *†#	2000
5	Everyone Says I Love You	Joe Berlin *†#	1996
6	Crimes and Misdemeanors	Cliff Stern *†#	1989
7	Casino Royale	Jimmy Bond/ Dr. Noah *#	1967
8	What's New, Pussycat?	Victor Skakapopulis *#	1965
9	Everything You Always Wanted to Know About Sex (But Were Afraid to Ask)	The Fool/ Fabrizio/Victor/ Sperm #1 *†#	1972
10	Sleeper	Miles Monroe *†#§	1973

* Actor
† Scriptwriter
# Director
§ Composer

Woody Allen provided the voice of neurotic ant Z-4195 in animated film *Antz* (1998), which, if included, would head the list. *Annie Hall* was the first film since 1941 for which one person was nominated for "Best Picture", "Best Actor", "Best Director", and "Best Screenplay" Academy Awards; he won "Best Picture" and "Best Screenplay" – which, characteristically, he did not bother to collect.

TOP 10 ALEC BALDWIN FILMS

	FILM	ROLE	YEAR
1	Pearl Harbor	Lt. Col. Doolittle	2001
2	The Hunt for Red October	Jack Ryan	1990
3	Notting Hill	Jeff King *	1999
4	Mercury Rising	Lt.Col. Kudrow	1998
5	Beetlejuice	Adam	1988
6	Working Girl	Mick Dugan	1988
7	The Juror	Teacher	1996
8	Malice	Dr. Jed Hill	1993
9	The Shadow	Lamont Cranston	1994
10	The Edge	Robert Green	1997

* Uncredited

Since 1998 Alec Baldwin has been the latest of several narrators of the US versions of the *Thomas the Tank Engine* videos. In 2001 he was the narrator of *The Royal Tenenbaums* and provided the voice of the dog Butch in the animated/live action *Cats & Dogs* and that of Captain Gray Edwards in the animated *Final Fantasy: The Spirits Within*.

TOP 10 DAN AYKROYD FILMS

	FILM	ROLE	YEAR
1	Pearl Harbor	Capt. Thurman	2001
2	Indiana Jones and the Temple of Doom	Weber	1984
3	Casper	Dr. Stantz	1995
4	Ghostbusters *	Dr. Stantz	1984
5	Ghostbusters II *	Dr. Stantz	1989
6	Driving Miss Daisy	Boolie Werthan	1989
7	Evolution	Governor Lewis	2001
8	Trading Places	L. Winthorpe III	1983
9	My Girl	Harry Sultenfuss	1991
10	Spies Like Us *	Austin Millbarge	1985

* Also writer

If Aykroyd's 20-second cameo appearance in *Indiana Jones and the Temple of Doom* is excluded, his next most successful film is *Dragnet* (1987). If his unbilled part in *Casper* is eliminated, cult success *The Blues Brothers* (1980) joins the list. His directorial debut with *Nothing But Trouble* (1991), in which he also starred, was one of his least commercially successful films. Aykroyd provided the voice of Chip, a wasp, in the animated film *Antz* (1998). Were it included, it would be in sixth place.

TOP 10 ANTONIO BANDERAS FILMS

	FILM	ROLE	YEAR
1	The Mask of Zorro	Alejandro Murrieta/Zorro	1998
2	Interview with the Vampire: The Vampire Chronicles	Armand	1994
3	Philadelphia	Miguel Alvarez	1993
4	Spy Kids	Gregorio Cortez	2001
5	Evita	Ché	1996
6	Spy Kids 2: Island of Lost Dreams	Gregorio Cortez	2002
7	Assassins	Miguel Bain	1995
8	The 13th Warrior	Ahmed Ibn Hamad	1999
9	Desperado	El Mariachi	1995
10	Frida	David Alfaro Siqueiros	2002

TOP 10 HUMPHREY BOGART FILMS

	FILM	ROLE	YEAR
1	The Caine Mutiny	Lt. Cdr. Philip Francis Queeg	1954
2	The African Queen	Charlie Allnut	1951
3	Casablanca	Richard "Rick" Blaine	1942
4 =	The Left Hand of God	Jim Carmody	1955
=	Sabrina	Linus Larrabee	1954
6	To Have and Have Not	Harry Morgan (Steve)	1944
7 =	The Barefoot Contessa	Harry Dawes	1954
=	Key Largo	Frank McCloud	1948
9 =	The Big Shot	Joseph "Duke" Berne	1942
=	Dark Passage	Vincent Parry	1947
=	We're No Angels	Joseph	1955

Humphrey Bogart's biggest-budget ($3.8 million) film, *The Treasure of the Sierra Madre* (1948), was one of his least successful, but is now regarded as a classic. Earnings from re-releases, TV screenings, and video/DVD releases make it a potential candidate for his Top 10.

TOP 10 MARLON BRANDO FILMS

	FILM	ROLE	YEAR
1	Superman	Jor-El	1978
2	The Godfather	Don Vito Corleone	1972
3	The Score	Max	2001
4	Apocalypse Now	Col. Walter E. Kurtz	1979
5	Don Juan DeMarco	Dr. Jack Mickler	1995
6	The Island of Dr. Moreau	Dr. Moreau	1996
7	Last Tango in Paris	Paul	1972
8	Sayonara	Maj. Lloyd Gruver	1957
9	The Freshman	Carmine Sabatini	1990
10	Candy	Grindl	1968

Often acclaimed as the greatest of all American actors, Marlon Brando made his screen debut in 1950 with *The Men*, gaining his first Oscar nomination for his second film, *A Streetcar Named Desire* (1951) and winning the "Best Actor" award for his sixth film, *On the Waterfront* (1954). For his role in *Superman*, Marlon Brando shrewdly negotiated a contract that paid him $3.7 million (out of a total budget of $55 million), plus 11.3 per cent of the film's domestic gross and 5.65 per cent of foreign grosses. Since it earned over $300 million worldwide, Brando ultimately made about $14 million for 12 days' filming, which ended up as 10 minutes of screen time.

TOP 10 MATTHEW BRODERICK FILMS

	FILM	ROLE	YEAR
1	Godzilla	Dr. Niko Tatopoulos	1998
2	Inspector Gadget	Officer John Brown/ Inspector Gadget/ Robo Gadget	1999
3	The Cable Guy	Steven M. Kovacs	1996
4	WarGames	David Lightman	1983
5	Ferris Bueller's Day Off	Ferris Bueller	1986
6	Addicted to Love	Sam	1997
7	Biloxi Blues	Eugene Morris Jerome	1988
8	Glory	Col. Robert Gould Shaw	1989
9	The Freshman	Clark Kellogg/ Narrator	1990
10	Project X	Jimmy Garrett	1987

Matthew Broderick supplied the voice of the adult Simba the lion in *The Lion King* (1994). If included, it would lead his Top 10.

TOP 10 MEL BROOKS FILMS

	FILM	ROLE	YEAR
1	Blazing Saddles *	Gov. William J. LePetomane Indian Chief/ WWI aviator	1974
2	The Muppet Movie	Professor Max Krassman	1979
3	The Little Rascals	Mr. Welling	1994
4	Spaceballs *	President Skroob/Yogurt	1987
5	Silent Movie *	Mel Funn	1976
6	Robin Hood: Men in Tights *	Rabbi Tuckman	1993
7	History of the World: Part I *	Moses/Comicus/ Torquemada/ Jacques/Louis XVI	1981
8	High Anxiety *	Dr. Richard Harpo Thorndyke	1978
9	To Be or Not To Be	Frederick Bronski	1983
10	Dracula: Dead and Loving It *	Dr. Abraham Van Helsing	1995

* Also writer and director

Mel Brooks has composed songs for several films, including the bad-taste classic "Springtime for Hitler" in *The Producers* (1968). He provided voices in several successful films, including the animated *The Prince of Egypt* (1998), *Look Who's Talking Too* (1990), and *Young Frankenstein* (1974).

TOP 10 PIERCE BROSNAN FILMS

	FILM	ROLE	YEAR
1	Mrs. Doubtfire	Stuart "Stu" Dunmeyer	1993
2	Die Another Day	James Bond	2002
3	The World is Not Enough	James Bond	1999
4	GoldenEye	James Bond	1995
5	Tomorrow Never Dies	James Bond	1997
6	Dante's Peak	Harry Dalton	1997
7	The Thomas Crown Affair	Thomas Crown	1999
8	Mars Attacks!	Professor Donald Kessler	1996
9	The Mirror Has Two Faces	Alex	1996
10	The Lawnmower Man	Dr. Lawrence Angelo	1992

Pierce Brosnan, now best known as James Bond, provided the voice of King Arthur in the animated *Quest for Camelot* (1998). If included, it would be ranked 9th. Each of the eight leading films in his Top 10 has earned in excess of $100 million worldwide.

TOP 10 STEVE BUSCEMI FILMS

	FILM	ROLE	YEAR
1	Armageddon	Rockhound	1998
2	Con Air	Garland "The Marietta Mangler" Greene	1997
3	Pulp Fiction	Buddy Holly	1994
4	Mr. Deeds	Crazy Eyes	2002
5	The Wedding Singer	David "Dave" Veltri (uncredited)	1998
6	Spy Kids 2: Island of Lost Dreams	Dr. Romero	2002
7	Rising Sun	Willy "The Weasel" Wilhelm	1993
8	28 Days	Cornell	2000
9	Desperado	Buscemi	1995
10	Fargo	Carl Showalter	1996

Best known as a character actor in Coen Brothers films such as *Fargo* (1996) and *The Big Lebowski* (1998), Steve Buscemi provided the voice of Randall Boggs in *Monsters, Inc.* (2001), which would rank second in his personal Top 10, while his critically acclaimed and award-winning supporting actor role in *Ghost World* (2001) failed to earn sufficient to rank. Prior to his acting career, he had served as a New York City fireman from 1980 to 1984. Immediately after the 11 September 2001 attacks on the World Trade Center, he returned, anonymously, to his firehouse and assisted in work on the site.

TOP 10 NICOLAS CAGE FILMS

	FILM	ROLE	YEAR
1	The Rock	Dr. Stanley Goodspeed	1996
2	Face/Off	Castor Troy/ Sean Archer	1997
3	Gone in 60 Seconds	Randall "Memphis" Raines	2000
4	Con Air	Cameron Poe	1997
5	City of Angels	Seth	1998
6	The Family Man	Jack Campbell	2000
7	Snake Eyes	Rick Santoro	1998
8	8MM	Tom Welles	1999
9	Moonstruck	Ronny Cammareri	1987
10	Windtalkers	Joe Enders	2002

Most of the films in Nicolas Cage's Top 10 earned $100 million or more worldwide – *The Rock* made in excess of $300 million – but *Captain Corelli's Mandolin* (2001) and *Leaving Las Vegas* (1995), for which he won a "Best Actor" Oscar, just fail to make the list.

TOP 10 MICHAEL CAINE FILMS

	FILM	ROLE	YEAR
1	Austin Powers in Goldmember	Nigel Powers	2002
2	Miss Congeniality	Victor Melling	2000
3	The Cider House Rules	Dr. Wilbur Larch	1999
4	A Bridge Too Far	Lt. Col. J.O.E. Vandeleur	1977
5	California Suite	Sidney Cochran	1978
6	On Deadly Ground	Michael Jennings	1994
7	Dirty Rotten Scoundrels	Lawrence Jamieson	1988
8	Hannah and Her Sisters	Elliot	1986
9	The Muppet Christmas Carol	Ebenezer Scrooge	1992
10	Dressed to Kill	Dr. Robert Elliott	1980

London-born Maurice Joseph Micklewhite adopted his stage name after seeing a sign promoting *The Caine Mutiny*. He had minor screen parts until his prominent role in *Zulu* (1964), since when he has made more than 100 films, receiving six Oscar nominations and winning two "Best Supporting Actor" awards, for *Hannah and Her Sisters* (1986) and *The Cider House Rules* (1999). He was knighted (as Sir Maurice Micklewhite) in 2000.

TOP 10 JIM CARREY FILMS

	FILM	ROLE	YEAR
1	Batman Forever	Riddler/ Edward Nygma	1995
2	Dr. Seuss's How the Grinch Stole Christmas	The Grinch	2000
3	The Mask	Stanley Ipkiss/ The Mask	1994
4	Liar Liar	Fletcher Reede	1997
5	The Truman Show	Truman Burbank	1998
6	Dumb & Dumber	Lloyd Christmas	1994
7	Ace Ventura: When Nature Calls	Ace Ventura	1995
8	Me, Myself & Irene	Charlie Baileygates/ Hank Evans	2000
9	Ace Ventura: Pet Detective	Ace Ventura	1994
10	The Cable Guy	The Cable Guy	1996

Jim Carrey is a member of an élite club of actors all of whose Top 10 films have earned more than $100 million worldwide. In fact, such is his international appeal that the average for the films in this list is $250 million.

TOP 10 GEORGE CLOONEY FILMS

	FILM	ROLE	YEAR
1	Ocean's Eleven	Danny Ocean	2001
2	The Perfect Storm	Capt. Billy Tyne	2000
3	Batman & Robin	Batman/Bruce Wayne	1997
4	Spy Kids	Devlin	2001
5	Three Kings	Maj. Archie Gates	1999
6	The Peacemaker	Col. Thomas Devoe	1997
7	One Fine Day	Jack Taylor	1996
8	The Thin Red Line	Capt. Charles Bosche	1998
9	Out of Sight	John Michael "Jack" Foley	1998
10	O Brother, Where Art Thou?	Ulysses Everett McGill	2000

Already well-known as Dr. Doug Ross in the TV series *ER* – as well as some best-forgotten early film parts, such as *Return of the Killer Tomatoes!* (1988) – George Clooney has appeared in a run of successful films during the past 10 years. He also provided voices for the animated *South Park: Bigger, Longer & Uncut* (1999).

TOP 10 SEAN CONNERY FILMS

	FILM	ROLE	YEAR
1	Indiana Jones and the Last Crusade	Prof. Henry Jones	1989
2	The Rock	John Patrick Mason	1996
3	Entrapment	Robert "Mac" MacDougal	1999
4	The Hunt for Red October	Capt. Marko Ramius	1990
5	The Untouchables	Jim Malone	1987
6	Thunderball	James Bond	1965
7	First Knight	King Arthur	1995
8	Goldfinger	James Bond	1964
9	Diamonds Are Forever	James Bond	1971
10	You Only Live Twice	James Bond	1967

Every one of Sean Connery's Top 10 films earned more than $100 million globally. If his fleeting (and uncredited) cameo appearance as King Richard II in the final two minutes of *Robin Hood: Prince of Thieves* (1991) were taken into account, it would be placed 2nd in the list. He also provided the dragon's voice in *Dragonheart* (1996), which, if included, would enter in 9th place.

TOP 10 KEVIN COSTNER FILMS

	FILM	ROLE	YEAR
1	Dances With Wolves *	Lt. John G. Dunbar	1990
2	The Bodyguard	Frank Farmer	1992
3	Robin Hood: Prince of Thieves	Robin of Locksley	1991
4	Waterworld	Mariner	1995
5	JFK	Jim Garrison	1991
6	The Untouchables	Eliot Ness	1987
7	A Perfect World	Butch Haynes	1993
8	Message in a Bottle	Garret Blake	1999
9	Tin Cup	Roy McAvoy	1996
10	Field of Dreams	Ray Kinsella	1989

* Academy Award for "Best Director"

Kevin Costner has appeared in a number of high-earning films – cumulatively his Top 10 have earned some $2.3 billion worldwide – but he has also acquired a reputation for appearing in and directing films such as *The Postman* (1997) that have failed to recoup their high budgets. Some, such as *Waterworld* and *A Perfect World*, however, have garnered relatively greater income beyond the US, thereby converting domestic losses into world profits.

TOP 10 RUSSELL CROWE FILMS

	FILM	ROLE	YEAR
1	Gladiator *	General Maximus Decimus Meridus	2000
2	A Beautiful Mind	John F. Nash	2001
3	L.A. Confidential	Officer Wendell "Bud" White	1997
4	The Insider	Jeffrey Wigand	1999
5	The Quick and the Dead	Cort	1995
6	Proof of Life	Terry Thorne	2000
7	Virtuosity	SID 6.7	1995
8	Mystery, Alaska	Sheriff John Biebe	1999
9	The Sum of Us	Jeff Mitchell	1994
10	Proof	Andy	1991

* Academy Award for "Best Actor"

By George!
George Clooney's Top 10 films alone have accumulated some $1.7 billion at the global box office, making him one of the world's most bankable stars.

TOP 10 TOM CRUISE FILMS

	FILM	ROLE	YEAR
1	Mission: Impossible 2	Ethan Hunt	2000
2	Mission: Impossible	Ethan Hunt	1996
3	Rain Man	Charlie Babbitt	1988
4	Top Gun	Lieutenant Pete "Maverick" Mitchell	1986
5	Minority Report	Detective John Anderton	2002
6	Jerry Maguire	Jerry Maguire	1996
7	The Firm	Mitch McDeere	1993
8	A Few Good Men	Lt. Daniel Alistair Kaffee	1992
9	Interview with the Vampire: The Vampire Chronicles	Lestat de Lioncourt	1994
10	Vanilla Sky	David Aames	2001

Tom Cruise (real name Thomas Cruise Mapother IV) built his career by playing a combination of handsome all-American heroes, military, and light comedy roles, but has shown himself equally at home with dramatic parts, for which he has been nominated for Oscars on three occasions. Few actors have matched his commercial success: every one of his Top 10 films has earned more than $200 million worldwide, a total of $3.3 billion.

TOP 10 ROBERT DE NIRO FILMS

	FILM	ROLE	YEAR
1	Meet the Parents	Jack Byrnes	2000
2	Heat	Neil McCauley	1995
3	The Untouchables	Al Capone	1987
4	Cape Fear	Max Cady	1991
5	Analyze This	Paul Vitti	1999
6	Sleepers	Father Bobby	1996
7	Backdraft	Lt. Rimgale	1991
8	Mary Shelley's Frankenstein	The Creature	1994
9	Casino	Sam Rothstein	1995
10	The Godfather, Part II	Vito Corleone	1974

All of Robert De Niro's Top 10 films have earned more than $100 million apiece at the world box office. He won the Academy Award for "Best Supporting Actor" for *The Godfather, Part II* (1974) – uniquely, playing the same part (Vito Corleone) for which Marlon Brando had won for *The Godfather* (1972) – and has been nominated for "Best Actor" on five occasions, winning for *Raging Bull* (1980).

TOP 10 LEONARDO DICAPRIO FILMS

	FILM	ROLE	YEAR
1	Titanic	Jack Dawson	1997
2	Catch Me If You Can	Frank Abagnale Jr.	2002
3	Gangs of New York	Amsterdam Vallon	2002
4	The Man in the Iron Mask	King Louis XIV/ Philippe	1998
5	The Beach	Richard	2000
6	Romeo + Juliet	Romeo	1996
7	The Quick and the Dead	Fee "The Kid" Herod	1995
8	Marvin's Room	Hank	1996
9	What's Eating Gilbert Grape	Arnie Grape	1993
10	Celebrity	Brandon Darrow	1998

A film career of less than 10 years has seen Leonardo DiCaprio star in six $100 million-plus earning films, including the biggest blockbuster of all time. His role in *What's Eating Gilbert Grape* gained him a "Best Supporting Actor" Oscar nomination.

TOP 10 MICHAEL DOUGLAS FILMS

	FILM	ROLE	YEAR
1	Basic Instinct	Det. Nick Curran	1992
2	Fatal Attraction	Dan Gallagher	1987
3	Disclosure	Tom Sanders	1994
4	Traffic	Robert Hudson Wakefield	2000
5	The Game	Nicholas Van Orton	1997
6	Black Rain	Nick Conklin	1989
7	A Perfect Murder	Steven Taylor	1998
8	Romancing the Stone	Jack Colton	1984
9	The American President	President Andrew Shepherd	1995
10	The War of the Roses	Oliver Rose	1989

Michael Douglas's first major success was not as an actor but as multi-Oscar-winning producer of *One Flew Over the Cuckoo's Nest*. He has since combined the role of producer and actor, winning a "Best Actor" Oscar for his role in *Wall Street* (1987), which falls short of a place in his Top 10, all of which are global $100 million-plus blockbusters.

TOP 10 CLINT EASTWOOD FILMS

	FILM	ROLE	YEAR
1	In the Line of Fire	Frank Horrigan	1993
2	The Bridges of Madison County *	Robert Kincaid	1995
3	Unforgiven *†	William Munny	1992
4	A Perfect World *	Red Garnett	1993
5	Space Cowboys *	Dr. Frank Corvin	2000
6	Every Which Way But Loose	Philo Beddoe	1978
7	Absolute Power *	Luther Whitney	1997
8	The Rookie *	Nick Pulovski	1990
9	Any Which Way You Can	Philo Beddoe	1980
10	Sudden Impact *	"Dirty" Harry Callahan	1983

* Also director
† Academy Award for "Best Director"

Clint Eastwood began his career with roles in B-movies, such as *Revenge of the Creature* and *Tarantula* (both 1955) before appearing as Rowdy Yates in the popular TV Western series *Rawhide* (1955–64). That led to his casting as "The Man with No Name" in Sergio Leone's Spaghetti Westerns (1964–66) and action films such as *Where Eagles Dare* (1968) before he starred in *Dirty Harry* and its sequels (1971–88).

TOP 10 RALPH FIENNES FILMS

	FILM	ROLE	YEAR
1	Schindler's List	Amon Goeth	1993
2	The English Patient	Laszlo de Almásy	1996
3	Red Dragon	Francis Dolarhyde	2002
4	Maid in Manhattan	Christopher Marshall	2002
5	The Avengers	John Steed	1998
6	Quiz Show	Charles Van Doren	1994
7	The End of the Affair	Maurice Bendrix	1999
8	Strange Days	Lenny Nero	1995
9	Sunshine	Ignatz Sonnenschein/ Adam Sors/ Ivan Sors	1999
10	Spider	Dennis "Spider" Cleg	2002

Ralph Fiennes provided the voice of the Pharaoh Rameses in the animated *The Prince of Egypt* (1998). If included, it would rank 3rd.

TOP 10 LAURENCE FISHBURNE FILMS

	FILM	ROLE	YEAR
1	The Matrix	Morpheus	1999
2	The Color Purple	Swain	1985
3	Apocalypse Now	Tyrone Miller/ "Mr. Clean"	1979
4	Just Cause	Tanny Brown	1995
5	Boyz N the Hood	Furious Styles	1991
6	Event Horizon	Captain Miller	1997
7	A Nightmare on Elm Street 3: Dream Warriors	Max	1987
8	What's Love Got to Do with It	Ike Turner, Sr.	1993
9	Higher Learning	Prof. Maurice Phipps	1995
10	Red Heat	Lt. Charlie Stobbs	1988

TOP 10 HARRISON FORD FILMS

	FILM	ROLE	YEAR
1	Star Wars: IV – A New Hope	Han Solo	1977
2	Star Wars: VI – Return of the Jedi	Han Solo	1983
3	Star Wars: V – The Empire Strikes Back	Han Solo	1980
4	Indiana Jones and the Last Crusade	Indiana Jones	1989
5	Raiders of the Lost Ark	Indiana Jones	1981
6	The Fugitive	Dr. Richard Kimble	1993
7	Indiana Jones and the Temple of Doom	Indiana Jones	1984
8	Air Force One	Pres. James Marshall	1997
9	What Lies Beneath	Dr. Norman Spencer	2000
10	Presumed Innocent	Rusty Sabich	1990

Uniquely in cinema history, every single one of Harrison Ford's Top 10 films has earned more than $220 million at the world box office, with the cumulative earnings of his Top 10 films alone totalling a remarkable $4.3 billion.

TOP 10 MORGAN FREEMAN FILMS

	FILM	ROLE	YEAR
1	Robin Hood: Prince of Thieves	Azeem	1991
2	Deep Impact	President Tom Beck	1998
3	Se7en	Det. Lt. William Somerset	1995
4	Outbreak	Brigadier General Billy Ford	1995
5	The Sum of All Fears	DCI William Cabot	2002
6	Unforgiven	Ned Logan	1992
7	Driving Miss Daisy	Hoke Colburn	1989
8	Along Came a Spider	Dr. Alex Cross	2001
9	Kiss the Girls	Dr. Alex Cross	1997
10	Amistad	Theodore Joadson	1997

Morgan Freeman was well known among children for his roles on the 1970s television series *The Electric Company* before embarking on a film career that has earned him three Oscar nominations.

TOP 10 RICHARD GERE FILMS

	FILM	ROLE	YEAR
1	Pretty Woman	Edward Lewis	1990
2	Runaway Bride	Ike Graham	1999
3	Chicago	Billy Flynn	2002
4	Sommersby	John Robert "Jack" Sommersby	1993
5	The Jackal	Declan Mulqueen	1997
6	An Officer and a Gentleman	Zack Mayo	1982
7	First Knight	Lancelot	1995
8	Primal Fear	Martin "Marty" Vail	1996
9	Unfaithful	Edward Sumner	2002
10	Autumn in New York	Will Keane	2000

Richard Gere's early acting career included a spell in London, where he appeared in the stage version of *Grease* and in Shakespeare at the Young Vic. His film work has spanned almost 30 years and has ranged from drama to comedy, not to mention biblical – he was oddly cast in the title role of the unmemorable 1985 mini-epic *King David*.

Did you know?

Two creatures have been named after Harrison Ford: a spider *Calponia harrisonfordi* (1993); and an ant *Pheidole harrisonfordi* (2002).

TOP 10 MEL GIBSON FILMS

	FILM	ROLE	YEAR
1	Signs	Graham Hess	2002
2	What Women Want	Nick Marshall	2000
3	Lethal Weapon 3	Det. Sgt. Martin Riggs	1992
4	Ransom	Tom Mullen	1996
5	Lethal Weapon 4	Det. Sgt. Martin Riggs	1998
6	Lethal Weapon 2	Det. Sgt. Martin Riggs	1989
7	The Patriot	Col. Benjamin Martin	2000
8	Braveheart *	William Wallace	1995
9	Maverick	Bret Maverick	1994
10	Payback	Porter	1999

* Also director; won Academy Award for "Best Director" and "Best Picture" (shared with Alan Ladd Jr. and Bruce Davey).
In addition to appearing in these 10, each of which earned upwards of $160 million worldwide, and more than 35 other films, Mel Gibson provided the voices of John Smith in *Pocahontas* (1995) and Rocky Rhodes in *Chicken Run* (2000), and appeared, uncredited, as himself in *Casper* (1995).

TOP 10 DANNY GLOVER FILMS

	FILM	ROLE	YEAR
1	Lethal Weapon 3	Det. Sgt. Roger Murtaugh	1992
2	Lethal Weapon 4	Det. Sgt. Roger Murtaugh	1998
3	Lethal Weapon 2	Det. Sgt. Roger Murtaugh	1989
4	The Color Purple	Albert	1985
5	The Royal Tenenbaums	Henry Sherman	2001
6	Witness	McFee	1985
7	Lethal Weapon	Sergeant Roger Murtaugh	1987
8	Predator 2	Lt. Mike Harrigan	1990
9	Angels in the Outfield	George Knox	1994
10	The Rainmaker	Judge Tyrone Kipler	1997

Danny Glover is in the unusual position of having had a minor, often uncredited, role in several films that would otherwise be included in his Top 10, among them *Maverick* (1994), where he appeared in a "blink and you'll miss it" scene as a bank robber, and as an unnamed inmate in *Escape from Alcatraz* (1979), while his scenes in *How Stella Got Her Groove Back* (1998) were deleted before release. Also in 1998, he supplied voices for two high-earning animated films, that of Jethro in *The Prince of Egypt* and Barbatus in *Antz*.

TOP 10 JEFF GOLDBLUM FILMS

	FILM	ROLE	YEAR
1	Jurassic Park	Dr. Ian Malcolm	1993
2	Independence Day	David Levinson	1996
3	The Lost World: Jurassic Park	Dr. Ian Malcolm	1997
4	Cats & Dogs	Prof. Dad Brody	2001
5	Nine Months	Sean Fletcher	1995
6	The Big Chill	Michael Goldman	1983
7	The Fly	Seth Brundle	1986
8	Silverado	Calvin Stanhope, aka "Slick"	1985
9	Powder	Donald Ripley	1995
10	Invasion of the Body Snatchers	Jack Bellicec	1978

Jeff Goldblum's career polarizes between starring roles in three of the highest-earning films of all time and appearances – often in minor roles – in many that achieved only negligible success. He was also one of some 70 people appearing fleetingly as themselves in *The Player* (1992), and can be heard as the voice of Aaron in the animated film, *The Prince of Egypt* (1998).

TOP 10 CUBA GOODING JR. FILMS

	FILM	ROLE	YEAR
1	Pearl Harbor	PO Doris "Dorie" Miller	2001
2	As Good As It Gets	Frank Sachs	1997
3	Jerry Maguire	Rod Tidwell	1996
4	A Few Good Men	Cpl. Carl Edward Hammaker	1992
5	Outbreak	Maj. Salt	1995
6	Snow Dogs	Dr. Ted "Teddy Bear" Brooks	2002
7	What Dreams May Come	Albert Lewis	1998
8	Men of Honor	BM2/Chief/ Mstr. Chief Carl Brashear	2000
9	Rat Race	Owen Templeton	2001
10	Boyz N the Hood	Tre Styles	1991

Were it included, Cuba Gooding Jr's debut film role – as a boy having his hair cut in *Coming to America* (1988) – would merit third place in this list, the top five entries in which have each earned over $180 million worldwide.

TOP 10 JOHN GOODMAN FILMS

	FILM	ROLE	YEAR
1	The Flintstones	Fred Flintstone	1994
2	Sea of Love	Detective Sherman	1989
3	Coyote Ugly	Bill	2000
4	Always	Al Yackey	1989
5	O Brother, Where Art Thou?	Big Dan Teague	2000
6	Arachnophobia	Delbert McClintock	1990
7	The Borrowers	Ocious P. Potter	1997
8	Revenge of the Nerds	Coach Harris	1984
9	King Ralph	Ralph Jones	1991
10	The Big Lebowski	Walter Sobchak	1998

John Goodman is also notable for supplying the voices of Pacha in *The Emperor's New Groove* (2000), Sulley in *Monsters, Inc.* (2001), and Baloo in *Jungle Book 2* (2003).

Star Wars Star

In 1994, having appeared in some of the highest-grossing films of all time, Harrison Ford was named the "Star of the Century" by the US NATO (National Alliance of Theatre Owners)/ShoWest Convention.

TOP 10 HUGH GRANT FILMS

	FILM	ROLE	YEAR
1	Notting Hill	William Thacker	1999
2	Bridget Jones's Diary	Daniel Cleaver	2001
3	Four Weddings and a Funeral	Charles	1994
4	Two Weeks Notice	George Wade	2002
5	Sense and Sensibility	Edward Ferrars	1995
6	Nine Months	Samuel Faulkner	1995
7	About a Boy	Will	2002
8	Mickey Blue Eyes	Michael Felgate	1999
9	Small Time Crooks	David Grant	2000
10	The Remains of the Day	Reginald Cardinal	1993

Hugh Grant has appeared in films for over twenty years, starring in several of the most successful British productions of all time at the US and international box office. He characteristically plays upper-class Englishman – indeed, his first film role (billed as "Hughie Grant") was that of Lord Adrian in *Privileged* (1982).

TOP 10 GENE HACKMAN FILMS

	FILM	ROLE	YEAR
1	Superman	Lex Luthor	1978
2	The Firm	Avery Tolar	1993
3	Enemy of the State	Edward "Brill" Lyle	1998
4	The Birdcage	Senator Kevin Keeley	1996
5	Unforgiven	Sheriff "Little Bill" Daggett	1992
6	Crimson Tide	Capt. Frank Ramsey	1995
7	The Mexican	Arnold Margolese	2001
8	Get Shorty	Harry Zimm	1995
9	Superman II	Lex Luthor	1980
10	The Poseidon Adventure	Rev. Frank Scott	1972

Gene Hackman also provided the voice of General Mandible in the animated film *Antz*. If counted, it would make 5th place in this list, which have all earned $100 million-plus worldwide.

State Secret

Gene Hackman turned down his role in *Enemy of the State* several times, until director Tony Scott persuaded him to take it. The film went on to earn over $250 million worldwide.

TOP 10 TOM HANKS FILMS

	FILM	ROLE	YEAR
1	Forrest Gump *	Forrest Gump	1994
2	Saving Private Ryan	Capt. John Miller	1998
3	Cast Away	Chuck Noland	2000
4	Apollo 13	Jim Lovell	1995
5	Catch Me If You Can	Carl Hanratty	2002
6	The Green Mile	Paul Edgecomb	1999
7	You've Got M@il	Joe Fox	1998
8	Sleepless in Seattle	Samuel "Sam" Baldwin	1993
9	Philadelphia *	Andrew Beckett	1993
10	Road to Perdition	Michael Sullivan	2002

* Academy Award for "Best Actor"

Tom Hanks also appeared in a voice-only part as Woody in *Toy Story 2* (1999) and *Toy Story* (1995). If included, these would be ranked in 2nd and 4th places respectively in his personal Top 10, the first nine of which have each earned more than $200 million worldwide.

TOP 10 ED HARRIS FILMS

	FILM	ROLE	YEAR
1	Apollo 13	Gene Kranz	1995
2	The Rock	Brig. Gen. Francis X. Hummel	1996
3	A Beautiful Mind	William Parcher	2001
4	The Truman Show	Christof	1998
5	The Firm	Wayne Tarrance	1993
6	Stepmom	Luke Harrison	1998
7	The Abyss	Virgil "Bud" Brigman	1989
8	Enemy at the Gates	Maj. König	2001
9	Absolute Power	Seth Frank	1997
10	Just Cause	Blair Sullivan	1995

Ed (Edward Allen) Harris has portrayed a range of all-American heroes – and, occasionally, villains – in parts that have earned him four Oscar nominations. Although a win has eluded him to date, a run of commercial successes means that half the films in his personal Top 10 have earned more than $250 million around the world.

TOP 10 CHARLTON HESTON FILMS

	FILM	ROLE	YEAR
1	True Lies	Spencer Trilby	1994
2	Any Given Sunday	AFFA Football Commissioner	1999
3	The Ten Commandments	Moses	1956
4	Earthquake	Stewart Graff	1974
5	Ben-Hur *	Judah Ben-Hur	1959
6	Tombstone	Henry Hooker	1993
7	Airport 1975	Alan Murdock	1974
8	Midway	Capt. Matthew Garth	1976
9	The Greatest Show on Earth	Marc Braden	1952
10	Planet of the Apes	George Taylor	1968

* "Best Actor" Academy Award

Charlton Heston has appeared in more than 100 films in a career that began over 60 years ago. Some of his recent parts (arguably including that in the film that leads his list) have been minor – for example, his cameo roles in *Wayne's World 2* (1993) and his uncredited appearance as Thade's father Zaius in the 2001 remake of the 1968 film in which he starred, *Planet of the Apes*. He has also narrated or provided voice-overs for several recent films, including *Hercules* (1997), *Armageddon* (1998), and *Cats & Dogs* (2001), all of which would qualify for places in his Top 10.

TOP 10 DUSTIN HOFFMAN FILMS

	FILM	ROLE	YEAR
1	Rain Man *	Raymond Babbitt	1988
2	Hook	Capt. James S. Hook	1991
3	Outbreak	Col. Sam Daniels	1995
4	Tootsie	Michael Dorsey/ Dorothy Michaels	1982
5	Sleepers	Danny Snyder	1996
6	Dick Tracy	Mumbles	1990
7	Kramer vs. Kramer *	Ted Kramer	1979
8	The Graduate	Benjamin Braddock	1967
9	Sphere	Dr. Norman Goodman	1998
10	Hero	Bernard "Bernie" Laplante	1992

* "Best Actor" Academy Award

Dustin Hoffman is notable for having successfully performed some very challenging film roles – as the autistic character in *Rain Man* (for which he won an Oscar); in drag in *Tootsie* and as the crippled Ratso Rizzo in *Midnight Cowboy* (1969), both of which gained him Oscar nominations; and as the 121-year-old Jack Crabb in *Little Big Man* (1970).

TOP 10 ANTHONY HOPKINS FILMS

	FILM	ROLE	YEAR
1	Hannibal	Dr. Hannibal Lecter	2001
2	The Silence of the Lambs *	Dr. Hannibal Lecter	1991
3	The Mask of Zorro	Don Diego de la Vega/Zorro	1998
4	Bram Stoker's Dracula	Prof. Abraham Van Helsing	1992
5	Red Dragon	Dr. Hannibal Lecter	2002
6	Legends of the Fall	Col. William Ludlow	1994
7	Meet Joe Black	William Parrish	1998
8	Amistad	John Quincy Adams	1997
9	A Bridge Too Far	Lt. Gen. John Frost	1977
10	Instinct	Ethan Powell	1999

* "Best Actor" Academy Award

Sir Anthony Hopkins appears in *Mission: Impossible 2* as Mission Commander Swanbeck, but his role is an uncredited cameo. His voice narrates *Dr. Seuss's How the Grinch Stole Christmas* (2000), which, if included, would be his 2nd highest-earning film ever.

Silence is Golden

Anthony Hopkins as Hannibal Lecter in *The Silence of the Lambs*. The film earned almost $300 million globally and he reprised the role in two sequels.

TOP 10 BOB HOSKINS FILMS

	FILM	ROLE	YEAR
1	Who Framed Roger Rabbit	Eddie Valiant	1988
2	Hook	Smee	1991
3	Maid in Manhattan	Lionel Bloch	2002
4	Michael	Vartan Malt	1996
5	Enemy at the Gates	Nikita Khrushchev	2001
6	Mermaids	Lou Landsky	1990
7	Super Mario Bros.	Mario Mario	1993
8	The Cotton Club	Owney Madden	1984
9	Pink Floyd: The Wall	Manager	1982
10	Lassiter	Insp. John Becker	1984

During the past 30 years, Bob Hoskins appeared in several notable high earners as well as a number that have achieved only moderate success. He appeared as himself in *Spice World* (1997); if included in his Top 10, it would be in 6th place.

TOP 10 SAMUEL L. JACKSON FILMS

	FILM	ROLE	YEAR
1	Star Wars: Episode I – The Phantom Menace	Mace Windu	1999
2	Jurassic Park	Arnold	1993
3	Star Wars: Episode II – Attack of the Clones	Mace Windu	2002
4	Die Hard: With a Vengeance	Zeus Carver	1995
5	xXx	Augustus Gibbons	2002
6	Unbreakable	Elijah Price	2000
7	Pulp Fiction	Jules Winnfield	1994
8	Patriot Games	Lt. Cmdr. Robert Jefferson "Robby" Jackson	1992
9	Deep Blue Sea	Russell Franklin	1999
10	A Time to Kill	Carl Lee Hailey	1996

Samuel L. (Leroy) Jackson's film career has seen him appear in a run of blockbusters: excluding those in which he had only a cameo role (as a hold-up man in *Coming to America*, 1988, for example), each of the 10 films listed here has earned more than $150 million globally, a total of $4 billion.

TOP 10 JAMES EARL JONES FILMS

	FILM	ROLE	YEAR
1	Coming to America	King Jaffe Joffer	1988
2	Clear and Present Danger	Admiral James Greer	1994
3	The Hunt for Red October	Admiral James Greer	1990
4	Patriot Games	Admiral James Greer	1992
5	Sommersby	Judge Isaacs	1993
6	Field of Dreams	Terence Mann	1989
7	Sneakers	Bernard Abbott	1992
8	Three Fugitives	Det. Dugan	1989
9	Conan the Barbarian	Thulsa Doom	1982
10	The Sandlot	Mr. Mertle	1993

James Earl Jones has appeared in numerous high-earning films, but none as successful as the first three in the *Star Wars* series (1977–83), to which he provides the voice of Darth Vader, and that of King Mufasa in *The Lion King* (1994), the biggest animated blockbuster to date, and as narrator in many other films. He also appeared, uncredited, as himself in a cameo role in *Naked Gun 33 ⅓: The Final Insult*.

TOP 10 TOMMY LEE JONES FILMS

	FILM	ROLE	YEAR
1	Men in Black	Agent K	1997
2	Men in Black II	Kevin Brown/Agent K	2002
3	The Fugitive	Samuel Gerard	1993
4	Batman Forever	Harvey Two-Face/Harvey Dent	1995
5	JFK	Clay Shaw	1991
6	Double Jeopardy	Travis Lehman	1999
7	Under Siege	William Stranix	1992
8	Space Cowboys	Col. William "Hawk" Hawkins	2000
9	Volcano	Mike Roark	1997
10	The Client	Roy Foltrigg	1994

Tommy Lee Jones supplied the voice of Major Chip Hazard in the part-animated *Small Soldiers* (1998). However, this film has been outearned by all the films in his Top 10, each of which has made over $100 million at the global box office, a total of over $2.6 billion in a movie career spanning over 30 years.

TOP 10 JACK LEMMON FILMS

	FILM	ROLE	YEAR
1	JFK	Jack Martin	1991
2	Grumpier Old Men	John Gustafson	1995
3	Grumpy Old Men	John Gustafson	1993
4	The Odd Couple	Felix Ungar	1968
5	The China Syndrome	Jack Godell	1979
6	Airport '77	Don Gallagher	1977
7	Out to Sea	Herb Sullivan	1997
8	Some Like It Hot	Jerry/Daphne	1959
9	My Fellow Americans	Pres. Russell O. Kramer	1996
10	The Great Race	Prof. Fate/ Prince Hapnik	1965

The first four of the films in Jack Lemmon's Top 10, plus *Out to Sea*, co-starred Walter Matthau. Their partnership began with *The Fortune Cookie* (1966) and also includes *The Front Page* (1974), *Buddy Buddy* (1981), *The Grass Harp* (1995), and *The Odd Couple II* (1998), as well as *Kotch* (1971), which Lemmon directed but in which he appeared only in a fleeting cameo role as a sleeping bus passenger. He also co-starred alongside Tony Curtis in *Some Like It Hot*, identified by the American Film Institute's poll as the funniest film of all time. He narrated and had a brief uncredited role in *The Legend of Bagger Vance* (2000), which, if counted, would rank in 6th place.

TOP 10 JOHN MALKOVICH FILMS

	FILM	ROLE	YEAR
1	Con Air	Cyrus "The Virus" Grissom	1997
2	In the Line of Fire	Mitch Leary/ John Booth/ James Carney	1993
3	The Man in the Iron Mask	Athos	1998
4	Johnny English	Pascal Sauvage	2003
5	The Messenger: The Story of Joan of Arc	Charles VII	1999
6	Dangerous Liaisons	Vicomte de Valmont	1988
7	Being John Malkovich	John Horatio Malkovich	1999
8	Places in the Heart	Mr. Will	1984
9	The Killing Fields	Al Rockoff	1984
10	Empire of the Sun	Basie	1987

Although uncredited, John Malkovich was the narrator of *Alive* (1993). If included, this would be in 6th place. He appears, uncredited, as himself in *Adaptation* (2003), which would be in 7th place.

Butterflies are Free

As in his role in *The Great Escape* 10 years earlier, Steve McQueen starred as a would-be prison escapee in *Papillon* (French for butterfly).

TOP 10 STEVE MARTIN FILMS

	FILM	ROLE	YEAR
1	Bringing Down the House	Peter Sanderson	2003
2	Parenthood	Gil Buckman	1989
3	Father of the Bride	George Stanley Banks	1991
4	Father of the Bride Part II	George Stanley Banks	1995
5	Bowfinger	Bobby Bowfinger	1999
6	The Jerk	Navin R. Johnson	1979
7	HouseSitter	Newton Davis	1992
8	Planes, Trains & Automobiles	Neal Page	1987
9	Dirty Rotten Scoundrels	Freddy Benson	1988
10	Roxanne	C.D. Bales	1987

Steve Martin provided the voice of Hotep in the animated *The Prince of Egypt* (1998). If this were included, it would head his Top 10, while *Fantasia/2000* (1999), in which he appeared as one of the hosts, would also merit a place. He had a cameo role as an unnamed heckler in *Remember the Titans* (2000), and was also one of the many "guest stars" in *The Muppet Movie* (1979).

TOP 10 WALTER MATTHAU FILMS

	FILM	ROLE	YEAR
1	JFK	Senator Long	1991
2	Dennis the Menace	George Wilson	1993
3	Grumpier Old Men	Max Goldman	1995
4	Grumpy Old Men	Max Goldman	1993
5	Hanging Up	Lou Mozell	2000
6	The Odd Couple	Oscar Madison	1968
7	California Suite	Marvin Michaels	1978
8	The Bad News Bears	Coach Morris Buttermaker	1976
9	Hello, Dolly!	Horace Vandergelder	1969
10	Out to Sea	Charlie Gordon	1997

Billed under his real name Walter Matuschanskayasky, Walter Matthau appeared in a brief cameo role in *Earthquake* (1974). Were it included, it would be in 3rd place in his Top 10.

TOP 10 STEVE McQUEEN FILMS

	FILM	ROLE	YEAR
1	The Towering Inferno	Chief O'Hallorhan	1974
2	Papillon	Henri "Papillon" Charrière	1973
3	Bullitt	Det. Lt. Frank Bullitt	1968
4	The Sand Pebbles	Jake Holman	1966
5	The Getaway	Carter "Doc" McCoy	1972
6	The Reivers	Boon Hogganbeck	1969
7	The Hunter	Papa Thorson	1980
8	The Thomas Crown Affair	Thomas Crown	1968
9	The Great Escape	Capt. Virgil Hilts	1963
10	Le Mans	Michael Delaney	1971

Steve McQueen (1930–80) made his first film in 1956, but it was not until his role in *The Magnificent Seven* (1960) that his star quality was recognized. He went on to achieve cult status with his famed motorcycle pursuit in *The Great Escape*, as a cool criminal mastermind in *The Thomas Crown Affair*, and for the celebrated car chase in *Bullitt*. His highest-earning film, *The Towering Inferno*, was created by merging the plots of two disaster novels, *The Tower* and *The Glass Inferno*. McQueen earned his sole Oscar nomination for *The Sand Pebbles*.

TOP 10 EDDIE MURPHY FILMS

	FILM	ROLE	YEAR
1	Beverly Hills Cop	Det. Axel Foley	1984
2	Beverly Hills Cop II	Det. Axel Foley	1987
3	Dr. Dolittle	Dr. John Dolittle	1998
4	Coming to America	Prince Akeem, *et al*	1988
5	The Nutty Professor	Prof. Sherman Klump, *et al*	1996
6	Dr. Dolittle 2	Dr. John Dolittle	2001
7	Nutty Professor II: The Klumps	Prof. Sherman Klump, *et al*	2000
8	Another 48 Hrs.	Reggie Hammond	1990
9	The Golden Child	Chandler Jarrell	1986
10	Boomerang	Marcus Graham	1992

Eddie Murphy also provided the voice of Donkey in the animated film *Shrek* (2001), which, were it included, would rank 1st in his Top 10, while *Mulan* (1998), for which he supplied the voice of Mushu, would appear in 2nd place. All 10 of his Top 10 have earned well over $100 million each worldwide, with both of the two *Beverly Hills Cop* films making over $300 million. In contrast, several of his recent films have achieved less success, with *The Adventures of Pluto Nash* (2002) notable for having failed to recoup more than a fraction of its $100-million production budget.

TOP 10 BILL MURRAY FILMS

	FILM	ROLE	YEAR
1	Ghostbusters	Dr. Peter Venkman	1984
2	Charlie's Angels	John Bosley/John David "J.D." Rage	2000
3	Ghostbusters II	Dr. Peter Venkman	1989
4	Tootsie	Jeff	1982
5	Groundhog Day	Phil Connors	1993
6	Stripes	John Winger	1981
7	The Royal Tenenbaums	Raleigh St. Clair	2001
8	Wild Things	Kenneth Bowden	1998
9	Scrooged	Francis Xavier Cross	1988
10	What About Bob?	Bob "Bobby" Wiley	1991

Bill Murray appeared, uncredited, as himself in *Space Jam* (1996). If included among his Top 10, it would appear in 3rd place.

Did you know?

Jack Nicholson has achieved a record 12 Oscar nominations and three wins in his 45-year film career.

TOP 10 LIAM NEESON FILMS

	FILM	ROLE	YEAR
1	Star Wars: Episode I – The Phantom Menace	Qui-Gon Jinn	1999
2	Schindler's List	Oskar Schindler	1993
3	Gangs of New York	Priest Vallon	2002
4	The Haunting	Dr. David Marrow	1999
5	Nell	Dr. Jerome "Jerry" Lovell	1994
6	Rob Roy	MacGregor	1995
7	K-19: The Widowmaker	Mikhail Polenin	2002
8	The Dead Pool	Peter Swan	1988
9	Michael Collins	Michael Collins	1996
10	Excalibur	Gawain	1981

Liam Neeson's voice is heard in *Star Wars: Episode II – Attack of the Clones* (2002), but he does not appear in it. Additionally, he acted as narrator of the documentary *Everest* (1998), the exceptional earnings of which would place it 5th in his Top 10.

TOP 10 PAUL NEWMAN FILMS

	FILM	ROLE	YEAR
1	Road to Perdition	John Rooney	2002
2	The Sting	Henry Gondorff/Mr. Shaw	1973
3	Message in a Bottle	Dodge Blake	1999
4	The Towering Inferno	Doug Roberts	1974
5	Butch Cassidy and the Sundance Kid	Butch Cassidy	1969
6	The Verdict	Frank Galvin	1982
7	The Color of Money *	Eddie	1986
8	Nobody's Fool	Donald "Sully" Sullivan	1994
9	Absence of Malice	Michael Colin Gallagher	1981
10	Fort Apache, the Bronx	Murphy	1981

* Academy Award for "Best Actor"

TOP 10 JACK NICHOLSON FILMS

	FILM	ROLE	YEAR
1	Batman	The Joker/Jack Napier	1989
2	As Good As It Gets *	Melvin Udall	1997
3	A Few Good Men	Col. Nathan R. Jessep	1992
4	Terms of Endearment	Garrett Breedlove	1983
5	Wolf	Will Randall	1994
6	One Flew Over the Cuckoo's Nest *	Randle Patrick McMurphy	1975
7	Mars Attacks!	President James Dale/Art Land	1996
8	About Schmidt	Warren Schmidt	2002
9	Anger Management	Dr. Buddy Rydell	2003
10	The Witches of Eastwick	Daryl Van Horne	1987

* Academy Award for "Best Actor"

PETER O'TOOLE FILMS

	FILM	ROLE	YEAR
1	The Last Emperor	Reginald F. Johnston ("R.J.")	1987
2	Lawrence of Arabia	T.E. Lawrence	1962
3	King Ralph	Lord Willingham	1991
4	The Bible...In the Beginning	The Three Angels	1966
5	Caligula	Tiberius	1979
6	The Lion in Winter	Henry II	1968
7	My Favorite Year	Alan Swann	1982
8	What's New, Pussycat?	Michael James	1965
9	Fairy Tale: A True Story	Sir Arthur Conan Doyle	1997
10	Supergirl	Zaltar	1984

Lawrence of Arabia has a prominent place in Peter O'Toole's Top 10 by virtue of the cumulative total earnings of its original release and re-releases. He also appeared (uncredited, as a Scottish piper) in *Casino Royale* (1967). Having been nominated for an Oscar on seven occasions without a single win, in 2003 he initially declined an honorary Academy Award, explaining that as his career was still active, he retained hopes of winning one for an acting role – but then graciously accepted it.

TOP 10 **AL PACINO FILMS**

	FILM	ROLE	YEAR
1	Heat	Vincent Hanna	1995
2	Dick Tracy	Big Boy Caprice	1990
3	The Devil's Advocate	John Milton	1997
4	The Godfather, Part III	Don Michael "Mike" Corleone	1990
5	The Godfather	Michael "Mike" Corleone	1972
6	Donnie Brasco	Benjamin "Lefty" Ruggerio	1997
7	Sea of Love	Det. Frank Keller	1989
8	The Godfather, Part II	Michael "Mike" Corleone	1974
9	Any Given Sunday	Tony D'Amato	1999
10	Insomnia	Will Dormer	2002

Al Pacino is celebrated for receiving eight Oscar nominations before finally winning, but his Golden Globe record is similarly erratic, with a total of 13 nominations but just two wins, for *Serpico* (1973) and *Scent of a Woman* (1992). He also won the Globes' prestigious Cecil B. DeMille Award in 2001.

Crime Pays

Brad Pitt's roles in crime and action films such as *Sleepers* (1996), which earned over $165 million worldwide, have made him one of the most highly rated of today's stars at the box office.

TOP 10 **BILL PAXTON FILMS**

	FILM	ROLE	YEAR
1	Titanic	Brock Lovett	1997
2	Twister	William "Bill" Harding	1996
3	True Lies	Simon	1994
4	Apollo 13	Fred Haise	1995
5	Vertical Limit	Elliot Vaughn	2000
6	Aliens	Pvt. W. Hudson	1986
7	U-571	Lt. Cmdr. Mike Dahlgren	2000
8	Spy Kids 2: Island of Lost Dreams	Dinky Winks	2002
9	Mighty Joe Young	Gregg O'Hara	1998
10	Tombstone	Morgan Earp	1993

Bill Paxton has taken supporting actor roles in several of the highest-earning films of all time, as well as numerous un-named cameo roles in others, including *Stripes* (1981) and *The Terminator* (1984).

TOP 10 **BRAD PITT FILMS**

	FILM	ROLE	YEAR
1	Ocean's Eleven	Rusty Ryan	2001
2	Se7en	Det. David Mills	1995
3	Interview with the Vampire: The Vampire Chronicles	Louis de Pointe du Lac	1994
4	Sleepers	Michael Sullivan	1996
5	Twelve Monkeys	Jeffrey Goines	1995
6	Legends of the Fall	Tristan Ludlow	1994
7	The Devil's Own	Rory Devaney/ Francis "Frankie" McGuire	1997
8	Meet Joe Black	Joe Black	1998
9	Seven Years in Tibet	Heinrich Harrer	1997
10	Spy Game	Tom Bishop	2001

Brad Pitt is a member of an élite group of actors all of whose 10 highest-earning films have made more than $100 million in total at the world box office.

TOP 10 ELVIS PRESLEY FILMS

	FILM	ROLE	YEAR
1	Blue Hawaii	Chad Gates	1961
2	Viva Las Vegas	Lucky Jackson	1964
3	Love Me Tender	Clint Reno	1956
4	Loving You	Deke Rivers	1957
5	Tickle Me	Lonnie Beale	1965
6	Harum Scarum	Johnny Tyronne	1965
7	G.I. Blues	Tulsa McLean	1960
8	Jailhouse Rock	Vince Everett	1957
9	Girl Happy	Rusty Wells	1965
10	Speedway	Steve Grayson	1968

From his first acting role in *Love Me Tender* (1956) to that of Dr. John Carpenter in *Change of Habit* (1970), Elvis made 32 films, also appearing as himself in *Elvis: That's The Way It Is* (1970) and *Elvis on Tour* (1972). Since his death he has continued to make appearances in archive footage in such major films as *Forrest Gump* (1994), while his songs figure in countless films.

Did you know?

Elvis Presley's only non-singing film role was in *Charro!* (1969), a Western directed by Charles Marquis Warren, the director of the *Rawhide* TV series that had brought Clint Eastwood to public attention.

TOP 10 KEANU REEVES FILMS

	FILM	ROLE	YEAR
1	The Matrix	Thomas A. Anderson/Neo	1999
2	Speed	Jack Traven	1994
3	Bram Stoker's Dracula	Jonathan Harker	1992
4	The Devil's Advocate	Kevin Lomax	1997
5	Parenthood	Tod Hawkes	1989
6	A Walk in the Clouds	Paul Sutton	1995
7	Chain Reaction	Eddie Kasalivich	1996
8	Johnny Mnemonic	Johnny Mnemonic	1995
9	Point Break	Johnny Utah	1991
10	Bill & Ted's Bogus Journey	Ted "Theodore" Logan	1991

The son of an English mother and part-Hawaiian, part-Chinese father, Keanu Reeves came to public attention in the late 1980s with films such as *Dangerous Liaisons* (1988) and *Bill & Ted's Excellent Adventure* (1989). After the huge international success of *The Matrix*, which made more than $450 million worldwide, he has been able to command a reputed per-picture salary of $15 million for the two big-budget sequels, *The Matrix Reloaded* and *The Matrix Revolutions*.

TOP 10 BILL PULLMAN FILMS

	FILM	ROLE	YEAR
1	Independence Day	President Thomas J. Whitmore	1996
2	Casper	Dr. James Harvey	1995
3	Sleepless in Seattle	Walter	1993
4	While You Were Sleeping	Jack Callaghan	1995
5	Sommersby	Orin Meecham	1993
6	A League of Their Own	Bob Hinson	1992
7	Ruthless People	Earl Mott	1986
8	Malice	Andy Safian	1993
9	Lake Placid	Jack Wells	1999
10	Spaceballs	Capt. Lone Starr	1987

The first six films in Bill Pullman's Top 10 each earned more than $100 million worldwide, with *Independence Day* making over $800 million, placing it among the highest-grossing films of all time.

TOP 10 ALAN RICKMAN FILMS

	FILM	ROLE	YEAR
1	Harry Potter and the Sorcerer's Stone	Prof. Severus Snape	2001
2	Harry Potter and the Chamber of Secrets	Prof. Severus Snape	2002
3	Robin Hood: Prince of Thieves	Sheriff of Nottingham	1991
4	Die Hard	Hans Grüber	1988
5	Sense and Sensibility	Colonel Brandon	1995
6	Galaxy Quest	Alexander "Alex" Dane/Dr. Lazarus	1999
7	Dogma	Metatron	1999
8	Michael Collins	Eamon De Valera	1996
9	Quigley Down Under	Elliott Marston	1990
10	January Man	Ed	1989

TOP 10 ROBERT REDFORD FILMS

	FILM	ROLE	YEAR
1	Indecent Proposal	John Gage	1993
2	Out of Africa	Denys Finch Hatton	1985
3	The Horse Whisperer	Tom Booker	1998
4	The Sting	Johnny Hooker/Kelly	1973
5	Spy Game	Nathan D. Muir	2001
6	Butch Cassidy and the Sundance Kid	The Sundance Kid (Harry Longbaugh)	1969
7	Up Close & Personal	Warren Justice	1996
8	All the President's Men	Bob Woodwardt	1976
9	Sneakers	Martin Bishop/Martin Brice	1992
10	A Bridge Too Far	Maj. Julian Cook	1977

Although best known as an actor, Robert Redford has been nominated for just one acting Oscar during his 40-year career, for his role in *The Sting* (1973), but has been nominated twice as "Best Director", winning for *Ordinary People* (1980). In 2002 he was presented with an Honorary Academy Award for his work as an actor, director, producer, and the creator of the Sundance Film Festival.

TOP 10 TIM ROBBINS FILMS

	FILM	ROLE	YEAR
1	Top Gun	Lt. Sam "Merlin" Wills	1986
2	Austin Powers: The Spy Who Shagged Me	The President	1999
3	Mission to Mars	Woodrow "Woody" Blake	2000
4	Nothing to Lose	Nick Beam	1997
5	The Shawshank Redemption	Andy Dufresne	1994
6	Bull Durham	Ebby Calvin "Nuke" LaLoosh	1988
7	Arlington Road	Oliver Lang/William Fenimore	1999
8	High Fidelity	Ian Raymond	2000
9	Jungle Fever	Jerry	1991
10	I.Q.	Ed Walters	1994

Tim Robbins' role in *Austin Powers: The Spy Who Shagged Me* is little more than a cameo. If it is discounted, *Jacob's Ladder* (1990), in which he plays the part of Jacob Singer, joins the list.

TOP 10 ADAM SANDLER FILMS

	FILM	ROLE	YEAR
1	Big Daddy	Sonny Koufax	1999
2	The Waterboy	Bobby Boucher	1998
3	Mr. Deeds	Longfellow Deeds	2002
4	The Wedding Singer	Robbie Hart	1998
5	Anger Management	Dave Buznik	2003
6	Little Nicky	Nicky	2000
7	Happy Gilmore	Happy Gilmore	1996
8	Billy Madison	Billy Madison	1995
9	Bulletproof	Archie Moses	1996
10	Coneheads	Carmine	1993

As well as starring in these films, Adam Sandler wrote the scripts for many of them. He was also executive producer of some of these and others in which he had cameo roles, including *The Animal* (2001) and *Hot Chicks* (2002), and provided voices to several characters in the animated *Eight Crazy Nights* (2002).

Did you know?

Arnold Schwarzenegger kills an estimated total of 383 people in his major films. He has made only three — *Twins* (1988), *Junior* (1994), and *Jingle All the Way* (1996) — in which he does not kill anyone.

TOP 10 ARNOLD SCHWARZENEGGER FILMS

	FILM	ROLE	YEAR
1	Terminator 2: Judgment Day	The Terminator (T-800 Model 101)	1991
2	True Lies	Harry Tasker	1994
3	Total Recall	Douglas Quaid	1990
4	Batman & Robin	Mr. Freeze/ Dr. Victor Fries	1997
5	Eraser	US Marshal John "The Eraser" Kruger	1996
6	Twins	Julius Benedict	1988
7	End of Days	Jericho Cane	1999
8	Kindergarten Cop	Det. John Kimble	1990
9	Jingle All the Way	Howard "Howie" Langston	1996
10	Last Action Hero	Jack Slater	1993

As well as this group of $100 million-plus earning films, Arnold Schwarzenegger (though uncredited) provided the voice of a white wolf in *Dr. Dolittle 2* (2001).

TOP 10 WILL SMITH FILMS

	FILM	ROLE	YEAR
1	Independence Day	Capt. Steven "Steve" Hiller	1996
2	Men in Black	Agent J/James Edwards	1997
3	Men in Black II	Agent J/James Edwards	2002
4	Enemy of the State	Robert Clayton Dean	1998
5	Wild Wild West	Capt. James "Jim" West	1999
6	Bad Boys	Mike Lowrey	1995
7	Made in America	Tea Cake Walters	1993
8	Ali	Cassius Clay/ Cassius X/ Muhammad Ali	2001
9	The Legend of Bagger Vance	Bagger Vance	2000
10	Six Degrees of Separation	Paul	1993

Achieving public recognition for his TV role in *The Fresh Prince of Bel-Air* (1990–96), Will (Willard) Smith made the move into film in 1992. He received Oscar as well as Golden Globe nominations for his title role in *Ali*, for which – as with *Men in Black II* – he earned $20 million.

TOP 10 KEVIN SPACEY FILMS

	FILM	ROLE	YEAR
1	American Beauty *	Lester Burnham	1999
2	Se7en	John Doe	1995
3	Outbreak	Maj. Casey Schuler	1995
4	A Time to Kill	D.A. Rufus Buckley	1996
5	L.A. Confidential	Sgt. Jack Vincennes	1997
6	The Negotiator	Lt. Chris Sabian	1998
7	Working Girl	Bob Speck	1988
8	K-PAX	Prot/Robert Porter	2001
9	See No Evil, Hear No Evil	Kirgo	1989
10	The Usual Suspects	Roger "Verbal" Kint	1995

* "Best Actor" Academy Award

Kevin Spacey appeared in a brief cameo role as himself in *Austin Powers in Goldmember* (2002), and supplied the voice of Hopper in the animated film *A Bug's Life* (1998), which were both high-earning films, but excluded from his personal Top 10.

TOP 10 SYLVESTER STALLONE FILMS

	FILM	ROLE	YEAR
1	Rambo: First Blood Part II	John J. Rambo	1985
2	Rocky IV	Rocky Balboa	1985
3	Cliffhanger	Gabe Walker	1993
4	Rambo III	John J. Rambo	1988
5	Rocky III	Rocky Balboa	1982
6	Rocky	Rocky Balboa	1976
7	The Specialist	Ray Quick	1994
8	Daylight	Kit Latura	1996
9	Rocky V	Rocky Balboa	1990
10	Judge Dredd	Judge Dredd	1995

All of Sylvester Stallone's Top 10 films earned more than $100 million each worldwide. He wrote the first six and the 9th in the list. He also supplied the voice of Weaver in the animated film *Antz* (1998), and had cameo roles in other high-earners, such as *Staying Alive* (1983). Stallone was nominated for both Oscars and Golden Globes for his acting roles and his scriptwriting for *Rocky*, but failed to win either – although the film won "Best Picture" awards from both organizations.

TOP 10 BEN STILLER FILMS

	FILM	ROLE	YEAR
1	There's Something About Mary	Ted Stroehmann	1998
2	Meet the Parents	Gaylord "Greg" Focker	2000
3	The Cable Guy	Sam Sweet/ Stan Sweet	1996
4	The Royal Tenenbaums	Chas Tenenbaum	2001
5	Zoolander	Derek Joseph Zoolander	2001
6	Keeping the Faith	Rabbi Jacob "Jake" Schram	2000
7	Mystery Men	Mr. Furious	1999
8	Empire of the Sun	Dainty	1987
9	Reality Bites	Michael Grates	1994
10	Stella	Jim Uptegrove	1990

As well as starring roles in a range of (mostly) comedy films, several of which he also directed, Ben Stiller appeared in cameos in *Happy Gilmore* (1996) and *Orange County* (2002).

JOHN TRAVOLTA FILMS

	FILM	ROLE	YEAR
1	Grease	Danny Zuko	1978
2	Look Who's Talking	James Ubriacco	1989
3	Saturday Night Fever	Tony Manero	1977
4	Face/Off	Sean Archer/ Castor Troy	1997
5	Pulp Fiction	Vincent Vega	1994
6	Phenomenon	George Malley	1996
7	The General's Daughter	Paul Brenner	1999
8	Broken Arrow	Maj. Vic Deakins	1996
9	Staying Alive	Tony Manero	1983
10	Swordfish	Gabriel Shear	2001

All John Travolta's Top 10 films earned more than $100 million each worldwide. He also appeared as himself in a cameo role in *Austin Powers in Goldmember* (2002). This has been discounted, but if included it would rank in third place.

Down to Earth

Oscar-winning actor Denzel Washington co-starred with Whitney Houston in the role of an earth-visiting angel in *The Preacher's Wife*.

DENZEL WASHINGTON FILMS

	FILM	ROLE	YEAR
1	Philadelphia	Joe Miller	1993
2	The Pelican Brief	Gray Grantham	1993
3	Crimson Tide	Lt. Cdr. Ron Hunter	1995
4	The Bone Collector	Lincoln Rhyme	1999
5	The Siege	Anthony "Hub" Hubbard	1998
6	Remember the Titans	Herman Boone	2000
7	Training Day *	Det. Alonzo Harris	2001
8	Courage Under Fire	Lt. Col. Nathaniel Serling	1996
9	The Preacher's Wife	Dudley	1996
10	John Q	John Quincy Archibald	2002

* "Best Actor" Academy Award

ROBIN WILLIAMS FILMS

	FILM	ROLE	YEAR
1	Mrs. Doubtfire	Daniel Hillard/ Mrs. Euphegenia Doubtfire	1993
2	Hook	Peter Banning/ Peter Pan	1991
3	Jumanji	Alan Parrish	1995
4	Dead Poets Society	John Keating	1989
5	Good Will Hunting	Sean Maguire	1997
6	Patch Adams	Hunter "Patch" Adams	1998
7	The Birdcage	Armand Goldman	1996
8	Flubber	Prof. Philip "Phil" Brainard	1997
9	Good Morning, Vietnam	A1C Adrian Cronauer	1987
10	Nine Months	Dr. Kosevich	1995

Robin Williams's entire Top 10 are $100-million-plus earning films. His voice appears as that of the Blue Genie of the Lamp in the animated blockbuster *Aladdin* (1992). If this were included, its earnings would place it at the head of the list.

BRUCE WILLIS FILMS

	FILM	ROLE	YEAR
1	The Sixth Sense	Malcolm Crowe	1999
2	Armageddon	Harry S. Stamper	1998
3	Die Hard: With a Vengeance	John McClane	1995
4	The Fifth Element	Korben Dallas	1997
5	Unbreakable	David Dunn	2000
6	Die Hard 2: Die Harder	John McClane	1990
7	Pulp Fiction	Butch Coolidge	1994
8	Twelve Monkeys	James "Jim" Cole	1995
9	The Jackal	The Jackal	1997
10	Death Becomes Her	Dr. Ernest Menville	1992

Each of Bruce Willis's Top 10 films has earned upwards of $150 million globally. Most were high-budget films that nonetheless saw a handsome return on their investment, but *Pulp Fiction* was exceptional in having (by Hollywood standards) a minute budget of $8 million, but made a worldwide gross of more than $200 million. Although discounted here – and ironically, in view of his tough-guy screen persona – Bruce Willis provided the voice of the baby Mikey in *Look Who's Talking* (1989), a worldwide blockbuster that earned almost $300 million.

TOP 10 JULIE ANDREWS FILMS

FILM	ROLE	YEAR
1 The Sound of Music	Maria	1965
2 The Princess Diaries	Clarisse Renaldi, Queen of Genovia	2001
3 Mary Poppins *	Mary Poppins	1964
4 10	"Sam" Taylor	1979
5 Hawaii	Jerusha Hale	1966
6 Thoroughly Modern Millie	Millie Dillmount	1967
7 Victor/Victoria	Count Victor Grezhinski/ Victoria Grant	1982
8 S.O.B.	Sally Miles	1981
9 The Man Who Loved Women	Marianna	1983
10 Torn Curtain	Sarah Sherman	1966

* "Best Actress" Academy Award
Among many other films directed by her husband Blake Edwards, Julie Andrews contributed her singing voice to the character Jarvis (played by Michael Robbins) in *The Pink Panther Strikes Again* (1976), which, if included, would be in 7th place. The opening sequence contains an animated parody of her most successful film, *The Sound of Music*.

TOP 10 DREW BARRYMORE FILMS

FILM	ROLE	YEAR
1 E.T. the Extra-Terrestrial	Gertie	1982
2 Batman Forever	Sugar	1995
3 Charlie's Angels	Dylan Sanders	2000
4 Scream	Casey Becker	1996
5 The Wedding Singer	Julia Sullivan	1998
6 Ever After: A Cinderella Story	Danielle De Barbarac	1998
7 Never Been Kissed	Josie Geller	1999
8 Wayne's World 2	Bjergen Kjergen	1993
9 Boys on the Side	Holly Pulchik	1995
10 Irreconcilable Differences	Casey Brodsky	1984

Granddaughter of Hollywood legend John Barrymore, Drew Barrymore's first film role was in *Altered States*, when she was five; by the time of her part in *E.T. the Extra-Terrestrial*, she was aged seven. Her bankability has increased in recent years to enable her to command a reputed $14 million for her role in *Charlie's Angels: Full Throttle* (2003).

TOP 10 KIM BASINGER FILMS

FILM	ROLE	YEAR
1 Batman	Vicki Vale	1989
2 8 Mile	Stephanie Smith	2002
3 L.A. Confidential	Lynn Bracken	1997
4 Wayne's World 2	Honey Hornée	1993
5 Never Say Never Again	Domino Petachi	1983
6 The Natural	Memo Paris	1984
7 Final Analysis	Heather Evans	1992
8 Blind Date	Nadia Gates	1987
9 Bless the Child	Maggie O'Connor	2000
10 The Getaway	Carol McCoy	1994

Kim Basinger moved from modelling to acting – her first roles were in TV movies during the late 1970s. She made her debut Hollywood film *Hard Country* in 1981 and became a "Bond girl", Domino Petachi, in *Never Say Never Again*, in 1983.

Femme Fatale

Kim Basinger won the "Best Supporting Actress" Oscar for her role in *L.A. Confidential*, a box office hit based on James Ellroy's detective story set in Los Angeles in the 1950s.

TOP 10 ANGELA BASSETT FILMS

FILM	ROLE	YEAR
1 Contact	Rachel Constantine	1997
2 The Score	Diane	2001
3 Waiting to Exhale	"Bernie" Harris	1995
4 Boyz N the Hood	Reva Devereaux	1991
5 Malcolm X	Betty Shabazz	1992
6 What's Love Got to Do with It	Tina Turner	1993
7 How Stella Got Her Groove Back	Stella Payne	1998
8 Vampire in Brooklyn	Rita Veder	1995
9 Music of the Heart	Janet Williams	1999
10 Supernova	Dr. Kaela Evers	2000

Angela Bassett had a cameo role as an air stewardess in *Kindergarten Cop* (1990). If it were included, it would head her personal Top 10.

TOP 10 KATHY BATES FILMS

FILM	ROLE	YEAR
1 Titanic	Margaret "Molly" Brown	1997
2 The Waterboy	Helen "Mama" Boucher	1998
3 Dick Tracy	Mrs. Green	1990
4 About Schmidt	Roberta Hertzel	2002
5 Fried Green Tomatoes †	Evelyn Couch	1991
6 Misery *	Annie Wilkes	1990
7 Diabolique	Shirley Voguel	1996
8 Dragonfly	Mrs. Belmont	2002
9 Dolores Claiborne	Dolores Claiborne	1995
10 Primary Colors	Libby Holden	1998

* "Best Actress" Academy Award
† Called *Fried Green Tomatoes at the Whistle Stop Cafe* in UK
In addition to the Top 10, Kathy Bates had uncredited cameo roles in several films, including The Squirrel Lady in *Rat Race* (2001) and as a judge in *A Civil Action* (1998). She was nominated for, but did not win, "Best Supporting Actress" Oscars for *Primary Colors* and *About Schmidt*.

TOP 10 INGRID BERGMAN FILMS

FILM	ROLE	YEAR
1 Murder on the Orient Express	Greta	1974
2 Cactus Flower	Stephanie Dickinson	1969
3 The Bells of St. Mary's	Sister Benedict	1945
4 For Whom the Bell Tolls	María	1943
5 Spellbound	Dr. Constance Peterson	1945
6 Notorious	Alicia Huberman	1946
7 Casablanca	Ilsa Lund Laszlo	1942
8 The Yellow Rolls Royce	Gerda Millett	1964
9 The Inn of the Sixth Happiness	Gladys Aylward	1958
10 Anastasia	Anastasia	1956

Ingrid Bergman (1915–82) had already made 10 films in her native Sweden before her first Hollywood appearance in *Intermezzo* (1939), a remake of the Swedish film in which she had starred in 1936. She was nominated for seven Oscars, winning "Best Actress" for *Gaslight* (1944) and *Anastasia* (1956), and "Best Supporting Actress" for *Murder in the Orient Express* (1974).

TOP 10 HALLE BERRY FILMS

	FILM	ROLE	YEAR
1	Die Another Day	Jinx	2002
2	The Flintstones	Sharon Stone	1994
3	X-Men	Storm/ Ororo Munroe	2000
4	Boomerang	Angela Lewis	1992
5	Executive Decision	Jean	1996
6	Swordfish	Ginger	2001
7	The Last Boy Scout	Cory	1991
8	Monster's Ball *	Leticia Musgrove	2001
9	Jungle Fever	Vivian	1991
10	Bulworth	Nina	1998

* "Best Actress" Academy Award

TOP 10 SANDRA BULLOCK FILMS

	FILM	ROLE	YEAR
1	Speed	Annie Porter	1994
2	Miss Congeniality	Gracie Hart	2000
3	Two Weeks Notice	Lucy Kelson	2002
4	While You Were Sleeping	Lucy Eleanor Moderatz	1995
5	Speed 2: Cruise Control	Annie Porter	1997
6	A Time to Kill	Ellen Roark	1996
7	The Net	Angela Bennett	1995
8	Forces of Nature	Sarah Lewis	1999
9	Practical Magic	Sally "Sal" Owens	1998
10	Hope Floats	Birdee Pruitt	1998

The voice of Miriam in the animated film *The Prince of Egypt* (1998) was provided by Sandra Bullock. If included, it would appear in second place in this list.

TOP 10 GLENN CLOSE FILMS

	FILM	ROLE	YEAR
1	Fatal Attraction	Alex Forrest	1987
2	Air Force One	Vice President Kathryn Bennett	1997
3	101 Dalmatians	Cruella De Vil	1996
4	102 Dalmatians	Cruella De Vil	2000
5	The Big Chill	Sarah	1983
6	The Natural	Iris Gaines	1984
7	Mars Attacks!	First Lady Marsha Dale	1996
8	The Paper	Alicia Clark	1994
9	Jagged Edge	Teddy Barnes	1985
10	Dangerous Liaisons	Marquise de Merteuil	1988

Glenn Close provided the voice of Kala in the animated film *Tarzan* (1999), which would score higher than any other in her acting Top 10. She also appeared uncredited (and unrecognisably) as Gutless, a pirate in *Hook* (1991), as herself in *In & Out* (1997), dubbed the voice of Andy MacDowell (whose accent was deemed unsuitable) in *Greystoke: The Legend of Tarzan, Lord of the Apes* (1984), and provided that of the Blue Fairy in the US version of the Italian film *Pinocchio* (2002), all of which would merit places in her Top 10. For these and other roles she received five Academy Award and six Golden Globe nominations — without ever winning.

TOP 10 COURTENEY COX FILMS

	FILM	ROLE	YEAR
1	Scream	Gale Weathers	1996
2	Scream 2	Gale Weathers	1997
3	Scream 3	Gale Weathers	2000
4	Ace Ventura: Pet Detective	Melissa Robinson	1994
5	Cocoon: The Return	Sara	1988
6	Masters of the Universe	Julie Winston	1987
7	3000 Miles to Graceland	Cybil Waingrow	2001
8	Mr. Destiny	Jewel Jagger	1990
9	The Opposite Sex and How to Live with Them	Carrie Davenport	1993
10	Commandments	Rachel Luce	1997

Although Courteney Cox is well known for her TV role in *Friends*, her film career is less memorable: while the first four films in her Top 10 are $100 million-plus earners, the rest have achieved considerably less at the box office, and she was nominated for a Golden Raspberry Award as "Worst Actress" for her role in *3000 Miles to Graceland*.

TOP 10 JAMIE LEE CURTIS FILMS

	FILM	ROLE	YEAR
1	True Lies	Helen Tasker	1994
2	A Fish Called Wanda	Wanda	1988
3	Forever Young	Claire Cooper	1992
4	Trading Places	Ophelia	1983
5	Halloween H20: 20 Years Later	Laurie Strode/ Keri Tate	1998
6	My Girl	Shelly DeVoto	1991
7	Halloween	Laurie Strode	1978
8	Fierce Creatures	Willa Weston	1997
9	Halloween: Resurrection	Laurie Strode	2002
10	Halloween II	Laurie Strode	1981

Jamie Lee Curtis was born into an acting dynasty as the daughter of actor Tony Curtis and actress Janet Leigh, and married *Spinal Tap* actor Christopher Guest, becoming Baroness Haden-Guest when he became a peer in 1996.

TOP 10 GEENA DAVIS FILMS

	FILM	ROLE	YEAR
1	Stuart Little	Eleanor Little	1999
2	Tootsie	April	1982
3	Stuart Little 2	Eleanor Little	2002
4	A League of Their Own	Dottie Hinson	1992
5	The Long Kiss Goodnight	Samantha Caine/ Charly Baltimore	1996
6	Beetlejuice	Barbara	1988
7	Hero	Gale Gayley	1992
8	Fletch	Larry	1985
9	Thelma & Louise	Thelma Dickinson	1991
10	The Fly	Veronica Quaife	1986

Unusually tall (1.83 m/6 ft) for a leading lady, Geena Davis's debut screen role was in *Tootsie*, which has maintained its place as one of her most commercially successful films. She received the "Best Supporting Actress" Oscar for her role as Muriel in *The Accidental Tourist* (1988), which just fails to enter her Top 10, and was nominated as "Best Actress" for her celebrated part in *Thelma & Louise*. Following her 1993 marriage to director Renny Harlin, she starred in his ill-fated *Cutthroat Island* (1995), one of the most notable high-budget flops of all time.

TOP 10 JUDI DENCH FILMS

	FILM	ROLE	YEAR
1	Die Another Day	M	2002
2	The World Is Not Enough	M	1999
3	GoldenEye	M	1995
4	Tomorrow Never Dies	M	1997
5	Shakespeare in Love	Queen Elizabeth I	1998
6	Chocolat	Armande Voizin	2000
7	Tea with Mussolini	Arabella	1999
8	A Room with a View	Eleanor Lavish	1986
9	The Shipping News	Agnis Hamm	2001
10	Mrs. Brown *	Queen Victoria	1997

* Retitled as *Her Majesty, Mrs. Brown* in the US

After 40 years in the business, Dame Judi Dench's most successful pictures have been the last four James Bond films, in which she plays "M", the head of MI6.

TOP 10 CAMERON DIAZ FILMS

	FILM	ROLE	YEAR
1	There's Something About Mary	Mary Jensen Matthews	1998
2	The Mask	Tina Carlyle	1994
3	My Best Friend's Wedding	Kimberly "Kim/Kimmy" Wallace	1997
4	Charlie's Angels	Natalie Cook	2000
5	Vanilla Sky	Julie Gianni	2001
6	Gangs of New York	Jenny Everdeane	2002
7	Any Given Sunday	Christina Pagniacci	1999
8	Being John Malkovich	Lotte Schwartz	1999
9	The Sweetest Thing	Christina Walters	2002
10	A Life Less Ordinary	Celine Naville	1997

Cameron Diaz's Top 10 films include several that are among the highest earning of recent years. She also provided the voice of Princess Fiona in *Shrek* (2001) – which has outearned all of them.

TOP 10 CARRIE FISHER FILMS

	FILM	ROLE	YEAR
1	Star Wars	Princess Leia Organa	1977
2	Star Wars: Episode VI – Return of the Jedi	Princess Leia Organa	1983
3	Star Wars: Episode V – The Empire Strikes Back	Princess Leia Organa	1980
4	Scream 3	Bianca Burnette	2000
5	When Harry Met Sally ...	Marie	1989
6	The Blues Brothers	Camille Ztdetelik	1980
7	Heartbreakers	Ms. Surpin	2001
8	Shampoo	Lorna	1975
9	Hannah and Her Sisters	April	1986
10	The 'burbs	Carol Peterson	1989

Carrie Fisher is perhaps best known for her role as Princess Leia in the first three films in the *Star Wars* series, but is also a bestselling author whose book *Postcards from the Edge* (1990) was made into a film starring Meryl Streep. She had unbilled cameo roles in *Hook* (1991) and *Austin Powers: International Man of Mystery* (1997).

TOP 10 BRIDGET FONDA FILMS

	FILM	ROLE	YEAR
1	The Godfather: Part III	Grace Hamilton	1990
2	Jackie Brown	Melanie Ralston	1997
3	Single White Female	Allison "Allie" Jones	1992
4	Kiss of the Dragon	Jessica	2001
5	Doc Hollywood	Nancy Lee Nicholson	1991
6	Lake Placid	Kelly Scott	1999
7	It Could Happen to You	Yvonne Biasi	1994
8	City Hall	Marybeth Cogan	1996
9	Point of No Return	Maggie Hayward/ Claudia Anne Joran/Nina	1993
10	Singles	Janet Livermore	1992

The daughter of Peter Fonda and niece of Jane Fonda, Bridget Fonda did not have a speaking role in a film until 1988, since when she has appeared in numerous low-budget low-profile films as well as some major productions, gaining particular acclaim for the role written specifically for her in *Single White Female*.

TOP 10 JANE FONDA FILMS

	FILM	ROLE	YEAR
1	On Golden Pond	Chelsea Thayer Wayne	1981
2	9 to 5	Judy Bernly	1980
3	California Suite	Hannah Warren	1978
4	The Electric Horseman	Alice "Hallie" Martin	1979
5	The China Syndrome	Kimberly Wells	1979
6	Fun with Dick and Jane	Jane Harper	1977
7	Coming Home *	Sally Hyde	1978
8	Julia	Lillian Hellman	1977
9	Agnes of God	Doctor Margaret Livingston	1985
10	The Morning After	Alex Sternbergen	1986

* "Best Actress" Academy Award

The daughter of Henry Fonda, with whom she appeared in *On Golden Pond*, Jane Fonda's work has ranged from comedy to drama – and even science-fiction, with *Barbarella* (1968), directed by her then husband Roger Vadim. She has received seven Oscar nominations, winning Best Actress for both *Coming Home* and *Klute* (1971).

JODIE FOSTER FILMS

	FILM	ROLE	YEAR
1	The Silence of the Lambs *	Clarice Starling	1991
2	Panic Room	Meg Altman	2002
3	Maverick	Annabelle Bransford	1994
4	Contact	Dr. Eleanor Ann "Ellie" Arroway	1997
5	Sommersby	Laurel Sommersby	1993
6	Anna and the King	Anna Leonowens	1999
7	Nell	Nell Kellty	1994
8	The Accused *	Sarah Tobias	1988
9	Little Man Tate	Dede Tate	1991
10	Taxi Driver	Iris Steensma	1976

* "Best Actress" Academy Award

Jodie Foster appeared in her debut Hollywood film at the age of nine, received her first Academy Award nomination at 13, and won both her "Best Actress" Oscars before she was 30.

Queen Crowned

Dame Judi Dench has been nominated for Oscars on four occasions, winning for her eight-minute supporting role as Queen Elizabeth I in *Shakespeare in Love*.

TOP 10 **WHOOPI GOLDBERG FILMS**

	FILM	ROLE	YEAR
1	Ghost	Oda Mae Brown	1990
2	Sister Act	Deloris Van Cartier/Sister Mary Clarence	1992
3	The Color Purple	Celie	1985
4	Star Trek: Generations	Guinan	1994
5	Made in America	Sarah Mathews	1993
6	Rat Race	Vera Baker	2001
7	Sister Act 2: Back in the Habit	Deloris Van Cartier/Sister Mary Clarence	1993
8	Star Trek X: Nemesis	Guinan	2002
9	The Little Rascals	Buckwheat's mother	1994
10	Boys on the Side	Jane Deluca	1995

Whoopi Goldberg provided the voice of Shenzi the Hyena in *The Lion King* (1994). If that were taken into the reckoning, it would appear at No. 1 position in her Top 10. Her voice was also that of Ranger Margaret in *The Rugrats Movie* (1998), which would appear in 4th position. She received the "Best Supporting Actress" Oscar for *Ghost*.

TOP 10 **MELANIE GRIFFITH FILMS**

	FILM	ROLE	YEAR
1	Working Girl	Tess McGill	1988
2	Nobody's Fool	Toby Roebuck	1994
3	Pacific Heights	Patty Palmer	1990
4	Now and Then	Tina "Teeny" Tercell	1995
5	One On One	The Hitchhiker	1977
6	Shining Through	Linda Voss	1992
7	Paradise	Lily Reed	1991
8	Milk Money	V	1994
9	Born Yesterday	Emma "Billy" Dawn	1993
10	The Bonfire of the Vanities	Maria Ruskin	1990

Melanie Griffith provided the voice of Margalo, a canary, in the animated film *Stuart Little 2*, which would appear at the top of her Top 10. Her part in *The Hitchhiker* was a minor supporting role; if discounted, *The Milagro Beanfield War* (1988), in which she played Flossie Devine, would join the list.

Making Whoopi

Whoopi Goldberg (born Caryn Johnson) in *Made in America*, one of several films in which she has starred that have earned over $100 million. She was the first woman to host the Oscars ceremony.

TOP 10 DARYL HANNAH FILMS

	FILM	ROLE	YEAR
1	Steel Magnolias	Annelle Dupuy Desoto	1989
2	Grumpier Old Men	Melanie Gustafson	1995
3	Grumpy Old Men	Melanie Gustafson	1993
4	Splash	Madison	1984
5	The Little Rascals	Miss Crabtree	1994
6	My Favorite Martian	Lizzie	1999
7	Legal Eagles	Chelsea Deardon	1986
8	Wall Street	Darien Taylor	1987
9	A Walk to Remember	Cynthia Carter	2002
10	Roxanne	Roxanne Kowalski	1987

TOP 10 GOLDIE HAWN FILMS

	FILM	ROLE	YEAR
1	The First Wives Club	Elise "Lisey" Eliot Atchison	1996
2	Death Becomes Her	Helen Sharp	1992
3	Bird on a Wire	Marianne Graves	1990
4	HouseSitter	Gwen	1992
5	Private Benjamin	Pvt. Judy Benjamin	1980
6	Shampoo	Jill	1975
7	Foul Play	Gloria Mundy	1978
8	Seems Like Old Times	Glenda Gardenia Parks	1980
9	Best Friends	Paula McCullen	1982
10	The Banger Sister	Suzette	2002

Goldie Hawn (born Goldie Jean Studlendgehawn) made her first appearance in 1968 in the long-running TV series *Rowan and Martin's Laugh-In*. She has effectively reprised her role as a zany, eternally youthful blonde in comedy films ever since, receiving an Academy Award nomination for "Best Actress" for her role in *Private Benjamin*.

TOP 10 SALMA HAYEK FILMS

	FILM	ROLE	YEAR
1	Wild Wild West	Rita Escobar	1999
2	Traffic	Rosario	2000
3	The Faculty	Nurse Rosa Harper	1998
4	From Dusk Till Dawn	Santanico Pandemonium	1996
5	Desperado	Carolina	1995
6	Frida	Frida Kahlo	2002
7	Fools Rush In	Isabel Fuentes	1997
8	Dogma	Serendipity	1999
9	Fair Game	Rita	1995
10	Fled	Cora	1996

Mexican actress Salma Hayek had only a minor role in *Traffic*. If that is omitted, *54* (1998), in which she appeared as Anita Randazzo, enters the list.

Did you know?

Breakfast at Tiffany's author Truman Capote urged Paramount to cast Marilyn Monroe in the role of Holly Golightly, but they chose Audrey Hepburn.

TOP 10 AUDREY HEPBURN FILMS

	FILM	ROLE	YEAR
1	Always	Hap	1985
2	My Fair Lady	Eliza Doolittle	1964
3	Wait Until Dark	Susy Hendrix	1967
4	Charade	Regina "Reggie" Lampert	1963
5	War and Peace	Natasha Rostov	1956
6	The Nun's Story	Sister Luke (Gabrielle van der Mal)	1959
7	Bloodline	Elizabeth Roffe	1979
8	Breakfast at Tiffany's	Holly Golightly (Lulamae Barnes)	1961
9	How to Steal a Million	Nicole Bonnet	1966
10	Robin and Marian	Lady Marian	1976

TOP 10 HELEN HUNT FILMS

	FILM	ROLE	YEAR
1	Twister	Dr. JoAnne Thornton-Harding	1996
2	Cast Away	Kelly Frears	2000
3	What Women Want	Darcy McGuire	2000
4	As Good As It Gets *	Carol Connelly	1997
5	Peggy Sue Got Married	Beth Bodell	1986
6	Pay It Forward	Arlene "Arley" McKinney	2000
7	Dr. T & the Women	Bree Davis	2000
8	Project X	Teri	1987
9	Rollercoaster	Tracy Calder	1977
10	Next of Kin	Jessie Gates	1989

* "Best Actress" Academy Award

TOP 10 HOLLY HUNTER FILMS

	FILM	ROLE	YEAR
1	The Firm	Tammy Hemphill	1993
2	Copycat	M.J. Monahan	1995
3	Always	Dorinda Durston	1989
4	O Brother, Where Art Thou?	Penny Wharvey McGill	2000
5	The Piano *	Ada McGrath	1993
6	Broadcast News	Jane Craig	1987
7	Raising Arizona	Ed	1987
8	Crash	Helen Remington	1996
9	Home for the Holidays	Claudia "Clyde" Larson	1995
10	A Life Less Ordinary	O'Reilly	1997

* "Best Actress" Academy Award

Unsually, both *Crash* and *A Life Less Ordinary* qualify for places in Holly Hunter's Top 10 through having earned considerably more outside the USA than at the domestic box office.

TOP 10 ANJELICA HUSTON FILMS

	FILM	ROLE	YEAR
1	The Addams Family	Morticia Addams	1991
2	Ever After: A Cinderella Story	Baroness Rodmilla De Ghent	1998
3	The Royal Tenenbaums	Dr. Etheline "Ethel" Tenenbaum-Sherman	2001
4	Addams Family Values	Morticia Addams	1993
5	Blood Work	Dr. Bonnie Fox	2002
6	Prizzi's Honor	Maerose Prizzi	1985
7	Crimes and Misdemeanors	Dolores Paley	1989
8	The Grifters	Lilly Dillon	1990
9	The Ice Pirates	Maida	1984
10	Manhattan Murder Mystery	Marcia Fox	1993

Along with a host of other stars, Anjelica Huston appeared as herself in *The Player* (1992). An earlier, and less well-known cameo role, was that of her hands, standing in for those of Deborah Kerr in the role of Agent Mimi in *Casino Royale* (1967), co-directed by Anjelica Huston's father, John Huston.

Fair Lady

Audrey Hepburn starred in five of the American Film Institute's Top 100 Love Stories: *Roman Holiday* (1953), *Sabrina* (1954), *Breakfast at Tiffany's* (1961), *My Fair Lady* (1964), and *Two for the Road* (1967).

TOP 10 ANGELINA JOLIE FILMS

	FILM	ROLE	YEAR
1	Lara Croft: Tomb Raider	Lara Croft	2001
2	Gone in Sixty Seconds	Sara "Sway" Wayland	2000
3	The Bone Collector	Amelia Donaghy	1999
4	Girl, Interrupted	Lisa Rowe	1999
5	Original Sin	Julia Russell	2001
6	Life or Something Like It	Lanie	2002
7	Pushing Tin	Mary Bell	1999
8	Hackers	Kate Libby ("Acid Burn")	1995
9	Playing by Heart	Joan	1998
10	Playing God	Claire	1997

Angelina Jolie is the daughter of the actor Jon Voight, who starred in, co-wrote, and co-produced her inauspicious screen debut *Lookin' to Get Out* (1982).

TOP 10 NICOLE KIDMAN FILMS

	FILM	ROLE	YEAR
1	Batman Forever	Dr. Chase Meridian	1995
2	Moulin Rouge!	Satine	2001
3	The Others	Grace Stewart	2001
4	Days of Thunder	Dr. Claire Lewicki	1990
5	Eyes Wide Shut	Alice Harford	1999
6	The Peacemaker	Dr. Julia Kelly	1997
7	Practical Magic	Gillian "Gilly-Bean" Owens	1998
8	Far and Away	Shannon Christie	1992
9	The Hours	Virginia Woolf	2002
10	Malice	Tracy Kennsinger	1993

Honolulu-born Nicole Kidman was raised in Australia, where she acted on TV before her break into film, in which she has pursued a highly successful career: six of her Top 10 films have earned over $100 million worldwide.

TOP 10 JENNIFER JASON LEIGH FILMS

	FILM	ROLE	YEAR
1	Road to Perdition	Annie Sullivan	2002
2	Backdraft	Jennifer Vaitkus	1991
3	Single White Female	Hedra "Hedy" Carlson	1992
4	Dolores Claiborne	Selena St. George	1995
5	Easy Money	Allison Capuletti	1983
6	Fast Times at Ridgemont High	Stacy Hamilton	1982
7	Short Cuts	Lois Kaiser	1993
8	A Thousand Acres	Caroline Cook	1997
9	Miami Blues	Susie Waggoner	1990
10	eXistenZ	Allegra Geller	1999

Jennifer Jason Leigh also supplied the voice of Bridget in the animated film *Hey Arnold! The Movie* (2002).

TOP 10 ANDIE MACDOWELL FILMS

	FILM	ROLE	YEAR
1	Four Weddings and a Funeral	Carrie	1994
2	Michael	Dorothy Winters	1996
3	Groundhog Day	Rita	1993
4	Greystoke: The Legend of Tarzan, Lord of the Apes	Jane Porter	1984
5	Green Card	Bronte Mitchell Faure	1990
6	St. Elmo's Fire	Dale Biberman	1985
7	Multiplicity	Laura Kinney	1996
8	sex, lies, and videotape	Ann	1989
9	Muppets From Space	Shelley Snipes	1999
10	Hudson Hawk	Anna Baragli	1991

TOP 10 MADONNA FILMS

	FILM	ROLE	YEAR
1	Dick Tracy	Breathless Mahoney	1990
2	A League of Their Own	Mae Mordabito	1992
3	Evita	Eva "Evita" Duarte de Perón	1996
4	Desperately Seeking Susan	Susan	1985
5	The Next Best Thing	Abbie Reynolds	2000
6	Body of Evidence	Rebecca Carlson	1993
7	Who's That Girl?	Nicole "Nikki" Finn	1987
8	Four Rooms *	Elspeth	1995
9	Shadows and Fog	Marie	1992
10	Shanghai Surprise	Gloria Tatlock	1986

* "The Missing Ingredient" segment
Madonna composed and sang songs in a number of the films in which she also acted. She has had cameo roles in several films, most notably *Die Another Day* (2002), and appeared as herself in the documentary *Madonna: Truth or Dare* (1991), which was a box office success.

TOP 10 FRANCES McDORMAND FILMS

	FILM	ROLE	YEAR
1	Primal Fear	Dr. Molly Arrington	1996
2	Fargo *	Marge Gunderson	1996
3	Almost Famous	Elaine Miller	2000
4	Mississippi Burning	Mrs. Pell	1988
5	Madeline	Miss Clavel	1998
6	Darkman	Julie Hastings	1990
7	Wonder Boys	Sara Gaskell	2000
8	City by the Sea	Michelle	2002
9	Raising Arizona	Dot	1987
10	The Man Who Wasn't There	Doris Crane	2001

* "Best Actress" Academy Award

Did you know?

At her death in 1962, Marilyn Monroe's estate was valued at $1.6 million. Since then, income from the licensing of her image has earned more than 10 times that amount every year, making her worth far more dead than alive.

TOP 10 BETTE MIDLER FILMS

	FILM	ROLE	YEAR
1	The First Wives Club	Brenda "'Bren'" Morelli Cushman	1996
2	Ruthless People	Barbara Stone	1986
3	Down and Out in Beverly Hills	Barbara Whiteman	1986
4	Beaches	Cecilia "CC" Carol Bloom	1988
5	Outrageous Fortune	Sandy Brozinsky	1987
6	Hocus Pocus	Winifred Sanderson	1993
7	Big Business	Sadie Ratliff/ Sadie Shelton	1988
8	The Rose	Mary Rose Foster	1979
9	Stella	Stella Claire	1990
10	For the Boys	Dixie Leonard	1991

Bette Midler had uncredited cameo roles in *What Women Want* (2000) and *Get Shorty* (1995). Her voice also appears in two animated films, as that of the character Georgette in *Oliver and Company* (1988) and as the singer of the song "God Help the Outcasts" in *The Hunchback of Notre Dame* (1996).

The Divine Miss M
Nominated for a leading actress Oscar twice, for *The Rose* and *For the Boys*, Hawaii-born singer-actress Bette Midler has appeared in numerous dramatic and comedy roles in her 30-year career.

TOP 10 MARILYN MONROE FILMS

	FILM	ROLE	YEAR
1	Some Like It Hot	Sugar Kane Kowalczyk	1959
2	How to Marry a Millionaire	Pola Debevoise	1953
3	The Seven Year Itch	The Girl	1955
4	Niagara	Rose Loomis	1953
5	Gentlemen Prefer Blondes	Lorelei Lee	1953
6	There's No Business Like Show Business	Vicky Hoffman/ Vicky Parker	1954
7	Bus Stop	Cherie	1956
8	The Misfits	Roslyn Taber	1961
9	River of No Return	Kay Weston	1954
10	All About Eve	Claudia Casswell	1950

Marilyn Monroe (born Norma Jean Mortensen) made as many unmemorable films as successful ones in a career that spanned barely a decade, but her turbulent life and early death have secured her a place among the Hollywood greats.

TOP 10 DEMI MOORE FILMS

	FILM	ROLE	YEAR
1	Ghost	Molly Jensen	1990
2	Indecent Proposal	Diana Murphy	1993
3	A Few Good Men	Lt. Cdr. JoAnne Galloway	1992
4	Disclosure	Meredith Johnson	1994
5	Striptease	Erin Grant	1996
6	G.I. Jane	Lt. Jordan "L.T." O'Neil	1997
7	The Juror	Annie Laird	1996
8	About Last Night…	Debbie	1986
9	St. Elmo's Fire	Jules Jacoby	1985
10	Now and Then	Samantha Albertson	1995

Each of the first four films in Demi Moore's Top 10 earned over $200 million worldwide. She also provided the voice of Esmerelda in the animated film *The Hunchback of Notre Dame* (1996) – and was one of the producers of all three of the *Austin Powers* films.

TOP 10 JULIANNE MOORE FILMS

	FILM	ROLE	YEAR
1	The Lost World: Jurassic Park	Dr. Sarah Harding	1997
2	The Fugitive	Dr. Anne Eastman	1993
3	Hannibal	Clarice Starling	2001
4	Nine Months	Rebecca Taylor/ Rebecca Faulkner	1995
5	The Hand That Rocks the Cradle	Marlene "Marl" Craven	1992
6	The Hours	Laura Brown	2002
7	Evolution	Dr. Allison Reed	2001
8	Assassins	Electra (Anna)	1995
9	Magnolia	Linda Partridge	1999
10	Boogie Nights	Amber Waves/ Maggie	1997

Michelle, Ma Belle

Dangerous Minds saw Michelle Pfeiffer take the role of a teacher in a problem highschool, for which she received an MTV Movie Award nomination as "Most Desirable Female".

TOP 10 GWYNETH PALTROW FILMS

	FILM	ROLE	YEAR
1	Se7en	Tracy Mills	1995
2	Hook	Young Wendy/ Angela Darling	1991
3	Shakespeare in Love *	Viola De Lesseps	1998
4	A Perfect Murder	Emily Bradford Taylor	1998
5	The Talented Mr. Ripley	Marge Sherwood	1999
6	Shallow Hal	Rosemary "Rosie" Shanahan	2001
7	The Royal Tenenbaums	Margot Helen Tenenbaum	2001
8	Sliding Doors	Helen Quilley	1998
9	Great Expectations	Estella	1998
10	Malice	Paula Bell	1993

* "Best Actress" Academy Award

TOP 10 SARAH JESSICA PARKER FILMS

	FILM	ROLE	YEAR
1	The First Wives Club	Shelly "Shell" Stewart	1996
2	Mars Attacks!	Nathalie Lake	1996
3	Footloose	Rusty	1984
4	Hocus Pocus	Sarah Sanderson	1993
5	Honeymoon in Vegas	Betsy/Donna	1992
6	L.A. Story	SanDeE	1991
7	Striking Distance	Jo Christman/ Det. Emily Harper	1993
8	Flight of the Navigator	Carolyn McAdams	1986
9	Extreme Measures	Jodie Trammel	1996
10	Dudley Do-Right	Nell Fenwick	1999

Sarah Jessica Parker was a child stage star, including among her credits the title role of *Annie* on Broadway, and had a productive film career before confirming her celebrity status as Carrie Bradshaw, the narrator and star of Emmy Award-winning TV series *Sex in the City* (1998–).

TOP 10 MICHELLE PFEIFFER FILMS

	FILM	ROLE	YEAR
1	Batman Returns	Catwoman/ Selina Kyle	1992
2	What Lies Beneath	Claire Spencer	2000
3	Dangerous Minds	Louanne Johnson	1995
4	Wolf	Laura Alden	1994
5	Up Close & Personal	Tally "Sallyanne" Atwater	1996
6	One Fine Day	Melanie Parker	1996
7	The Witches of Eastwick	Sukie Ridgemont	1987
8	I Am Sam	Rita Harrison	2001
9	The Story of Us	Katie Jordan	1999
10	Scarface	Elvira Hancock	1983

Michelle Pfeiffer also provided the voice of Tzipporah in the animated film *The Prince of Egypt* (1998), which would rate in third place in her Top 10.

TOP 10 JULIA ROBERTS FILMS

	FILM	ROLE	YEAR
1	Pretty Woman	Vivian "Viv" Ward	1990
2	Ocean's Eleven	Tess Ocean	2001
3	Notting Hill	Anna Scott	1999
4	Runaway Bride	Maggie Carpenter	1999
5	Hook	Tinkerbell	1991
6	My Best Friend's Wedding	Julianne "Jules" Potter	1997
7	Erin Brockovich *	Erin Brockovich	2000
8	The Pelican Brief	Darby Shaw	1993
9	Sleeping with the Enemy	Sara Waters/ Laura Burney	1991
10	Stepmom	Isabel Kelly	1998

* "Best Actress" Academy Award

Did you know?

All of Julia Roberts' Top 10 films earned more than $150 million worldwide, a total of almost $3 billion, a record unmatched by any other actress.

TOP 10 RENE RUSSO FILMS

	FILM	ROLE	YEAR
1	Lethal Weapon 3	Lorna Cole	1992
2	Ransom	Kate Mullen	1996
3	Lethal Weapon 4	Lorna Cole	1998
4	Outbreak	Robby Keough	1995
5	In the Line of Fire	Lilly Raines	1993
6	The Thomas Crown Affair	Catherine Olds Banning	1999
7	Get Shorty	Karen Flores	1995
8	Tin Cup	Dr. Molly Griswold	1996
9	Showtime	Chase Renzi	2002
10	Major League	Lynn Wells	1989

TOP 10 MEG RYAN FILMS

	FILM	ROLE	YEAR
1	Top Gun	Carole Bradshaw	1986
2	You've Got M@il	Kathleen Kelly	1998
3	Sleepless in Seattle	Annie Reed	1993
4	City of Angels	Maggie Rice	1998
5	When Harry Met Sally...	Sally Albright	1989
6	French Kiss	Kate	1995
7	Courage Under Fire	Capt. Karen Emma Walden	1996
8	When a Man Loves a Woman	Alice Green	1994
9	Addicted to Love	Maggie	1997
10	Joe Versus the Volcano	DeDe/Angelica/ Patricia	1990

Meg Ryan also provided the voice of Anastasia in the 1997 film of that title. If included, it would appear in fifth place.

Secret of Success

Rene Russo as a Secret Service agent in *In the Line of Fire*, one of seven of her films that has earned more than $100 million globally.

Funny Girl/Serious Boy
Right Barbra Streisand poses as a boy in *Yentl*, which won her Golden Globes as "Best Director" and for "Best Picture".

TOP 10 WINONA RYDER FILMS

	FILM	ROLE	YEAR
1	Bram Stoker's Dracula	Mina Murray/ Elisabeta	1992
2	Mr. Deeds	Babe Bennett	2002
3	Alien: Resurrection	Annalee Call	1997
4	Edward Scissorhands	Kim Boggs	1990
5	Beetlejuice	Lydia	1988
6	Little Women	Jo March	1994
7	Autumn in New York	Charlotte Fielding	2000
8	Mermaids	Charlotte Flax	1990
9	Girl, Interrupted	Susanna Kaysen	1999
10	The Age of Innocence	May Welland	1993

TOP 10 SUSAN SARANDON FILMS

	FILM	ROLE	YEAR
1	The Rocky Horror Picture Show	Janet Weiss	1975
2	The Client	Reggie Love	1994
3	Stepmom	Jacqueline "Jackie" Harrison	1998
4	Dead Man Walking *	Sister Helen Prejean	1995
5	The Witches of Eastwick	Jane Spofford	1987
6	Little Women	Mrs. March	1994
7	Thelma & Louise	Louise Sawyer	1991
8	Bull Durham	Annie Savoy/ narrator	1988
9	The Banger Sisters	Lavinia	2002
10	The Other Side of Midnight	Catherine Alexander Douglas	1977

* "Best Actress" Academy Award

TOP 10 SISSY SPACEK FILMS

	FILM	ROLE	YEAR
1	JFK	Liz Garrison	1991
2	Coal Miner's Daughter *	Loretta Webb/ Lynn	1980
3	In the Bedroom	Ruth Fowler	2001
4	Blast from the Past	Helen Thomas Webber	1999
5	Carrie	Carrie White	1976
6	Crimes of the Heart	Babe Magrath	1986
7	Tuck Everlasting	Mae Tuck	2002
8	Missing	Beth Horman	1982
9	The River	Mae Garvey	1984
10	The Straight Story	Rose Straight	1999

* "Best Actress" Academy Award

TOP 10   SHARON STONE FILMS

	FILM	ROLE	YEAR
1	Basic Instinct	Catherine Tramell	1992
2	Total Recall	Lori	1990
3	The Specialist	May Munro/ Adrian Hastings	1994
4	Sliver	Carly Norris	1993
5	Casino	Ginger McKenna	1995
6	Sphere	Dr. Beth Halperin	1998
7	Diabolique	Nicole Horner	1996
8	The Quick and the Dead	Ellen	1995
9	Irreconcilable Differences	Blake Chandler/ Amanda	1984
10	Intersection	Sally Eastman	1994

Sharon Stone's first film role was a fleeting appearance in Woody Allen's *Stardust Memories* (1980), where she appears credited only as "Pretty girl on train". She provided the voice of Bala in the animated *Antz* (1998), earnings from which would place it third in her Top 10, and made a cameo appearance in *Last Action Hero* (1993).

TOP 10   MERYL STREEP FILMS

	FILM	ROLE	YEAR
1	Out of Africa	Karen Blixen-Finecke	1985
2	The Bridges of Madison County	Francesca Johnson	1995
3	Death Becomes Her	Madeline Ashton	1992
4	Kramer vs. Kramer	Joanna Kramer	1979
5	The River Wild	Gail	1994
6	The Hours	Clarissa Vaughan	2002
7	The Deer Hunter	Linda	1978
8	Manhattan	Jill	1979
9	Postcards from the Edge	Suzanne Vale	1990
10	Silkwood	Karen Silkwood	1983

TOP 10   BARBRA STREISAND FILMS

	FILM	ROLE	YEAR
1	The Prince of Tides *	Susan Lowenstein	1991
2	A Star Is Born	Esther Hoffman	1976
3	The Mirror Has Two Faces *	Rose Morgan	1996
4	What's Up, Doc?	Judy Maxwell	1972
5	Funny Girl †	Fanny Brice	1968
6	The Way We Were	Katie Morosky	1973
7	The Main Event	Hillary Kramer	1979
8	Yentl *	Yentl/Anshel	1983
9	Funny Lady	Fanny Brice	1975
10	Nuts	Claudia Draper	1987

* Also director
† "Best Actress" Academy Award (shared with Katharine Hepburn) for *The Lion in Winter*

TOP 10 ELIZABETH TAYLOR FILMS

	FILM	ROLE	YEAR
1	The Flintstones	Pearl Slaghoople	1994
2	Cleopatra	Cleopatra	1963
3	Giant	Leslie Lynnton Benedict	1956
4	Who's Afraid of Virginia Woolf? *	Martha	1966
5	Cat on a Hot Tin Roof	Maggie "The Cat" Pollitt	1958
6	Butterfield 8 *	Gloria Wandrous	1960
7	The Sandpiper	Laura Reynolds	1965
8	Suddenly, Last Summer	Catherine Holly	1959
9	Ivanhoe	Rebecca	1952
10	Raintree County	Susanna Drake	1957

* "Best Actress" Academy Award

TOP 10 UMA THURMAN FILMS

	FILM	ROLE	YEAR
1	Batman & Robin	Poison Ivy/ Dr. Pamela Isley	1997
2	Pulp Fiction	Mia Wallace	1994
3	The Truth About Cats & Dogs	Noelle	1996
4	The Avengers	Emma Peel	1998
5	Final Analysis	Diana Baylor	1992
6	Dangerous Liaisons	Cécile de Volanges	1988
7	Beautiful Girls	Andera	1996
8	Les Misérables	Fantine	1998
9	Johnny Be Good	Georgia Elkans	1988
10	Gattaca	Irene Cassini	1997

Although featuring in her Top 10 by virtue of their global box office income, neither *The Avengers* nor *Gattaca* earned back their substantial production budgets, and may thus be regarded as flops. Conversely, *Pulp Fiction* had a budget of some $8 million, but went on to make more than $200 million worldwide.

Did you know?

Elizabeth Taylor has appeared in *The Simpsons* both as herself and providing the voice of the baby Maggie – who normally never speaks – on two occasions.

Honourable Mention

Kathleen Turner starred as a professional assassin in *Prizzi's Honor* (shown right). Her debut film *Body Heat* also saw her cast in the role of a ruthless killer.

TOP 10 KATHLEEN TURNER FILMS

	FILM	ROLE	YEAR
1	Romancing the Stone	Joan Wilder	1984
2	The War of the Roses	Barbara Rose	1989
3	The Jewel of the Nile	Joan Wilder	1985
4	Peggy Sue Got Married	Peggy Sue	1986
5	Baby Geniuses	Elena	1999
6	The Accidental Tourist	Sarah	1988
7	Prizzi's Honor	Irene Walker	1985
8	Body Heat	Matty Walker	1981
9	Undercover Blues	Jane Blue	1993
10	V.I. Warshawski	Victoria "V.I." Warshawski	1991

Kathleen Turner also provided the voice of Jessica Rabbit in part-animated *Who Framed Roger Rabbit* (1988), which has outearned all those in her Top 10.

TOP 10 SIGOURNEY WEAVER FILMS

	FILM	ROLE	YEAR
1	Ghostbusters	Dana Barrett	1984
2	Ghostbusters II	Dana Barrett	1989
3	Alien	Lt. Ellen Ripley	1979
4	Aliens	Lt. Ellen Ripley	1986
5	Alien: Resurrection	Lt. Ellen Ripley Clone #8	1997
6	Alien³	Lt. Ellen Ripley	1992
7	Galaxy Quest	Gwen DeMarco/ Lt. Madison	1999
8	Copycat	Helen Hudson	1995
9	Dave	Ellen Mitchell	1993
10	Working Girl	Katherine Parker	1988

Ripley, Believe it or Not …

In her *Alien³* reprise of her role as Lt. Ellen Ripley, Sigourney Weaver confronts the malevolent alien for the third time. Despite her demise in the film, she was to return, courtesy of cloning, in the sequel.

TOP 10 RACHEL WEISZ FILMS

	FILM	ROLE	YEAR
1	The Mummy Returns	Evelyn Carnahan O'Connell/ Princess Nefertiri	2001
2	The Mummy	Evelyn Carnahan	1999
3	About a Boy	Rachel	2002
4	Enemy at the Gates	Tania Chernova	2001
5	Chain Reaction	Dr. Lily Sinclair	1996
6	Sunshine	Greta	1999
7	Stealing Beauty	Miranda	1996
8	Confidence	Lily	2003
9	The Land Girls	Ag (Agapanthus)	1998
10	Swept from the Sea	Amy Foster	1997

TOP 10 KATE WINSLET FILMS

	FILM	ROLE	YEAR
1	Titanic	Rose DeWitt Bukater	1997
2	Sense and Sensibility	Marianne Dashwood	1995
3	The Life of David Gale	Elizabeth (Bitsey) Bloom	2003
4	Quills	Madeleine LeClerc	2000
5	Iris	Young Iris Murdoch	2001
6	A Kid in King Arthur's Court	Princess Sarah	1995
7	Enigma	Hester Wallace	2001
8	Hamlet	Ophelia	1996
9	Heavenly Creatures	Juliet Hulme	1994
10	Hideous Kinky	Julia	1998

TOP 10 RENÉE ZELLWEGER FILMS

	FILM	ROLE	YEAR
1	Bridget Jones's Diary	Bridget Jones	2001
2	Jerry Maguire	Dorothy Maguire	1996
3	Chicago	"Roxie" Hart	2002
4	Me, Myself & Irene	Irene P. Waters	2000
5	Nurse Betty	Betty Sizemore	2000
6	One True Thing	Ellen Gulden	1998
7	The Bachelor	Anne Arden	1999
8	Reality Bites	Tami	1994
9	8 Seconds	Buckle Bunny	1994
10	White Oleander	Claire Richards	2002

TOP 10 DEBRA WINGER FILMS

	FILM	ROLE	YEAR
1	Terms of Endearment	Emma Greenway Horton	1983
2	An Officer and a Gentleman	Paula Pokrifki	1982
3	Forget Paris	Ellen Andrews	1995
4	Legal Eagles	Laura Kelly	1986
5	Urban Cowboy	Sissy Davis	1980
6	Shadowlands	Joy Gresham	1993
7	Betrayed	Katie Phillips/ Cathy Weaver	1988
8	Leap of Faith	Jane	1992
9	Black Widow	"Alex" Barnes	1987
10	Thank God It's Friday	Jennifer	1978

TOP 10 REESE WITHERSPOON FILMS

	FILM	ROLE	YEAR
1	Sweet Home Alabama	Melanie Carmichael /Melanie Smooter	2002
2	Legally Blonde	Elle Woods	2001
3	Cruel Intentions	Annette Hargrove	1999
4	Little Nicky	Holly	2000
5	Pleasantville	Jennifer Wagner	1998
6	Twilight	Mel Ames	1998
7	American Psycho	Evelyn Williams	2000
8	Fear	Nicole Walker	1996
9	The Importance of Being Earnest	Cecily	2002
10	Election	Tracy Enid Flick	1999

TOP 10 CATHERINE ZETA-JONES FILMS

	FILM	ROLE	YEAR
1	Chicago	Velma Kelly	2002
2	The Mask of Zorro	Elena Montero/ Elena Murrieta	1998
3	Entrapment	Virginia Baker	1999
4	Traffic	Helena Ayala	2000
5	The Haunting	Theodora "Theo"	1999
6	America's Sweethearts	Gwen Harrison	2001
7	High Fidelity	Charlie Nicholson	2000
8	The Phantom	Sala	1996
9	Christopher Columbus: The Discovery	Beatriz	1992
10	Splitting Heirs	Kitty	1993

The role of the director is crucial not only in the making of every film, but often in determining its success or failure, whether measured by critical acclaim or commercial success. It is the director who puts his personal stamp on the film to such an extent that some are released with their director's names appended to their titles – hence Fellini's *8½*. Here, such topics as the Top 10 highest-earning and biggest budget films of women directors and the most successful productions of actor-directors are followed by the Top 10s of some 40 directors from Alfred Hitchcock to Ridley Scott. Screenwriters too – some unfamiliar to the public at large, while others, such as Stephen King and George Lucas, celebrities in their own right – play a pivotal and sometimes little-regarded part in the process of filmmaking, and are considered here.

Pointing the Way
Steven Spielberg on the set of *A.I.: Artificial Intelligence* (2001). His prodigious output of blockbusters has confirmed his place as the most successful director of all time.

TOP 10 DIRECTORS WITH THE HIGHEST CUMULATIVE US EARNINGS

	DIRECTOR	FILMS	HIGHEST-EARNER	ALL FILMS, US ($)
1	Steven Spielberg	21	E.T. the Extra-Terrestrial	3,151,000,000
2	Robert Zemeckis	12	Forrest Gump	1,540,700,000
3	Chris Columbus	11	Harry Potter and the Sorcerer's Stone	1,538,800,000
4	George Lucas	5	Star Wars	1,320,200,000
5	Ron Howard	14	Dr. Seuss's How the Grinch Stole Christmas	1,301,000,000
6	Richard Donner	15	Lethal Weapon 2	1,194,000,000
7	James Cameron	7	Titanic	1,135,000,000
8	Ivan Reitman	12	Ghostbusters	974,100,000
9	Tim Burton	9	Batman	909,400,000
10	Barry Sonnenfeld	8	Men in Black	807,900,000

While the cumulative total US box office income of all the films of these directors provides a comparative view of the overall earning power of the group, the most impressive representative is George Lucas, with relatively few but extremely high-grossing releases at a per-picture average of $264 million.

TOP 10 FILMS DIRECTED BY NON-US DIRECTORS

	FILM	DIRECTOR	BIRTH PLACE	YEAR
1	Titanic *	James Cameron	Kapuskasing, Canada	1997
2	Lord of the Rings: The Two Towers	Peter Jackson	Pukerua Bay, New Zealand	2002
3	Lord of the Rings: The Fellowship of the Ring	Peter Jackson	Pukerua Bay, New Zealand	2001
4	Independence Day	Roland Emmerich	Stuttgart, Germany	1996
5	The Sixth Sense	M. Night Shyamalan	Pondicherry, India	1999
6	Star Wars: Episode VI – Return of the Jedi	Richard Marquand	Cardiff, Wales	1983
7	Mission: Impossible 2	John Woo	Guangzhou, China	2000
8	Twister	Jon de Bont	Eindhoven, The Netherlands	1996
9	Gladiator	Ridley Scott	South Shields, England	2000
10	The Bodyguard	Mick Jackson	Aveley, England	1992

* Won "Best Picture" Oscar

Although American-born directors dominate the film industry, all these films were made by non-US-born directors. All 10 are in the all-time Top 50 at the global box office, having earned more than $400 million each.

Stealing the Show

With its US income alone amounting to more than $260 million, *Dr. Seuss's How the Grinch Stole Christmas* was high-grossing director Ron Howard's top-earning film.

TOP 10 FILMS DIRECTED BY WOMEN

	FILM	DIRECTOR	YEAR
1	Shrek *	Victoria Jenson †	2001
2	What Women Want	Nancy Meyers	2000
3	Deep Impact	Mimi Leder	1998
4	Look Who's Talking	Amy Heckerling	1989
5	Dr. Dolittle	Betty Thomas	1998
6	Bridget Jones's Diary	Sharon Maguire	2001
7	You've Got M@il	Nora Ephron	1998
8	Sleepless in Seattle	Nora Ephron	1993
9	The Prince of Egypt *	Brenda Chapman #	1998
10	Wayne's World	Penelope Spheeris	1992

* Animated
† Co-director with Andrew Adamson and Scott Marshall
# Co-director with Steve Hickner and Simon Wells
The films in this list made upwards of $200 million each globally, with the total for *Shrek* approaching $500 million and *What Women Want* $400 million.

TOP 10 BIGGEST BUDGET FILMS DIRECTED BY WOMEN

	FILM	DIRECTOR	YEAR	BUDGET ($)
1	K-19: The Widowmaker	Kathryn Bigelow	2002	100,000,000
2	Spirit: Stallion of the Cimarron *	Kelly Asbury/ Lorna Cook	2002	80,000,000
3	Deep Impact	Mimi Leder	1998	75,000,000
4	Dr. Dolittle	Betty Thomas	1998	71,500,000
5	I Spy	Betty Thomas	2002	70,000,000
6 =	Lucky Numbers	Nora Ephron	2000	65,000,000
=	You've Got M@il	Nora Ephron	1998	65,000,000
=	What Women Want	Nancy Meyers	2000	65,000,000
9 =	The Prince of Egypt *	Brenda Chapman †	1998	60,000,000
=	Shrek *	Vicky Jenson #	2001	60,000,000

* Animated
† Co-director with Steve Hickner and Simon Wells
# Co-director with Andrew Adamson and Scott Marshall

TOP 10 FILMS DIRECTED BY UK DIRECTORS

	FILM	DIRECTOR	BIRTH PLACE	YEAR
1	Star Wars: Episode VI – Return of the Jedi	Richard Marquand	Cardiff	1983
2	Gladiator	Ridley Scott	South Shields	2000
3	The Bodyguard	Mick Jackson	Aveley	1992
4	Hannibal	Ridley Scott	South Shields	2001
5	American Beauty	Sam Mendes	Reading	1999
6	Top Gun	Tony Scott	Stockton-on-Tees	1986
7	Indecent Proposal	Adrian Lyne	Peterborough	1993
8	Fatal Attraction	Adrian Lyne	Peterborough	1987
9	Beverly Hills Cop II	Tony Scott	Stockton-on-Tees	1987
10	Saturday Night Fever	John Badham	Luton	1977

TOP 10 FILMS IN WHICH THE DIRECTOR HAS ALSO ACTED

	FILM	DIRECTOR/ACTOR ROLE	YEAR
1	The Sixth Sense	M. Night Shyamalan – Dr. Hill	1999
2	Armageddon	Michael Bay – NASA scientist	1998
3	Pretty Woman	Garry Marshall – Bum "Tour Guide"	1990
4	Dances With Wolves	Kevin Costner – Lt. John G. Dunbar/Dances With Wolves	1990
5	Dr. Seuss's How the Grinch Stole Christmas	Ron Howard – Townsperson	2000
6	A Beautiful Mind	Ron Howard – Man at ball	2001
7	The Runaway Bride	Gary Marshall – Softball player	1997
8	Rocky IV	Sylvester Stallone – Rocky Balboa	1985
9	Scary Movie	Keenan Ivory Waynans – Slave	2000
10	Waterworld	Kevin Costner – Mariner	1995

The role of actor-director has a long cinema tradition, numbering such luminaries as Charlie Chaplin, Buster Keaton, Orson Welles, and John Huston among its ranks. All those in this Top 10 have combined the two professions in the same film, each of which has earned more than $250 million at the world box office – although with such notable exceptions as Kevin Costner and Sylvester Stallone, few of their roles have been more than (often uncredited) cameos. Alfred Hitchcock famously appeared in cameo roles in all the films he directed from *The Lodger* (1927) to his last, *Family Plot* (1976).

In the Arena

British director Ridley Scott with Russell Crowe on the set of *Gladiator* (2000), winner of the "Best Picture" Oscar and second highest-earning film of the year.

TOP 10 FILMS DIRECTED BY WOODY ALLEN

	FILM	YEAR
1	Manhattan	1979
2	Hannah and Her Sisters	1986
3	Annie Hall *	1977
4	Small Time Crooks	2000
5	Everyone Says I Love You	1996
6	Deconstructing Harry	1997
7	Mighty Aphrodite	1995
8	Crimes and Misdemeanors	1989
9	Love and Death	1975
10	The Curse of the Jade Scorpion	2001

* "Best Director" Oscar; film won "Best Picture" Oscar

TOP 10 FILMS DIRECTED BY ROBERT ALTMAN

	FILM	YEAR
1	Gosford Park	2001
2	M*A*S*H	1970
3	Popeye	1980
4	The Player	1992
5	Dr. T & the Women	2000
6	Prêt-à-Porter	1994
7	Cookie's Fortune	1999
8	Short Cuts	1993
9	Nashville	1975
10	California Split	1974

TOP 10 FILMS DIRECTED BY MICHAEL APTED

	FILM	YEAR
1	The World Is Not Enough	1999
2	Nell	1994
3	Coal Miner's Daughter	1980
4	Enough	2002
5	Gorillas in the Mist	1988
6	Class Action	1991
7	Thunderheart	1992
8	Extreme Measures	1996
9	Critical Condition	1987
10	Blink	1994

TOP 10 FILMS DIRECTED BY JOHN G. AVILDSEN

	FILM	YEAR
1	Rocky V	1990
2	Rocky *	1976
3	The Karate Kid, Part II	1986
4	The Karate Kid	1984
5	The Karate Kid III	1989
6	Lean on Me	1989
7	Neighbors	1981
8	8 Seconds	1994
9	Joe	1970
10	For Keeps	1988

* "Best Director" Oscar; film won "Best Picture" Oscar

TOP 10 FILMS DIRECTED BY MEL BROOKS

	FILM	YEAR
1	Blazing Saddles	1974
2	Young Frankenstein	1974
3	Robin Hood: Men in Tights	1993
4	Spaceballs	1987
5	Silent Movie	1976
6	History of the World: Part I	1981
7	High Anxiety	1978
8	Dracula: Dead and Loving It	1995
9	The Twelve Chairs	1970
10	Life Stinks	1991

The Great Director

The British-born actor, director, and writer Charlie Chaplin's "Little Tramp" character is one of the most enduring icons in the history of cinema.

TOP 10 FILMS DIRECTED BY JOHN CARPENTER

	FILM	YEAR
1	Halloween	1978
2	Escape from L.A.	1996
3	Vampire$	1998
4	Starman	1984
5	Escape from New York	1981
6	The Fog	1980
7	Christine	1983
8	Memoirs of an Invisible Man	1992
9	Prince of Darkness	1987
10	The Thing	1982

Made on a budget of just $325,000, *Halloween* went on to generate some $47 million at the US box office alone, spawning a series of successful sequels with which Carpenter has been involved, but has not directed.

THE 10 FIRST FEATURE FILMS DIRECTED BY CHARLIE CHAPLIN

	FILM	US RELEASE
1	The Kid	6 Feb 1921
2	The Pilgrim	23 Feb 1923
3	A Woman of Paris	1 Oct 1923
4	The Gold Rush	26 Jun 1925
5	The Circus	6 Jan 1928
6	City Lights	6 Feb 1931
7	Modern Times	5 Feb 1936
8	The Great Dictator	15 Oct 1940
9	Monsieur Verdoux	11 Apr 1947
10	Limelight	23 Oct 1952

As well as his innumerable silent shorts (he made 34 in 1914 alone), Charlie Chaplin (1889–1977) directed 13 feature films, in most of them also taking the role of producer, writer, and occasionally composer, and acting in all of them (although his role in *A Woman of Paris* was an uncredited cameo as a porter). He also directed and appeared in *A King in New York*, which was made and released in Europe in 1957, but remained unscreened in the US until 21 December 1973. Chaplin followed this with his last feature, *A Countess from Hong Kong* (1967), in which he had a minor part as an elderly steward aboard an ocean liner.

TOP 10 FILMS DIRECTED BY CHRISTOPHER COLUMBUS

	FILM	YEAR
1	Harry Potter and the Sorcerer's Stone	2001
2	Harry Potter and the Chamber of Secrets	2002
3	Home Alone	1990
4	Mrs. Doubtfire	1993
5	Home Alone 2: Lost in New York	1992
6	Stepmom	1998
7	Nine Months	1995
8	Bicentennial Man	1999
9	Adventures in Babysitting	1987
10	Only the Lonely	1991

With US earnings of his Top 10 films exceeding $1.5 billion, and a worldwide total approaching $3.5 billion, Christopher Columbus has been responsible for some of the highest-grossing films of all time.

TOP 10 FILMS DIRECTED BY FRANCIS FORD COPPOLA

	FILM	YEAR
1	Bram Stoker's Dracula	1992
2	The Godfather, Part III	1990
3	The Godfather *	1972
4	The Godfather, Part II *†	1974
5	Jack	1996
6	Apocalypse Now	1979
7	The Rainmaker	1997
8	Peggy Sue Got Married	1986
9	The Cotton Club	1984
10	The Outsiders	1983

* "Best Picture" Oscar
† "Best Director" Oscar
The earnings of re-releases of *Apocalypse Now* and *Apocalypse Now Redux* (2001) have not been taken into account, but even if they were, its position in Francis Ford Coppola's Top 10 would be unchanged.

TOP 10 FILMS DIRECTED BY WES CRAVEN

	FILM	YEAR
1	Scream	1996
2	Scream 2	1997
3	Scream 3	2000
4	New Nightmare	1994
5	Vampire in Brooklyn	1995
6	The People Under the Stairs	1991
7	A Nightmare On Elm Street	1984
8	The Serpent and the Rainbow	1988
9	Shocker	1989
10	Music of the Heart	1999

Along with John Carpenter, Wes (Wesley Earl) Craven is one of the few directors whose name has become a "brand" to identify a genre of horror film; several of these titles are prefixed with "Wes Craven's ...".

TOP 10 FILMS DIRECTED BY DAVID CRONENBERG

	FILM	YEAR
1	The Fly	1986
2	Crash	1996
3	The Dead Zone	1983
4	Scanners	1981
5	eXistenZ	1999
6	Dead Ringers	1988
7	Spider	2002
8	Naked Lunch	1991
9	Videodrome	1983
10	M. Butterfly	1993

Canadian director Cronenberg has been honoured with awards at Berlin and Cannes and by several US critics' organizations, but to date has failed even to be nominated for an Oscar or a Golden Globe.

Triple Triumph
With *The Godfather, Part II*, Francis Ford Coppola became one of only four people ever to win "Best Director", "Best Picture", and "Best Screenplay" Oscars for the same film.

TOP 10 FILMS DIRECTED BY JONATHAN DEMME

	FILM	YEAR
1	The Silence of the Lambs *	1991
2	Philadelphia	1993
3	Beloved	1998
4	Married to the Mob	1988
5	Something Wild	1986
6	Swing Shift	1984
7	The Truth About Charlie	2002
8	Melvin and Howard	1980
9	Last Embrace	1979
10	Swimming to Cambodia	1987

* "Best Director" Oscar; film won "Best Picture" Oscar

TOP 10 FILMS DIRECTED BY BRIAN DE PALMA

	FILM	YEAR
1	Mission: Impossible	1996
2	The Untouchables	1987
3	Mission to Mars	2000
4	Snake Eyes	1998
5	Scarface	1983
6	Carlito's Way	1993
7	Carrie	1976
8	Dressed to Kill	1980
9	Raising Cain	1992
10	The Fury	1978

TOP 10 FILMS DIRECTED BY RICHARD DONNER

	FILM	YEAR
1	Lethal Weapon 3	1992
2	Superman	1978
3	Lethal Weapon 4	1998
4	Lethal Weapon 2	1989
5	Maverick	1994
6	Conspiracy Theory	1997
7	Assassins	1995
8	Scrooged	1988
9	Lethal Weapon	1987
10	The Goonies	1985

TOP 10 FILMS DIRECTED BY CLINT EASTWOOD

	FILM	YEAR
1	The Bridges of Madison County	1995
2	Unforgiven *	1992
3	A Perfect World	1993
4	Space Cowboys	2000
5	Absolute Power	1997
6	The Rookie	1990
7	Sudden Impact	1983
8	Firefox	1982
9	Heartbreak Ridge	1986
10	Pale Rider	1985

* "Best Director" Oscar; film won "Best Picture" Oscar
Clint Eastwood made his directorial debut with *Play Misty for Me* in 1971, and it is as a director of over 20 films that he has received the critical acclaim that has been lacking in his work as an actor: he gained a "Best Director" Oscar and Golden Globe for *Unforgiven* (1992) and another Globe for *Bird* (1988), but has never won an actor award from either organization.

TOP 10 FILMS DIRECTED BY BLAKE EDWARDS

	FILM	YEAR
1	10	1979
2	A Shot in the Dark	1964
3	The Return of the Pink Panther	1975
4	Blind Date	1987
5	The Pink Panther Strikes Again	1976
6	Victor/Victoria	1982
7	Micki + Maude	1984
8	The Great Race	1965
9	Operation Petticoat	1959
10	Skin Deep	1989

Blake Edwards is best known for the *Pink Panther* films with Peter Sellers as bungling Inspector Jacques Clouseau, and, although it fails to make a showing in his Top 10, *Breakfast at Tiffany's* (1961). Two of the films that feature prominently here – *10* and *Victor/Victoria* – starred Blake Edwards's wife Julie Andrews, whose singing voice also appeared in *The Pink Panther Strikes Again*.

TOP 10 FILMS DIRECTED BY ALFRED HITCHCOCK

	FILM	YEAR
1	Psycho	1960
2	Rear Window	1954
3	North by Northwest	1959
4	The Birds	1963
5	Family Plot	1976
6	Torn Curtain	1966
7	Frenzy	1972
8	Vertigo	1958
9	The Man Who Knew Too Much	1956
10	Spellbound	1945

Despite being nominated for "Best Director" Oscars on six occasions, Alfred Hitchcock never won, but in 1968 he was awarded the Irving G. Thalberg Memorial Award.

TOP 10 FILMS DIRECTED BY RON HOWARD

	FILM	YEAR
1	Dr. Seuss's How the Grinch Stole Christmas	2000
2	Apollo 13	1995
3	A Beautiful Mind *	2001
4	Ransom	1996
5	Backdraft	1991
6	Parenthood	1989
7	Cocoon	1985
8	Far and Away	1992
9	Splash	1984
10	Willow	1988

* Best Director" Oscar; film won "Best Picture" Oscar

Master of Suspense
Regarded as the doyen of the thriller, Sir Alfred Hitchcock made the first of his more than 50 films in England in the 1920s and 30s, moving to Hollywood in 1939.

NORMAN JEWISON

	FILM	YEAR
1	Moonstruck	1987
2	Fiddler on the Roof	1971
3	The Hurricane	1999
4	Best Friends	1982
5	And Justice for All	1979
6	Rollerball	1975
7	Other People's Money	1991
8	Agnes of God	1985
9	Jesus Christ Superstar	1973
10	In the Heat of the Night *	1967

* "Best Picture" Oscar

Canadian director Norman Jewison has been nominated for "Best Director" Oscars on four occasions without winning, but in 1999 received the Irving G. Thalberg Memorial Award.

STANLEY KUBRICK

	FILM	YEAR
1	2001: A Space Odyssey	1968
2	Eyes Wide Shut	1999
3	Full Metal Jacket	1987
4	The Shining	1980
5	Spartacus	1960
6	A Clockwork Orange	1971
7	Barry Lyndon	1975
8	Dr. Strangelove, or How I Learned to Stop Worrying and Love the Bomb	1964
9	Lolita	1962
10	Paths of Glory	1957

In an almost 50-years long career, director, writer, and producer Stanley Kubrick received 13 Oscar nominations, including four as "Best Director", winning only for special effects in 2001: A Space Odyssey.

SPIKE LEE

	FILM	YEAR
1	Malcolm X	1992
2	The Original Kings of Comedy	2000
3	Jungle Fever	199
4	Do the Right Thing	1989
5	He Got Game	1998
6	Summer of Sam	1999
7	Mo' Better Blues	1990
8	25th Hour	2002
9	School Daze	1988
10	Crooklyn	1994

Although falling outside his Top 10, Spike (Shelton Jackson) Lee's first feature film, She's Gotta Have It, made on a budget of $600,000, went on to earn more than $7 million in the US. He has also written and taken small roles in many of his films, many of which have gained awards, with Do The Right Thing nominated for the Palme d'Or.

TOP 10 FILMS DIRECTED BY GARY MARSHALL

	FILM	YEAR
1	Pretty Woman	1990
2	Runaway Bride	1999
3	The Princess Diaries	2001
4	Beaches	1988
5	Nothing in Common	1986
6	The Other Sister	1999
7	Young Doctors in Love	1982
8	Frankie and Johnny	1991
9	Overboard	1987
10	The Flamingo Kid	1984

Gary Marshall neatly started and ended the 1990s with his two highest-earning films (which grossed almost $800 million between them); he appeared in minor roles in both.

TOP 10 FILMS DIRECTED BY JOHN McTIERNAN

	FILM	YEAR
1	Die Hard: With a Vengeance	1995
2	The Hunt for Red October	1990
3	Die Hard	1988
4	The Thomas Crown Affair	1999
5	Last Action Hero	1993
6	Predator	1987
7	The 13th Warrior	1999
8	Medicine Man	1992
9	Rollerball	2002
10	Nomads	1986

Although Nomads, his directorial debut, was his least successful film, John McTiernan has since made a run of action blockbusters, among them remakes of two films, The Thomas Crown Affair and Rollerball.

TOP 10 FILMS DIRECTED BY PHILLIP NOYCE

	FILM	YEAR
1	Clear and Present Danger	1994
2	Patriot Games	1992
3	The Saint	1997
4	The Bone Collector	1999
5	Sliver	1993
6	The Quiet American	2002
7	Rabbit-Proof Fence	2002
8	Dead Calm	1989
9	Blind Fury	1989
10	Echoes of Paradise	1987

Phillip Noyce has made films that range from big-budget action films to those takling such issues as racial injustice in his native Australia in Rabbit-Proof Fence.

TOP 10 FILMS DIRECTED BY FRANK OZ

	FILM	YEAR
1	In & Out	1997
2	Bowfinger	1999
3	The Score	2001
4	HouseSitter	1992
5	What About Bob?	1991
6	Dirty Rotten Scoundrels	1988
7	The Indian in the Cupboard	1995
8	The Dark Crystal	1982
9	Little Shop of Horrors	1986
10	The Muppets Take Manhattan	1984

Frank Oz has directed films since The Dark Crystal, but is equally famed as an actor. As one of the creators of The Muppets, he provided the voice of such well-known characters as Miss Piggy, as well as

TOP 10 FILMS DIRECTED BY ALAN J. PAKULA

	FILM	YEAR
1	Presumed Innocent	1990
2	The Pelican Brief	1993
3	The Devil's Own	1997
4	All the President's Men	1976
5	Starting Over	1979
6	Sophie's Choice	1982
7	Consenting Adults	1992
8	The Sterile Cuckoo	1969
9	Klute	1971
10	Rollover	1981

The Sterile Cuckoo, starring Liza Minnelli marked the directorial debut of Alan J. Pakula (1928–98). Of the 16 films he directed, Presumed Innocent was the highest-earning, making over $220

TOP 10 FILMS DIRECTED BY ALAN PARKER

	FILM	YEAR
1	Evita	1996
2	Mississippi Burning	1988
3	Midnight Express	1978
4	Angela's Ashes	1999
5	The Commitments	1991
6	The Life of David Gale	2002
7	Pink Floyd: The Wall	1982
8	Fame	1980
9	Angel Heart	1987
10	The Road to Wellville	1994

British director Alan (now Sir Alan) Parker, has directed 17 films, several of them with a strong musical content, including his highest-earner, Evita, based on the stage musical by Tim Rice and

TOP 10 FILMS DIRECTED BY ROMAN POLANSKI

	FILM	YEAR
1	The Pianist	2002
2	The Ninth Gate	1999
3	Rosemary's Baby	1968
4	Chinatown	1974
5	Tess	1979
6	Death and the Maiden	1994
7	Frantic	1988
8	Bitter Moon	1992
9	Pirates	1986
10	The Fearless Vampire Killers or: Pardon Me, But Your Teeth Are in My Neck	1976

Roman Ruler
1933 born Roman Polanski won the Cannes film festival's Palme d'Or and "Best Director" Oscar – his third nomination after *Chinatown* (1974) and *Tess* (1979) – for *The Pianist*.

Although Roman Polanski's *Pirates* is included in his Top 10 based on the box office grosses of his films, it failed to recoup more than a fraction of its $40 million budget, and hence was a notable flop.

TOP 10 FILMS DIRECTED BY SYDNEY POLLACK

	FILM	YEAR
1	The Firm	1993
2	Out of Africa *	1985
3	Tootsie	1982
4	Sabrina	1995
5	Random Hearts	1999
6	The Way We Were	1973
7	Jeremiah Johnson	1972
8	The Electric Horseman	1979
9	Three Days of the Condor	1975
10	Absence of Malice	1981

* "Best Director" Oscar; film won "Best Picture" Oscar
Actor, producer, and director Sydney Pollack appears twice in the American Film Institute's list of 100 greatest love stories, with *The Way We Were* at No.6 and *Out of Africa* at No.13.

TOP 10 FILMS DIRECTED BY ROB REINER

	FILM	YEAR
1	A Few Good Men	1992
2	The American President	1995
3	When Harry Met Sally ...	1989
4	Misery	1990
5	The Story of Us	1999
6	Stand by Me	1986
7	The Princess Bride	1987
8	The Sure Thing	1985
9	Ghosts of Mississippi	1996
10	North	1994

As well as some high-earning films – *A Few Good Men* earned over $200 million worldwide, and the next two in his list more than $100 million each – Rob Reiner also directed *North*, which had a budget of $40 million, but barely recouped a fifth of that amount. He was also responsible for cult classic "mockumentary" *Spinal Tap* (1984), which just fails to make his Top 10.

TOP 10 FILMS DIRECTED BY IVAN REITMAN

	FILM	YEAR
1	Ghostbusters	1984
2	Twins	1988
3	Ghostbusters II	1989
4	Kindergarten Cop	1990
5	Six Days Seven Nights	1998
6	Evolution	2001
7	Junior	1994
8	Stripes	1981
9	Dave	1993
10	Legal Eagles	1986

Czechoslovakian-born Ivan Reitman grew up in Canada, and since his debut with *Meatballs* (1979) has followed an impressive Hollywood career as the director of commercial comedy films. He was also the producer of *National Lampoon's Animal House* (1978).

TOP 10 FILMS DIRECTED BY JOEL SCHUMACHER

	FILM	YEAR
1	Batman Forever	1995
2	Batman & Robin	1997
3	A Time to Kill	1996
4	The Client	1994
5	8MM	1999
6	Flawless	1999
7	Flatliners	1990
8	Falling Down	1993
9	Bad Company	2002
10	St. Elmo's Fire	1985

TOP 10 FILMS DIRECTED BY MARTIN SCORSESE

	FILM	YEAR
1	Cape Fear	1991
2	Gangs of New York	2002
3	Casino	1995
4	The Color of Money	1986
5	Goodfellas	1990
6	The Age of Innocence	1993
7	Taxi Driver	1976
8	Raging Bull	1980
9	Bringing Out the Dead	1999
10	Alice Doesn't Live Here Anymore	1974

TOP 10 FILMS DIRECTED BY RIDLEY SCOTT

	FILM	YEAR
1	Gladiator *	2000
2	Hannibal	2001
3	Alien	1979
4	Black Hawk Down	2001
5	Black Rain	1989
6	G.I. Jane	1997
7	Thelma & Louise	1991
8	Blade Runner	1982
9	Legend	1985
10	1492: Conquest of Paradise	1992

* Film won "Best Picture" Oscar

TOP 10 FILMS DIRECTED BY TONY SCOTT

	FILM	YEAR
1	Top Gun	1986
2	Beverly Hills Cop II	1987
3	Enemy of the State	1998
4	Days of Thunder	1990
5	Crimson Tide	1995
6	Spy Game	2001
7	The Last Boy Scout	1991
8	The Fan	1996
9	Revenge	1990
10	True Romance	1993

Like his elder brother Ridley, British director Tony Scott has made a number of highly successful films since his debut with *The Hunger* (1983), sharing with him an Emmy as producers of made-for-TV movie *The Gathering Storm* (2002).

TOP 10 FILMS DIRECTED BY STEVEN SODERBERGH

	FILM	YEAR
1	Ocean's Eleven	2001
2	Erin Brockovich	2000
3	Traffic *	2000
4	Out of Sight	1998
5	sex, lies, and videotape	1989
6	Solaris	2002
7	The Limey	1999
8	Full Frontal	2002
9	Kafka	1991
10	King of the Hill	1993

* "Best Director" Oscar

TOP 10 FILMS DIRECTED BY STEVEN SPIELBERG

	FILM	YEAR
1	Jurassic Park	1993
2	E.T. the Extra-Terrestrial	1982
3	The Lost World: Jurassic Park	1997
4	Indiana Jones and the Last Crusade	1989
5	Saving Private Ryan *	1998
6	Jaws	1975
7	Raiders of the Lost Ark	1981
8	Minority Report	2002
9	Close Encounters of the Third Kind	1977
10	Catch Me If You Can	2002

* "Best Director" Oscar

TOP 10 FILMS DIRECTED BY OLIVER STONE

	FILM	YEAR
1	JFK	1991
2	Born on the Fourth of July *	1989
3	Platoon * †	1986
4	Any Given Sunday	1999
5	Natural Born Killers	1994
6	Wall Street	1987
7	The Doors	1991
8	Nixon	1995
9	U-Turn	1997
10	Heaven & Earth	1993

* "Best Director" Oscars
† Film won "Best Picture" Oscar

TOP 10 FILMS DIRECTED BY PETER WEIR

	FILM	YEAR
1	The Truman Show	1998
2	Dead Poets Society	1989
3	Witness	1985
4	Green Card	1990
5	The Mosquito Coast	1986
6	The Year of Living Dangerously	1982
7	Fearless	1993
8	Gallipoli	1981
9	Picnic at Hanging Rock	1975
10	The Last Wave	1977

TOP 10 FILMS DIRECTED BY BILLY WILDER

	FILM	YEAR
1	Irma la Douce	1963
2	Some Like It Hot	1959
3	The Front Page	1974
4	The Apartment *	1960
5	The Seven Year Itch	1955
6	The Lost Weekend *	1945
7	Sabrina	1954
8	The Emperor Waltz	1948
9	Buddy Buddy	1981
10	Witness for the Prosecution	1957

* "Best Director" Oscar; film won "Best Picture" Oscar

TOP 10 FILMS DIRECTED BY ROBERT ZEMECKIS

	FILM	YEAR
1	Forrest Gump *	1994
2	Cast Away	2000
3	Back to the Future	1985
4	Who Framed Roger Rabbit	1988
5	Back to the Future Part II	1989
6	What Lies Beneath	2000
7	Back to the Future Part III	1990
8	Contact	1997
9	Death Becomes Her	1992
10	Romancing the Stone	1984

* "Best Director" Oscar; film won "Best Picture" Oscar

Heart of Stone

Oliver Stone directs Kevin Costner as DA Jim Garrison in *JFK*, his exploration of the Kennedy assassination. The real Jim Garrison played Chief Justice Earl Warren in the film.

TOP 10 FILMS WRITTEN BY RONALD BASS

	FILM	YEAR
1	Rain Man	1988
2	Waiting to Exhale	1995
3	My Best Friend's Wedding	1997
4	Entrapment	1999
5	Dangerous Minds	1995
6	Sleeping With the Enemy	1991
7	Stepmom	1998
8	What Dreams May Come	1998
9	When a Man Loves a Woman	1994
10	How Stella Got Her Groove Back	1998

As with certain other writers featured here, Ron Bass has pursued his career writing both original screenplays and adapting the work of other writers. He has also produced some of the same films, while other writers have extended their roles even further by also directing films for which they have provided scripts.

TOP 10 FILMS WRITTEN BY ROBERT BENTON

	FILM	YEAR
1	Superman	1978
2	Kramer vs. Kramer *	1979
3	What's Up, Doc?	1972
4	Bonnie and Clyde	1967
5	Nobody's Fool *	1994
6	Places in the Heart *	1984
7	Twilight *	1998
8	Still of the Night *	1982
9	Nadine *	1987
10	The Late Show *	1977

* Also director

TOP 10 FILMS WRITTEN BY MICHAEL CRICHTON*

	FILM	YEAR
1	Jurassic Park †	1993
2	The Lost World: Jurassic Park	1997
3	Twister	1996
4	Jurassic Park III	2001
5	Disclosure	1994
6	Congo	1995
7	Sphere	1998
8	Rising Sun	1993
9	The 13th Warrior #	1999
10	Coma §	1978

* Including novels adapted for the screen by himself and others
† Wrote the novel *Jurassic Park*; co-wrote screenplay with David Koepp
# Novel titled *Eaters of the Dead*
§ Also director

TOP 10 FILMS WRITTEN BY STEVEN E. DE SOUZA

	FILM	YEAR
1	The Flintstones	1994
2	Die Hard 2	1990
3	Another 48 Hrs.	1990
4	Die Hard	1988
5	Beverly Hills Cop III	1994
6	Street Fighter *	1994
7	48 Hrs.	1982
8	The Running Man	1987
9	Commando	1985
10	Jumpin' Jack Flash †	1986

* Also director
† Uncredited

TOP 10 FILMS WRITTEN BY NORA EPHRON

	FILM	YEAR
1	You've Got M@il	1998
2	Sleepless in Seattle	1993
3	Michael	1996
4	When Harry Met Sally ...	1989
5	Hanging Up	2000
6	Silkwood	1983
7	My Blue Heaven	1990
8	Heartburn	1986
9	Mixed Nuts	1994
10	This is My Life	1992

Heart to Heart
Three-times Oscar-nominated writer Nora Ephron's account of the break-up of her marriage to Watergate journalist Carl Bernstein was the basis of *Heartburn*, in which her character was played by Meryl Streep.

TOP 10 FILMS WRITTEN BY WILLIAM GOLDMAN

	FILM	YEAR
1	Maverick	1994
2	The General's Daughter	1999
3	Butch Cassidy and the Sundance Kid	1969
4	Absolute Power	1997
5	The Ghost and the Darkness	1996
6	All the President's Men	1976
7	Misery	1990
8	Dreamcatcher *	2003
9	A Bridge Too Far	1977
10	The Princess Bride	1987

* Co-written with Lawrence Kasdan

TOP 10 FILMS WRITTEN BY JOHN HUGHES

	FILM	YEAR
1	Home Alone	1990
2	101 Dalmatians	1996
3	Home Alone 2: Lost in New York	1992
4	Flubber	1997
5	Maid in Manhattan *	2002
6	Dennis the Menace	1993
7	Beethoven *	1992
8	Beethoven's 2nd *	1993
9	National Lampoon's Christmas Vacation	1989
10	Ferris Bueller's Day Off	1986

* Written under the name "Edmond Dantès"

TOP 10 FILMS WRITTEN BY RUTH PRAWER JHABVALA

	FILM	YEAR
1	Howards End	1992
2	The Remains of the Day	1993
3	A Room With a View	1986
4	Mr. & Mrs. Bridge	1990
5	The Golden Bowl	2000
6	Surviving Picasso	1996
7	Madame Sousatzka	1988
8	Jefferson in Paris	1995
9	A Soldier's Daughter Never Cries	1998
10	Heat and Dust	1983

TOP 10 FILMS WRITTEN BY STEPHEN KING*

	FILM	YEAR
1	The Green Mile	1999
2	Misery	1990
3	Dreamcatcher	2003
4	The Shawshank Redemption †	1994
5	Pet Sematary	1989
6	Stand by Me #	1986
7	Dolores Claiborne	1995
8	The Shining	1980
9	The Running Man	1987
10	Sleepwalkers	1992

* Adapted for the screen from his novels unless otherwise stated
† Short story *Rita Hayworth and the Shawshank Redemption*
# Novella *The Body*
For more than a quarter of a century, Stephen King's novels and stories have formed the basis of a film industry of their own, with *The Green Mile* by far the highest-earning to date. He dissociated himself from *The Lawnmower Man* (1992), which cannot be claimed as a film of his novel of the same title. *Lawnmower Man 2* and *Pet Sematary 2* similarly have no direct connection with King's work.

TOP 10 FILMS WRITTEN BY MARK ROSENTHAL

	FILM	YEAR
1	Planet of the Apes	2001
2	Star Trek VI: The Undiscovered Country	1991
3	Mercury Rising	1998
4	The Jewel of the Nile	1985
5	Mighty Joe Young	1998
6	The Beverly Hillbillies	1993
7	Superman IV: The Quest for Peace	1987
8	For Love or Money	1993
9	The Legend of Billie Jean	1985
10	Desperate Hours	1990

TOP 10 FILMS WRITTEN BY DAVID KOEPP

	FILM	YEAR
1	Jurassic Park *	1993
2	Spider-Man	2002
3	The Lost World: Jurassic Park *	1997
4	Mission: Impossible	1996
5	Panic Room	2002
6	Death Becomes Her	1992
7	Snake Eyes	1998
8	Carlito's Way	1993
9	The Paper	1994
10	The Shadow	1994

* Screenplay co-written with Michael Crichton

TOP 10 FILMS WRITTEN BY GEORGE LUCAS

	FILM	YEAR
1	Star Wars: Episode I – The Phantom Menace *	1999
2	Star Wars *†	1977
3	Star Wars: Episode II – Attack of the Clones *	2002
4	Star Wars: Episode VI – Return of the Jedi	1983
5	Star Wars: Episode V – The Empire Strikes Back	1980
6	Indiana Jones and the Last Crusade	1989
7	Raiders of the Lost Ark	1981
8	Indiana Jones and the Temple of Doom	1984
9	American Graffiti *	1973
10	Willow	1988

* Also director
† Later retitled *Star Wars: Episode IV – A New Hope*
George Lucas's Top 10, which have cumulatively earned almost $5 billion worldwide, includes films written by others based on stories by him and screenplays co-written with others.

Kid's Stuff

As writer, director, and producer of some of the most popular family films of all time, one-man film industry George Lucas has achieved a unique place in cinematic history.

TOP 10 FILMS WRITTEN BY LAWRENCE KASDAN

	FILM	YEAR
1	Star Wars: Episode VI – Return of the Jedi	1983
2	Star Wars: Episode V – The Empire Strikes Back	1980
3	The Bodyguard	1992
4	Raiders of the Lost Ark	1981
5	Dreamcatcher *†	2003
6	The Big Chill *	1983
7	Grand Canyon *	1991
8	The Accidental Tourist *	1988
9	Silverado *	1985
10	Wyatt Earp *	1994

* Also director
† Co-written with William Goldman and Stephen King (novel)
Each of the first three films in this list made more than $400 million worldwide, placing them among the top 50 of all time. Those he also directed have earned considerably less, with *Wyatt Earp* failing to recoup even half its $63 million budget.

From galaxy to battlefield, from haunted castle to football stadium, the subject matter of film has become so diverse that a wealth of evocative places and times await you every time you start watching a film. From the beginning of the industry, when the number of genres was limited to a handful of such recognizable types as Westerns, there has been an increasing tendency to classify films into themes and sub-themes, so that an overall genre such as crime may encompass films that feature the police, courtroom dramas, the Mafia, or a host of other allied subjects. In the Top 10 lists, these and many others are identified, among them action, animation, comedy, and disaster films; animals from bugs and mice to apes to dinosaurs; documentaries, superheroes, vampires and werewolves, musicals, and science fiction films. Within this topic, we also consider some of the Top 10 examples of the varied sources of film stories, including comics, books, plays, and even computer games.

May the Force Be With You
Science fiction is one of the most popular of all film genres. The *Star Wars* phenomenon leads the field with cumulative global earnings of more than $3.5 billion.

TOP 10 ANIMATED FILMS OF ALL TIME

	FILM	US RELEASE	WORLD GROSS ($)
1	The Lion King *	15 Jun 1994	771,900,000
2	Monsters, Inc. *	28 Oct 2001	529,000,000
3	Aladdin *	11 Nov 1992	502,400,000
4	Toy Story 2 *	13 Nov 1999	485,800,000
5	Shrek	16 May 2001	469,700,000
6	Tarzan *	17 Jun 1999	435,300,000
7	Ice Age	15 Mar 2002	365,000,000
8	A Bug's Life *	14 Nov 1998	363,400,000
9	Toy Story *	22 Nov 1995	361,500,000
10	Dinosaur *	19 May 2000	356,100,000

* Disney

TOP 10 ANIMATED FILMS OF THE 1930s TO 1970s

	FILM	YEAR
1	Bambi	1942
2	One Hundred and One Dalmatians	1961
3	The Jungle Book	1967
4	Snow White and the Seven Dwarfs	1937
5	Mary Poppins *	1964
6	Lady and The Tramp	1955
7	Peter Pan	1953
8	Pinocchio	1940
9	Fantasia	1940
10	Song of the South *	1946

* Part-animated/part-live action

It is interesting that animated films from the 1930s, 1940s, 1950s, and 1960s have all outearned those from the 1970s, only one of which, *The Aristocats* (1970), comes close, with *Robin Hood* (1973) and *The Rescuers* (1977) trailing close behind.

TOP 10 ANIMATED FILMS OF THE 1980s

	FILM	YEAR
1	Who Framed Roger Rabbit *	1988
2	The Little Mermaid	1989
3	Oliver & Company	1988
4	The Land Before Time	1988
5	An American Tail	1986
6	The Fox and the Hound	1981
7	All Dogs Go to Heaven	1989
8	The Great Mouse Detective	1986
9	The Care Bears Movie	1985
10	The Black Cauldron	1985

* Part-animated/part-live action

TOP 10 ANIMATED FILMS OF THE 1990s

	FILM	YEAR
1	The Lion King	1994
2	Aladdin	1992
3	Toy Story 2	1999
4	Tarzan	1999
5	A Bug's Life	1998
6	Toy Story	1995
7	Beauty and The Beast	1991
8	Pocahontas	1995
9	The Hunchback of Notre Dame	1996
10	Mulan	1998

TOP 10 ANIMATED FILMS OF THE 2000s

	FILM	YEAR
1	Monsters, Inc.	2001
2	Shrek	2001
3	Ice Age	2002
4	Dinosaur	2000
5	Lilo & Stitch	2002
6	Cats & Dogs *	2001
7	Chicken Run	2000
8	Atlantis: The Lost Empire	2001
9	The Emperor's New Groove	2000
10	Rugrats in Paris: The Movie – Rugrats II	2000

* Part-animated/part-live action

TOP 10 ANIMATED FILMS IN THE UK

	FILM	YEAR	UK GROSS (£)
1	Toy Story 2	2000	44,306,070
2	Monsters, Inc.	2002	37,687,826
3	Chicken Run	2000	29,509,150
4	A Bug's Life	1999	29,478,093
5	Shrek	2001	29,004,582
6	The Lion King	1994	23,144,442
7	Cats & Dogs *	2001	23,013,391
8	Toy Story	1996	22,297,733
9	Tarzan	1999	18,158,801
10	Aladdin	1992	16,416,742

* Part-animated/part-live action

TOP 10 DISNEY ANIMATED FEATURE FILMS

	FILM	US RELEASE	WORLD GROSS ($)
1	The Lion King	15 Jun 1994	771,900,000
2	Monsters, Inc.	28 Oct 2001	529,000,000
3	Aladdin	11 Nov 1992	502,400,000
4	Toy Story 2	13 Nov 1999	485,800,000
5	Tarzan	17 Jun 1999	449,400,000
6	A Bug's Life	14 Nov 1998	363,400,000
7	Toy Story	22 Nov 1995	361,500,000
8	Dinosaur	13 May 2000	356,100,000
9	Beauty and the Beast	22 Nov 1991	352,900,000
10	Who Framed Roger Rabbit *	21 Jun 1988	349,100,000

* Part-animated/part-live action

Book Mark

The Jungle Book earned more than $200 million worldwide, while its subsequent video release became one of the bestselling of all time.

TOP 10 NON-DISNEY ANIMATED FEATURE FILMS

	FILM	PRODUCTION COMPANY	YEAR	WORLD GROSS ($)
1	Shrek	DreamWorks	2001	477,000,000
2	Ice Age	Fox Animation	2002	366,300,000
3	Casper *	Amblin Entertainment	1995	282,300,000
4	Space Jam *	Warner Bros.	1996	225,400,000
5	Chicken Run	DreamWorks	2000	224,900,000
6	The Prince of Egypt	DreamWorks	1998	218,300,000
7	Cats & Dogs *	Warner Bros.	2001	200,400,000
8	Antz	DreamWorks	1998	181,700,000
9	Mononoke-hime	Dentsu Inc.	1997	159,400,000
10	Pokémon: The First Movie	4 Kids Entertainment, etc.	1999	155,700,000

* Part-animated/part-live action

TOP 10 ANIMATED FILMS RANKED BY BUDGET

	FILM	YEAR	BUDGET ($)
1 =	Tarzan	1999	150,000,000
=	The Polar Express	2004	150,000,000
3	Treasure Planet	2002	140,000,000
4	Final Fantasy: The Spirits Within	2001	137,000,000
5	Dinosaur	2000	128,000,000
6	Monsters, Inc.	2001	115,000,000
7	The Emperor's New Groove	2000	100,000,000
8	The Road to El Dorado	2000	95,000,000
9	Finding Nemo	2003	94,000,000
10	The Incredibles	2004	92,000,000

In 1937, *Snow White and the Seven Dwarfs* had a budget of $1,490,000. *Robin Hood* (1973), set a record with $15,000,000 that remained unbroken until 1985, when *The Black Cauldron* (1985) became the first to break the $25,000,000 barrier. Since the 1990s, budgets of $50,000,000 or more have become common-place: *The Lion King* (1994) cost $79,300,000, and *Tarzan* became the first to break through $100,000,000.

TOP 10 PART-ANIMATION/PART-LIVE ACTION FILMS

	FILM	YEAR
1	Who Framed Roger Rabbit	1988
2	Casper	1995
3	Space Jam	1996
4	Cats & Dogs	1980
5	9 to 5	1980
6	Mary Poppins	1964
7	Fantasia/2000	2000
8	Small Soldiers	1998
9	Song of the South	1946
10	James and the Giant Peach	1996

Many films now contain computer-generated images alongside live action, but these are the highest earning that combine traditional animation and live action as a key element. *Fantasia* (1940) may arguably warrant a place in the list, but the only combination sequence is a brief encounter between Mickey Mouse and the conductor Leopold Stokowski in what is otherwise an animated film.

THE 10 FIRST DISNEY CARTOONS

	FILM	FIRST RELEASE
1	Little Red Riding Hood	29 Jul 1922
2	The Four Musicians of Bremen	1 Aug 1922
3	Jack and the Beanstalk	4 Sep 1922
4	Goldie Locks and the Three Bears	5 Oct 1922
5	Puss in Boots	3 Nov 1922
6 =	Cinderella	6 Dec 1922
=	Tommy Tucker's Tooth	6 Dec 1922
8	Alice's Day at Sea *	1 Mar 1924
9	Alice's Spooky Adventure *	1 Apr 1924
10	Alice's Wild West Show *	1 May 1924

* Live-action/cartoon combination

THE 10 FIRST SILLY SYMPHONIES CARTOONS

	FILM	FIRST RELEASE
1	The Skeleton Dance	22 Aug 1929
2	El Terrible Toreador	7 Sep 1929
3	Springtime	24 Oct 1929
4	Hell's Bells	30 Oct 1929
5	The Merry Dwarfs	16 Dec 1929
6	Summer	6 Jan 1930
7	Autumn	13 Feb 1930
8	Cannibal Capers	13 Mar 1930
9	Frolicking Fish	8 May 1930
10	Arctic Antics	5 Jun 1930

Silly Symphonies was created by Walt Disney to exploit the coming of sound and introduced such perennial cartoon characters as Donald Duck and Pluto. All films in this list are black and white.

THE 10 FIRST COLUMBIA CARTOONS

	FILM	FIRST RELEASE
1	Ratskin	15 Aug 1929
2	Canned Music	12 Sep 1929
3	Port Whines	10 Oct 1929
4	Sole Mates	7 Nov 1929
5	Farm Relief	30 Dec 1929
6	The Cat's Meouw	2 Jan 1930
7	Spook Easy	30 Jan 1930
8	Slow Beau	27 Feb 1930
9	Desert Sunk	27 Mar 1930
10	An Old Flame	24 Apr 1930

All these cartoons featured Krazy Kat. He had already been established as a cartoon character with another studio, International Film Service, Inc., with the release of *Introducing Krazy Kat and Ignatz Mouse* on 18 February 1916.

THE 10 FIRST WALTER LANTZ CARTOONS

	FILM	FIRST RELEASE
1	Ozzie of the Circus	5 Jan 1929
2	Stage Stunt	13 May 1929
3	Stripes and Stars	27 May 1929
4	Wicked West	10 Jun 1929
5	Nuts and Bolts	24 Jun 1929
6	Ice Man's Luck	8 Jul 1929
7	Jungle Jingles	22 Jul 1929
8	Weary Willies	5 Aug 1929
9	Saucy Sausages	19 Aug 1929
10	Race Riot	2 Sep 1929

These were all black-and-white cartoons featuring Oswald the Lucky Rabbit. Walter Lantz (1900–94) took the character over from Walt Disney, who had been making them since 1927. Lantz later made the first ever Technicolor cartoon, the opening sequence to live-action *The King of Jazz* (1930).

THE 10 FIRST VAN BEUREN CARTOONS

	FILM	FIRST RELEASE
1	Dinner Time	1 Sep 1928
2	Concentrate	4 May 1929
3	The Jail Breakers	6 May 1929
4	Woodchoppers	9 May 1929
5	The Faithful Pup	12 May 1929
6	Presto-Chango	20 May 1929
7	Skating Hounds	27 May 1929
8	Stage Struck	25 Jun 1929
9	House Cleaning Time	23 Jul 1929
10	A Stone Age Romance	1 Aug 1929

Van Beuren Productions was founded by Amadee J. Van Beuren (1879–1937), who took over Fables Studio in 1928 and decided to make exclusively sound cartoons. *Dinner Time* was thus the first short cartoon with sound (Disney's *Steamboat Willie* is heralded as the first, but was made as a silent film, with sound added before release).

THE 10 FIRST DISNEY ANIMATED FEATURES

	FILM	FIRST RELEASE
1	Snow White and the Seven Dwarfs	21 Dec 1937
2	Pinocchio	7 Feb 1940
3	Fantasia	12 Nov 1940
4	Dumbo	23 Oct 1941
5	Bambi	9 Aug 1942
6	The Three Caballeros	3 Feb 1945
7	Make Mine Music	15 Aug 1946
8	Fun and Fancy Free	27 Sep 1947
9	Melody Time	27 May 1948
10	The Adventures of Ichabod and Mr. Toad	5 Oct 1949

THE 10 FIRST TERRYTOONS CARTOONS

	FILM	FIRST RELEASE
1	Caviar	23 Feb 1930
2	Pretzels	9 Mar 1930
3	Spanish Onions	23 Mar 1930
4	Indian Pudding	6 Apr 1930
5	Roman Punch	20 Apr 1930
6 =	Hot Turkey	4 May 1930
=	Hawaiian Pineapple	4 May 1930
8	Swiss Cheese	18 May 1930
9	Codfish Balls	1 Jun 1930
10	Hungarian Goulash	15 Jun 1930

Former newspaper cartoonist Paul Terry (1887–1971) worked on Van Beuren's first sound cartoon, *Dinner Time*, in 1928. After leaving in 1929, he went into partnership with Frank Moser (1886–1974) to form the animation studio Terrytoons, whose productions were distributed by Fox Pictures. Their first 25 films all took foods as their titles.

THE 10 FIRST LOONEY TUNES CARTOONS

	FILM	FIRST RELEASE
1	Sinkin' in the Bathtub	30 May 1930
2	Congo Jazz	30 Sep 1930
3	Hold Anything	30 Oct 1930
4	The Booze Hangs High	30 Nov 1930
5	Box Car Blues	30 Dec 1930
6	Big Man from the North	31 Jan 1931
7	Ain't Nature Grand!	Feb 1931
8	Ups 'n' Downs	31 Mar 1931
9	Dumb Patrol	31 Apr 1931
10	Yodelling Yokels	31 May 1931

Looney Tunes, a "homage" to Disney's Silly Symphonies series, was the name given to the cartoons Warner Bros. commissioned from former Disney animators Hugh Harman (1903–82) and Rudolf Ising (1903–92). These early films were originally made in black and white, but later remade, not always successfully, in colour.

THE 10 FIRST UB IWERKS CARTOONS

	FILM	FIRST RELEASE
1	Fiddlesticks	16 Aug 1930
2	Flying Fists	6 Sep 1930
3	The Village Barber	27 Sep 1930
4	Cuckoo Murder Case	18 Oct 1930
5 =	Little Orphan Willie	31 Dec 1930
=	Puddle Pranks	31 Dec 1930
7 =	The Soup Song	31 Jan 1931
=	The Village Smitty	31 Jan 1931
9	Laughing Gas	14 Mar 1931
10	Ragtime Romeo	2 May 1931

Ub Iwerks (formerly Ubbe Ert Iwwerks, 1901–71) was originally in partnership with Walt Disney, with whom he produced the first ever sketches of Mickey Mouse. During his subsequent career, he pioneered many animation techniques, founding his own studio in 1930, all the initial productions of which featured the character Flip the Frog.

THE 10 FIRST FAMOUS STUDIOS CARTOONS

	FILM	CHARACTERS	FIRST RELEASE
1	You're a Sap. Mr. Jap	Popeye	7 Aug 1942
2	Alona on the Sarong Seas	Popeye	4 Sep 1942
3	Japoteurs	Superman	18 Sep 1942
4 =	A Hull of a Mess	Popeye	16 Oct 1942
=	Showdown	Superman	16 Oct 1942
6 =	Eleventh Hour	Superman	20 Nov 1942
=	Scrap the Japs	Popeye	20 Nov 1942
8 =	Destruction, Inc.	Superman	25 Dec 1942
=	Me Musical Nephews	Popeye	25 Dec 1942
10	Spinach Fer Britain	Popeye	22 Jan 1943

The first cartoons produced by the Famous Studios division of Paramount all featured all-American heroes Popeye and Superman – and, perhaps inevitably, given the dates, several were pro-Allies/anti-Axis propaganda films.

THE 10 FIRST UPA CARTOONS

	FILM/SERIES	CHARACTERS	FIRST RELEASE
1	Robin Hoodlum	Fox and Crow	23 Dec 1948
2	The Magic Fluke	Fox and Crow	27 Mar 1949
3	Ragtime Bear	Jolly Frolics/Mr. Magoo	8 Sep 1949
4	Punchy De Leon	Jolly Frolics/Mr. Magoo	12 Jan 1950
5	Spellbound Hound	Mr. Magoo	16 Mar 1950
6	The Miner's Daughter	Jolly Frolics	25 May 1950
7	Giddyap	Jolly Frolics	27 Jul 1950
8	Trouble Indemnity	Mr. Magoo	4 Sep 1950
9	The Popcorn Story	Jolly Frolics	30 Nov 1950
10	Bungled Bungalow	Mr. Magoo	28 Dec 1950

UPA – United Productions of America – a cartoon studio distributed by Columbia, introduced the character Mr. Magoo (voiced by Jim Backus). These films became the company's mainstay during the 1950s, winning Oscars in 1954 (*When Magoo Flew*) and 1956 (*Mr. Magoo's Puddle Jumper*). Mr. Magoo also starred in UPA's first feature-length cartoon film, *1001 Arabian Nights* (1959).

Winning by a Nose
Made with a then record budget of $2.6 million, *Pinocchio*, Disney's second animated feature film, was the highest-earning film of 1940, winning Oscars for "Best Original Score" and "Best Song".

THE 10 FIRST HAPPY HARMONY CARTOONS

	FILM	FIRST RELEASE
1	The Discontented Canary	1 Sep 1934
2	The Old Pioneer	29 Sep 1934
3	A Tale of the Vienna Woods	27 Oct 1934
4	Bosko's Parlor Pranks	24 Nov 1934
5	Toyland Broadcast	22 Dec 1934
6	Hey-Hey Fever	9 Jan 1935
7	When the Cat's Away	16 Feb 1935
8	The Lost Chick	9 Mar 1935
9	The Calico Dragon	30 Mar 1935
10	The Good Little Monkeys	13 Apr 1935

These were the first of the Happy Harmonies series, produced for MGM by Hugh Harman and Rudolf Ising. They produced a total of 36 films up to 1938.

THE 10 FIRST MERRIE MELODIES CARTOONS

	FILM	FIRST RELEASE
1	Lady, Play Your Mandolin!	31 Aug 1931
2	Smile, Darn Ya, Smile!	5 Sep 1931
3	One More Time	3 Oct 1931
4	You Don't Know What You're Doin!	31 Oct 1931
5	Hittin' the Trail for Hallelujah Land	28 Nov 1931
6	Red-Headed Baby	26 Dec 1931
7	Pagan Moon	23 Jan 1932
8	Freddy the Freshman	20 Feb 1932
9	Crosby, Columbo, and Vallee	19 Mar 1932
10	Goopy Geer	16 Apr 1932

Following the success of their Looney Tunes series, Hugh Harman and Rudolf Ising launched Merrie Melodies cartoons, the first three of which featured the character Foxy. Over the next 60 years, more than 500 Merrie Melodies cartoons were released, giving birth to such animation immortals as Bugs Bunny.

Steaming Ahead
Mickey Mouse in Walt Disney's *Steamboat Willie*, the first
sound cartoon, released at the Colony Theatre, New York, on
18 November 1928. This date has since been regarded as
Mickey's birthdate. In the film, Mickey whistles but does not
talk and does not wear his trademark white gloves.

© Disney Enterprises, Inc.

THE 10 FIRST MICKEY MOUSE CARTOONS

	FILM	DISNEY DELIVERY DATE
1	Plane Crazy	15 May 1928
2	Steamboat Willie	29 Jul 1928
3	Gallopin' Gaucho	2 Aug 1928
4	The Barn Dance	14 Mar 1929
5	The Opry House	20 Mar 1929
6	When the Cat's Away	3 May 1929
7	The Plow Boy	28 Jun 1929
8	The Barnyard Battle	2 Jul 1929
9	The Karnival Kid	31 Jul 1929
10	Mickey's Follies	28 Aug 1929

Walt Disney's iconic Mickey Mouse first appeared in *Plane Crazy*,
a silent film in which he copies the exploits of aviator Charles
Lindbergh in an attempt to impress Minnie Mouse. *Steamboat
Willie* was the first Mickey Mouse cartoon with sound. He went on
to appear in some 130 films, including a starring role in *Fantasia*
(1940), while *Lend a Paw* won an Oscar in 1941. He made only
occasional appearances after the 1950s, but guested in *Who
Framed Roger Rabbit* (1988), *A Goofy Movie* (1995), and *Fantasia/
2000* (2000). *The Search for Mickey Mouse* is scheduled for 2004.

THE 10 FIRST BUGS BUNNY CARTOONS

	FILM	FIRST THEATRICAL RELEASE
1	Porky's Hare Hunt	30 Apr 1938
2	Hare-um Scare-um	12 Aug 1939
3	Elmers's Candid Camera	2 Mar 1940
4	A Wild Hare	27 Jul 1940
5	Elmer's Pet Rabbit	4 Jan 1941
6	Tortoise Beats Hare	15 Mar 1941
7	Hiawatha's Rabbit Hunt	7 Jun 1941
8	The Heckling Hare	5 Jul 1941
9	All This and Rabbit Stew	13 Sep 1941
10	Wabbit Twouble	20 Dec 1941

Bugs Bunny's debut was as a co-star with Porky Pig in *Porky's Hare
Hunt*, but he was not named until the release of *Elmer's Pet Rabbit*.
A Wild Hare was the first cartoon in which he said the trademark line,
"Eh, what's up, Doc?", voiced, along with over 200 sequels, by Mel
Blanc (1908–89). The film was nominated for an Oscar, as were
Hiawatha's Rabbit Hunt and *Knighty-Knight Bugs* (1958); the latter
won the award. One of most enduring of all cartoon characters, Bugs
Bunny made a "guest" appearance in *Who Framed Roger Rabbit* (1988)
and *Space Jam* (1996), and stars in *Looney Tunes: The Movie* (2003).

THE 10 FIRST CASPER THE GHOST CARTOONS

	FILM	FIRST THEATRICAL RELEASE
1	The Friendly Ghost	16 Nov 1945
2	There's Good Boos Tonight	23 Apr 1948
3	A-Haunting We Will Go	13 May 1949
4	Casper's Spree Under the Sea	13 Oct 1950
5	Once Upon a Rhyme	15 Dec 1950
6	Boo-Hoo Baby	30 Mar 1951
7	Too Boo or Not to Boo	8 Jun 1951
8	Boo Scout	27 Jul 1951
9	Casper Comes to Clown	10 Aug 1951
10	Casper Takes a Bow-Wow	7 Dec 1951

Illustrator Joe Oriolo and writer Seymour V. Reit submitted their story
about a friendly ghost to Paramount's Famous Studios. After the
success of the first three cartoons, and the ghost's appearance from
1949 as a comic book, Casper starred in more than 50 cartoons,
culminating in 1995 with a part-live action/part-computer animated
film, which earned almost $300 million at the world box office.

THE 10 FIRST TOM AND JERRY CARTOONS

	FILM	FIRST THEATRICAL RELEASE
1	Puss Gets The Boot *	20 Feb 1940
2	The Midnight Snack	19 Jul 1941
3	The Night Before Christmas *	6 Dec 1941
4	Fraidy Cat	17 Jan 1942
5	Dog Trouble	18 Apr 1942
6	Puss 'N' Toots	30 May 1942
7	The Bowling Alley-Cat	18 Jul 1942
8	Fine Feathered Friend	10 Oct 1942
9	Sufferin' Cats!	16 Jan 1943
10	The Lonesome Mouse	22 May 1943

* Academy Award nomination

When MGM launched the cartoon in 1940, Tom was called Jasper, and the mouse unnamed. The names "Tom and Jerry" were chosen from a selection submitted by their employees, but the pairing has a literary origin with "Corinthian Tom" and "Jerry Hawthorn", the disorderly characters in Pierce Egan's rumbustious novel *Life in London* (1821). Creators William Hanna and Joseph Barbera directed over 100 cartoons featuring them from 1940 to 1958, when MGM closed its animation department. In the period 1943–53, Tom and Jerry cartoons received 13 Oscar nominations, winning on seven occasions. In 1960–62 Gene Deitch and, in 1963, Chuck Jones, made further films before Hannah and Barbera re-acquired the rights in 1975. Tom and Jerry also appeared in 1992 in *Tom and Jerry: The Movie*, a full-length film – and the only one in which the eternal adversaries are heard to speak to each other.

THE 10 FIRST WOODY WOODPECKER CARTOONS

	FILM	FIRST THEATRICAL RELEASE
1	Knock Knock	25 Nov 1940
2	Woody Woodpecker (aka The Cracked Nut)	17 Jul 1941
3	The Screwdriver	11 Aug 1941
4	What's Cookin'? (aka Pantry Panic)	24 Nov 1941
5	Hollywood Matador	9 Feb 1942
6	Ace in the Hole	22 Jun 1942
7	The Loan Stranger	19 Oct 1942
8	The Screwball	15 Feb 1943
9	The Dizzy Acrobat *	21 May 1943
10	Ration Bored	26 Jul 1943

* Academy Award nomination

Woody Woodpecker debuted as an incidental character in the Andy Panda cartoon *Knock Knock*, and was first named in his second outing. His voice was originally that of Mel Blanc, until Blanc signed an exclusive contract with Warner Bros., where he became the voice of Bugs Bunny and other characters. From 1952, the hyperactive woodpecker's tones were created by Grace Stafford (1903–92), wife of animation studio boss Walter Lantz (1899–1994). Woody starred in some 200 cartoons up to 1972, his last role being an appearance in the animated/live-action *Who Framed Roger Rabbit* (1988).

THE 10 FIRST POPEYE CARTOONS

	FILM	FIRST THEATRICAL RELEASE
1	Popeye the Sailor with Betty Boop	14 Jul 1933
2	I Yam What I Yam	29 Sep 1933
3	Blow Me Down!	27 Oct 1933
4	I Eats My Spinach	17 Nov 1933
5	Seasin's Greetinks	17 Dec 1933
6	Wild Elephinks	29 Dec 1933
7	Sock-A-Bye Baby	19 Jan 1934
8	Let's You and Him Fight	16 Feb 1934
9	The Man on the Flying Trapeze	16 Mar 1934
10	Can You Take It	27 Apr 1934

Popeye originated on 17 January 1929 as a newspaper comic strip, the brainchild of Elzie Crisler Segar (1894–1938). Animator Max Fleischer (1883–1972) acquired the rights and introduced the character alongside established cartoon star Betty Boop in his 1933 screen debut, with Popeye's voice provided by William Costello. The ever-popular cartoons continued until 1957, were revived as a TV series in 1978–83, and appeared in a final outing as a spoof TV series, *Popeye and Son* (1987–88). The live-action *Popeye* (1980), directed by Robert Altman, starred Robin Williams in the title role, one of his earliest screen performances.

Did you know?

The Hollywood Forever Cemetery grave of Mel Blanc, the voice of cartoon characters from Bugs Bunny to the Flintstones' Barney Rubble, is headed by the Looney Tunes sign-off, "That's All Folks".

Duck Tale

Disney's perennial character Donald Duck has appeared in cartoons, including the feature-length *DuckTales: The Movie – Treasure of the Lost Lamp* (1990), across eight decades.

THE 10 FIRST DONALD DUCK CARTOONS

	FILM	FIRST THEATRICAL RELEASE
1	The Wise Little Hen	9 Jun 1934
2	Orphan's Benefit	11 Aug 1934
3	The Dognapper	17 Nov 1934
4	The Band Concert	23 Feb 1935
5	Mickey's Service Station	16 Mar 1935
6	Mickey's Fire Brigade	3 Aug 1935
7	On Ice	28 Sep 1935
8	Mickey's Polo Team	4 Jan 1936
9	Orphans' Picnic	15 Feb 1936
10	Mickey's Grand Opera	7 Mar 1936

Donald Duck's voice preceded the character, when Walt Disney heard Clarence Nash (1904–85) reading "Mary Had a Little Lamb" in a comic voice. Nash went on to provide the voice for 50 years. Such was the character's fame that by 1943 Trevor Howard in *Brief Encounter* remarks "Thank heaven for Donald Duck", while the anti-Hitler Donald Duck film, *Der Fuehrer's Face* (1943), won an Oscar. Donald went on to star in over 150 cartoons, transferring successfully to television, as well as appearing in feature films including *Who Framed Roger Rabbit* (1988) and *Fantasia/2000* (2000).

© Disney Enterprises, Inc.

Runaway Success
Mel Gibson as Bret Maverick Jr. in *Maverick*, a big-screen film derived from a 1950s TV series starring James Garner – who appears in the film as Bret Maverick Sr.

TOP 10 COWBOY AND WESTERN FILMS

	FILM	YEAR
1	Dances With Wolves	1990
2	The Mask of Zorro	1998
3	Wild Wild West	1999
4	Maverick	1994
5	City Slickers	1991
6	Legends of the Fall	1994
7	Unforgiven	1992
8	Blazing Saddles	1974
9	Spirit: Stallion of the Cimarron	2002
10	Butch Cassidy and the Sundance Kid	1969

Westerns have a history that dates back to the birth of cinema: *The Great Train Robbery* (1903), which is credited as the first narrative film ever made, was also the first ever Western. Once one of Hollywood's most popular genres, they have been less prominent in recent years, although each of those in the Top 10 have yielded $100 million or more globally.

TOP 10 MARTIAL ARTS FILMS

	FILM	YEAR
1	Rush Hour 2	2001
2	Rush Hour	1998
3	Crouching Tiger, Hidden Dragon	2000
4	Teenage Mutant Ninja Turtles	1990
5	Mortal Kombat	1995
6	The Karate Kid, Part II	1986
7	Shanghai Noon	2000
8	The Karate Kid	1984
9	Teenage Mutant Ninja Turtles II: The Secret of the Ooze	1991
10	Romeo Must Die	2000

Japanese Director Akira Kurosawa's *Sugata Sanshiro*, aka *Judo Saga* (1943) is one of the earliest to feature martial arts. As well as films in which it is central to the theme, karate and other martial arts also play a part in many James Bond films, comic book derived *Blade* (1998) and *Blade II* (2002), Jackie Chan's action comedy *Tuxedo* (2002), and even such animated films as *Mulan* (1998).

Did you know?

Chinese martial arts exponent Kwan Tak-Hing appeared in the first kung fu film made in Hong Kong in 1949, and went on to play the same character, real-life martial arts master Wong Fei-Hung, in almost 100 films.

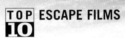

TOP 10 THRILLERS SELECTED BY THE AMERICAN FILM INSTITUTE*

	FILM	YEAR
1	Psycho	1960
2	Jaws	1975
3	The Exorcist	1973
4	North by Northwest	1959
5	Silence of the Lambs	1991
6	Alien	1979
7	The Birds	1963
8	The French Connection	1971
9	Rosemary's Baby	1968
10	Raiders of the Lost Ark	1981

* The Top of the Top 100 selected in 2000 by more than 1,500
leaders of the American movie community
Source: American Film Institute

TOP 10 RACE AND CHASE FILMS

	FILM	YEAR
1	Gone in 60 Seconds	2000
2	The Fast and the Furious	2001
3	Smokey and the Bandit	1977
4	Rat Race	2001
5	The Cannonball Run	1981
6	Smokey and the Bandit II	1980
7	It's a Mad, Mad, Mad Mad World	1963
8	Midnight Run	1988
9	Thelma and Louise	1991
10	Driven	2001

Car chases are commonplace in action films – those in *Bullitt*
(1968) and *The French Connection* (1971) are regarded as two of
the most exciting in cinema history – but films with entire plots
revolving around cross-country pursuits, car rallies, and illegal
street racing have also proved popular Hollywood vehicles.

TOP 10 ESCAPE FILMS

	FILM	YEAR
1	The Fugitive	1993
2	Face/Off	1997
3	Chicken Run *	2000
4	Con Air	1997
5	A Perfect World	1993
6	U.S. Marshals	1998
7	Stir Crazy	1980
8	O Brother, Where Art Thou?	2000
9	Tango & Cash	1989
10	Papillon	1973

* Animated

Thrillers featuring escapes from prisons, prison transport trains and
planes, and prisoner-of-war camps and the consequent pursuit of
prisoners are an enduring theme that has also given us such earlier
classics as *La Grande Illusion* (1937) and *The Great Escape* (1963)
– scenes from which are parodied in the animated *Chicken Run*.

On the Run

Cary Grant attempts to evade his pursuers in
Alfred Hitchcock's *North by Northwest*, identified
by the American Film Institute as one of the
greatest thrillers of all time.

TOP 10 MOUNTAINS AND MOUNTAINEERING FILMS

	FILM	YEAR
1	Cliffhanger	1993
2	Vertical Limit	2000
3	Seven Years in Tibet	1997
4	Everest	1998
5	Alive	1993
6	The Eiger Sanction	1975
7	K2	1991
8	Courage Mountain	1989
9	Gran Paradiso	2000
10	Five Days One Summer	1982

Mountain climbing has figured in films since German filmmaker
Arnold Fanck created the genre in the 1920s, directing such classics
as *White Hell of Pitz Palu* (1929), starring Leni Riefenstahl – who
herself went on to direct many notable mountain-based films.

TOP 10 JACKIE CHAN FILMS

	FILM	ROLE	YEAR
1	Rush Hour 2	Chief Inspector Lee	2001
2	Rush Hour	Detective Inspector Lee	1998
3	Shanghai Noon	Chon Wang	2000
4	Rumble in the Bronx	Ah Keung	1996
5	The Tuxedo	Jimmy Tong	2002
6	Shanghai Knights	Chon Wang	2003
7	Shuang long hui *	Ma Yau/Die Hard	1992
8	Jing cha gu shi IV: Jian dan ren wu	Jackie Chan Ka Kui	1996
9	Mr. Nice Guy	Jackie	1998
10	Cannonball Run II	Jackie	1984

* Named *Twin Dragons* in the English version; the roles played were John Ma/Boomer.
Jackie Chan appeared uncredited as "First Subaru driver" in *The Cannonball Run*
(1981); in its 1984 sequel, his part was at least named – as "Jackie".

TOP 10 LIVE-ACTION TALKING ANIMAL FILMS

	FILM	YEAR
1	101 Dalmatians	1996
2	Stuart Little	1999
3	Dr. Dolittle	1998
4	Babe	1995
5	Cats & Dogs	2001
6	102 Dalmatians	2000
7	Dr. Dolittle 2	2001
8	Stuart Little 2	1999
9	Snow Dogs	2002
10	Kangaroo Jack	2003

Anthropomorphic animals are a mainstay of animated films, but they also feature prominently in the realm of live action. Talking cats and dogs (and, with the two *Babe* films, pigs and other farmyard animals) predominate, while the *Dr. Dolittle* films present an entire menagerie of chatty creatures. Falling just outside the Top 10, *Paulie* (1998) is surprisingly one of the few films starring an animal that really does talk – a parrot.

TOP 10 CREEPY-CRAWLY FILMS

	FILM	YEAR	CREATURE(S)
1	A Bug's Life *	1998	Various
2	Antz *	1998	Ants
3	Arachnophobia	1990	Spiders
4	The Fly	1986	Housefly
5	Mimic	1997	Mutant insects
6	James and the Giant Peach †	1996	Various
7	Microcosmos #	1996	Insects
8	The Fly II	1989	Housefly
9	Kingdom of the Spiders	1977	Tarantulas
10	The Swarm	1978	Bees

* Animated
† Part-animated/part-live action
# Documentary
The creatures featured in these films range from the cute to the terrifying, many of them exploiting our widespread phobias relating to insects and spiders.

TOP 10 KILLER CREATURE FILMS*

	FILM	YEAR	ANIMAL(S)
1	Jaws	1975	Shark
2	Jaws 2	1978	Shark
3	Deep Blue Sea	1999	Sharks
4	Anaconda	1997	Snake
5	The Ghost and the Darkness	1996	Lions
6	Arachnophobia	1990	Spiders
7	Eight Legged Freaks	2002	Spiders
8	Lake Placid	1999	Alligator
9	Jaws 3-D	1983	Shark
10	Cujo	1983	Rabid dog

* Excluding dinosaurs and fantasy creatures such as dragons and werewolves

TOP 10 DOG FILMS

	FILM	YEAR
1	101 Dalmatians	1996
2	Scooby-Doo	2002
3	One Hundred and One Dalmatians *	1961
4	Cats & Dogs	2001
5	102 Dalmatians	2000
6	Snow Dogs	2002
7	Lady and the Tramp *	1955
8	Beethoven	1992
9	Oliver & Company	1988
10	Beethoven's 2nd	1993

* Animated

TOP 10 DINOSAUR FILMS

	FILM	YEAR
1	Jurassic Park	1993
2	The Lost World: Jurassic Park	1997
3	Godzilla	1998
4	Jurassic Park III	2001
5	Dinosaur *	2000
6	Fantasia *†	1940
7	T-Rex: Back to the Cretaceous	1998
8	The Flintstones in Viva Rock Vegas	2000
9	The Land Before Time *	1988
10	Super Mario Bros.	1993

* Animated; the others are live-action films with mechanical or computer-generated animation sequences
† Igor Stravinsky's "Rite of Spring" sequence
Since *Gertie the Dinosaur* (1914), the first cartoon manifestation of a cinematic fascination with dinosaurs, over 100 films featuring these creatures have been released. The first film in the *Jurassic Park* trilogy is the fourth highest-earning film of all time, with a global income in excess of $920 million, while its sequels have earned $615 million and $366 million respectively.

Mouse Clicks
Voiced by Michael J. Fox, *Stuart Little* and its sequel lead the Top 10 of films in which mice play prominent roles.

King Rules
Although it was made over 70 years ago, *King Kong* made a then record $90,000 on its opening weekend. Its frequent re-releases have earned enough to compete with many recent ape films.

TOP 10 APE FILMS*

	FILM	YEAR
1	Tarzan †	1999
2	Planet of the Apes	2001
3	Every Which Way But Loose	1978
4	Mighty Joe Young	1998
5	Any Which Way You Can	1980
6	King Kong	1933
7	King Kong	1976
8	Greystoke: The Legend of Tarzan, Lord of the Apes	1984
9	Planet of the Apes	1968
10	Gorillas in the Mist: The Story of Dian Fossey	1988

* Includes gorillas, chimpanzees, and orang-utans
† Animated; has earned over $400 million worldwide

TOP 10 MOUSE FILMS

	FILM	YEAR
1	Stuart Little	1999
2	Stuart Little 2	2002
3	Mouse Hunt	1997
4	An American Tail *	1986
5	The Rescuers Down Under *	1999
6	An American Tail: Fievel Goes West	1991
7	Adventures of the Great Mouse Detective *	1986
8	The Rescuers *	1977
9	The Secret of NIMH *	1982
10	Dumbo *	1941

* Animated

TOP 10 HIGHEST-EARNING JAMES BOND FILMS

	FILM	BOND ACTOR	YEAR	WORLDWIDE ($)
1	Die Another Day	Pierce Brosnan	2002	393,400,000
2	The World Is Not Enough	Pierce Brosnan	1999	354,800,000
3	GoldenEye	Pierce Brosnan	1995	353,300,000
4	Tomorrow Never Dies	Pierce Brosnan	1997	346,600,000
5	Moonraker	Roger Moore	1979	210,300,000
6	The Living Daylights	Timothy Dalton	1987	191,200,000
7	For Your Eyes Only	Roger Moore	1981	187,400,000
8	The Spy Who Loved Me	Roger Moore	1977	185,400,000
9	Octopussy	Roger Moore	1983	183,700,000
10	Licence to Kill	Timothy Dalton	1990	156,200,000

Ian Fleming wrote twelve James Bond novels, only two of which, *Moonraker* (1955) and *The Spy Who Loved Me* (1962), figure in this Top 10. After his death in 1964, *For Your Eyes Only*, *Octopussy*, *The Living Daylights*, and *GoldenEye* were developed by other writers from his short stories, while subsequent releases were written without reference to Fleming's writings. *Casino Royale* (book 1953, film 1967), featuring 56-year-old David Niven as the retired spy Sir James Bond, is an oddity in that it was presented as a comedy. This and *Never Say Never Again* (1983), effectively a remake of *Thunderball*, are not considered "official" Bond films, making the 2002 release *Die Another Day* the 20th in the canonical series.

Bond is Back

Chosen as the second James Bond film after President Kennedy nominated the book as one of his ten all-time favourites, *From Russia With Love* was the last film he ever saw. It was the first in which Desmond Llewelyn appeared as gadget expert Q, and the only one in which Bond author Ian Fleming makes a fleeting cameo appearance.

TOP 10 MOST VIOLENT JAMES BOND FILMS

	FILM	YEAR	KILLS
1	Moonraker	1979	208
2	Octopussy	1983	204
3	Dr. No	1962	196
4	GoldenEye	1995	156
5	The Spy Who Loved Me	1977	135
6	Diamonds are Forever	1971	44
7	You Only Live Twice	1967	35
8	Tomorrow Never Dies	1997	34
9	Thunderball	1965	28
10 =	From Russia With Love	1963	25
=	The World Is Not Enough	1999	25

Source: SCMS

World Class

James Bond (Pierce Brosnan) races downhill in the Chamonix, France, skiing sequence in *The World Is Not Enough*. The film took its title from the translation of Bond's family motto, *Orbis non sufficit*.

THE 10 FIRST BOND VILLAINS*

	BOND VILLAIN	ACTOR	FILM	YEAR
1	Dr. Julius No	Joseph Wiseman	Dr. No	1962
2	Ernst Stavro Blofeld	Eric Pohlmann †	From Russia With Love	1963
3	Auric Goldfinger	Gert Fröbe	Goldfinger	1964
4	Emilio Largo	Adolfo Celi	Thunderball	1965
5	Ernst Stavro Blofeld	Donald Pleasence	You Only Live Twice	1967
6	Ernst Stavro Blofeld	Telly Savalas	Majesty's Secret Serivce	1969
7	Ernst Stavro Blofeld	Charles Gray	Diamonds are Forever	1971
8	Kananga/Mr. Big	Yaphet Kotto	Live and Let Die	1973
9	Francisco Scaramanga	Christopher Lee	The Man With the Golden Gun	1974
10	Karl Stromberg	Kurt Jurgens	The Spy Who Loved Me	1977

* Main character only, excluding henchmen and women
† Uncredited voice only

Max von Sydow also appeared as arch-villain Ernst Stavro Blofeld in *Never Say Never Again* (1983), which is not considered part of the official James Bond series. Christopher Lee, memorable for his title role as *The Man With the Golden Gun*, was the cousin of James Bond creator Ian Fleming (Lee's stepfather Harcourt Rose was the brother of Ian Fleming's mother Evelyn St. Croix Rose).

THE 10 FIRST BOND GIRLS*

	BOND GIRL	ACTRESS	FILM	YEAR
1	Honey Ryder	Ursula Andress	Dr. No	1962
2	Tatiana Romanova	Daniela Bianchi	From Russia With Love	1963
3	Pussy Galore	Honor Blackman	Goldfinger	1964
4	Domino Derval	Claudine Auger	Thunderball	1965
5	Kissy Suzuki	Mie Hama	You Only Live Twice	1967
6	Tracy Draco	Diana Rigg	On Her Majesty's Secret Service	1969
7	Tiffany Case	Jill St. John	Diamonds are Forever	1971
8	Solitaire	Jane Seymour	Live and Let Die	1973
9	Mary Goodnight	Britt Ekland	The Man With the Golden Gun	1974
10	Major Anya Amasova	Barbara Bach	The Spy Who Loved Me	1977

* Principals only; minor roles omitted

Kim Basinger appeared as Domino in *Never Say Never Again* (1983), which is not included in the Bond franchise.

THE 10 FIRST BOND CARS*

	BOND CAR	FILM	YEAR
1	Aston Martin DB5	Goldfinger	1964
		Thunderball	1965
2	Aston Martin DBS †	On Her Majesty's Secret Service	1969
3	Lotus Esprit	The Spy Who Loved Me	1977
4	Lotus Esprit Turbo	For Your Eyes Only	1981
5	Aston Martin V8 Vantage	The Living Daylights	1987
6	Aston Martin DB5	GoldenEye	1995
7	BMW Z3	GoldenEye	1995
8	BMW 750iL	Tomorrow Never Dies	1997
9	BMW Z8	The World Is Not Enough	1999
10	Aston Martin Vanquish	Die Another Day	2002

*This list is of Q-modified cars only and excludes standard production vehicles driven by Bond, such as the Ford Mustang in *Diamonds are Forever* or the Citroen 2CV in *For Your Eyes Only*.
† No gadgets used in the film; the car also appears in the background in Q's workshop in *Diamonds are Forever*.

Did you know?

Although *Dr. No* was the first of the 20 Bond films, *Casino Royale* was screened eight years earlier, when CBS broadcast it on 21 October 1954 as a one-hour live TV play.

FILM	YEAR
1 Some Like It Hot	1959
2 Tootsie	1982
3 Dr. Strangelove, or How I Learned to Stop Worrying and Love the Bomb	1964
4 Annie Hall	1977
5 Duck Soup	1933
6 Blazing Saddles	1974
7 M*A*S*H	1970
8 It Happened One Night	1934
9 The Graduate	1967
10 Airplane!	1980

Source: American Film Institute

This list is the cream of the 500 titles nominated and 100 selected by a panel of 1,500 film experts for the AFI's "100 Years 100 Laughs" list, published on 13 June 2000.

FILM	YEAR
1 Forrest Gump	1994
2 Men in Black	1997
3 Home Alone	1990
4 Ghost	1990
5 Pretty Woman	1990
6 Ocean's Eleven	2001
7 Men in Black II	2002
8 Mrs. Doubtfire	1993
9 What Women Want	2001
10 Notting Hill	1999

* Excluding animated

Since the earliest days of Hollywood, comedy has consistently performed well at the box office: all those in the Top 10 have earned more than $350 million worldwide, while each of the first four has earned in excess of half a billion dollars globally.

FILM	YEAR
1 Ghost	1990
2 Pretty Woman	1990
3 What Women Want	2000
4 Notting Hill	1999
5 There's Something About Mary	1998
6 My Big Fat Greek Wedding	2002
7 As Good As It Gets	1998
8 Runaway Bride	1999
9 Look Who's Talking	1989
10 Meet the Parents	2000

Almost all the Top 10 films in this eternally popular genre have each earned more than $300 at the world box office.

TOP 10 NATIONAL LAMPOON FILMS

FILM	YEAR
1 National Lampoon's Animal House	1978
2 National Lampoon's Christmas Vacation	1989
3 National Lampoon's Vacation	1983
4 National Lampoon's European Vacation	1985
5 National Lampoon's Vegas Vacation	1997
6 National Lampoon's Loaded Weapon 1	1993
7 National Lampoon's Van Wilder	2002
8 National Lampoon's Class Reunion	1982
9 National Lampoon's Senior Trip	1995
10 National Lampoon's The Joy of Sex	1984

The magazine *National Lampoon*, a spin-off from America's oldest humour publication, *Harvard Lampoon* (founded 1876), was established in 1969. With US box office income of more than $140 million, *Animal House*, the first *National Lampoon* film, remains the franchise's highest earner. It was written by *National Lampoon* founder editor Douglas Kennedy, who also appears in the film.

Comedy Classic

Clark Gable and Claudette Colbert in Frank Capra's *It Happened One Night*. The film won "Best Picture", "Best Director", "Best Actor", and "Best Actress" Oscars, and was recognized by the American Film Institute as one of the 10 funniest of all time.

	FILM	GENRES SPOOFED	YEAR
1	Austin Powers: the Spy Who Shagged Me	James Bond	1999
2	Austin Powers in Goldmember	James Bond	2002
3	Scary Movie	Various	2000
4	Hot Shots!	Top Gun	1991
5	Scream	Slasher horror	1996
6	Scream 2	Slasher horror	1997
7	Scream 3	Slasher horror	2000
8	Scary Movie 2	Various	2001
9	Last Action Hero	Action films	1993
10	Blazing Saddles	Westerns	1974

THE 10 FIRST "CARRY ON" FILMS

	FILM	YEAR
1	Carry On Sergeant	1958
2	Carry On Nurse	1959
3	Carry On Teacher	1959
4	Carry On Constable	1960
5	Carry On Regardless	1960
6	Carry On Cruising	1962
7	Carry On Cabby	1963
8	Carry On Jack	1964
9	Carry On Spying	1964
10	Carry On Cleo	1964

This original series of hugely successful British comedy films spanned 20 years. The first 10 were followed by 19 more films, each starting with the title, *Carry on …* of which the last, *Carry On Emanuelle*, was released in 1978. *Carry on Columbus* (1992) was an attempt to revive the series.

Groovy, Baby

Mike Myers starred in both title roles in sixties spy spoof *Austin Powers in Goldmember*, the top gross-out comedy of the 21st century.

TOP 10 CRIME COMEDY FILMS

	FILM	YEAR
1	Ocean's Eleven	2001
2	Rush Hour 2	2001
3	Lethal Weapon 3	1993
4	Beverly Hills Cop	1984
5	Beverly Hills Cop II	1987
6	Lethal Weapon 4	1998
7	Rush Hour	1998
8	Sister Act	1992
9	Lethal Weapon 2	1989
10	Miss Congeniality	2000

Crime capers, mafia movies, and police actions films with a
comedy component make up this Top 10 of films that have earned

TOP 10 HORROR SPOOF FILMS

	FILM	YEAR
1	Scary Movie	2000
2	Scream	1996
3	Scream 2	1997
4	Scream 3	2000
5	Scary Movie 2	2001
6	Young Frankenstein	1974
7	Love at First Bite	1979
8	An American Werewolf in London	1981
9	An American Werewolf in Paris	1997
10	Fright Night	1985

TOP 10 GROSS-OUT COMEDY FILMS*

	FILM	YEAR
1	There's Something About Mary	1998
2	Austin Powers: the Spy who Shagged Me	1999
3	Austin Powers in Goldmember	2002
4	Scary Movie	2000
5	American Pie 2	2001
6	Dumb & Dumber	1994
7	Big Daddy	1999
8	American Pie	1999
9	The Waterboy	1998
10	Nutty Professor II: The Klumps	2000

* "Gross-out" films represent a new wave of films featuring outrageous comedy for teens and adults, generally revolving round disgusting behaviour and often involving bodily functions. Their popularity is exemplified by their earning power: all those in the list have grossed(!) more than $100 million at the worldwide box office, with *There's Something About Mary* more than $360 million. Director Bobby Farrelly has made something of a speciality of this genre: Nos. 1, 4, and 9 in this list were his work.

Against the Law
US Marshall Samuel Gerard (Tommy Lee Jones), shown here, in a dramatic encounter with Dr. Richard Kimble (Harrison Ford) in director Andrew Davis' *The Fugitive*, the most successful of all cop blockbusters.

TOP 10 COP FILMS

	FILM	YEAR
1	The Fugitive	1993
2	Die Hard: With a Vengeance	1995
3	Basic Instinct	1992
4	Se7en	1995
5	Rush Hour 2	2002
6	Lethal Weapon 3	1993
7	Beverly Hills Cop	1984
8	Beverly Hills Cop II	1987
9	Lethal Weapon 4	1998
10	Speed	1994

Films in which a central character is a policeman have never been among the most successful of all time. However, all those within this list have made more than $280 million apiece worldwide. They range from films with a comic slant, such as the *Beverly Hills Cop* films, to darker thrillers, such as *Basic Instinct* and *Se7en*. Films with FBI and CIA agents have been excluded from the reckoning, hence eliminating blockbusters such as *Mission: Impossible*.

TOP 10 PIRATE FILMS

	FILM	YEAR
1	Hook	1991
2	Six Days Seven Nights	1998
3	Treasure Planet	2002
4	Peter Pan *	1953
5	Peter Pan: Return to Never Land *	2002
6	The Goonies	1985
7	Muppet Treasure Island	1996
8	Swiss Family Robinson	1960
9	The Princess Bride	1987
10	The Island	1980

* Animated

While *Treasure Planet* appears here on the basis of its earnings, it was actually a huge flop. Roman Polanski's *Pirates* (1986), made with a budget $40,000,000 recouped less than 5 per cent at the US box office, while *Cutthroat Island* (1995), with Geena Davis as a female pirate, earned barely 10 per cent of its $92,000,000 budget.

TOP 10 COURTROOM DRAMA AND LAWYER FILMS

	FILM	YEAR
1	Erin Brockovich	2000
2	A Few Good Men	1992
3	Presumed Innocent	1990
4	Philadelphia	1993
5	Sleepers	1996
6	The Devil's Advocate	1997
7	A Time to Kill	1996
8	Legally Blonde	2001
9	The Client	1994
10	Kramer vs. Kramer	1979

The courtroom closely resembles a theatre – as the "Razzle Dazzle" scene in the musical *Chicago* portrays – and is thus a natural focus for many successful films (it is also worth noting that a courtroom set represents a relatively inexpensive component of a production budget). The court is a major element of those in the Top 10, all of which have earned $100 million-plus worldwide.

TOP 10 — MAFIA FILMS

	FILM	YEAR
1	The Firm	1993
2	The Untouchables	1987
3	Analyze This	1999
4	Road to Perdition	2002
5	The Godfather, Part III	1990
6	The Godfather	1972
7	Donnie Brasco	1997
8	The Client	1994
9	The Godfather, Part II	1974
10	The Whole Nine Yards	2000

Although *The Godfather* trilogy represents the apogee of the Mafia movie, its history dates back to the silent era. In recent years, comedies in which organized crime and Mafia stereotypes are satirized have been especially popular, as exemplified by several entries in this Top 10 (all of which have earned at least $100 million worldwide) and by others falling just outside it, such as *Kangaroo Jack* (2003) and *Mickey Blue Eyes* (1999).

TOP 10 — PRISON FILMS

	FILM	YEAR
1	The Green Mile	1999
2	Con Air	1997
3	The Man in the Iron Mask	1998
4	Stir Crazy	1980
5	Dead Man Walking	1995
6	Out of Sight	1998
7	Life	1999
8	Tango & Cash	1989
9	Just Cause	1995
10	The Shawshank Redemption	1994

This Top 10 includes films where prisons and prisoners are central to the theme, but excludes prisoner-of-war films and those in which ex-cons feature or the prison scenes are incidental to but do not comprise the entire plot, such as *Ocean's Eleven* (2001) and *Chicago* (2002).

TOP 10 — SPY AND SECRET AGENT FILMS

	FILM	YEAR
1	Mission: Impossible 2	2000
2	Mission: Impossible	1996
3	Die Another Day	2002
4	True Lies	1994
5	The World Is Not Enough	1999
6	GoldenEye	1995
7	Tomorrow Never Dies	1997
8	Austin Powers: The Spy Who Shagged Me	1999
9	Austin Powers in Goldmember	2002
10	Charlie's Angels	2000

Spies, secret agents, and espionage have proved popular themes for films since the 1930s, and gained further appeal during the Cold War era. All those in the Top 10 have earned more than $250 million worldwide, with the *James Bond* series achieving four entries. They, in turn, have spawned spoofs and rivals in the form of the *Austin Powers* films and *xXx* (2002).

Did you know?

The real Erin Brockovich appears in the hugely successful film that bears her name, in a cameo as a waitress called Julia, while the real Julia (Roberts) appears as Erin Brockovich.

You Can Call Me Al

Robert De Niro threw himself into his role as Mafia boss Al Capone in *The Untouchables* by wearing clothes made by Capone's own tailor and gaining weight by gorging on Italian food.

TOP 10 DISASTER FILMS

	FILM	YEAR	DISASTER
1	Titanic	1997	Shipwreck
2	Armageddon	1998	Asteroid impact
3	Twister	1996	Tornado
4	Die Hard: With a Vengeance	1995	Terrorist bomber
5	Apollo 13	1995	Space capsule explosion
6	Deep Impact	1998	Comet impact
7	The Perfect Storm	2000	Storm at sea
8	Die Hard 2: Die Harder	1990	Terrorists at airport
9	Outbreak	1995	Epidemic
10	Dante's Peak	1997	Volcano

Excluding science-fiction subjects (alien attacks, rampaging dinosaurs, and other fantasy themes), disasters involving blazing buildings, natural disasters such as volcanoes, earthquakes, tidal waves, train and air crashes, sinking ships, and terrorist attacks, have long been a staple of Hollywood films, while latterly asteroid impact, tornadoes, exploding space capsules, and killer viruses have been added to the genre. The list comprises films that have earned an average of almost $500 million worldwide.

TOP 10 NATURAL DISASTER FILMS

	FILM	YEAR	DISASTER
1	Armageddon	1998	Asteroid impact
2	Twister	1996	Tornado
3	Deep Impact	1998	Comet impact
4	The Perfect Storm	2000	Storm at sea
5	Outbreak	1995	Epidemic
6	Dante's Peak	1997	Volcano
7	Twelve Monkeys	1995	Virus
8	Volcano	1997	Volcano
9	Earthquake	1974	Earthquake
10	Joe Versus the Volcano	1990	Volcano

This Top 10 list concentrates on natural disaster films based on real scientific possibilities; "science-fiction" disaster films involving mutant creatures and the like have been excluded. Nonetheless, a number of the most commercially successful examples of the natural disaster genre – which includes some of the highest-earning films of all time – contain elements of science fiction (such as time travel in *Twelve Monkeys*).

TOP 10 SHIPWRECK AND MARINE DISASTER FILMS

	FILM/CIRCUMSTANCES	YEAR
1	Titanic: The true story of the Titanic hitting an iceberg and sinking on its maiden voyage, plus a love story sub-plot	1997
2	The Perfect Storm: The fishing vessel Andrea Gail founders in a storm	2000
3	Speed 2: Cruise Control: The Seaborn Legend cruise liner is hijacked, eventually ploughing into a coastal resort	1997
4	The Poseidon Adventure: The Poseidon liner turns turtle and survivors have to escape before it sinks	1972
5	Das Boot (The Boat): Life aboard World War II German submarine U-96, finally sunk by aircraft attack	1981
6	K-19: The Widowmaker: A Soviet nuclear submarine suffers a reactor failure	2002
7	Swiss Family Robinson: A family is shipwrecked on a desert island, surviving Robinson Crusoe-style	1960
8	The Unsinkable Molly Brown: A musical based on the real-life story of Titanic survivor Molly Brown	1964
9	Gray Lady Down: Nuclear submarine USS Neptune is rammed by a cargo ship	1978
10	Raise the Titanic: An attempt is made to salvage the Titanic to recover a rare mineral that it was carrying	1980

No fewer than three of the films listed here, including the highest-earner of all time, re-tell the story of the sinking in 1912 of the *Titanic*. To these may be added several outside the Top 10, including, most remarkably, a German film about the disaster, *In Nacht und Eis* (*In Night and Ice*, 1912), which was released within months of the sinking of the liner. Believed lost, it resurfaced following the publicity generated by the 1997 film. Another German account, *Titanic* (1953), made during World War II as a pro-German propaganda film, was partly shot on board the liner *Cap Arcona*, which was itself sunk in 1945 killing some 5,000 – far more than the 1,517 who were lost in the *Titanic* disaster itself. This was followed by the US-made *Titanic* (1953) and the British *A Night to Remember* (1958).

TOP 10 AIR CRASH FILMS

	FILM/CIRCUMSTANCES	YEAR
1	Cast Away: A FedEx plane crashes into the sea off a desert island, stranding sole survivor Chuck Noland (Tom Hanks)	2000
2	Jurassic Park III: A plane crashes on dinosaur island	2001
3	Die Hard 2: Die Harder Terrorists cause an airliner to crash at Washington Dulles Airport	1990
4	Broken Arrow: A plane is deliberately crashed in a desert	1996
5	Final Destination: A boy has premonitions of an airliner crash	2000
6	U.S. Marshals: A convict plane crashes into a lake	1998
7	Random Hearts: A man and a woman's respective partners are killed in a plane crash	1999
8	La Bamba: Bio-pic re-enactment of the plane crash that killed singer Ritchie Valens	1987
9	Alive: Based on a true incident, when the Uruguayan rugby team's plane crashed in the Andes and the survivors resorted to cannibalism	1993
10	Bounce: A passenger switches tickets with another, whose plane crashes, killing him	2000

Dramatic plane crashes have occurred on film for more than 70 years, with these outstanding as the 10 highest-earning films in which an air crash is pivotal, rather than incidental, to the plot. The ultimate crashing of hijacked aircraft provides the denouement, rather than the principal theme, of several action films, including *Con Air* and *Air Force One*, both of which were released in 1997. True air disasters have occasionally been re-enacted as made-for-TV films, but have only rarely been featured on the big screen. Other than the two that appear in the Top 10, *The Hindenburg* (1975), which re-tells the story of the catastrophic 6 May 1937 explosion of the giant Zeppelin airship at Lakehurst, New Jersey, USA, with the loss of 36 lives, is the only notable exception.

TOP 10 FILMS INVOLVING TERRORIST ATTACKS

	FILM	MODUS OPERANDI	YEAR
1	Mission: Impossible 2 *	Deadly virus	2000
2	True Lies *	Nuclear weapon	1994
3	Die Hard: With a Vengeance	City bomber	1995
4	The Rock *	Nerve gas	1996
5	Air Force One	US President's plane seized	1997
6	Die Hard 2: Die Harder	Airport seized	1990
7	Con Air	Aircraft seized	1997
8	Patriot Games	Assasination plot	1992
9	The Sum of All Fears *	Nuclear weapon at Super Bowl	2002
10	The Jackal *	Assasination of US President's wife	1997

* The intended disaster is averted in these films

Terrorism has been brought to the fore since the events of 11 September 2001, but terrorist activities have been a theme of films for at least 40 years, with such releases as *Cry Terror!* (1958), the forerunners of a wave of films of the 1970s, when the Cold War and nuclear threats were at their height. Each of the films in this Top 10 has earned more than $150 million worldwide.

Never Say Die

John McClane (Bruce Willis) combats terrorist bomber Peter Grüber (Jeremy Irons) in the third outing for the *Die Hard* franchise, *Die Hard: With a Vengeance*.

TOP 10 FILMS FEATURING HISTORICAL LEADERS AND RULERS

	FILM	YEAR	SUBJECT
1	The Patriot	2000	Col. Benjamin Martin
2	Braveheart	1995	William Wallace
3	Anna and the King	1999	King Mongku
4	The Ten Commandments	1956	Moses
5	The Madness of King George	1994	King George III
6	The Messenger: The Story of Joan of Arc	1999	Joan of Arc
7	Gandhi	1982	Mahatma Gandhi
8	The Last Emperor	1987	Emperor Pu Yi
9	Lawrence of Arabia	1962	T. E. Lawrence
10	Spartacus	1960	Spartacus

The central characters in all these films are real military leaders and national rulers – fictitious leaders, such as Robin Hood and *Gladiator* hero Maximus Decimus Meridus are thus excluded.

Commanding Heights

Moses (Charlton Heston) lays down the law in *The Ten Commandments*, the highest-earning live action film of the 1950s. In 1923, director Cecil B. DeMille had made a silent version with the same title.

Did you know?

In *The Adventures of Robin Hood* (1938), Maid Marian (Olivia de Havilland) rides a horse called Golden Cloud. It was later bought by cowboy actor Roy Rogers, who renamed it Trigger, starring alongside it in all his films.

TOP 10 SWASHBUCKLER FILMS

	FILM	YEAR
1	Robin Hood, Prince of Thieves	1991
2	The Mask of Zorro	1998
3	The Man in the Iron Mask	1998
4	The Count of Monte Cristo	2002
5	The Three Musketeers	1993
6	Rob Roy	1995
7	Robin Hood: Men in Tights	1993
8	Robin Hood *	1973
9	The Three Musketeers	1974
10	The Four Musketeers: Milady's Revenge	1974

* Animated

Established in the 1920s and developed over the next two decades by such stars as Douglas Fairbanks and Errol Flynn, the swashbuckler film, a genre dominated by *Robin Hood* and *The Three Musketeers*, revolves around the exploits of heroes skilled in swordfighting. This is a strictly European list, hence excluding the Oriental equivalent exemplified by films such as *Crouching Tiger, Hidden Dragon* (2000).

TOP 10 FILMS INVOLVING TERRORIST ATTACKS

	FILM	MODUS OPERANDI	YEAR
1	Mission: Impossible 2 *	Deadly virus	2000
2	True Lies *	Nuclear weapon	1994
3	Die Hard: With a Vengeance	City bomber	1995
4	The Rock *	Nerve gas	1996
5	Air Force One	US President's plane seized	1997
6	Die Hard 2: Die Harder	Airport seized	1990
7	Con Air	Aircraft seized	1997
8	Patriot Games	Assasination plot	1992
9	The Sum of All Fears *	Nuclear weapon at Super Bowl	2002
10	The Jackal *	Assasination of US President's wife	1997

* The intended disaster is averted in these films

Terrorism has been brought to the fore since the events of 11 September 2001, but terrorist activities have been a theme of films for at least 40 years, with such releases as *Cry Terror!* (1958), the forerunners of a wave of films of the 1970s, when the Cold War and nuclear threats were at their height. Each of the films in this Top 10 has earned more than $150 million worldwide.

Never Say Die

John McClane (Bruce Willis) combats terrorist bomber Peter Grüber (Jeremy Irons) in the third outing for the *Die Hard* franchise, *Die Hard: With a Vengeance*.

TOP 10 DOCUMENTARIES*

	FILM	SUBJECT	YEAR
1	The Dream is Alive	Space shuttle	1985
2	Mysteries of Egypt	Archaeology	1998
3	To Fly	History of flying	1976
4	Grand Canyon: The Hidden Secrets	Exploration	1984
5	Everest	Mountaineering expedition	1998
6	Blue Planet	The Earth seen from space	1990
7	Antarctica	Exploration	1991
8	Into the Deep	Underwater exploration	1994
9	Space Station	Space exploration	2002
10	In Search of Noah's Ark	Archaeology	1977

* Including history, adventure, exploration, and nature; excluding biography, performance, and sport

TOP 10 SPORT DOCUMENTARIES

	FILM	SUBJECT	YEAR
1	Extreme	Extreme sports	1999
2	To the Limit	Extreme sports	1989
3	Michael Jordan to the Max	Basketball	2000
4	Endless Summer	Surfing	1966
5	Dirt	Motorcycle racing	1979
6	Hoop Dreams	Basketball	1994
7	ESPN's Ultimate X	Extreme sports	2002
8	Fifty	Winter sports	1999
9	Ride	Snowboarding	2000
10	When We Were Kings	Boxing (Muhammad Ali and George Foreman)	1996

Remarkably, sport documentaries have been made since 1899, when the Sigmund Lubin and Edison companies made films re-enacting boxing matches between the celebrated fighters of the day.

Did you know?

One of the earliest colour documentaries was *The Durbar at Delhi*, a 2-hour 6-minute film of the Indian celebrations marking the coronation of King George V. It was made in the primitive Kinemacolor process and released in 1912.

On Top of the World

Everest is one of the highest-earning IMAX film of all time, with international earnings in excess of $100 million. It is a documentary of a 1996 expedition, and features Jamling Tenzing Norgay, the son of Tenzing Norgay, the "Sherpa Tenzing", celebrated in 1953 as one of the first two people ever to climb the world's tallest mountain.

TOP 10 — BIOGRAPHY DOCUMENTARIES*

	FILM/SUBJECT	YEAR
1	In Search of Historic Jesus	1980
2	Michael Jordan to the Max	2000
3	Imagine: John Lennon	1988
4	Crumb (on cartoonist Robert Crumb)	1994
5	Unzipped (on fashion designer Isaac Mizrahi)	1995
6	The Endurance (on Ernest Shackleton)	2000
7	Mark Twain's America in 3D	1998
8	A Brief History of Time (on Stephen Hawking)	1992
9	Blue (on filmmaker Derek Jarman)	1993
10	Thirty Two Short Films About Glenn Gould (on pianist Glenn Gould)	1993

* Excluding sport and performance

TOP 10 — MOCKUMENTARIES*

	FILM	YEAR
1	To Die For	1995
2	Best in Show	2000
3	Drop Dead Gorgeous	1999
4	Husbands and Wives	1992
5	Zelig	1983
6	A Mighty Wind	2003
7	Sweet and Lowdown	1999
8	Bob Roberts	1992
9	This Is Spinal Tap	1984
10	Waiting for Guffman	1997

* Spoof documentaries

Three Hours of Peace and Music
Some 193,200 m (120 miles) of film of the three-day Woodstock Festival in 1969 were edited down to three hours, winning *Woodstock* the Oscar for "Best Documentary".

TOP 10 — IMAX FILMS

	FILM	YEAR
1	The Dream Is Alive *	1985
2	Mysteries of Egypt *	1998
3	Fantasia 2000	2000
4	To Fly *	1976
5	Grand Canyon: The Hidden Secrets *	1984
6	Everest *	1998
7	T-Rex: Back to the Cretaceous	1998
8	Blue Planet *	1990
9	Into the Deep *	1994
10	Antarctica *	1991

* Documentary subject
The IMAX® ("Image Maximum") process was developed in Canada by William C. Shaw and P.R.W. Jones and first demonstrated in 1970. Its use of 70-mm film projected on to a large curved screen is ideally suited to documentary subjects such as space travel and portrayals of panoramic landcapes.

TOP 10 — LIVE PERFORMANCE DOCUMENTARIES

	FILM	SUBJECT	YEAR
1	Eddie Murphy Raw	Comedy	1987
2	The Original Kings of Comedy	Comedy	2000
3	Richard Pryor Live on the Sunset Strip	Comedy	1982
4	Woodstock	Rock festival	1970
5	Cirque du Soleil – Journey of Man	Stage show	2000
6	Martin Lawrence Live: Runteldat	Comedy	2002
7	Buena Vista Social Club	Cuban musicians	1999
8	Madonna: Truth or Dare	Concert tour	1991
9	Richard Pryor Here and Now	Comedy	1983
10	Richard Pryor Live in Concert	Comedy	1979

TOP 10 FILMS FEATURING HISTORICAL LEADERS AND RULERS

	FILM	YEAR	SUBJECT
1	The Patriot	2000	Col. Benjamin Martin
2	Braveheart	1995	William Wallace
3	Anna and the King	1999	King Mongku
4	The Ten Commandments	1956	Moses
5	The Madness of King George	1994	King George III
6	The Messenger: The Story of Joan of Arc	1999	Joan of Arc
7	Gandhi	1982	Mahatma Gandhi
8	The Last Emperor	1987	Emperor Pu Yi
9	Lawrence of Arabia	1962	T. E. Lawrence
10	Spartacus	1960	Spartacus

The central characters in all these films are real military leaders and national rulers – fictitious leaders, such as Robin Hood and *Gladiator* hero Maximus Decimus Meridus are thus excluded.

Commanding Heights

Moses (Charlton Heston) lays down the law in *The Ten Commandments*, the highest-earning live action film of the 1950s. In 1923, director Cecil B. DeMille had made a silent version with the same title.

Did you know?

In *The Adventures of Robin Hood* (1938), Maid Marian (Olivia de Havilland) rides a horse called Golden Cloud. It was later bought by cowboy actor Roy Rogers, who renamed it Trigger, starring alongside it in all his films.

TOP 10 SWASHBUCKLER FILMS

	FILM	YEAR
1	Robin Hood, Prince of Thieves	1991
2	The Mask of Zorro	1998
3	The Man in the Iron Mask	1998
4	The Count of Monte Cristo	2002
5	The Three Musketeers	1993
6	Rob Roy	1995
7	Robin Hood: Men in Tights	1993
8	Robin Hood *	1973
9	The Three Musketeers	1974
10	The Four Musketeers: Milady's Revenge	1974

* Animated

Established in the 1920s and developed over the next two decades by such stars as Douglas Fairbanks and Errol Flynn, the swash-buckler film, a genre dominated by *Robin Hood* and *The Three Musketeers*, revolves around the exploits of heroes skilled in swordfighting. This is a strictly European list, hence excluding the Oriental equivalent exemplified by films such as *Crouching Tiger, Hidden Dragon* (2000).

TOP 10 BIBLICAL HERO FILMS*

	FILM	YEAR	SUBJECT
1	The Prince of Egypt †	1998	Moses
2	The Ten Commandments	1956	Moses, et al.
3	The Bible … In the Beginning	1966	Noah, et al.
4	History of the World Part I #	1981	Moses
5	Samson and Delilah	1949	Samson
6	Jonah: A Veggie Tales Movie †	2002	Jonah
7	Solomon and Sheba	1959	Solomon
8	David and Bathsheba	1951	King David
9	The Ten Commandments	1923	Moses, et al.
10	King David	1985	King David

* Based on the Old Testament
† Animated
# One segment

TOP 10 KING ARTHUR FILMS

	FILM	YEAR	ARTHUR ACTOR
1	First Knight	1991	Sean Connery
2	Dragonheart	1996	John Gielgud *
3	Quest for Camelot †	1998	Pierce Brosnan *
4	Excalibur	1981	Nigel Terry
5	Camelot	1967	Richard Harris
6	The Sword in the Stone †	1963	Richard & Robert Reitherman *
7	A Kid in King Arthur's Court	1995	Joss Ackland
8	Monty Python and the Holy Grail	1975	Graham Chapman
9	Knights of the Round Table	1953	Mel Ferrer
10	A Connecticut Yankee in King Arthur's Court	1949	Cedric Hardwicke

* Voice only
† Animated

Caped Crusader

Michael Keaton takes the title role of *Batman*, the first and most successful of four films featuring the superhero. He reprised his part in *Batman Returns*, but was replaced respectively by Val Kilmer and George Clooney in the sequels.

TOP 10 SUPERHERO FILMS

	FILM	YEAR
1	Spider-Man	2002
2	Batman	1989
3	Batman Forever	1995
4	The Mask	1994
5	Superman	1978
6	X-Men	2000
7	Batman Returns	1992
8	Batman & Robin	1997
9	Teenage Mutant Ninja Turtles	1990
10	Daredevil	2003

* Animated
Superman makes a single showing in this Top 10, since it is in the unusual situation where the first film made a large amount (in excess of $300 million) at the world box office, while each of its three sequels made progressively less.

Sob Story
Ryan O'Neal and Ali McGraw co-starred in *Love Story*, the top-earning film of 1970. Before its release, Erich Segal turned his script into one of the bestselling novels of all time.

This Top 10 is derived from the American Film Institute's 2002 poll of "100 Years ... 100 Passions – America's Greatest Love Stories".

* Animated

Plenty of films, *Titanic* (1997) and *Pearl Harbor* (2001) among them, contain a romantic element alongside a dramatic theme, but these films are blockbusters in which the romantic theme is the dominant one.

These are all films where a wedding or weddings are central, rather than incidental, to the plot.

TOP 10 BABY FILMS

	FILM	YEAR
1	Look Who's Talking	1989
2	Three Men and a Baby	1993
3	The Rugrats Movie *	1982
4	Nine Months	1999
5	The Hand That Rocks the Cradle	2001
6	Rugrats in Paris: The Movie *	1990
7	Junior	1993
8	Look Who's Talking Too	1994
9	Fools Rush In	1985
10	Where the Heart Is	2002

* Animated

These are the most successful films in which pregnancy or babies are pivotal to the plot. There are many other high-earning films that focus on toddlers and older children, among them *3 Men and a Little Lady* (1990) and *Honey, I Blew Up the Kid* (1992).

TOP 10 DIVORCE AND MARITAL BREAKDOWN FILMS

	FILM	YEAR
1	Mrs. Doubtfire	1993
2	The First Wives Club	1996
3	Kramer vs. Kramer	1979
4	The War of the Roses	1989
5	Hope Floats	1998
6	The Royal Tenenbaums	2001
7	Best Friends	1982
8	Nothing in Common	1986
9	Far From Heaven	2002
10	Heartburn	1986

After Hollywood's focus on idealized nuclear families in the 1950s, the themes of marital drama, separation, divorce, and battles over children came to the fore in the 1960s along with the rise in divorce rates.

Tug-of-love

Dustin Hoffman and Justin Henry in "Best Picture" Oscar-winning *Kramer vs. Kramer*. The film's central themes of divorce and child custody touched a chord with audiences, earning the film more than $100 million in the US alone.

Did you know?

My Big Fat Greek Wedding has broken several box office records, in 2002 overtaking *The Blair Witch Project* to become the highest-earning independent film ever, and passing *Dances With Wolves* as the highest-grossing film never to reach No. 1 in the US.

MONSTER & HORROR

THE LON CHANEY
10 HORROR FILMS

	FILM	US RELEASE
1	The Penalty	14 Nov 1920
2	The Blind Bargain	3 Dec 1922
3	While Paris Sleeps	21 Jan 1923
4	The Hunchback of Notre Dame	2 Sep 1923
5	The Monster	16 Mar 1925
6	The Unholy Three	30 May 1925
7	The Phantom of the Opera	15 Nov 1925
8	The Unknown	13 Jun 1927
9	London After Midnight	17 Dec 1927
10	The Unholy Three	12 Jul 1930

Although American character actor Lon (Alonso) Chaney (1883–1930) is best known for his repertoire of monster roles, he actually made only 10 horror films, all of them in the last decade of his life.

Fright Night at the Opera

Based on Gaston Leroux's novel, horror masterpiece *The Phantom of the Opera* (1925) starred Lon Chaney in the iconic title role. He also personally directed the masked ball scene, shown here.

TOP GHOST FILMS
10

	FILM	YEAR
1	The Sixth Sense	1999
2	Ghost	1990
3	Ghostbusters	1984
4	Casper *	1995
5	What Lies Beneath	2000
6	Ghostbusters II	1989
7	Sleepy Hollow	1999
8	The Haunting	1999
9	The Others	2001
10	Scary Movie 2	2001

* Part-animated/part-live action

TOP DRAGON FILMS
10

	FILM	YEAR
1	Shrek *	1999
2	Mulan *	1990
3	Dragonheart	1984
4	Reign of Fire	1995
5	Dungeons & Dragons	2000
6	Quest for Camelot	1989
7	The NeverEnding Story	1999
8	Dragonslayer	1999
9	The Pagemaster	2001
10	The Wonderful World of the Brothers Grimm	2001

* Animated

TOP 10 FRIDAY THE 13TH FILMS

	FILM	YEAR
1	Friday the 13th	1980
2	Friday the 13th Part III: 3D	1982
3	Friday the 13th Part IV: The Final Chapter	1984
4	Friday the 13th Part V: A New Beginning	1985
5	Friday the 13th Part II	1981
6	Friday the 13th Part VI: Jason Lives	1986
7	Friday the 13th Part VII: The New Blood	1988
8	Jason Goes to Hell: The Final Friday	1993
9	Friday the 13th Part VIII: Jason Takes Manhattan	1989
10	Jason X	2002

The first film in the 22-year *Friday the 13th* horror franchise was the most successful, but its sequels have all earned respectable income at the world box office. The series continues with the release of *Friday the 13th Part XI* – appropriately scheduled for release on Friday 13th June 2003.

Dressed to Kill

Hooded killer Jason Voorhees returns to wreak vengeance at a summer camp in the first sequel in the *Friday the 13th* saga.

TOP 10 VAMPIRE FILMS

	FILM	YEAR
1	Interview with the Vampire: The Vampire Chronicles	1994
2	Bram Stoker's Dracula	1992
3	Blade II	2002
4	Blade	1998
5	From Dusk Till Dawn	1996
6	Love at First Bite	1979
7	Wes Craven Presents Dracula 2000	2000
8	Queen of the Damned	2002
9	The Lost Boys	1987
10	John Carpenter's Vampire$	1998

Of the more than 400 vampire films made, the German film *Nächte des Grauens* (1916) was the first, *The Great London Mystery* (1920) the first in English, and the Hungarian film *Drakula halála* (1921) the first adaptation of Bram Stoker's *Dracula*.

TOP 10 HORROR FILMS

	TITLE	YEAR
1	Jurassic Park	1993
2	The Sixth Sense	1999
3	The Lost World: Jurassic Park	1997
4	Jaws	1975
5	The Mummy Returns	2001
6	The Mummy	1999
7	Signs	2002
8	Godzilla	1998
9	Jurassic Park III	2001
10	Hannibal	2001

This list encompasses supernatural and science-fiction horror and monster creatures such as dinosaurs and oversized sharks. It has long been a successful genre: each of the films listed has earned $350 million or more at the world box office.

TOP 10 WEREWOLF FILMS

	FILM	YEAR
1	Wolf	1999
2	Teen Wolf	1990
3	An American Werewolf in London	2001
4	An American Werewolf in Paris	2001
5	The Howling	2000
6	Silver Bullet	1989
7	Wolfen	1999
8	Teen Wolf Too	1999
9	The Company of Wolves	2001
10	The Monster Squad	2001

TOP 10 MYTHS & LEGENDS FILMS

	FILM	YEAR
1	Aladdin *	1992
2	Hercules *	1997
3	Fantasia *†	1940
4	Clash of the Titans	1981
5	Sinbad and the Eye of the Tiger	1977
6	The 7th Voyage of Sinbad	1958
7	Hercules	1983
8	The Golden Voyage of Sinbad	1974
9	Hercules	1959
10	The Thief of Bagdad [sic]	1924

* Animated
† Pastoral Symphony sequence

TOP 10 FAIRYTALE FILMS

	FILM	YEAR
1	Aladdin *	1992
2	Shrek *	2001
3	Beauty and the Beast *	1991
4	The Little Mermaid *	1989
5	Snow White and the Seven Dwarfs *	1937
6	The Princess Diaries	2001
7	Ever After: A Cinderella Story	1998
8	Pinocchio *	1940
9	Willow	1988
10	Sleeping Beauty *	1959

The sources of fairytale stories range across traditional collections such as Arabian Nights (*Aladdin*), original tales by "Carlo Collodi"/ Carlo Lorenzini (*Pinocchio*) and Hans Christian Andersen (*The Little Mermaid*), and those collected by the Brothers Grimm (*Snow White and the Seven Dwarfs*) and Charles Perrault (*Sleeping Beauty* and *Cinderella*). *Cinderella*, often claimed as the most-filmed story of all time, became a successful animated film (1950) – though just missing a place in this list – and was also the basis of *Ever After*.

TOP 10 SWORD & SORCERY FILMS

	FILM	YEAR
1	The Lord of the Rings: The Two Towers	2002
2	The Lord of the Rings: The Fellowship of the Ring	2001
3	Dragonheart	1996
4	Willow	1988
5	Dungeons & Dragons	2000
6	Conan the Barbarian	1982
7	The Sword and the Sorcerer	1982
8	Conan the Destroyer	1984
9	The Lord of the Rings *	1978
10	The Black Cauldron *	1985

* Animated

The fantasy sub-genre "sword and sorcery" was named in 1960 by science-fiction writer Fritz Leiber (1910–92) to describe the *Conan the Barbarian* stories that Robert E. Howard (1906–36) had written in the 1930s. Also known as "heroic fantasy", they take place in an imaginary past world and commonly feature an heroic swordsman who embarks on a quest and vanquishes an evil supernatural force. The genre has been especially successful with the *Lord of the Rings* series, but not all have achieved such dizzy heights: *Red Sonja* (1985), based on a story by Robert E. Howard and starring Brigitte Nielsen, the former wife of Sylvester Stallone, cost an estimated $17.9 million to make, but earned barely $7 million at the box office.

Angelic Couple

Robin Williams and Annabella Sciorra become angels in *What Dreams May Come*. The film won an Oscar for its visual effects.

TOP 10 ANGEL FILMS

	FILM	YEAR
1	City of Angels	1998
2	Michael	1996
3	Heaven Can Wait	1978
4	What Dreams May Come	1998
5	The Preacher's Wife	1996
6	Always	1989
7	Down to Earth	2001
8	Oh, God!	1977
9	Angels in the Outfield	1994
10	Dogma	1999

Angels and other divine manifestations coming to Earth and interacting with the living have proved a popular theme in countless films. In contrast to the genre known as *film noir*, some critics have dubbed them *film blanc*. *It's a Wonderful Life* (1947) is perhaps one of the most celebrated, but fails to earn a place in this Top 10.

TOP 10 DEVIL FILMS

	FILM	YEAR	DEVIL
1	The Exorcist	1973	Linda Blair
2	End of Days	1999	Gabriel Byrne
3	The Devil's Advocate	1997	Al Pacino
4	The Golden Child	1986	Charles Dance
5	Bedazzled	2000	Elizabeth Hurley
6	The Witches of Eastwick	1987	Jack Nicholson
7	Little Nicky	2000	Harvey Keitel
8	The Omen	1976	Harvey Stephens
9	The Natural	1984	Robert Prosky
10	Exorcist II: The Heretic	1977	Linda Blair

The Devil has appeared in films since the silent period. As well as these 10 high-earners, he also appears in *The Exorcist III* (1990), but on this occasion uncredited, and only in the form of a voice (spoken by Colleen Dewhurst). In *Oh, God! You Devil* (1984), George Burns plays the unique dual role of God and the Devil.

TOP 10 WITCHES & WIZARDS/ MAGIC FILMS

	FILM	YEAR
1	Harry Potter and the Sorcerer's Stone	2001
2	The Lord of the Rings: The Two Towers	2002
3	Harry Potter and the Chamber of Secrets	2002
4	The Lord of the Rings: The Fellowship of the Ring	2001
5	Shrek *	2001
6	Beauty and the Beast *	1991
7	The Blair Witch Project	1999
8	Sleepy Hollow	1999
9	Snow White and the Seven Dwarfs *	1937
10	Fantasia/2000 *	1999

* Animated

Little Devil

Five-year-old Harvey Stephens received a Golden Globe nomination for his acting debut as the demonic Damien in *The Omen*, one of the most popular films of 1976.

Did you know?

In a 1999 poll, *The Exorcist* came out top of a poll of the "Scariest Movies of All Time". Its 1973 release had been notorious for causing mass hysteria among audiences.

TOP 10 MUSICALS

	FILM	YEAR
1	Grease	1978
2	Saturday Night Fever	1977
3	Chicago	2002
4	8 Mile	2002
5	Moulin Rouge!	2001
6	The Sound of Music	1965
7	Evita	1996
8	The Rocky Horror Picture Show	1975
9	Staying Alive	1983
10	Mary Poppins	1964

Traditional musicals (films in which the cast actually sing) and films in which a musical soundtrack is a major component are included here. In recent years animated films with musical content appear to have taken over from the musical – *Beauty and the Beast*, *Aladdin*, *The Lion King*, *Pocahontas*, *The Prince of Egypt*, and *Tarzan* all won "Best Original Song" Oscars.

TOP 10 MUSICIAN FILM BIOGRAPHIES

	FILM	SUBJECT	YEAR
1	The Sound of Music	Von Trapp family	1965
2	Shine	David Helfgott	1996
3	Coal Miner's Daughter	Loretta Lynn	1980
4	La Bamba	Ritchie Valens	1987
5	Amadeus	Wolfgang Amadeus Mozart	1984
6	What's Love Got to Do with It	Tina Turner	1993
7	Selena	Selena Quintanilla	1997
8	The Doors	The Doors	1991
9	Lady Sings the Blues	Billie Holiday	1972
10	The Glenn Miller Story	Glenn Miller	1954

Biopics on the lives of famous musicians have been a Hollywood staple for over 50 years. Those within and outside the Top 10 have encompassed both classical and popular musicians, including such artists as Jerome Kern (*Till the Clouds Roll By*, 1946), Hank Williams (*Your Cheatin' Heart*, 1964), Peter Tchaikovsky (*The Music Lovers*, 1970), Buddy Holly (*The Buddy Holly Story*, 1978), John Lennon (*Imagine: John Lennon*, 1988), Jerry Lee Lewis (*Great Balls of Fire*, 1989), Ludwig van Beethoven (*Immortal Beloved*, 1994), and Jacqueline du Pré (*Hilary and Jackie*, 1998).

TOP 10 POP STAR FILM DEBUTS

	STAR	FILM	YEAR
1	Whitney Houston	The Bodyguard	1992
2	Eminem	8 Mile	2002
3	Meatloaf	The Rocky Horror Picture Show	1975
4	Dolly Parton	Nine to Five	1980
5	Spice Girls	Spice World	1998
6	Jennifer Lopez	Money Train	1995
7	Aaliyah	Romeo Must Die	2000
8	Britney Spears	Crossroads	2002
9	Ice Cube	Boyz N the Hood	1991
10	Barbra Streisand	Funny Girl	1968

TOP 10 MUSICALS ADAPTED FROM STAGE VERSIONS

	MUSICAL	THEATRE OPENING	FILM YEAR
1	Grease	1972	1978
2	Chicago	1975	2002
3	The Sound of Music	1959	1965
4	Evita	1978	1996
5	The Rocky Horror Picture Show	1973	1975
6	Fiddler on the Roof	1964	1971
7	My Fair Lady	1956	1964
8	The Best Little Whorehouse in Texas	1978	1982
9	Annie	1977	1982
10	West Side Story	1957	1961

MGM MUSICALS

	FILM	YEAR
1	Victor/Victoria	1982
2	The Unsinkable Molly Brown	1964
3	Gigi	1958
4	I'll Cry Tomorrow	1955
5	High Society	1956
6	Meet Me in St. Louis	1944
7	Show Boat	1951
8	Seven Brides For Seven Brothers	1954
9	The Wonderful World of The Brothers Grimm	1962
10	The Wizard of Oz	1939

From the earliest years of talking pictures, MGM established itself as the pre-eminent studio for musicals, making some 200 and winning the first "Best Picture" Oscar for *The Broadway Melody* (1929), and subsequently for *The Great Ziegfeld* (1936), *An American in Paris* (1951), and *Gigi* (1958). MGM's *That's Entertainment* (1974) earned more than any of those in the Top 10, but, like its two sequels, it was a compilation rather than a single narrative film.

FILM WITH TITLES DERIVED FROM SONG TITLES

	FILM	SONG*	FILM YEAR
1	American Pie	1972	1999
2	Sweet Home Alabama	1976	2002
3	Bad Boys	1983	1995
4	Sea of Love	1959	1989
5	One Fine Day	1963	1996
6	My Girl	1965	1991
7	Something to Talk About	1991	1995
8	When a Man Loves a Woman	1966	1994
9	The Crying Game	1964	1992
10	Addicted to Love	1986	1997

* Release of first hit version

The first song that gave its name to a film title was "How Would You Like to Be the Ice Man?", appropriated for a film released on 21 April 1899! Films with titles that are not identical to those of the songs that may have inspired them have been ignored here, hence excluding the song "Oh Pretty Woman" (1964) and film *Pretty Woman* (1990).

Song and Dance
Margaret O'Brien and Judy Garland in *Meet Me in St. Louis*, MGM's hit musical of 1944. Garland married the film's director, Vincente Minnelli, the following year.

The Hills are Alive ...
... with *The Sound of Music*, one of the most successful musicals and top music biopic of all time. It won five Oscars, including "Best Picture".

TOP 10 "BEST SONG" OSCAR-WINNING SINGLES IN THE UK

	SONG	ARTIST	FILM	YEAR
1	I Just Called to Say I Love You	Stevie Wonder	The Woman in Red	1984
2	Fame	Irene Cara	Fame	1980
3	Take My Breath Away	Berlin	Top Gun	1986
4	My Heart Will Go On	Celine Dion	Titanic	1997
5	What a Feeling	Irene Cara	Flashdance	1983
6	Evergreen	Barbra Streisand	A Star Is Born	1976
7	Streets of Philadelphia	Bruce Springsteen	Philadelphia	1994
8	Moon River	Danny Williams	Breakfast at Tiffany's	1961
9	Whatever Will Be, Will Be	Doris Day	The Man Who Knew Too Much	1956
10	Raindrops Keep Fallin' on My Head	Sacha Distel	Butch Cassidy and the Sundance Kid	1969

Source: Music Information Database

TOP 10 "BEST SONG" OSCAR-WINNING SINGLES IN THE US

	SONG	ARTIST	FILM	YEAR
1	You Light Up My Life	Debby Boone	You Light Up My Life	1977
2	Up Where We Belong	Joe Cocker and Jennifer Warnes	An Officer and a Gentleman	1982
3	Evergreen	Barbra Streisand	A Star Is Born	1976
4	My Heart Will Go On	Celine Dion	Titanic	1997
5	I Just Called to Say I Love You	Stevie Wonder	The Woman in Red	1984
6	Arthur's Theme (Best That You Can Do)	Christopher Cross	Arthur	1981
7	The Way We Were	Barbra Streisand	The Way We Were	1973
8	A Whole New World	Peabo Bryson and Regina Belle	Aladdin	1992
9	Raindrops Keep Fallin' on My Head	B.J. Thomas	Butch Cassidy and the Sundance Kid	1969
10	(I've had the) Time of My Life	Bill Medley and Jennifer Warnes	Dirty Dancing	1987

Source: Music Information Database

TOP 10 ORIGINAL SOUNDTRACK ALBUMS IN THE UK

	ALBUM	YEAR
1	The Bodyguard	1992
2	Dirty Dancing	1998
3	Titanic	1997
4	Bridget Jones's Diary	2001
5	Trainspotting	1996
6	The Commitments	1991
7	The Full Monty	1997
8	Top Gun	1986
9	Evita	1996
10	Buster	1988

Source: The Music Information Database

TOP 10 ORIGINAL SOUNDTRACK ALBUMS IN THE US

	ALBUM	YEAR
1	The Bodyguard	1992
2	Purple Rain	1984
3	Forrest Gump	1994
4 =	Dirty Dancing	1987
=	Titanic	1997
6	The Lion King	1994
7 =	Top Gun	1986
=	Footloose	1984
9	Grease	1978
10	Saturday Night Fever	1977

Source: RIAA

Did you know?

Recorded by Gordon MacRea and the cast, the soundtrack album from the 1955 film *Oklahoma!* stayed in the US charts for 255 weeks, becoming the first ever album to sell one million copies.

Going for a Song

Featuring tracks by Whitney Houston and others, *The Bodyguard* is the bestselling original film soundtrack album of all time on both sides of the Atlantic, selling over 17 million copies in the US alone.

TOP 10 ELVIS PRESLEY FILM SONGS IN THE UK

	SONG	FILM	YEAR
1	Jailhouse Rock	Jailhouse Rock	1957
2	Wooden Heart	G.I. Blues	1960
3	Return to Sender	Girls! Girls! Girls!	1962
4	Can't Help Falling in Love	Blue Hawaii	1961
5	Teddy Bear	Loving You	1957
6	King Creole	King Creole	1958
7	Let's Have a Party	Loving You	1957
8	Hard Headed Woman	King Creole	1958
9	I Just Can't Help Believing	Elvis – That's The Way It Is	1970
10	Always on My Mind	Elvis On Tour	1972

Source: MRIB

The title song from his first film, *Love Me Tender*, though a multi-million seller in the US, was a much smaller hit in Britain, and would fall at No. 14 if this list were extended.

TOP 10 ELVIS PRESLEY FILM SONGS IN THE US

	SONG	FILM	YEAR
1	Love Me Tender	Love Me Tender	1956
2	Jailhouse Rock	Jailhouse Rock	1957
3	Teddy Bear	Loving You	1957
4	Return to Sender	Girls! Girls! Girls!	1962
5	Can't Help Falling in Love	Blue Hawaii	1961
6	Hard Headed Woman	King Creole	1958
7	Bossa Nova Baby	Fun In Acapulco	1963
8	One Broken Heart For Sale	It Happened at the World's Fair	1963
9	Follow That Dream	Follow That Dream	1962
10	I'm Yours	Tickle Me	1965

Source: MRIB

Elvis's film-extracted singles from 1963–69, which actually formed the bulk of his releases during this period, ironically sold much less well than those from the 1950s, when his recording career was paramount, or from the 1970s, when he was concentrating on live performance.

TOP 10 JAMES BOND FILM THEMES IN THE UK

	SONG	ARTIST	YEAR
1	A View to a Kill	Duran Duran	1985
2	We Have All the Time in the World (from On Her Majesty's Secret Service)	Louis Armstrong	1994
3	The Living Daylights	a-ha	1987
4	Licence to Kill	Gladys Knight	1989
5	Nobody Does it Better (from The Spy Who Loved Me)	Carly Simon	1977
6	For Your Eyes Only	Sheena Easton	1981
7	Live and Let Die	Paul McCartney and Wings	1973
8	GoldenEye	Tina Turner	1995
9	You Only Live Twice	Nancy Sinatra	1967
10	Die Another Day	Madonna	2002

TOP 10 JAMES BOND FILM THEMES IN THE US

	SONG	ARTIST	YEAR
1	A View to a Kill	Duran Duran	1985
2	Nobody Does It Better (from The Spy Who Loved Me)	Carly Simon	1977
3	Live and Let Die	Paul McCartney and Wings	1973
4	For Your Eyes Only	Sheena Easton	1981
5	Goldfinger	Shirley Bassey	1965
6	Thunderball	Tom Jones	1966
7	All Time High (from Octopussy)	Rita Coolidge	1983
8	You Only Live Twice	Nancy Sinatra	1967
9	Diamonds Are Forever	Shirley Bassey	1972
10	Die Another Day	Madonna	2002

King-sized Hit
The title track from *Jailhouse Rock*, Elvis Presley's third film, became his 14th million-selling single.

TOP 10 FILMS BASED ON PLAYS*

	FILM	YEAR	AUTHOR
1	You've Got M@il	1998	Miklós László
2	A Few Good Men	1992	Aaron Sorkin
3	The Birdcage	1996	Jean Poiret
4	My Big Fat Greek Wedding	2002	Nia Vardalos
6	Driving Miss Daisy	1989	Alfred Uhry
6	Romeo + Juliet	1996	William Shakespeare
7	A Perfect Murder	1998	Frederick Knott
8	On Golden Pond	1981	Ernest Thompson
9	Heaven Can Wait	1978	Harry Segall
10	Sabrina	1995	Samuel Taylor

* Excluding musicals

You've Got M@il and *The Shop Around the Corner* (1940) were both adapted from *Parfumerie*, a play by Miklós Laszlo, while the play *Heaven Can Wait* (aka *Halfway to Heaven*) by Harry Segall had even more incarnations, having inspired *Here Comes Mr. Jordan* (1941), *Down to Earth* (2001), the musical version *Down to Earth* (1947), and the musical *Xanadu* (1980).

TOP 10 FILMS BASED ON CLASSIC BRITISH NOVELS

	FILM	YEAR	NOVELIST	YEAR*
1	Dracula	1992	Bram Stoker	1897
2	Sense and Sensibility	1995	Jane Austen	1811
3	The Time Machine	2002	H.G. Wells	1895
4	Frankenstein	1994	Mary Shelley	1818
5	Great Expectations	1998	Charles Dickens	1860–61
6	Emma	1996	Jane Austen	1816
7	Howards End	1992	E.M. Forster	1910
8	A Room with a View	1986	E.M. Forster	1908
9	The Portrait of a Lady	1996	Henry James	1881
10	The Wings of the Dove	1997	Henry James	1902

* Of publication

This Top 10 features British novels published at least 90 years prior to the release of the film based on them, but excludes films inspired by, but not following, the text and storyline of such novels as Joseph Conrad's *Heart of Darkness* (1902), on which *Apocalypse Now* (1979) was loosely based, the heavily adapted versions of novels by Charles Dickens, such as *Scrooged* and *Oliver!*, animated films that have taken considerable liberties with original stories, such as *Oliver and Company*, from Dickens' *Oliver Twist*, or *Treasure Planet*, which was derived from Robert Louis Stevenson's *Treasure Island*, and films based on short stories, including the many animated and live-action re-tellings of Rudyard Kipling's *The Jungle Book*.

TOP 10 LIVE-ACTION FILMS BASED ON A TV SERIES

	FILM	TV SERIES*	YEAR
1	Mission: Impossible 2	1966	2000
2	Mission: Impossible	1966	1996
3	The Fugitive	1963	1993
4	The Flintstones	1960	1994
5	Scooby-Doo	1969	2002
6	Charlie's Angels	1976	2000
7	Bean	1989	1997
8	Wild Wild West	1965	1999
9	Traffic †	1989	2000
10	The Addams Family	1964	1991

* Launched on TV in the USA
† UK TV series *Traffik*

A Great View
Helena Bonham Carter and Julian Sands in *A Room with a View*, an Oscar-winning adaptation of the E.M. Forster novel.

TOP 10 FILMS BASED ON POPULAR NOVELS

	FILM	YEAR	NOVELIST
1	Harry Potter and the Sorcerer's Stone *	2001	J.K. Rowling
2	Jurassic Park	1993	Michael Crichton
3	The Lord of the Rings: The Two Towers	2002	J.R.R. Tolkien
4	Harry Potter and the Chamber of Secrets	2002	J.K. Rowling
5	The Lord of the Rings: The Fellowship of the Ring	2001	J.R.R. Tolkien
6	Forrest Gump	1994	Winston Groom
7	The Lost World: Jurassic Park	1997	Michael Crichton
8	Jaws	1975	Peter Benchley
9	Tarzan †	1999	Edgar Rice Burroughs
10	Dances With Wolves	1990	Michael Blake

* Book title *Harry Potter and the Philosopher's Stone*
† Animated

TOP 10 FILMS BASED ON COMPUTER GAMES

	FILM	GAME*	YEAR
1	Lara Croft: Tomb Raider	1996	2001
2	Mortal Kombat	1992	1995
3	Street Fighter	1987	1994
4	Final Fantasy: The Spirits Within	1987	2001
5	Resident Evil	1996	2002
6	Mortal Kombat: Annihilation	1992	1997
7	Super Mario Bros	1985	1993
8	Ballistic: Ecks vs. Sever	2001	2002
9	Wing Commander	1990	1999
10	Double Dragon	1987	1993

* Original, if series

A Troubled Mind
Russell Crowe in "Best Picture" Oscar-winning *A Beautiful Mind*, directed by Ron Howard. The film was based on the true life story of disturbed mathematician John Nash.

TOP 10 FILMS BASED ON COMICS

	FILM*	YEAR	PUBLISHED†
1	Spider-Man	2002	1962
2	Men in Black	1997	1990
3	Batman	1989	1939
4	The Mask	1994	1991
5	Superman	1978	1938
6	X-Men	2000	1963
7	Casper #	1995	1949
8	Teenage Mutant Ninja Turtles	1990	1984
9	The Addams Family	1991	1937
10	Dick Tracy	1990	1931

* If series, highest-earning only
† Year of first publication of comic
# Original film made 1946

TOP 10 FILMS BASED ON DC COMICS

	FILM	YEAR
1	Batman	1989
2	Batman Forever	1995
3	Superman	1978
4	Batman Returns	1992
5	Batman & Robin	1997
6	Superman II	1980
7	Superman III	1983
8	Superman IV: The Quest for Peace	1987
9	Supergirl	1984
10	Batman: Mask of the Phantasm	1993

National Allied Publications, later DC (Detective Comics), launched its first comics in 1935, introducing Superman in 1938 and Batman in 1940. Superman made his screen debut in 1941 and Batman in 1943.

TOP 10 FILMS BASED ON TRUE STORIES

	FILM	YEAR
1	Titanic	1997
2	Pearl Harbor	2001
3	Apollo 13	1995
4	Pocahontas *	1995
5	Catch Me if You Can	2002
6	The Perfect Storm	2000
7	Schindler's List	1993
8	A Beautiful Mind	2001
9	Chicago	2000
10	Erin Brockovich	2000

* Animated
Filmmakers' licence is inevitably employed in such films, with, for example, romantic sub-plots superimposed on the sinking of the *Titanic*, but they broadly represent accurate accounts. Each of those appearing in this Top 10 has made more than $200 million worldwide.

TOP 10 SCIENCE FICTION FILMS

	FILM	YEAR
1	Star Wars: Episode I – The Phantom Menace	1999
2	Jurassic Park	1993
3	Independence Day	1996
4	Spider-Man	2002
5	Star Wars *	1977
6	E.T. the Extra-Terrestrial	1982
7	Star Wars: Episode II – Attack of the Clones	2002
8	The Lost World: Jurassic Park	1997
9	Men in Black	1997
10	Star Wars: Episode VI – Return of the Jedi	1983

* Later retitled *Star Wars: Episode IV – A New Hope*
The first five films in this list are also in the all-time Top 10 films, and all 10 are among the 18 most successful films ever, having earned over $570 million each – a total of more than $7.4 billion at the world box office.

Old Master
Yoda, the 900-year-old Jedi master, has appeared in all the *Star Wars* blockbusters since *The Empire Strikes Back* (1980).

TOP 10 ALIEN INVADERS FILMS

	FILM	YEAR
1	Independence Day	1996
2	Men in Black	1997
3	Men in Black II	2002
4	Signs	2002
5	The Fifth Element	1997
6	The X Files: Fight the Future	1998
7	Star Trek: First Contact	1996
8	Starship Troopers	1997
9	Species	1995
10	Mars Attacks!	1996

This Top 10 – all of them $100 million-plus earners – excludes benign alien visitors, such as those in *Close Encounters of the Third Kind* (1977), focusing on films in which Earth and its inhabitants come under threat of or actual attack by alien beings.

TOP 10 ASTRONAUT AND SPACE TRAVEL FILMS

	FILM	YEAR
1	Independence Day	1996
2	Armageddon	1998
3	Planet of the Apes	2001
4	Deep Impact	1998
5	Total Recall	1990
6	Moonraker	1979
7	Stargate	1994
8	Alien	1979
9	Aliens	1986
10	Alien Resurrection	1997

This Top 10 is limited to films featuring human astronauts and imaginary space travel by humans from Earth, hence excluding other world fantasies such as the *Star Wars* series and films concerned with alien visitors to Earth, such as *E.T. the Extra-Terrestrial*, *Men in Black*, and *Close Encounters of the Third Kind*.

Space Invaders
Secret military base Area 51, Nevada, comes under fire in *Independence Day*, one of the highest-earning films of all time.

TOP 10 SCIENCE FICTION COMEDY FILMS

	FILM	YEAR
1	Men in Black	1997
2	Men in Black II	2002
3	Back to the Future	1985
4	Back to the Future Part II	1989
5	The Nutty Professor	1996
6	Back to the Future Part III	1990
7	Lilo & Stitch *	2002
8	Space Jam	1996
9	Honey, I Shrunk the Kids	1989
10	Wild Wild West	1999

* Animated

The fantasy inherent in science fiction often borders on comedy, and serious science fiction films often contain comedic episodes, but these high-earners (all $200 million-plus worldwide) were made with comedy at their heart. Supernatural subjects – even those such as *Ghostbusters* that employ scientific paraphernalia – have been excluded.

TOP 10 TIME TRAVEL FILMS

	FILM	YEAR
1	Terminator II: Judgment Day	1991
2	Planet of the Apes	2002
3	Back to the Future	1985
4	Back to the Future Part II	1989
5	Austin Powers: The Spy Who Shagged Me	2000
6	Austin Powers in Goldmember	2002
7	Back to the Future Part III	1990
8	Twelve Monkeys	1995
9	Star Trek: First Contact	1996
10	Lost in Space	1998

Time travel has been a popular film theme since the silent period, with such releases as *A Connecticut Yankee in King Arthur's Court* (1921). Films based on H.G. Wells's classic novel *The Time Machine* (1895) have been remade often, the first being a TV movie in 1949. Each film in this list has earned more than $135 million worldwide.

TOP 10 SCIENCE FICTION FILM REMAKES*

	ORIGINAL	YEAR	REMAKE	YEAR
1	Planet of the Apes	1968	Planet of the Apes	2001
2	Gojira (Japan)	1954	Godzilla	1998
3	The Nutty Professor	1963	The Nutty Professor	1996
4	Abre Los Ojos (Spain)	1997	Vanilla Sky	2001
5	La Jetée (France)	1965	Twelve Monkeys	1995
6	The Time Machine	1960	The Time Machine	2002
7	The Fly	1958	The Fly	1986
8	Flash Gordon	1936	Flash Gordon	1980
9	Invasion of the Body Snatchers	1956	Invasion of the Body Snatchers	1978
10	Rollerball	1975	Rollerball	2002

* Ranked by comparative world total box office gross of remake

TOP 10 ANIMATED SCIENCE FICTION FILMS

	FILM	YEAR
1	Lilo & Stitch	2002
2	Atlantis: The Lost Empire	2002
3	Pokémon: The First Movie	1999
4	Pokémon: Power of One	2000
5	Jimmy Neutron: Boy Genius	2001
6	Treasure Planet	2002
7	Final Fantasy: The Spirits Within	2002
8	Titan A.E.	2000
9	The Iron Giant	1999
10	Heavy Metal	1981

Although this list is ranked according to global box office income, it contains several entries, most notably *Treasure Planet*, that failed to recoup their substantial production costs, and hence must be regarded as commercial flops.

TOP 10 SPORT FILMS

	FILM	YEAR	SPORT
1	Rocky IV	1985	Boxing
2	Jerry Maguire *	1996	American football
3	Space Jam	1996	Basketball
4	The Waterboy	1998	American football
5	Days of Thunder	1990	Stock car racing
6	Cool Runnings	1993	Bobsleighing
7	A League of Their Own	1992	Baseball
8	Remember the Titans	2000	American football
9	Rocky III	1982	Boxing
10	Rocky V	1990	Boxing

* While the film is set in the world of sports, American football itself is incidental to its plot, which is about a sports agent and his client, who happens to be an American football player.

Led by Sylvester Stallone's *Rocky* series, the boxing ring dominates Hollywood's most successful sports-based epics (based on worldwide box office income), with all those in the Top 10 having made at least $120 million. Were *Forrest Gump* (1994) considered in this category on the grounds that American football and table-tennis are featured in it, it would top the list.

TOP 10 WINTER SPORTS FILMS

	FILM	YEAR	SPORT
1	Cool Runnings	1993	Bobsleighing
2	Snow Dogs	2002	Sled dog racing
3	The Mighty Ducks	1992	Ice hockey
4	Sudden Death *	1995	Ice hockey
5	D2: The Mighty Ducks	1994	Ice hockey
6	D3: The Mighty Ducks	1996	Ice hockey
7	Slap Shot	1977	Ice hockey
8	The Cutting Edge	1992	Ice skating
9	Iron Will	1994	Sled dog racing
10	Ice Castles	1978	Ice skating

* Terrorist attack at ice hockey venue

One Jump Ahead
Wesley Snipes co-stars with Woody Harrelson in the Ron Shelton-directed comedy *White Men Can't Jump*, one of the highest-grossing basketball films. The pair also won the MTV Award for "Best On-screen Duo".

TOP 10 THEMES OF SPORT FILMS

	SPORT	FILMS
1	Boxing	204
2	Horse racing	139
3	American football	123
4 =	Baseball	85
=	Motor racing	85
6	Basketball	41
7	Athletics	33
8	Golf	24
9	Wrestling	20
10	Motorcycle racing	15

Source: Patrick Robertson, *Film Facts* (2001)
A survey of feature films with competitive sports as their principal themes produced in Hollywood from 1910 to 2000 identified a total of 891 films, with boxing accounting for 22.9 per cent of the total.

TOP 10 BASKETBALL FILMS

	FILM	YEAR
1	Space Jam	1996
2	White Men Can't Jump	1998
3	Eddie	2000
4	Hoosiers	1999
5	Love & Basketball	1991
6	Air Bud	2000
7	Blue Chips	1986
8	He Got Game	1991
9	Michael Jordan to the Max *	1993
10	The Air Up There	1994

* Documentary

TOP 10 AMERICAN FOOTBALL FILMS

	FILM	YEAR
1	The Waterboy	1998
2	Remember the Titans	2000
3	Any Given Sunday	1999
4	Varsity Blues	1999
5	The Replacements (Scabs)	2000
6	Semi-Tough	1977
7	Wildcats	1986
8	Necessary Roughness	1991
9	North Dallas Forty	1979
10	The Program	1993

American football has provided the background to well over 200 feature films. It also figures incidentally in such successful films as *Jerry Maguire* (1996) and *The Last Boy Scout* (1991), while *Bring It On* (2000) focuses on football cheerleaders rather than players.

TOP 10 BOXING FILMS

	FILM	YEAR
1	Rocky IV	1985
2	Rocky III	1982
3	Rocky V	1990
4	Rocky	1976
5	Fight Club	1999
6	Snake Eyes	1998
7	Rocky II	1979
8	Ali	2001
9	The Hurricane	1999
10	Undisputed	2002

TOP 10 MOTOR RACING FILMS

	FILM	YEAR
1	The Fast and the Furious *	2001
2	Days of Thunder	1990
3	The Cannonball Run *	1981
4	The Love Bug	1969
5	Driven	2001
6	Cannonball Run II *	1984
7	Grand Prix	1966
8	Winning	1969
9	Herbie Goes to Monte Carlo	1977
10	The Gumball Rally *	1976

* Illegal street or cross-country racing

TOP 10 BASEBALL FILMS

	FILM	YEAR
1	A League of Their Own	1992
2	The Rookie	2002
3	Field of Dreams	1989
4	Rookie of the Year	1993
5	Angels in the Outfield	1994
6	Bull Durham	1988
7	Major League	1989
8	The Natural	1984
9	For Love of the Game	1999
10	Hardball	2001

A League of Their Own, starring Tom Hanks, Geena Davis, and Madonna, is unusual in depicting a team in the All American Girls Baseball League.

Packing a Punch
Starring, written, and directed by Sylvester Stallone, *Rocky IV* has earned over $300 million worldwide, making it the most successful sport film ever.

TOP 10 PRISONER-OF-WAR FILMS

	FILM	YEAR
1	Schindler's List	1993
2	Rambo: First Blood Part II	1985
3	Behind Enemy Lines	1986
4	The Deer Hunter	1978
5	The Bridge on the River Kwai	1957
6	Sophie's Choice	1982
7	Missing in Action	1984
8	Empire of the Sun	1987
9	Von Ryan's Express	1965
10	The Great Escape	1963

This list includes missing-in-action and concentration camp films, but excludes those in which imprisonment is an incidental theme, thus eliminating *Seven Years in Tibet* (1997), which would otherwise be in third place.

TOP 10 SUBMARINE FILMS

	FILM	YEAR
1	The Hunt for Red October	1990
2	Crimson Tide	1995
3	U-571	2000
4	Das Boot *	1981
5	K-19: The Widowmaker	2002
6	Down Periscope	1996
7	Operation Petticoat	1959
8	Gray Lady Down	1978
9	Destination Tokyo	1943
10	Below	2002

* Including 1997 re-release

Films featuring military submarines have been made since the silent era, while latterly submarine action during the Cold War has proved a popular theme. Films including submarines that are incidental to the plot, such as *Raiders of the Lost Ark* (1981), or those featuring non-military subs used in underwater exploration, such as *Titanic* (1997), are excluded from this list.

TOP 10 AMERICAN CIVIL WAR FILMS*

	FILM	YEAR
1	Dances With Wolves	1990
2	Gone With the Wind	1939
3	How the West Was Won	1962
4	The Outlaw Josey Wales	1976
5	Glory	1989
6	The Birth of a Nation	1915
7	Shenandoah	1965
8	Gods and Generals	2003
9	The Good, the Bad and the Ugly	1966
10	Raintree County	1957

* Films set in and depicting events of this war

Soldiers of Fortune

Winner of five Oscars, including "Best Picture" and "Best Director", *Platoon* went on to earn some $150 million internationally.

TOP 10 WORLD WAR I FILMS

	FILM	YEAR
1	Legends of the Fall	1994
2	Lawrence of Arabia	1962
3	The Four Horsemen of the Apocalypse	1921
4	In Love and War	1997
5	The Blue Max	1966
6	The Big Parade	1925
7	A Farewell to Arms	1957
8	The African Queen	1951
9	What Price Glory	1926
10	Hearts of the World	1918

This is an unusual list in that several entries are World War I films that were made not long after the end of the Great War, when the events they depicted would have been fresh in the minds of their audiences. Such was the success of some – *The Four Horsemen of the Apocalypse*, for example, was one of the most popular films of the silent era – that they have well outearned many similarly themed films made since.

TOP 10 WORLD WAR II FILMS*

	FILM	YEAR
1	Saving Private Ryan	1998
2	Pearl Harbor	2001
3	Schindler's List	1993
4	The English Patient	1996
5	Life Is Beautiful (La Vita è bella)	1997
6	U-571	2000
7	The Pianist	2002
8	Enemy at the Gates	2001
9	The Thin Red Line	1998
10	Patton	1970

* Includes WWII action films as well as films set during the war

Guinness Is Good for You
Alec Guinness won the "Best Actor" Oscar, one of seven awarded for David Lean's prisoner-of-war film *The Bridge on the River Kwai*. Guinness co-starred with William Holden and Jack Hawkins.

TOP 10 VIETNAM FILMS

	FILM	YEAR
1	Rambo: First Blood Part II	1985
2	Born on the Fourth of July	1989
3	Platoon	1986
4	Good Morning, Vietnam	1987
5	We Were Soldiers	2002
6	Apocalypse Now	1979
7	The Deer Hunter	1978
8	Full Metal Jacket	1987
9	Air America	1990
10	Uncommon Valor	1983

Vietnam has inevitably been a source of numerous action films – a genre that began while the war still raged, with movies such as John Wayne's *Green Berets* (1968) – of which these have proved the most successful. The Top 10 includes films set in Vietnam during or after the war, but excludes those in which a character's 'Nam experiences are only one plot element, hence excluding *Forrest Gump* (1994), which would otherwise head the list. Perhaps the most curious aspect of this list is that only one film actually contains the almost taboo word "Vietnam" in its title. Note also that *M*A*S*H* (1970) is excluded: despite the widespread belief that it is set in the Vietnam War, the action takes place during the earlier Korean War.

AWARDS, POLLS, BESTS, & WORSTS

Few industries are as award-conscious as the film business, and no other awards attract the same kudos or popular fascination as the world's major movie accolades: it is reckoned that the annual Academy Awards – "Oscars" – ceremony is watched by a global TV audience of more than a billion people. In exploring this glittering realm, numerous statistical Top 10 lists compare the leading nominees and winners, the oldest and youngest recipients, and all the acting Oscar winners – best actors, actresses, winners for supporting roles, pictures directors, and for music categories. Other major award winners include the Cannes Palme d'Or, the Golden Globes, a range of international professional awards, polls of popular favourites, and last (and in some ways, least) Top 10s of the "worst" actors, actresses, and films.

Beautiful Dream
Roberto Benigni celebrates winning the "Best Actor" Oscar for *Life Is Beautiful* (1997), which also won the award for Best Foreign Language Film.

10 TOP OSCAR "BEST PICTURES"

THE 10 "BEST PICTURE" OSCARS – 1930s

	FILM	DIRECTOR	YEAR
1	All Quiet on the Western Front	Lewis Milestone	1930
2	Cimarron	Wesley Ruggles *	1931
3	Grand Hotel	Edmund Goulding *	1932
4	Cavalcade	Frank Lloyd *	1933
5	It Happened One Night †	Frank Capra	1934
6	Mutiny on the Bounty	Frank Lloyd *	1935
7	The Great Ziegfeld	Robert Z. Leonard *	1936
8	The Life of Emile Zola	William Dieterle *	1937
9	You Can't Take it With You	Frank Capra	1938
10	Gone With The Wind	Victor Fleming	1939

* Did not also win "Best Director" Oscar
† Winner of Oscars for "Best Director", "Best Actor", "Best Actress", and "Best Screenplay"
The first Academy Awards, popularly known as Oscars, were presented at a ceremony at the Hollywood Roosevelt Hotel on 16 May 1929, and were for films released in the period 1927–28. *Wings*, directed by William A. Wellman, the first film to be honoured as "Best Picture", was silent. A second ceremony held at the Ambassador Hotel on 31 October of the same year was for films released in 1928–29, and was won by *Broadway Melody*, directed by Harry Beaumont, the first talkie and the first musical to win an Oscar. The film was also a novelty in containing some sequences shot in a primitive form of two-colour (red/green) Technicolor. *Gone With The Wind* was the first all-colour winner of the "Best Picture" award.

THE 10 "BEST PICTURE" OSCARS – 1940s

	FILM	DIRECTOR	YEAR
1	Rebecca	Alfred Hitchcock *	1940
2	How Green Was My Valley	John Ford	1941
3	Mrs. Miniver	William Wyler	1942
4	Casablanca	Michael Curtiz	1943
5	Going My Way	Leo McCarey	1944
6	The Lost Weekend	Billy Wilder	1945
7	The Best Years of Our Lives	William Wyler	1946
8	Gentleman's Agreement	Elia Kazan	1947
9	Hamlet	Laurence Olivier †	1948
10	All the King's Men	Robert Rossen *	1949

* Did not also win "Best Director" Oscar
† Did not also win "Best Director" Oscar, but won as producer
Several "Best Picture" winners are now regarded as film classics, many critics numbering *Casablanca* among the greatest films of all time. *Mrs. Miniver* (which won six Oscars) and *The Best Years of Our Lives* (seven Oscars) were both directed by William Wyler and reflected the concerns of wartime and post-war life respectively. *How Green Was My Valley* and *Going My Way* each won five Oscars. *Rebecca* (Alfred Hitchcock's first US-made film) and *Hamlet* both starred Laurence Olivier, who also directed the latter, winning both "Best Picture" and "Best Actor" Oscars. "Best Picture" Oscars are awarded to the producer, but directors are noted here – they are especially interesting where the "Best Picture" did not also win for "Best Director".

As Time Goes By ...
Released during World War II, *Casablanca* has established itself as a timeless classic, one of the best-loved and most quoted films of all time.

THE 10 "BEST PICTURE" OSCARS – 1950s

	FILM	DIRECTOR	YEAR
1	All About Eve	Joseph L. Mankiewicz	1950
2	An American in Paris	Vincente Minnelli *	1951
3	The Greatest Show on Earth	Cecil B. DeMille †	1952
4	From Here to Eternity	Fred Zinnemann	1953
5	On the Waterfront	Elia Kazan	1954
6	Marty	Delbert Mann	1955
7	Around the World in 80 Days	Michael Anderson *	1956
8	The Bridge on the River Kwai	David Lean	1957
9	Gigi	Vincente Minnelli	1958
10	Ben-Hur	William Wyler	1959

* Did not also win "Best Director" Oscar
† Did not also win "Best Director" Oscar, but DeMille was also the film's producer, so was awarded "Best Picture". The first film of the 1950s, *All About Eve*, received the most nominations (14), while the last, *Ben-Hur*, won the most (11).

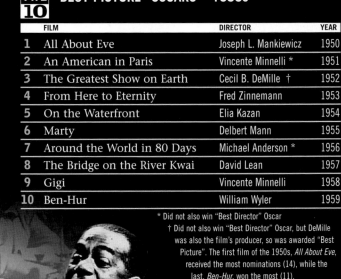

THE 10 "BEST PICTURE" OSCARS – 1960s

	FILM	DIRECTOR	YEAR
1	The Apartment	Billy Wilder	1960
2	West Side Story	Robert Wise and Jerome Robbins	1961
3	Lawrence of Arabia	David Lean	1962
4	Tom Jones	Tony Richardson	1963
5	My Fair Lady	George Cukor	1964
6	The Sound of Music	Robert Wise	1965
7	A Man for All Seasons	Fred Zinnemann	1966
8	In the Heat of the Night	Norman Jewison *	1967
9	Oliver!	Carol Reed	1968
10	Midnight Cowboy	John Schlesinger	1969

* Did not also win "Best Director" Oscar

The 1960s was the decade of the movie musical, with no fewer than four winning "Best Picture" Oscars. The 1960 winner, *The Apartment*, was the last black and white film to receive the "Best Picture" Oscar until *Schindler's List* (1993).

THE 10 "BEST PICTURE" OSCARS – 1970s

	FILM	DIRECTOR	YEAR
1	Patton	Franklin J. Schaffner	1970
2	The French Connection	William Friedkin	1971
3	The Godfather	Francis Ford Coppola *	1972
4	The Sting	George Roy Hill	1973
5	The Godfather, Part II	Francis Ford Coppola	1974
6	One Flew Over the Cuckoo's Nest †	Milos Forman	1975
7	Rocky	John G. Avildsen	1976
8	Annie Hall	Woody Allen	1977
9	The Deer Hunter	Michael Cimino	1978
10	Kramer vs. Kramer	Robert Benton	1979

* Did not also win "Best Director" Oscar
† Winner of Oscars for "Best Actor", "Best Actress", and "Best Screenplay"

THE 10 "BEST PICTURE" OSCARS – 1980s

	FILM	DIRECTOR	YEAR
1	Ordinary People	Robert Redford	1980
2	Chariots of Fire	Hugh Hudson *	1981
3	Gandhi	Richard Attenborough	1982
4	Terms of Endearment	James L. Brooks	1983
5	Amadeus	Milos Forman	1984
6	Out of Africa	Sydney Pollack	1985
7	Platoon	Oliver Stone	1986
8	The Last Emperor	Bernardo Bertolucci	1987
9	Rain Man	Barry Levinson	1988
10	Driving Miss Daisy	Bruce Beresford *	1989

* Did not also win "Best Director" Oscar

Last But Not Least

Winner of nine Oscars, including "Best Picture", *The Last Emperor* achieved critical acclaim that was not mirrored by its box office success.

THE 10 "BEST PICTURE" OSCARS – 1990s

	FILM	DIRECTOR	YEAR
1	Dances With Wolves	Kevin Costner	1990
2	The Silence of the Lambs	Jonathan Demme	1991
3	Unforgiven	Clint Eastwood	1992
4	Schindler's List	Steven Spielberg	1993
5	Forrest Gump	Robert Zemeckis	1994
6	Braveheart	Mel Gibson	1995
7	The English Patient	Anthony Minghella	1996
8	Titanic	James Cameron	1997
9	Shakespeare in Love	John Madden*	1998
10	American Beauty	Sam Mendes	1999

* Did not also win "Best Director" Oscar

Winners in the 21st century have been: *Gladiator* (2000) directed by Ridley Scott who failed to win "Best Director", *A Beautiful Mind* (2001) directed by Ron Howard, and *Chicago* (2002) directed by Rob Marshall who also failed to win "Best Director", which went to Roman Polanski for *The Pianist*.

TOP 10 HIGHEST-EARNING "BEST PICTURES" OF ALL TIME*

	FILM	YEAR †
1	Titanic	1997
2	Forrest Gump	1994
3	Gladiator	2000
4	Dances With Wolves	1990
5	Rain Man	1988
6	Gone With the Wind	1939
7	American Beauty	1999
8	Schindler's List	1993
9	A Beautiful Mind	2001
10	Shakespeare in Love	1998

* Ranked by world box office income
† Of release; Oscars are awarded the following year
The precise monitoring of global box office income for recent films – and certain exceptional films of the past, such as *Gone With the Wind* – makes it possible to rank these according to all-time world income.

TOP 10 HIGHEST-EARNING "BEST PICTURES" OF 1940s*

	FILM	YEAR
1	The Best Years of Our Lives	1946
2	Going My Way	1944
3	Mrs. Miniver	1942
4	Casablanca	1943
5	The Lost Weekend	1945
6	Gentleman's Agreement	1947
7	Hamlet	1948
8	Rebecca	1940
9	How Green Was My Valley	1941
10	All the King's Men	1949

* Ranked by US rental income
Prior to the 1960s – and in some contexts up to the present – US rental income (the amount paid by exhibitors to distributors) was the conventional way of comparing the relative success of films.

TOP 10 HIGHEST-EARNING "BEST PICTURES" OF 1950s*

	FILM	YEAR
1	Ben-Hur	1959
2	Around the World in 80 Days	1956
3	The Bridge on the River Kwai	1957
4	The Greatest Show on Earth	1952
5	From Here to Eternity	1953
6	Gigi	1958
7	An American in Paris	1951
8	On the Waterfront	1954
9	All About Eve	1950
10	Marty	1955

* Ranked by US rental income

Top of the List

Box office hit *Schindler's List* provided director Steven Spielberg with his only "Best Picture" Oscar, although he won as "Best Director" for another film set in World War II, *Saving Private Ryan* (1998).

TOP 10 HIGHEST-EARNING "BEST PICTURES" OF 1960s*

	FILM	YEAR
1	The Sound of Music	1965
2	My Fair Lady	1964
3	Midnight Cowboy	1969
4	West Side Story	1961
5	Tom Jones	1963
6	Lawrence of Arabia	1962
7	Oliver!	1968
8	A Man For All Seasons	1966
9	In the Heat of the Night	1967
10	The Apartment	1960

* Ranked by US box office income

By the 1960s, accurate box office income reports were issued in the United States, enabling comparisons to be made between the winners of the decade. The latest reported US figure for *The Sound of Music* is $163,214,286.

TOP 10 HIGHEST-EARNING "BEST PICTURES" OF 1970s*

	FILM	YEAR
1	The Sting	1973
2	The Godfather	1972
3	Rocky	1976
4	One Flew Over the Cuckoo's Nest	1975
5	Kramer vs. Kramer	1979
6	Patton	1970
7	The Godfather, Part II	1974
8	The Deer Hunter	1978
9	The French Connection	1971
10	Annie Hall	1977

* Ranked by US box office income

Although *The Sting* was the most successful Oscar-winning film of the decade, it was outearned in its release year by *The Exorcist*, and subsequently by even more commercial hits in the form of *Jaws* (1975) and *Star Wars* (1977).

Rain and Sun
Dustin Hoffman and Tom Cruise as incongruous brothers in *Rain Man*. Cruise is said to have boosted world sales of his trademark Ray-Ban® Wayfarer sunglasses by 15 per cent.

Did you know?

Provided the film is still on release, a "Best Picture" Oscar means an instant increase in box office income: the first weekend following the win by *Chicago*, its income leapt in the USA by 25% and in the UK by 30%, while sales of the soundtrack album received a similar boost.

TOP 10 HIGHEST-EARNING "BEST PICTURES" OF 1980s*

	FILM	YEAR
1	Rain Man	1988
2	Platoon	1986
3	Terms of Endearment	1983
4	Driving Miss Daisy	1989
5	Out of Africa	1985
6	Chariots of Fire	1981
7	Ordinary People	1980
8	Gandhi	1982
9	Amadeus	1984
10	The Last Emperor	1987

* Ranked by US box office income

The first four films listed each made more than $100 million at the US box office, and even more overseas. *Rain Man* was one of the highest-earning films of the decade worldwide, generating more than $400 million.

TOP 10 HIGHEST-EARNING "BEST PICTURES" OF 1990s*

	FILM	YEAR
1	Titanic	1997
2	Forrest Gump	1994
3	Dances With Wolves	1990
4	American Beauty	1999
5	Schindler's List	1993
6	Shakespeare in Love	1998
7	The Silence of the Lambs	1991
8	The English Patient	1996
9	Braveheart	1995
10	Unforgiven	1992

* Ranked by world box office income

Since the late 1980s, it has become possible to compare worldwide film income. If the winners of the 21st century were integrated here using the same criterion, all those to date – *Gladiator* (2000), *A Beautiful Mind* (2001), and *Chicago* (2002) – would occupy prominent places in the list.

THE 10 FILMS TO WIN THE MOST OSCARS

	FILM	YEAR	NOMINATIONS	WINS
1 =	Ben-Hur	1959	12	11
=	Titanic	1997	14	11
3	West Side Story	1961	11	10
4 =	Gigi	1958	9	9
=	The Last Emperor	1987	9	9
=	The English Patient	1996	12	9
7 =	Gone With the Wind †	1939	13	8
=	From Here to Eternity	1953	13	8
=	On the Waterfront	1954	12	8
=	My Fair Lady	1964	12	8
=	Cabaret	1972	10	8
=	Gandhi	1982	11	8
=	Amadeus	1984	11	8

† Two special awards in addition to the wins given here

Ten other films have won seven Oscars each: *Going My Way* (1944), *The Best Years of Our Lives* (1946), *The Bridge on the River Kwai* (1957), *Lawrence of Arabia* (1962), *Patton* (1970), *The Sting* (1973), *Out of Africa* (1985), *Dances With Wolves* (1991), *Schindler's List* (1993), and *Shakespeare in Love* (1998). *Titanic* (1997) matched the previous record of 14 nominations of *All About Eve* (1950), but outshone it by winning 11, compared with the latter's six.

THE 10 FILMS NOMINATED FOR THE MOST OSCARS

	FILM	YEAR	WINS	NOMINATIONS
1 =	All About Eve	1950	6	14
=	Titanic	1997	11	14
3 =	Gone With the Wind *	1939	8	13
=	From Here to Eternity	1953	8	13
=	Shakespeare in Love	1998	7	13
=	Mary Poppins †	1964	5	13
=	Who's Afraid of Virginia Woolf? †	1966	5	13
=	Forrest Gump	1994	6	13
=	The Lord of the Rings: The Fellowship of the Ring	2001	4	13
=	Chicago	2002	6	13

* Two special awards in addition to the wins given here
† Did not win "Best Picture"

None Out of Ten

Gangs of New York was nominated for 10 Academy Awards, including "Best Picture" and "Best Director" (Martin Scorsese), but failed to win any.

THE 10 LATEST YEARS IN WHICH "BEST PICTURE" AND "BEST DIRECTOR" WERE WON BY DIFFERENT FILMS

	"BEST PICTURE"	"BEST DIRECTOR" FILM	YEAR
1	Chicago	The Pianist	2002
2	Gladiator	Traffic	2000
3	Shakespeare in Love	Saving Private Ryan	1998
4	Driving Miss Daisy	Born on the Fourth of July	1989
5	Chariots of Fire	Reds	1981
6	The Godfather	Cabaret	1972
7	In the Heat of the Night	The Graduate	1967
8	Around the World in 80 Days	Giant	1956
9	The Greatest Show on Earth	The Quiet Man	1952
10	An American in Paris	A Place in the Sun	1951

THE 10 FILMS WITH MOST OSCAR WINS IN MAJOR CATEGORIES*

	FILM	YEAR	WINS
1	Going My Way	1944	6
2 =	It Happened One Night	1934	5
=	Gone With the Wind	1939	5
=	Mrs. Miniver	1942	5
=	The Best Years of Our Lives	1946	5
=	From Here to Eternity	1953	5
=	On the Waterfront	1954	5
=	One Flew over the Cuckoo's Nest	1975	5
=	Kramer vs. Kramer	1979	5
=	Terms of Endearment	1983	5
=	The Silence of the Lambs	1991	5

* Includes "Best Picture/Director/Actor/Actress/Supporting Actor/Supporting Actress/Writing"

THE 10 FILMS WITH MOST NOMINATIONS BUT NO WIN

	FILM	NOMINATIONS	YEAR
1 =	The Turning Point	1977	11
=	The Color Purple	1985	11
3	Gangs of New York	2002	10
4 =	The Little Foxes	1941	9
=	Peyton Place	1957	9
6 =	Quo Vadis?	1951	8
=	The Nun's Story	1959	8
=	The Sand Pebbles	1966	8
=	The Elephant Man	1980	8
=	Ragtime	1981	8
=	The Remains of the Day	1993	8

THE 10 FILMS TO WIN MOST OSCARS BUT NOT "BEST PICTURE"

	FILM	YEAR	WINS
1	Cabaret	1972	8
2 =	A Place in the Sun	1951	6
=	Star Wars	1977	6
4 =	Wilson	1944	5
=	The Bad and The Beautiful	1952	5
=	The King and I	1956	5
=	Mary Poppins	1964	5
=	Doctor Zhivago	1965	5
=	Who's Afraid of Virginia Woolf?	1966	5
=	Saving Private Ryan	1998	5

THE 10 STUDIOS WITH THE MOST OSCARS (IN ALL CATEGORIES)

	STUDIO	WINS
1	MGM	190
2	20th Century Fox	18
3	Paramount	180
4	Warner Bros.	163
5	Columbia	154
6	United Artists	149
7	Universal	8
8	RKO Radio	56
9	Buena Vista	4
10	Miramax	39

THE 10 STUDIOS WITH THE MOST "BEST PICTURE" NOMINATIONS

	STUDIO	NOMINATIONS
1	Warner Bros.	61
2	MGM	57
3	Paramount	55
4	20th Century Fox	54
5 =	Columbia	51
=	United Artists	51
7	Universal	25
8	RKO Radio	19
9	Miramax	14
10	Fox	7

THE 10 STUDIOS WITH THE MOST OSCAR NOMINATIONS*

	STUDIO	NOMINATIONS
1	Paramount	895
2	20th Century Fox	857
3	Warner Bros.	843
4	MGM	834
5	Columbia	747
6	United Artists	743
7	Universal	434
8	RKO Radio	330
9	Buena Vista	205
10	Miramax	194

THE 10 STUDIOS WITH THE MOST "BEST PICTURE" OSCARS

	STUDIO	WINS
1 =	Columbia	12
=	United Artists	12
3	Paramount	1
4	MGM	9
5	20th Century Fox	
6 =	Universal	6
=	Warner Bros.	6
8	Orion	
9	DreamWorks	3
10 =	Miramax	

Victor Victorious

Victor Fleming directs Vivien Leigh in *Gone With the Wind*, the direction of which he took over from George Cukor. Among its 10 wins, he received the Oscar for "Best Director", while she won "Best Actress".

"BEST DIRECTOR" OSCARS – 1930s*

	DIRECTOR	FILM	YEAR
1	Lewis Milestone	All Quiet on the Western Front	1930
2	Norman Taurog	Skippy	1931
3	Frank Borzage	Bad Girl	1932
4	Frank Lloyd	Cavalcade	1933
5	Frank Capra	It Happened One Night	1934
6	John Ford	The Informer	1935
7	Frank Capra	Mr. Deeds Goes to Town	1936
8	Leo McCarey	The Awful Truth	1937
9	Frank Capra	You Can't Take It With You	1938
10	Victor Fleming	Gone With the Wind	1939

* The joint winners of the "Best Director" Oscar in the first year of the Academy Awards (1929) were Lewis Milestone for *Two Arabian Knights* (1927) and Frank Borzage for *Seventh Heaven* (1927). Frank Lloyd won "Best Director" for *The Divine Lady* in 1929.

"BEST DIRECTOR" OSCARS – 1940s

	DIRECTOR	FILM	YEAR
1	John Ford	The Grapes of Wrath	1940
2	John Ford	How Green Was My Valley	1941
3	William Wyler	Mrs. Miniver	1942
4	Michael Curtiz	Casablanca	1943
5	Leo McCarey	Going My Way	1944
6	Billy Wilder	The Lost Weekend	1945
7	William Wyler	The Best Years of Our Lives	1946
8	Elia Kazan	Gentleman's Agreement	1947
9	John Huston	The Treasure of the Sierra Madre	1948
10	Joseph L. Mankiewicz	A Letter to Three Wives	1949

William Wyler's two wins in the decade were followed by a third for *Ben-Hur* (1959) in the next, each of them also winning "Best Picture". His record 12 nominations spanned 29 years from 1936 to 1965.

"BEST DIRECTOR" OSCARS – 1950s

	DIRECTOR	FILM	YEAR
1	Joseph L. Mankiewicz	All About Eve	1950
2	George Stevens	A Place in the Sun	1951
3	John Ford	The Quiet Man	1952
4	Fred Zinnemann	From Here to Eternity	1953
5	Elia Kazan	On the Waterfront	1954
6	Delbert Mann	Marty	1955
7	George Stevens	Giant	1956
8	David Lean	The Bridge on the River Kwai	1957
9	Vincente Minnelli	Gigi	1958
10	William Wyler	Ben-Hur	1959

During the decade, there was a correlation between "Best Director" and "Best Picture" on seven occasions, the exceptions being those for 1951, 1952, and 1956, which were beaten to "Best Picture" by, respectively, *An American in Paris*, *The Greatest Show on Earth*, and *Around the World in 80 Days*.

"BEST DIRECTOR" OSCARS – 1960s

	DIRECTOR	FILM	YEAR
1	Billy Wilder	The Apartment	1960
2	Robert Wise and Jerome Robbins	West Side Story	1961
3	David Lean	Lawrence of Arabia	1962
4	Tony Richardson	Tom Jones	1963
5	George Cukor	My Fair Lady	1964
6	Robert Wise	The Sound of Music	1965
7	Fred Zinnemann	A Man for All Seasons	1966
8	Mike Nichols	The Graduate	1967
9	Carol Reed	Oliver!	1968
10	John Schlesinger	Midnight Cowboy	1969

Although Mike Nichols won his Oscar as "Best Director" for *The Graduate*, the film lost out as "Best Picture" to *In the Heat of the Night* (1967), directed by Norman Jewison. Billy Wilder gained his second win, having been nominated as "Best Director" on a total of eight occasions between 1944 and 1960.

"BEST DIRECTOR" OSCARS – 1970s

	DIRECTOR	FILM	YEAR
1	Franklin J. Schaffner	Patton	1970
2	William Friedkin	The French Connection	1971
3	Bob Fosse	Cabaret	1972
4	George Roy Hill	The Sting	1973
5	Francis Ford Coppola	The Godfather, Part II	1974
6	Milos Forman	One Flew Over the Cuckoo's Nest	1975
7	John G. Avildsen	Rocky	1976
8	Woody Allen	Annie Hall	1977
9	Michael Cimino	The Deer Hunter	1978
10	Robert Benton	Kramer vs. Kramer	1979

All the winners of the 1970s coincided with the "Best Picture" winners, with the notable exception of Bob Fosse's *Cabaret*, which lost out to *The Godfather* (1972). The latter's director, Francis Ford Coppola, was honoured two years later for the sequel, *The Godfather, Part II*.

"BEST DIRECTOR" OSCARS – 1980s

	DIRECTOR	FILM	YEAR
1	Robert Redford	Ordinary People	1980
2	Warren Beatty	Reds	1981
3	Richard Attenborough	Gandhi	1982
4	James L. Brooks	Terms of Endearment	1983
5	Milos Forman	Amadeus	1984
6	Sydney Pollack	Out of Africa	1985
7	Oliver Stone	Platoon	1986
8	Bernardo Bertolucci	The Last Emperor	1987
9	Barry Levinson	Rain Man	1988
10	Oliver Stone	Born on the Fourth of July	1989

Two "Best Director"-winning films of the decade failed to win in the "Best Picture" category as well: *Reds* was beaten by *Chariots of Fire* (1981), directed by Hugh Hudson, while *Born on the Fourth of July* lost to *Driving Miss Daisy* (1989), directed by Bruce Beresford.

"BEST DIRECTOR" OSCARS – 1990s

	DIRECTOR	FILM	YEAR
1	Kevin Costner	Dances With Wolves	1990
2	Jonathan Demme	The Silence of the Lambs	1991
3	Clint Eastwood	Unforgiven	1992
4	Steven Spielberg	Schindler's List	1992
5	Robert Zemeckis	Forrest Gump	1994
6	Mel Gibson	Braveheart	1995
7	Anthony Minghella	The English Patient	1996
8	James Cameron	Titanic	1997
9	Steven Spielberg	Saving Private Ryan	1998
10	Sam Mendes	American Beauty	1999

Academy Awards for "Best Director" in the 21st century went to Steven Soderbergh for *Traffic* (2000), Ron Howard for *A Beautiful Mind* (2001), and Roman Polanski for *The Pianist* (2002).

Direct Action

Although it lost to *Shakespeare in Love* as "Best Picture", Steven Spielberg won the "Best Director" Academy Award for his action-packed war film, *Saving Private Ryan*.

Directorial Debut
Orson Welles was the first director ever nominated for an Oscar for his first feature film, *Citizen Kane* (1941) in which he also took the title role. The film received nine nominations, but won only for the script – which Welles co-wrote.

THE 10 FIRST DIRECTORS NOMINATED FOR A "BEST DIRECTOR" OSCAR FOR THEIR DEBUT FILM*

	DIRECTOR	FILM	YEAR
1	Orson Welles	Citizen Kane	1941
2	Delbert Mann †	Marty	1955
3	Sidney Lumet	12 Angry Men	1957
4	Jack Clayton	Room at the Top	1959
5	Jerome Robbins †	West Side Story	1961
6	Frank Perry	David and Lisa	1962
7	Mike Nichols	Who's Afraid of Virginia Woolf?	1966
8	Warren Beatty/Buck Henry	Heaven Can Wait	1978
9	Robert Redford †	Ordinary People	1980
10	James L. Brooks †	Terms of Endearment	1983

* Excluding short films
† Won "Best Director" Oscar

THE 10 DIRECTORS WITH THE MOST "BEST DIRECTOR" OSCAR NOMINATIONS

	DIRECTOR	WINS	YEARS	NOMINATIONS
1	William Wyler	5	1936–65	12
2	Billy Wilder	2	1944–60	8
3 =	David Lean	2	1946–84	7
=	Fred Zinnemann	2	1948–77	7
4 =	Woody Allen	1	1977–97	6
=	Clarence Brown	0	1929/30–46	6
=	Frank Capra	3	1923/33–46	6
7 =	Robert Altman	0	1970–2001	5
=	George Cukor	1	1932/33	5
=	John Ford	4	1935–52	5
=	Alfred Hitchcock	0	1940–60	5
=	John Huston	1	1948–85	5
=	Elia Kazan	2	1947–63	5
=	Frank Lloyd	2	1928/29–35	5
=	Steven Spielberg	2	1977–98	5
=	George Stevens	2	1942–63	5
=	King Vidor	0	1927/28–56	5

THE 10 OLDEST OSCAR-WINNING DIRECTORS

	DIRECTOR	FILM	YEAR	AGE
1	Roman Polanski	The Pianist	2002	69y 7m 5d
2	George Cukor	My Fair Lady	1965	65y 8m 29d
3	Clint Eastwood	Unforgiven	1992	62y 9m 29d
4	Carol Reed	Oliver!	1968	62y 3m 15d
5	Fred Zinnemann	A Man for All Seasons	1966	60y 0m 12d
6	Richard Attenborough	Gandhi	1982	59y 7m 13d
7	John Ford	The Quiet Man	1953	59y 1m 18d
8	William Wyler	Ben-Hur	1960	57y 9m 13d
9	Michael Curtiz	Casablanca	1942	57y 2m 9d
10	Vincente Minnelli	Gigi	1958	57y 1m 6d

THE 10 YOUNGEST OSCAR-WINNING DIRECTORS

	DIRECTOR	FILM	YEAR	AGE
1	William Friedkin	The French Connection	1971	32y 8m 1d
2	Norman Taurog	Skippy	1931	32y 8m 15d
3	Sam Mendes	American Beauty	1999	34y 7m 25d
4	Lewis Milestone	All Quiet on the Western Front	1930	35y 1m 5d
5	Michael Cimino	The Deer Hunter	1978	35y 4m 23d
6	Tony Richardson	Tom Jones	1963	35y 10m 8d
7	Delbert Mann	Marty	1955	35y 11m 22d
8	Francis Ford Coppola	The Godfather, Part II	1974	36y 0m 1d
9	Kevin Costner	Dances With Wolves	1990	36y 2m 2d
10	Mike Nichols	The Graduate	1967	36y 5m 4d

In 1929, the Oscars's first year, there was no single "Best Director" award; Lewis Milestone (33 years 7 months 16 days) won an Oscar for directing the best comedy, *Two Arabian Knights* (1927) and Frank Borzage (36 years 0 months and 23 days) won for directing the best dramatic production, *Seventh Heaven* (1927).

THE 10 PEOPLE WITH THE MOST OSCARS*

	NAME	PROFESSION	YEARS	WINS
1	Walt Disney	Producer	1931/32	20
2	Cedric Gibbons	Art direction	1928/29–56	11
3	Alfred Newman	Musical score	1938–67	9
4 =	Edith Head	Costume design	1949–73	8
=	Alan Menken	Musical score/Original song	1989–95	8
=	Edwin B. Willis	Art direction	1941–56	8
7 =	Richard Day	Art direction	1935–54	7
=	Frederick Quimby	Producer	1943–52	7
=	Gary Rydstrom	Sound	1991–98	7
=	Douglas Shearer	Sound	1929/30–51	7

* In all categories

TOP 10 OSCARS HOSTS

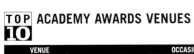

	HOST*	YEARS	APPEARANCES
1	Bob Hope	1939–77	20
2	Billy Crystal	1989–99	7
3	Johnny Carson	1978–83	5
4 =	Whoopi Goldberg	1983–2001	4
=	Jack Lemmon	1957–84	4
6 =	Jane Fonda	1968–85	3
=	Jerry Lewis	1955–58	3
=	Conrad Nagel	1929/30–52	3
=	David Niven	1957–73	3
=	Frank Sinatra	1962–74	3

* Including co-hosts

TOP 10 ACADEMY AWARDS VENUES

	VENUE	OCCASIONS
1	Dorothy Chandler Pavilion	25
2	RKO Pantages Theatre	11
3	Shrine Civic Auditorium	10
4	Santa Monica Civic Auditorium	8
5	The Biltmore Bowl, Biltmore Hotel	7
6 =	The Cocoanut Grove, Ambassador Hotel	3
=	Fiesta Room, Ambassador Hotel	3
=	Grauman's Chinese Theatre	3
9	Kodak Theatre	2
10 =	Blossom Room, Hollywood Roosevelt Hotel	1
=	Sala D'Oro, Biltmore Hotel	1
=	Academy Award Theater	1

Hope Springs Eternal

The winner of four honorary Academy Awards and the prestigious Jean Hersholt Humanitarian Award, Bob Hope presented the ceremony on a record 20 occasions. In anticipation of his 100th birthday on 29 May 2003, Hollywood honoured the British-born veteran comedian by declaring him "Citizen of the Century".

THE 10 "BEST ACTOR" OSCARS – 1930s

	ACTOR	FILM	YEAR
1	George Arliss	Disraeli	1930
2	Lionel Barrymore	A Free Soul	1931
3	Wallace Beery	The Champ	1932
4	Charles Laughton	The Private Life of Henry VIII	1933
5	Clarke Gable	It Happened One Night *	1934
6	Victor McLaglen	The Informer	1935
7	Paul Muni	The Story of Louis Pasteur	1938
8	Spencer Tracy	Captains Courageous	1937
9	Spencer Tracy	Boys Town	1938
10	Robert Donat	Goodbye, Mr. Chips	1939

* "Best Picture", "Best Director", "Best Actress", and "Best Screenplay" Oscars
The first winner of an Oscar for "Best Actor" was Emil Jannings for his roles in two silent films, *The Way of All Flesh* (1927) and *The Last Command* (1928). Swiss-born Jannings' German accent proved a stumbling block when talkies arrived, and he settled in Germany where he appeared opposite Marlene Dietrich in the 1930 film *Der Blaue Engel* (*The Blue Angel*) and went on to make Nazi propaganda films. Although cleared by the War Crimes Commission, he was unable to resume his film career after World War II, and he died in Austria in 1950. Warner Baxter won the second "Best Actor" award for his role as The Cisco Kid, a Mexican bandit, in the film *In Old Arizona* (1929).

Fifth Time Lucky

After receiving four Oscar nominations in the 1940s, Gregory Peck finally won "Best Actor" for his powerful performance as lawyer Atticus Finch in the 1962 film *To Kill a Mockingbird*, based on Harper Lee's Pulitzer Prize-winning novel.

THE 10 "BEST ACTOR" OSCARS – 1940s

	ACTOR	FILM	YEAR
1	James Stewart	The Philadelphia Story	1940
2	Gary Cooper	Sergeant York	1941
3	James Cagney	Yankee Doodle Dandy	1942
4	Paul Lukas	Watch on the Rhine	1943
5	Bing Crosby	Going My Way *	1944
6	Ray Milland	The Lost Weekend *	1945
7	Fredric March	The Best Years of Our Lives *	1946
8	Ronald Colman	A Double Life	1947
9	Laurence Olivier	Hamlet *	1948
10	Broderick Crawford	All the King's Men *	1949

* "Best Picture" Oscar
James Stewart gained his only acting Oscar for *The Philadelphia Story*, although he was nominated on four other occasions, and at the 1984 event was presented with an Honorary Award to celebrate his 50 years in films. Laurence Olivier's Oscar was the first win for a British actor in a British film.

THE 10 "BEST ACTOR" OSCARS – 1950s

	ACTOR	FILM	YEAR
1	José Ferrer	Cyrano de Bergerac	1950
2	Humphrey Bogart	The African Queen	1951
3	Gary Cooper	High Noon	1952
4	William Holden	Stalag 17	1953
5	Marlon Brando	On the Waterfront *	1954
6	Ernest Borgnine	Marty *	1955
7	Yul Brynner	The King and I	1956
8	Alec Guinness	The Bridge on the River Kwai *	1957
9	David Niven	Separate Tables	1958
10	Charlton Heston	Ben-Hur *	1959

* "Best Picture" Oscar
Five-times nominee and double winner Gary Cooper also received an Honorary Award in 1960, but was unable to attend through illness; it was accepted by James Stewart, and Cooper died a month later.

THE 10 "BEST ACTOR" OSCARS – 1960s

	ACTOR	FILM	YEAR
1	Burt Lancaster	Elmer Gantry	1960
2	Maximilian Schell	Judgment at Nuremberg	1961
3	Gregory Peck	To Kill a Mockingbird	1962
4	Sidney Poitier	Lilies of the Field	1963
5	Rex Harrison	My Fair Lady *	1964
6	Lee Marvin	Cat Ballou	1965
7	Paul Scofield	A Man for All Seasons *	1966
8	Rod Steiger	In the Heat of the Night *	1967
9	Cliff Robertson	Charly	1968
10	John Wayne	True Grit	1969

* "Best Picture" Oscar
Sydney Poitier was the first black actor to win an Academy Award; it was not until 2001 that an African-American actress, Halle Berry, won the coveted award.

THE 10 "BEST ACTOR" OSCARS – 1970s

	ACTOR	FILM	YEAR
1	George C. Scott	Patton *	1970
2	Gene Hackman	The French Connection *	1971
3	Marlon Brando	The Godfather *	1972
4	Jack Lemmon	Save the Tiger	1973
5	Art Carney	Harry and Tonto	1974
6	Jack Nicholson	One Flew Over the Cuckoo's Nest *	1975
7	Peter Finch	Network	1976
8	Richard Dreyfus	The Goodbye Girl	1977
9	Jon Voight	Coming Home	1978
10	Dustin Hoffman	Kramer vs. Kramer *	1979

* "Best Picture" Oscar

Peter Finch was the first (and so far only) "Best Actor" to be honoured posthumously: he died on 14 January 1977 and the award was announced at the 1976 ceremony held on 28 March 1977. He was not the first posthumous winner of any Academy Award, however: that distinction went to Sidney Howard for his screenplay for *Gone With the Wind*. Howard died on 23 August 1939, and at the award ceremony on 29 February 1940, the Nobel Prize-winning novelist Sinclair Lewis received the Oscar on his behalf.

THE 10 "BEST ACTOR" OSCARS – 1980s

	ACTOR	FILM	YEAR
1	Robert De Niro	Raging Bull	1980
2	Henry Fonda	On Golden Pond	1981
3	Ben Kingsley	Gandhi *	1982
4	Robert Duvall	Tender Mercies	1983
5	F. Murray Abraham	Amadeus *	1984
6	William Hurt	Kiss of the Spider Woman	1985
7	Paul Newman	The Color of Money	1986
8	Michael Douglas	Wall Street	1987
9	Dustin Hoffman	Rain Man *	1988
10	Daniel Day-Lewis	My Left Foot	1989

* "Best Picture" Oscar

Paul Newman's role as "Fast Eddie" Felson in *The Color of Money* was a reprise of the role he had played in *The Hustler* (1961), for which he had also been nominated. This, his only acting Oscar, came after he had been nominated in leading roles seven times from 1958 onwards, although he had won an Honorary Award the previous year, and he was to receive the Academy's Jean Hersholt Humanitarian Award in 1994, as well as two further non-winning nominations. He was nominated for "Best Picture" as the producer of *Rachel, Rachel* (1968), which was also his directorial debut.

THE 10 "BEST ACTOR" OSCARS – 1990s

	ACTOR	FILM	YEAR
1	Jeremy Irons	Reversal of Fortune	1990
2	Anthony Hopkins	The Silence of the Lambs *	1991
3	Al Pacino	Scent of a Women	1992
4	Tom Hanks	Philadelphia	1993
5	Tom Hanks	Forrest Gump *	1994
6	Nicholas Cage	Leaving Las Vegas	1995
7	Geoffrey Rush	Shine	1996
8	Jack Nicholson	As Good As It Gets	1997
9	Roberto Benigni	Life Is Beautiful	1998
10	Kevin Spacey	American Beauty *	1999

* "Best Picture" Oscar

Tom Hanks shares the honour of two consecutive wins with Spencer Tracy (1937 and 1938). Only four other actors have ever won twice: Marlon Brando (1954; 1972), Gary Cooper (1941; 1952), Dustin Hoffman (1979; 1988), and Jack Nicholson (1975; 1997). Subsequent "Best Actor" Oscar winners are Russell Crowe for *Gladiator* (which also won "Best Picture") in 2000, Denzel Washington for *Training Day* in 2001, and Adrien Brody for *The Pianist* in 2002.

As Good As Gold

Jack Nicholson gained his second "Best Actor" Oscar for *As Good As It Gets*. He has been nominated on 12 occasions from 1969 (for *Easy Rider*) to 2002 (for *About Schmidt*).

Did you know?

George C. Scott was the first winner to refuse an Oscar, for his performance in *Patton* (1970). Marlon Brando refused his for *The Godfather* (1972), sending Maria Cruz, an actress posing as a Native American Indian called Sacheen Littlefeather, to receive it for him.

THE 10 "BEST ACTRESS" OSCARS – 1930s

	ACTRESS	FILM	YEAR
1	Norma Shearer	The Divorcee	1930
2	Marie Dressler	Min and Bill	1931
3	Helen Hayes	The Sin of Madelon Claudet	1932
4	Katharine Hepburn	Morning Glory	1933
5	Claudette Colbert	It Happened One Night *	1934
6	Bette Davis	Dangerous	1935
7	Luise Rainer	The Great Zeigfeld *	1936
8	Luise Rainer	The Good Earth	1937
9	Bette Davis	Jezebel	1938
10	Vivien Leigh	Gone With the Wind *	1939

* "Best Picture" Oscar

The first winner of a "Best Actress" Oscar was Janet Gaynor for her roles in three films, *Seventh Heaven* (1927), *Sunrise* (1927), and *Street Angel* (1928), and the second was Mary Pickford for *Coquette* (1929).

THE 10 "BEST ACTRESS" OSCARS – 1940s

	ACTRESS	FILM	YEAR
1	Ginger Rogers	Kitty Foyle	1940
2	Joan Fontaine	Suspicion	1941
3	Greer Garson	Mrs. Miniver *	1942
4	Jennifer Jones	The Song of Bernadette	1943
5	Ingrid Bergman	Gaslight	1944
6	Joan Crawford	Mildred Pierce	1945
7	Olivia de Havilland	To Each His Own	1946
8	Loretta Young	The Farmer's Daughter	1947
9	Jane Wyman	Johnny Belinda	1948
10	Olivia de Havilland	The Heiress	1949

* "Best Picture" Oscar

Joan Fontaine and double winner Olivia de Havilland are the only sisters to win "Best Actress in a Leading Role" Oscars. Other sibling Oscar winners include Warren Beatty and Shirley MacLaine.

Sophia's Choice

Sophia Loren was so convinced she would not win the "Best Actress" Oscar for her role in the Italian-made *Two Women* that she did not attend the ceremony, and a previous winner, Greer Garson, accepted the award on her behalf.

THE 10 "BEST ACTRESS" OSCARS – 1950s

	ACTRESS	FILM	YEAR
1	Judy Holiday	Born Yesterday	1950
2	Vivien Leigh	A Streetcar Named Desire	1951
3	Shirley Booth	Come Back, Little Sheba	1952
4	Audrey Hepburn	Roman Holiday	1953
5	Grace Kelly	The Country Girl	1954
6	Anna Magnani	The Rose Tattoo	1955
7	Ingrid Bergman	Anastasia	1956
8	Joanne Woodward	The Three Faces of Eve	1957
9	Susan Hayward	I Want to Live!	1958
10	Simone Signoret	Room at the Top	1959

Uniquely in the 1960s, not one Oscar win for an actress in a lead role coincided with a win for the picture in which she appeared. This is partly a reflection of the very masculine bias of some of the "Best Picture" winners in this period, including *On the Waterfront* (1954), *The Bridge on the River Kwai* (1957), and *Ben-Hur* (1959), none of which produced a single nomination for a woman.

THE 10 "BEST ACTRESS" OSCARS – 1960s

	ACTRESS	FILM	YEAR
1	Elizabeth Taylor	Butterfield 8	1960
2	Sophia Loren	Two Women	1961
3	Anne Bancroft	The Miracle Worker	1962
4	Patricia Neal	Hud	1963
5	Julie Andrews	Mary Poppins	1964
6	Julie Christie	Darling	1965
7	Elizabeth Taylor	Who's Afraid of Virginia Woolf?	1966
8	Katharine Hepburn	Guess Who's Coming to Dinner	1967
9	Katharine Hepburn/ Barbra Streisand *	The Lion in Winter/ Funny Girl	1968
10	Maggie Smith	The Prime of Miss Jean Brody	1969

* The only tie for "Best Actress"

THE 10 "BEST ACTRESS" OSCARS – 1970s

	ACTRESS	FILM	YEAR
1	Glenda Jackson	Women in Love	1970
2	Jane Fonda	Klute	1971
3	Liza Minnelli	Cabaret	1972
4	Glenda Jackson	A Touch of Class	1973
5	Ellen Burstyn	Alice Doesn't Live Here Anymore	1974
6	Louise Fletcher	One Flew Over the Cuckoo's Nest *	1975
7	Faye Dunaway	Network	1976
8	Diane Keaton	Annie Hall *	1977
9	Jane Fonda	Coming Home	1978
10	Sally Field	Norma Rae	1979

* "Best Picture" Oscar
British actress Glenda Jackson's two wins were garnered from a total of four nominations for leading role Oscars during the decade; the other two were for *Sunday, Bloody Sunday* (1971) and *Hedda* (1975).

THE 10 "BEST ACTRESS" OSCARS – 1980s

	ACTRESS	FILM	YEAR
1	Sissy Spacek	Coal Miner's Daughter	1980
2	Katharine Hepburn	On Golden Pond	1981
3	Meryl Streep	Sophie's Choice	1982
4	Shirley MacLaine	Terms of Endearment *	1983
5	Sally Field	Places in the Heart	1984
6	Geraldine Page	The Trip to Bountiful	1985
7	Marlee Matlin	Children of a Lesser God	1986
8	Cher	Moonstruck	1987
9	Jodie Foster	The Accused	1988
10	Jessica Tandy	Driving Miss Daisy *	1989

* "Best Picture" Oscar
Youngest-ever "Best Actress" winner Marlee Matlin's performance in the film version of the stage play *Children of a Lesser God* was especially remarkable, since not only was it her debut film, but as she plays the part of a deaf-mute, she has no spoken dialogue.

THE 10 "BEST ACTRESS" OSCARS – 1990s

	ACTRESS	FILM	YEAR
1	Kathy Bates	Misery	1990
2	Jodie Foster	The Silence of the Lambs *	1991
3	Emma Thompson	Howard's End	1992
4	Holly Hunter	The Piano	1993
5	Jessica Lange	Blue Sky	1994
6	Susan Sarandon	Dead Man Walking	1995
7	Frances McDormand	Fargo	1996
8	Helen Hunt	As Good As It Gets	1997
9	Gwyneth Paltrow	Shakespeare in Love *	1998
10	Hilary Swank	Boys Don't Cry	1999

* "Best Picture" Oscar
The "Best Actress" Oscar winners in the 21st century are Julia Roberts for *Erin Brockovich* (2000), Halle Berry for *Monster's Ball* (2001), and Nicole Kidman for *The Hours* (2002). Halle Berry was the first African-American actress to win a "Best Actress" Oscar; coincidentally, in the same year Denzel Washington, an African-American actor, won "Best Actor" for *Training Day*.

Foster Child

Jodie Foster had been nominated for an Oscar for her supporting role in *Taxi Driver* (1976), when she was just 13, and won for her lead role in controversial courtroom drama *The Accused* (1988).

10 TOP OSCAR "BEST SUPPORTING ACTORS"

THE 10 "BEST SUPPORTING ACTOR" OSCARS – 1940s

	ACTOR	FILM	YEAR
1	Walter Brennan	The Westerner	1940
2	Donald Crisp	How Green Was My Valley	1941
3	Van Heflin	Johnny Eager	1942
4	Charles Coburn	The More the Merrier	1943
5	Barry Fitzgerald	Going My Way	1944
6	James Dunn	A Tree Grows in Brooklyn	1945
7	Harold Russell	The Best Years of Our Lives	1946
8	Edmund Gwenn	Miracle on 34th Street	1947
9	Walter Huston	The Treasure of the Sierra Madre	1948
10	Dean Jagger	Twelve O'Clock High	1949

The Oscar for "Best Actor in a Supporting Role" was first awarded for films of 1936, when it was won by Walter Brennan for *Come and Get It*. Subsequent 1930s winners were Joseph Schildkraut for *The Life of Emile Zola* (1937), Walter Brennan for *Kentucky* (1938), and Thomas Mitchell for *Stagecoach* (1939).

Artistic Endeavour

Anthony Quinn as painter Paul Gauguin in *Lust for Life* (1956), one of the shortest roles ever to win an Oscar. Both his Oscar wins were achieved in the 1950s, but he received further nominations in 1957 and 1964.

THE 10 "BEST SUPPORTING ACTOR" OSCARS – 1950s

	ACTOR	FILM	YEAR
1	George Sanders	All About Eve	1950
2	Karl Malden	A Streetcar Named Desire	1951
3	Anthony Quinn	Viva Zapata!	1952
4	Frank Sinatra	From Here to Eternity	1953
5	Edmond O'Brien	The Barefoot Contessa	1954
6	Jack Lemmon	Mister Roberts	1955
7	Anthony Quinn	Lust for Life	1956
8	Red Buttons	Sayonara	1957
9	Burl Ives	The Big Country	1958
10	Hugh Griffith	Ben-Hur	1959

Jack Lemmon was the first actor to win Oscars as both supporting and lead actor: his 1955 supporting win was followed by one for his lead role in *Save the Tiger* (1973). Only five others – Gene Hackman, Robert De Niro, Jack Nicholson, Denzel Washington, and Kevin Spacey – have emulated this achievement.

THE 10 "BEST SUPPORTING ACTOR" OSCARS – 1960s

	ACTOR	FILM	YEAR
1	Peter Ustinov	Spartacus	1960
2	George Chakiris	West Side Story	1961
3	Ed Begley	Sweet Bird of Youth	1962
4	Melvyn Douglas	Hud	1963
5	Peter Ustinov	Topkapi	1964
6	Martin Balsam	A Thousand Clowns	1965
7	Walter Matthau	The Fortune Cookie	1966
8	George Kennedy	Cool Hand Luke	1967
9	Jack Albertson	The Subject was Roses	1968
10	Gig Young	They Shoot Horses, Don't They?	1969

With his win for *Topkapi* (1964), Peter Ustinov joined a small band of actors who won two awards for supporting roles. Walter Brennan was the first – and the only winner of three Oscars in this category – and Anthony Quinn the second. Since Ustinov, only Melvyn Douglas, Jason Robards, and Michael Caine have replicated this success.

THE 10 "BEST SUPPORTING ACTOR" OSCARS – 1970s

	ACTOR	FILM	YEAR
1	John Mills	Ryan's Daughter	1970
2	Ben Johnson	The Last Picture Show	1971
3	Joel Grey	Cabaret	1972
4	John Houseman	The Paper Chase	1973
5	Robert De Niro	The Godfather, Part II	1974
6	George Burns	The Sunshine Boys	1975
7	Jason Robards	All the President's Men	1976
8	Jason Robards	Julia	1977
9	Christopher Walken	The Deer Hunter	1978
10	Melvyn Douglas	Being There	1979

Two of the winners in the 1970s – Joel Grey and George Burns – received their awards with their first and only nominations. Although veteran actor Burns had appeared in films in the 1930s, he had moved into television and prior to *The Sunshine Boys* (1975) had not acted in a film since 1939.

THE 10 "BEST SUPPORTING ACTOR" OSCARS – 1980s

	ACTOR	FILM	YEAR
1	Timothy Hutton	Ordinary People	1980
2	John Gielgud	Arthur	1981
3	Louis Gossett Jr.	An Officer and a Gentleman	1982
4	Jack Nicholson	Terms of Endearment	1983
5	Haing S. Ngor	The Killing Fields	1984
6	Don Ameche	Cocoon	1985
7	Michael Caine	Hannah and Her Sisters	1986
8	Sean Connery	The Untouchables	1987
9	Kevin Kline	A Fish Called Wanda	1988
10	Denzel Washington	Glory	1989

THE 10 "BEST SUPPORTING ACTOR" OSCARS – 1990s

	ACTOR	FILM	YEAR
1	Joe Pesci	GoodFellas	1990
2	Jack Palance	City Slickers	1991
3	Gene Hackman	Unforgiven	1992
4	Tommy Lee Jones	The Fugitive	1993
5	Martin Landau	Ed Wood	1994
6	Kevin Spacey	The Usual Suspects	1995
7	Cuba Gooding Jr.	Jerry Maguire	1996
8	Robin Williams	Good Will Hunting	1997
9	James Coburn	Affliction	1998
10	Michael Caine	The Cider House Rules	1999

The winners in the 2000s were Benicio Del Toro for *Traffic* (2000), Jim Broadbent for *Iris* (2001), and Chris Cooper for *Adaptation* (2002).

Quiet Victory
John Mills won his only Oscar for his role as a deaf mute in *Ryan's Daughter* (1970). The first silent winner in the sound era, he accepted his award in silence.

Success Story

Although she won with her sole Oscar nomination for her role as Anita in *West Side Story*, Rita Moreno's other work gained her a Grammy (1972), a Tony (1975), and two Emmy awards (1977 and 1978).

THE 10 "BEST SUPPORTING ACTRESS" OSCARS – 1940s

	ACTRESS	FILM	YEAR
1	Jane Darwell	The Grapes of Wrath	1940
2	Mary Astor	The Great Lie	1941
3	Teresa Wright	Mrs. Miniver	1942
4	Katina Paxinou	For Whom the Bell Tolls	1943
5	Ethel Barrymore	None but the Lonely Heart	1944
6	Anne Revere	National Velvet	1945
7	Anne Baxter	The Razor's Edge	1946
8	Celeste Holm	Gentleman's Agreement	1947
9	Claire Trevor	Key Largo	1948
10	Mercedes McCambridge	All the King's Men	1949

The Oscar for "Best Actress in a Supporting Role" was first awarded for films of 1936, when it was won by Gale Sondergaard for *Anthony Adverse*. Subsequent 1930s winners were Alice Brady for *In Old Chicago* (1937), Fay Bainter for *Jezebel* (1938), and Hattie McDaniel for *Gone With the Wind* (1939).

THE 10 "BEST SUPPORTING ACTRESS" OSCARS – 1950s

	ACTRESS	FILM	YEAR
1	Josephine Hull	Harvey	1950
2	Kim Hunter	A Streetcar Named Desire	1951
3	Gloria Grahame	The Bad and the Beautiful	1952
4	Donna Reed	From Here to Eternity	1953
5	Eva Marie Saint	On the Waterfront	1954
6	Jo Van Fleet	East of Eden	1955
7	Dorothy Malone	Written on the Wind	1956
8	Miyoshi Umeki	Sayonara	1957
9	Wendy Hiller	Separate Tables	1958
10	Shelley Winters	The Diary of Anne Frank	1959

Only three of the winners in the 1950s – Grahame, Hiller, and Winters – ever received another Oscar nomination, while two of the winners of the decade – Hunter and Hiller – were not present to collect their awards, which were accepted on their respective behalves by actress Bette Davis and producer Harold Hecht.

THE 10 "BEST SUPPORTING ACTRESS" OSCARS – 1960s

	ACTRESS	FILM	YEAR
1	Shirley Jones	Elmer Gantry	1960
2	Rita Moreno	West Side Story	1961
3	Patty Duke	The Miracle Worker	1962
4	Margaret Rutherford	The V.I.P.s	1963
5	Lila Kedrova	Zorba the Greek	1964
6	Shelley Winters	A Patch of Blue	1965
7	Sandy Dennis	Who's Afraid of Virginia Woolf?	1966
8	Estelle Parsons	Bonnie and Clyde	1967
9	Ruth Gordon	Rosemary's Baby	1968
10	Goldie Hawn	Cactus Flower	1969

THE 10 "BEST SUPPORTING ACTRESS" OSCARS – 1970s

	ACTRESS	FILM	YEAR
1	Helen Hayes	Airport	1970
2	Cloris Leachman	The Last Picture Show	1971
3	Eileen Heckart	Butterflies Are Free	1972
4	Tatum O'Neal	Paper Moon	1973
5	Ingrid Bergman	Murder on the Orient Express	1974
6	Lee Grant	Shampoo	1975
7	Beatrice Straight	Network	1976
8	Vanessa Redgrave	Julia	1977
9	Maggie Smith	California Suite	1978
10	Meryl Streep	Kramer vs. Kramer	1979

Nominated for her debut film role, 10-year-old Tatum O'Neal is the youngest-ever winner of an acting Oscar, rather than an honorary award. Beatrice Straight's 5 minute 40 second winning performance in *Network* was also notable as the shortest ever to win an Oscar.

THE 10 "BEST SUPPORTING ACTRESS" OSCARS – 1980s

	ACTRESS	FILM	YEAR
1	Mary Steenburgen	Melvin and Howard	1980
2	Maureen Stapleton	Reds	1981
3	Jessica Lange	Tootsie	1982
4	Linda Hunt	The Year of Living Dangerously	1983
5	Peggy Ashcroft	A Passage to India	1984
6	Anjelica Huston	Prizzi's Honor	1985
7	Dianne Wiest	Hannah and Her Sisters	1986
8	Olympia Dukakis	Moonstruck	1987
9	Geena Davis	The Accidental Tourist	1988
10	Brenda Fricker	My Left Foot	1989

Linda Hunt's win was the first for an actress playing the part of a man. Anjelica Huston's was memorable for her being the third generation of Oscar-winning Hustons, her grandfather Walter having won a "Best Supporting Actor" Oscar for *The Treasure of the Sierra Madre* (1948), for which her father John won as "Best Director" and for his screenplay.

Did you know?

Hattie McDaniel's "Best Supporting Actress" win for her role as Mammy in *Gone With the Wind* (1939) was the first for an African-American. Her Oscar statuette was bequeathed to Howard University, but was stolen and has never been recovered.

THE 10 "BEST SUPPORTING ACTRESS" OSCARS – 1990s

	ACTRESS	FILM	YEAR
1	Whoopi Goldberg	Ghost	1990
2	Mercedes Ruehl	The Fisher King	1991
3	Marisa Tomei	My Cousin Vinny	1992
4	Anna Paquin	The Piano	1993
5	Dianne Wiest	Bullets Over Broadway	1994
6	Mira Sorvino	Mighty Aphrodite	1995
7	Juliette Binoche	The English Patient	1996
8	Kim Basinger	L.A. Confidential	1997
9	Judi Dench	Shakespeare in Love	1998
10	Angelina Jolie	Girl, Interrupted	1999

The winners in the 2000s were Marcia Gay Harden for *Pollock* (2000), Jennifer Connelly for *A Beautiful Mind* (2001), and Catherine Zeta-Jones for *Chicago* (2002).

Title Role
Vanessa Redgrave as the eponymous heroine of *Julia*. The film received 11 Oscar nominations and won three, but her "Best Supporting Actress" award is her sole win out of six nominations.

THE 10 LATEST STARS TO RECEIVE TWO NOMINATIONS IN THE SAME YEAR

	ACTOR/ACTRESS	FILMS	YEAR
1	Julianne Moore	Far From Heaven/The Hours *	2002
2 =	Holly Hunter	The Piano †/The Firm *	1993
=	Emma Thompson	The Remains of the Day/In the Name of the Father *	1993
4	Al Pacino	Scent of a Woman †/Glengarry Glen Ross *	1992
5	Sigourney Weaver	Gorillas in the Mist/Working Girl *	1988
6	Jessica Lange	Frances/Tootsie †	1982
7	Teresa Wright	Pride of the Yankees/Mrs. Miniver *†	1942
8 =	George Arliss	Disraeli †/The Green Goddess	1929/30
=	Maurice Chevalier	The Love Parade/The Big Pond	1929/30
=	Ronald Colman	Bulldog Drummond/Condemned	1929/30
=	Greta Garbo	Anna Christie/Romance	1929/30
=	Norma Shearer	The Divorcee †/Their Own Desire	1929/30

* Supporting
† Won
The only other double nominees were in the very first year of the Oscars, 1927/28, when Richard Barthelmess and Emil Jannings were each nominated for two films, and Janet Gaynor for three; only Jannings and Gaynor won their awards. In subsequent years, wins were for single films only.

THE 10 STARS WITH THE MOST CONSECUTIVE ACTING NOMINATIONS

	ACTOR/ACTRESS	YEARS	NOMINATIONS
1 =	Bette Davis	1938–42	5
=	Greer Garson	1941–45	5
3 =	Jennifer Jones	1943–46	4
=	Marlon Brando	1951–54	4
=	Al Pacino	1972–75	4
=	Elizabeth Taylor	1957–60	4
7 =	Spencer Tracy	1936–38	3
=	Gary Cooper	1941–43	3
=	Ingrid Bergman	1943–45	3
=	Gregory Peck	1945–47	3
=	Deborah Kerr	1956–58	3
=	Richard Burton	1964–66	3
=	Jack Nicholson	1973–75	3
=	Jane Fonda	1977–79	3
=	Meryl Streep	1981–83	3
=	Glenn Close	1982–84	3
=	William Hurt	1985–87	3
=	Russell Crowe	1999–2001	3

Moore the Merrier
Four times Oscar nominee Julianne Moore had the distinction of being nominated in the same year for her roles in *Far From Heaven* and *The Hours*.

THE 10 ACTRESSES WITH THE MOST NOMINATIONS*

	ACTOR	SUPPORTING WINS	BEST WINS	NOMINATIONS
1	Meryl Streep	1	1	13
2	Katharine Hepburn	0	4	12
3	Bette Davis	0	2	10
4	Geraldine Page	0	1	8
5 =	Ingrid Bergman	1	2	7
=	Jane Fonda	0	2	7
=	Greer Garson	0	1	7
8 =	Ellen Burstyn	0	1	6
=	Deborah Kerr	0	0	6
=	Jessica Lange	1	1	6
=	Vanessa Redgrave	1	0	6
=	Thelma Ritter	0	0	6
=	Norma Shearer	0	0	6
=	Maggie Smith	1	1	6
=	Sissy Spacek	0	1	6

* In all acting categories

Scent of Victory

Al Pacino was nominated eight times before scoring a same-year double nomination, for *Glengarry Glen Ross* as "Best Supporting Actor" and *Scent of a Woman* as "Best Actor"(both 1992), winning for his role in the latter.

THE 10 ACTORS WITH THE MOST NOMINATIONS*

	ACTOR	SUPPORTING	BEST	NOMINATIONS
1	Jack Nicholson	1	3	12
2	Laurence Olivier	0	1	10
3	Paul Newman	0	1	9
=	Spencer Tracy	0	2	9
5	Marlon Brando	0	2	8
=	Jack Lemmon	1	1	8
=	Al Pacino	0	1	8
8 =	Richard Burton	0	0	7
=	Dustin Hoffman	0	2	7
=	Peter O'Toole	0	0	7

* In all acting categories

THE 10 LATEST NOMINATIONS FOR STARS IN NON-ENGLISH LANGUAGE PERFORMANCES

	ACTOR/ACTRESS	FILM	LANGUAGE	YEAR
1	Javier Bardem	Before Night Falls	Spanish	2000
2 =	Roberto Benigni *	Life Is Beautiful	Italian	1998
=	Fernanda Montenegro	Central Station	Portuguese	1998
4	Massimo Troisi	Il Postino	Italian	1995
5	Catherine Deneuve	Indochine	French	1992
6	Gérard Depardieu	Cyrano de Bergerac	French	1990
7	Isabelle Adjani	Camille Claudel	French	1989
8	Max von Sydow	Pelle the Conqueror	Swedish	1988
9	Marcello Mastroianni	Dark Eyes	Italian	1987
10	Marlee Matlin *	Children of a Lesser God	Sign language	1986

* Won Oscar

THE 10 STARS WITH THE MOST NOMINATIONS WITHOUT WINNING

	ACTOR/ACTRESS	WINS	NON-WINNING NOMINATIONS
1	Meryl Streep	2	11
2 =	Jack Nicholson	3	9
=	Laurence Olivier	1*	9
4 =	Bette Davis	2	8
=	Katharine Hepburn	4	8
=	Paul Newman	1	8
7 =	Richard Burton	0	7
=	Peter O'Toole	0	7
=	Al Pacino	1	7
=	Geraldine Page	1	7
=	Spencer Tracy	2	7

* Also one win as Producer

THE 10 FIRST NOMINATIONS FOR STARS IN NON-ENGLISH LANGUAGE PERFORMANCES

	ACTOR/ACTRESS	FILM	LANGUAGE	YEAR
1	Sophia Loren *	Two Women	Italian	1961
2 =	Marcello Mastroianni	Divorce – Italian Style	Italian	1962
=	Sophia Loren	Divorce – Italian Style	Italian	1962
4 =	Anouk Aimée	A Man and a Woman	French	1966
=	Ida Kaminska	The Shop on Main Street	Czech	1966
6	Liv Ullmann	The Emigrants	Swedish	1972
7	Robert De Niro *	The Godfather, Part II	Italian	1974
8	Marie-Christine Barrault	Cousin, Cousine	French	1976
9	Marcello Mastroianni	A Special Day	Italian	1977
10	Ingrid Bergman	Autumn Sonata	Swedish	1978

* Won Oscar

THE 10 FIRST STARS TO WIN TWO "BEST ACTOR"/ "BEST ACTRESS" OSCARS

	ACTOR/ACTRESS	FIRST WIN	YEAR	SECOND WIN	YEAR
1	Luise Rainer	The Great Ziegfeld	1936	The Good Earth	1937
2 =	Bette Davis	Dangerous	1935	Jezebel	1938
=	Spencer Tracy	Captains Courageous	1937	Boys Town	1938
4	Fredric March	Dr. Jekyll and Mr. Hyde	1931/32	The Best Years of Our Lives	1946
5	Olivia de Havilland	To Each His Own	1946	The Heiress	1949
6	Vivien Leigh	Gone With the Wind	1939	A Streetcar Named Desire	1951
7	Gary Cooper	Sergeant York	1941	High Noon	1952
8	Ingrid Bergman	Gaslight	1944	Anastasia	1956
9	Elizabeth Taylor	Butterfield 8	1960	Who's Afraid of Virginia Woolf?	1966
10	Katharine Hepburn	Morning Glory	1932/33	Guess Who's Coming to Dinner	1967

THE 10 LONGEST WAITS: THE 10 BIGGEST GAPS BETWEEN 1ST NOMINATION AND 1ST AWARD*

	ACTOR/ACTRESS	FIRST NOMINATION	WINNING FILM	YEAR	INTERVAL (YEARS)
1	Henry Fonda	1940	On Golden Pond	1981	41
2	Geraldine Page	1953	The Trip to Bountiful	1985	32
3	Paul Newman	1958	The Color of Money	1986	28
4	Shirley MacLaine	1958	Terms of Endearment	1983	25
5 =	Al Pacino	1972	Scent of a Woman	1992	20
=	John Wayne	1949	True Grit	1969	20
7	Ronald Colman	1929	A Double Life	1947	18
8	Gregory Peck	1945	To Kill a Mockingbird	1962	17
9	Susan Sarandon	1981	Dead Man Walking	1995	14
10	Rod Steiger	1954	In the Heat of the Night	1967	13

* "Best Actor/Actress" Oscar wins only

THE 10 LATEST WINNERS OF AN ACADEMY AWARD FOR THEIR DEBUT FILM*

	ACTOR/ACTRESS	FILM	FILM YEAR
1	Anna Paquin †	The Piano	1993
2	Marlee Matlin #	Children of a Lesser God	1986
3	Haing S. Ngor †	The Killing Fields	1984
4	Timothy Hutton †	Ordinary People	1980
5	Tatum O'Neal †	Paper Moon	1973
6	Barbra Streisand #	Funny Girl	1968
7	Julie Andrews #	Mary Poppins	1964
=	Lila Kedrova †	Zorba The Greek	1964
9	Miyoshi Umeki †	Sayonara	1957
10	Anna Magnani #	The Rose Tatoo	1955

* In a film eligible for a "Best Actor/Actress" or "Best Supporting Actor/Actress" Oscar win (hence excluding previous TV movies, etc)
† "Best Supporting Actor/Actress"
# "Best Actor/Actress"

Twice Shy

Ingrid Bergman's rare second Oscar win came 12 years after her first. Her award, for her title role in *Anastasia*, was accepted by Cary Grant.

THE 10 YOUNGEST OSCAR WINNERS

	ACTOR/ACTRESS	AWARD	YEAR	AGE
1	Shirley Temple	Special Award (outstanding contribution during 1934)	1934	6y 10m 4d
2	Vincent Winter	Special Award (*The Little Kidnappers*)	1954	7y 3m 1d
3	Margaret O'Brien	Special Award (outstanding child actress of 1944)	1944	8y 2m 0d
4	Jon Whiteley	Special Award (*The Little Kidnappers*)	1954	10y 1m 11d
5	Tatum O'Neal	Best Supporting Actress (*Paper Moon*)	1973	10y 4m 27d
6	Anna Paquin	Best Supporting Actress (*The Piano*)	1993	11y 7m 28d
7	Ivan Jandl	Special Award (*The Search*)	1948	12y 0m 27d
8	Claude Jarman Jr.	Special Award (*The Yearling*)	1946	12y 5m 16d
9	Bobby Driscoll	Special Award (outstanding juvenile actor)	1949	13y 0m 20d
10	Hayley Mills	Special Award (outstanding juvenile performance)	1960	13y 11m 29d

The Academy Awards ceremony takes place in the year following that in which the film was released, so the winners are generally a year older when they receive their Oscars than when they acted in the films. Hayley Mills, the 12th and last winner of the "Special Award" miniature Oscar, won it one day before her 14th birthday. Subsequent winners have had to compete on the same basis as the adults. Tatum O'Neal is thus the youngest winner of – as well as the youngest-ever nominee for – an "adult" Oscar. Jackie Cooper was nine at the time of his nomination as "Best Actor" for *Skippy* (1930–31 Academy Awards), but the youngest winner was, surprisingly, more than 20 years older, Richard Dreyfuss (for *The Goodbye Girl* in the 1977 Awards). Justin Henry, 8, is the youngest nominee for "Best Supporting Actor", *Kramer vs. Kramer* (1979), but the youngest winner is Timothy Hutton, aged 20 when he won in the 1980 Awards for *Ordinary People*. The youngest "Best Actress" Award winner is Marlee Matlin, aged 21, for *Children of a Lesser God* (1986), and the youngest nominee Isabelle Adjani, 20, for *The Story of Adèle H* (1975).

THE 10 OLDEST OSCAR WINNERS

	ACTOR/ACTRESS	AWARD	YEAR	AGE
1	Jessica Tandy	Best Actress (*Driving Miss Daisy*)	1989	80y 9m 21d
2	George Burns	Best Supporting Actor (*The Sunshine Boys*)	1975	80y 2m 9d
3	Melvyn Douglas	Best Supporting Actor (*Being There*)	1979	79y 0m 9d
4	John Gielgud	Best Supporting Actor (*Arthur*)	1981	77y 11m 15d
5	Don Ameche	Best Supporting Actor (*Cocoon*)	1985	77y 9m 24d
6	Peggy Ashcroft	Best Supporting Actress (*A Passage to India*)	1984	77y 3m 3d
7	Henry Fonda	Best Actor (*On Golden Pond*)	1981	76y 10m 13d
8	Katharine Hepburn	Best Actress (*On Golden Pond*)	1981	74y 4m 11d
9	Edmund Gwenn	Best Supporting Actor (*Miracle on 34th Street*)	1947	72y 5m 24d
10	Ruth Gordon	Best Supporting Actress (*Rosemary's Baby*)	1968	72y 5m 15d

Jessica Tandy holds the record as both the oldest nominee and oldest winner of a "Best Actor" or "Best Actress" Oscar. Among those senior citizens who received nominations but did not win Oscars are Gloria Stuart, aged 87, for "Best Supporting Actress" in *Titanic* (1997), and Ralph Richardson, 82, for "Best Supporting Actor" in *Greystoke: The Legend of Tarzan* (1984). The oldest non-winning "Best Actor" nominee was Richard Farnsworth, aged 80, for *The Straight Story* (1999). May Robson was 75 when she was nominated as "Best Actress" in *Lady for a Day* (1933).

THE 10 FIRST ACTORS TO WIN A "BEST ACTOR" OSCAR WITH THEIR ONE AND ONLY NOMINATION

	ACTOR	FILM	YEAR
1	Warner Baxter	In Old Arizona	1928/29
2	Lionel Barrymore	A Free Soul	1930/31
3	Paul Lukas	Watch on the Rhine	1943
4	Ray Milland	The Lost Weekend	1945
5	Broderick Crawford	All the King's Men	1949
6	Ernest Borgnine	Marty	1955
7	Yul Brynner	The King and I	1956
8	David Niven	Separate Tables	1958
9	Charlton Heston	Ben-Hur	1959
10	Lee Marvin	Cat Ballou	1965

In the first year of the Academy Awards, Emil Jannings won for two films, but since single-film nominations have been the norm, all the actors listed won a "Best Actor" Academy Award after being nominated once and never again. Subsequent one-off winners are Cliff Robertson, *Charly* (1968), Art Carney, *Harry and Tonto* (1976), F. Murray Abraham, *Amadeus* (1984), Michael Douglas, *Wall Street* (1987), Jeremy Irons, *Reversal of Fortune* (1990), Roberto Benigni, *La Vita è Bela/Life is Beautiful* (1998), and Adrien Brody, *The Pianist* (2002). Eight of the single winners are living, so could yet repeat their success.

THE 10 FIRST ACTRESSES TO WIN A "BEST ACTRESS" OSCAR WITH THEIR ONE AND ONLY NOMINATION

	ACTRESS	FILM	FILM YEAR
1	Mary Pickford	Coquette	1928/29
2	Ginger Rogers	Kitty Foyle	1940
3	Judy Holliday	Born Yesterday	1950
4	Shirley Booth	Come Back, Little Sheba	1952
5	Grace Kelly	The Country Girl	1954
6	Louise Fletcher	One Flew Over the Cuckoo's Nest	1975
7	Marlee Matlin	Children of a Lesser God	1986
8	Helen Hunt	As Good As It Gets	1997
9	Gwyneth Paltrow	Shakespeare in Love	1998
10	Hilary Swank	Boys Don't Cry	1999

Before actors and actresses were nominated for one film only, Janet Gaynor won a "Best Actress" Oscar for three films, *Seventh Heaven*, *Sunrise* (both 1927), and *Street Angel* (1928). The first five listed died without ever again receiving a "Best Actress" nomination – although in 1976, at the age of 84, Mary Pickford was presented with an honorary award. The only other sole-nomination winner is Halle Berry for *Monster's Ball* (2001). The six latest winners are still active, so they have every opportunity to win further awards.

175

"BEST SONG" OSCARS – 1940s

	SONG	FILM	YEAR
1	When You Wish Upon a Star	Pinocchio	1940
2	The Last Time I Saw Paris	Lady be Good	1941
3	White Christmas	Holiday Inn	1942
4	You'll Never Know	Hello, Frisco, Hello	1943
5	Swinging on a Star	Going My Way	1944
6	It Might as Well be Spring	State Fair	1945
7	On the Atchison, Topeka and Santa Fé	The Harvey Girls	1946
8	Zip-A-Dee-Doo-Dah	Song of the South	1947
9	Buttons and Bows	The Paleface	1948
10	Baby, It's Cold Outside	Neptune's Daughter	1949

The "Best Song" Oscar was instituted at the 1934 Academy Awards ceremony, when it was won by "The Continental" from the film *The Gay Divorcee*. The other five winners from the rest of the 1930s were 1935: "Lullaby of Broadway" from *Gold Diggers of 1935*; 1936: "The Way You Look Tonight" from *Swing Time*; 1937: "Sweet Leilani" from *Waikiki Wedding*; 1938: "Thanks for the Memory" from *Big Broadcast of 1938*; and 1939: "Over the Rainbow" from *The Wizard of Oz*.

Clean Sweep
Dick Van Dyke as Bert the chimney sweep sings Oscar-winning Song "Chim Chim Cheree" in *Mary Poppins*. The film also won the Oscar for "Best Original Score".

"BEST SONG" OSCARS – 1950s

	SONG	FILM	YEAR
1	Mona Lisa	Captain Carey	1950
2	In the Cool, Cool, Cool of the Evening	Here Comes the Groom	1951
3	High Noon (Do Not Forsake Me, Oh My Darling)	High Noon	1952
4	Secret Love	Calamity Jane	1953
5	Three Coins in the Fountain	Three Coins in the Fountain	1954
6	Love is a Many-splendored Thing	Love is a Many-splendored Thing	1955
7	Que Sera, Sera	The Man Who Knew Too Much	1956
8	All the Way	The Joker is Wild	1957
9	Gigi	Gigi	1958
10	High Hopes	A Hole in the Head	1959

Doris Day benefited strongly from these Oscars, scoring million-selling singles with "Secret Love" and "Whatever Will Be, Will Be", both from films in which she starred.

"BEST SONG" OSCARS – 1960s

	SONG	FILM	YEAR
1	Never on Sunday	Never on Sunday	1960
2	Moon River	Breakfast at Tiffany's	1961
3	Days of Wine and Roses	Days of Wine and Roses	1962
4	Call Me Irresponsible	Papa's Delicate Condition	1963
5	Chim Chim Cheree	Mary Poppins	1964
6	The Shadow of Your Smile	The Sandpiper	1965
7	Born Free	Born Free	1966
8	Talk to the Animals	Dr. Doolittle	1967
9	The Windmills of Your Mind	The Thomas Crown Affair	1968
10	Raindrops Keep Falling on My Head	Butch Cassidy and the Sundance Kid	1969

"BEST SONG" OSCARS – 1970s

	SONG	FILM	YEAR
1	For All We Know	Lovers and Other Strangers	1970
2	Theme from Shaft	Shaft	1971
3	The Morning After	The Poseidon Adventure	1972
4	The Way We Were	The Way We Were	1973
5	We May Never Love Like This Again	The Towering Inferno	1974
6	I'm Easy	Nashville	1975
7	Evergreen	A Star is Born	1976
8	You Light up My Life	You Light up My Life	1977
9	Last Dance	Thank God it's Friday	1978
10	It Goes Like it Goes	Norma Rae	1979

Barbra Streisand became the first artist since Frank Sinatra to win two Oscar song awards in the same decade, with "The Way We Were" and "Evergreen", both of which went on to become huge international hits. Isaac Hayes' memorable "Theme from *Shaft*", in addition to being a rare "non-ballad" winner, became an influential milestone in both film and TV theme music, often copied but never equalled during the rest of the decade.

THE 10 "BEST SONG" OSCARS – 1980s

	SONG	FILM	YEAR
1	Fame	Fame	1980
2	Up Where We Belong	An Officer and a Gentleman	1981
3	Arthur's Theme (Best That You Can Do)	Arthur	1982
4	Flashdance	Flashdance	1983
5	I Just Called to Say I Love You	The Woman in Red	1984
6	Say You, Say Me	White Nights	1985
7	Take My Breath Away	Top Gun	1986
8	(I've Had) The Time of My Life	Dirty Dancing	1987
9	Let the River Run	Working Girl	1988
10	Under the Sea	The Little Mermaid	1989

THE 10 "BEST SONG" OSCARS – 1990s

	SONG	FILM	YEAR
1	Sooner or Later (I Always Get My Man)	Dick Tracy	1990
2	Beauty and the Beast	Beauty and the Beast	1991
3	Whole New World	Aladdin	1992
4	Streets of Philadelphia	Philadelphia	1993
5	Can You Feel the Love Tonight	The Lion King	1994
6	Colors of the Wind	Pocahontas	1995
7	You Must Love Me	Evita	1996
8	My Heart Will Go On	Titanic	1997
9	When You Believe	The Prince of Egypt	1998
10	You'll Be in My Heart	Tarzan	1999

Subsequent 21st-century winners have been – 2000: "Things Have Changed" from *Wonder Boys*; 2001: "If I Didn't Have You" from *Monsters, Inc.*; and 2002: "Lose Yourself" from *8 Mile*.

TOP 10 ARTISTS WITH THE MOST "BEST SONG" OSCAR NOMINATIONS

	ARTIST/WINS	YEARS	NOMINATIONS
1	Sammy Cahn (4)	1942–75	26
2	Johnny Mercer (4)	1938–71	18
3 =	Paul Francis Webster (3)	1944–76	16
=	Alan and Marilyn Bergman (2)	1968–95	16
5	James Van Heusen (4)	1944–68	14
6 =	Henry Mancini (2)	1961–86	11
=	Ned Washington (1)	1940–61	11
8 =	Sammy Fain (2)	1937–77	10
=	Alan Menken (4)	1986–97	10
=	Randy Newman (1)	1981–2001	10
=	Leo Robin (1)	1934–53	10
=	Jule Styne (1)	1940–68	10
=	Henry Warren (3)	1935–57	10

It was not until the 7th year of the Academy Awards, in 1934, that the category of "Best Song" was added to the other accolades bestowed on the previous year's films. The Awards are usually multiple in that they include both writers of the music or, as in the case of Sammy Cahn, the lyrics. His unmatched total of 26 nominations includes such classics as "Three Coins in the Fountain" (1954), while his closest rival Johnny Mercer's catalogue of successes includes "Moon River" from *Breakfast at Tiffany's* (1961). Both of them received nominations over a period spanning 33 years. James Van Heusen, Alan and Marilyn Bergman, and Ned Washington all accomplished the additional feat of winning "Best Song" Oscars on the first occasion they were nominated, while Randy Newman holds the record for the greatest number of nominations (10) before achieving an Award. Several of the artists listed were also nominated and in some instances won further Oscars for "Best Original Score".

I Could Have Danced All Night

Gregory Hines in *White Nights*. Composed and sung by Lionel Richie, the film's theme song "Say You, Say Me" also won the Golden Globe for "Best Song" and became a No. 1 chart hit in the US.

THE 10 PALME D'OR WINNERS – 1950s

	FILM	LANGUAGE	DIRECTOR	YEAR*
1	No festival			1950
2 =	Fröken Julie (Miss Julie)	Swedish	Alf Sjöberg	1951
=	Miracolo a Milano (Miracle in Milan)	Italian	Vittorio De Sica	1951
3 =	Due soldi di speranza (Two Pennyworth of Hope)	Italian	Renato Castellani	1952
=	Othello	English	Orson Welles	1952
4	Le salaire de la peur (Wages of Fear)	French/English Spanish/German	Henri-Georges Clouzot	1953
5	Jigokumon (Gate of Hell)	Japanese	Teinosuke Kinugasa	1954
6	Marty	English	Delbert Mann	1955
7	Le monde du silence (The Silent World)	French	Jacques-Yves Cousteau and Louis Malle	1956
8	Friendly Persuasion	English	William Wyler	1957
9	Letjat Zhuravli (The Cranes Are Flying)	Russian	Mikhail Kalatozov	1958
10	Orfeu Negro (Black Orpheus)	Portuguese	Marcel Camus	1959

*Of award. The festival includes films released in the current as well as the preceding year. Although the Cannes Film Festival was established in 1939, the Second World War delayed its inaugural ceremony until 1946. In that year and in 1947, there was no single "Best Film" prize, several films being honoured jointly including such unlikely bedfellows as David Lean's Brief Encounter (1946) and Walt Disney's Dumbo (1941). There was no Festival in 1948 or 1950.

THE 10 PALME D'OR WINNERS – 1960s

	FILM	LANGUAGE	DIRECTOR	YEAR
1	La Dolce Vita	Italian	Federico Fellini	1960
2 =	Une aussi longue absence (The Long Absence)	French	Henri Colpi	1961
=	Viridiana	Spanish	Luis Buñuel	1961
3	O Pagador de Promessas (The Given Word)	Portuguese	Anselmo Duarte	1962
4	Il Gattopardo (The Leopard)	Italian	Luchino Visconti	1963
5	Les parapluies de Cherbourg (The Umbrellas of Cherbourg)	French	Jacques Demy	1964
6	The Knack ... and How to Get It	English	Richard Lester	1965
7 =	Un homme et une femme (A Man and a Woman)	French	Claude Lelouch	1966
=	Signore e Signori (The Birds, the Bees, and the Italians)	Italian	Pietro Germi	1966
9	Blowup	English	Michelangelo Antonioni	1967
10	If ...	English	Lindsay Anderson	1969

Glittering Prize-winner
Il Gattopardo (The Leopard), the film of the classic novel by Giuseppe Tomasi Di Lampedusa, starring Claudia Cardinale (on the right) and Burt Lancaster, won the 1963 Palme d'Or.

FILM	LANGUAGE	DIRECTOR	YEAR
1 M*A*S*H	English	Robert Altman	1970
2 The Go-Between	English	Joseph Losey	1971
3 = Il Caso Mattei (The Mattei Affair)	Italian	Francesco Rosi	1972
= La Classe operaia va in Paradiso (The Working Class Goes to Heaven)	Italian	Elio Petri	1972
4 = The Hireling	English	Alan Bridges	1973
= Scarecrow	English	Jerry Schatzberg	1973
5 The Conversation	English	Francis Ford Coppola	1974
6 Chronique des années de braise (Chronicle of the Years of Fire)	Arabic	Mohammed Lakhdar-Hamina	1975
7 Taxi Driver	English	Martin Scorsese	1976
8 Padre Padrone (My Father My Master)	Italian	Paolo Taviani/ Vittorio Taviani	1977
9 L'Albero Degli Zoccoli (The Tree of Wooden Clogs)	Italian	Ermanno Olmi	1978
10 = Apocalypse Now	English, French, Vietnamese	Francis Ford Coppola	1979
= Die Blechtrommel (The Tin Drum)	German, Polish, Russian	Völker Schlöndorff	1979

FILM	LANGUAGE	DIRECTOR	YEAR
1 = All That Jazz	English	Bob Fosse	1980
= Kagemusha (Shadow Warrior)	Japanese	Akira Kurosawa	1980
2 Czlowiek z zelaza (Man of Iron)	Polish	Andrzej Wajda	1981
3 = Missing	English/Spanish	Costa-Gavras	1982
= Yol	Turkish	Serif Gören/ Yilmaz Güney	1982
4 Narayama bushiko (The Ballad of Narayama)	Japanese	Shohei Imamura	1983
5 Paris, Texas	English	Wim Wenders	1984
6 Otac na sluzbenom putu (When Father was Away on Business)	Serbo-Croatian	Emir Kusturica	1985
7 The Mission	English	Rolland Joffé	1986
8 Sous le soleil de Satan (Under the Sun of Satan)	French	Maurice Pialat	1987
9 Pelle Erobreren (Pelle the Conqueror)	Danish/Swedish	Bille August	1988
10 sex, lies and videotape	English	Steven Soderbergh	1989

THE 10 PALME D'OR WINNERS – 1990s

FILM	LANGUAGE	DIRECTOR	YEAR
1 Wild at Heart	English	David Lynch	1990
2 Barton Fink	English	Joel Coen	1991
3 Den Goda Viljan (The Best Intentions)	Swedish	Bille August	1992
4 = The Piano	English/Maori	Jane Campion	1993
= Ba wang bie ji (Farewell My Concubine)	Mandarin	Kaige Chen	1993
5 Pulp Fiction	English	Quentin Tarantino	1994
6 Underground	Serbo-Croatian/ German	Emir Kusturica	1995
7 Secrets & Lies	English	Mike Leigh	1996
8 = Unagi (The Eel)	Japanese	Shohei Imamura	1997
= Ta'me guilass (Taste of Cherry)	Farsi	Abbas Kiarostami	1997
9 Mia Eoniotita Ke Mia Mera (Eternity and A Day)	Greek	Theo Angelopoulos	1998
10 Rosetta	French	Jean-Pierre Dardenne/ Luc Dardenne	1999

The Palme d'Or went to *Dancer in the Dark* by Lars von Trier (2000), *The Son's Room* by Nanni Moretti (2001), *The Pianist* by Roman Polanski (2002), and *Elephant* by Gus Van Sant (2003).

Japanese Epic
Tatsuya Nakadai took the title role in Akira Kurosawa's historical saga *Kagemusha*, joint-winner of the 1980 Palm d'Or. The most expensive film ever made in Japan, it is regarded as one of the classics of modern cinema.

THE 10 FIRST "BEST PICTURE" AWARDS

	FILM	YEAR*
1	The Song of Bernadette	1943
2	Going My Way	1944
3	The Lost Weekend	1945
4	The Best Years of Our Lives	1946
5	Gentleman's Agreement	1947
6	Treasure of Sierra Madre *and* Johnny Belinda	1948
7	All the King's Men	1949
8	Sunset Boulevard	1950
9	A Place in the Sun	1951
10	The Greatest Show on Earth	1952

* Of film; award ceremonies take place the following year

The Golden Globe Awards are presented annually by the Hollywood Foreign Press Association, a group of US-based journalists who report on the entertainment industry for the world's press. They are often seen as a prediction of Oscars to come: in the "Best Picture" category, their awards were identical six times out of 10 in the first 10 years, a coincidence rate that has continued ever since. From the 1952 ceremony onwards, a distinction was made between "Drama" and "Musical or Comedy"; the above awards are for Dramas for the film years 1951–52, when the Musical or Comedy category winners were *An American in Paris* (1951) and *With a Song in My Heart* (1952).

THE 10 LATEST "BEST MUSICAL OR COMEDY" AWARDS

	FILM	YEAR
1	Chicago	2002
2	Moulin Rouge!	2001
3	Almost Famous	2000
4	Toy Story 2 *	1999
5	Shakespeare in Love	1998
6	As Good As It Gets	1997
7	Evita	1996
8	Babe	1995
9	The Lion King *	1994
10	Mrs. Doubtfire	1993

* Animated

While the similarity of identity between the Golden Globes and Oscars is notable among the Drama awards and those films' leading actors and actresses, the Musical or Comedy awards tend to be presented to films that have received popular and commercial success, but seldom also receive the critical accolade of an Academy Award. During the past 10 years, with the single exception of *Almost Famous*, all the Golden Globe awards in this category went to films that earned (often considerably) in excess of $100 million each.

Happy Hours

After two previous wins for a comedy and a musical, Nicole Kidman gained her first Golden Globe award for a drama with her performance as Virginia Woolf in *The Hours*.

THE 10 LATEST "BEST DRAMA" AWARDS

	FILM	YEAR
1	The Hours	2002
2	A Beautiful Mind	2001
3	Gladiator	2000
4	American Beauty	1999
5	Saving Private Ryan	1998
6	Titanic	1997
7	The English Patient	1996
8	Sense and Sensibility	1995
9	Forrest Gump	1994
10	Schindler's List	1993

Did you know?

The Golden Globe award, a globe encircled by a strip of film, was not presented until 1946: previous winners received only a simple scroll.

THE 10 LATEST "BEST ACTOR, DRAMA" AWARDS

	ACTOR	FILM	YEAR
1	Jack Nicholson	About Schmidt	2002
2	Russell Crowe	A Beautiful Mind	2001
3	Tom Hanks	Cast Away	2000
4	Denzel Washington	The Hurricane	1999
5	Jim Carrey	The Truman Show	1998
6	Peter Fonda	Ulee's Gold	1997
7	Geoffrey Rush	Shine	1996
8	Nicolas Cage	Leaving Las Vegas	1995
9	Tom Hanks	Forrest Gump	1994
10	Tom Hanks	Philadelphia	1993

THE 10 LATEST "BEST ACTRESS, DRAMA" AWARDS

	ACTRESS	FILM	YEAR
1	Nicole Kidman	The Hours	2002
2	Sissy Spacek	In the Bedroom	2001
3	Julia Roberts	Erin Brockovich	2000
4	Hilary Swank	Boys Don't Cry	1999
5	Cate Blanchett	Elizabeth	1998
6	Judi Dench	Mrs. Brown *	1997
7	Brenda Blethyn	Secrets & Lies	1996
8	Sharon Stone	Casino	1995
9	Jessica Lange	Blue Sky	1994
10	Holly Hunter	The Piano	1993

* US title *Her Majesty, Mrs. Brown*

THE 10 LATEST "BEST ACTOR, MUSICAL OR COMEDY" AWARDS

	ACTRESS	FILM	YEAR
1	Richard Gere	Chicago	2002
2	Gene Hackman	The Royal Tenenbaums	2001
3	George Clooney	O Brother, Where Art Thou?	2000
4	Jim Carrey	Man on the Moon	1999
5	Michael Caine	Little Voice	1998
6	Jack Nicholson	As Good As It Gets	1997
7	Tom Cruise	Jerry Maguire	1996
8	John Travolta	Get Shorty	1995
9	Hugh Grant	Four Weddings and a Funeral	1994
10	Robin Williams	Mrs. Doubtfire	1993

THE 10 LATEST "BEST ACTRESS, MUSICAL OR COMEDY" AWARDS

	ACTRESS	FILM	YEAR
1	Renée Zellweger	Chicago	2002
2	Nicole Kidman	Moulin Rouge!	2001
3	Renée Zellweger	Nurse Betty	2000
4	Janet McTeer	Tumbleweeds	1999
5	Gwyneth Paltrow	Shakespeare in Love	1998
6	Helen Hunt	As Good As It Gets	1997
7	Madonna	Evita	1996
8	Nicole Kidman	To Die For	1995
9	Jamie Lee Curtis	True Lies	1994
10	Angela Bassett	What's Love Got to Do with It	1993

Although romantic comedies feature predominantly among the winners, a number of the successful actresses in this category received their awards for roles in movies that are either traditional musicals or have a high musical content, including two musical biographies, *Evita*, the film version of Tim Rice and Andrew Lloyd Webber's stage show on the life of Eva Peron, and *What's Love Got To Do With It*, which portrays the life story of singer Tina Turner.

All That Jazz

Renée Zellweger as murderess Roxie Hart and Richard Gere as lawyer Billy Flynn in the Rob Marshall-directed musical *Chicago*, based on the 1975 Broadway hit of the same name: both stars and the film won Golden Globe awards.

THE 10 LATEST "BEST DIRECTORS" AWARDS

	DIRECTOR	FILM	YEAR
1	Martin Scorsese	Gangs of New York	2002
2	Robert Altman	Gosford Park	2001
3	Ang Lee	Crouching Tiger, Hidden Dragon	2000
4	Sam Mendes	American Beauty	1999
5	Steven Spielberg	Saving Private Ryan	1998
6	James Cameron	Titanic	1997
7	Milos Forman	The People vs. Larry Flynt	1996
8	Mel Gibson	Braveheart	1995
9	Robert Zemeckis	Forrest Gump	1994
10	Steven Spielberg	Schindler's List	1993

THE 10 LATEST "BEST FOREIGN LANGUAGE FILM" AWARDS

	FILM	COUNTRY	YEAR
1	Talk to Her	Spain	2002
2	No Man's Land	Bosnia	2001
3	Crouching Tiger, Hidden Dragon	Taiwan	2000
4	All About My Mother	Spain	1999
5	Central Station	Brazil	1998
6	Ma Vie en Rose	Belgium	1997
7	Kolya	Czech Republic	1996
8	Les Misérables	France	1995
9	Farinelli	Belgium	1994
10	Farewell My Concubine	Hong Kong	1993

Patient's Reward
Ralph Fiennes as the eponymous English Patient. Despite the title, Fiennes plays the part of a Hungarian Count, Laszlo de Almásy. The film won BAFTA, Oscar, and Golden Globe awards for best film.

THE 10 LATEST WINNERS OF THE BAFTA "BEST FILM" AWARD

	FILM	YEAR
1	The Pianist	2002
2	The Lord of the Rings: The Fellowship of the Ring	2001
3	Gladiator	2000
4	American Beauty	1999
5	Shakespeare in Love	1998
6	The Full Monty	1997
7	The English Patient	1996
8	Sense and Sensibility	1995
9	Four Weddings and a Funeral	1994
10	Schindler's List	1993

The British Academy of Film and Television Arts (BAFTA) awards have been presented since 1947.

THE 10 LATEST WINNERS OF THE BAFTA "BEST ACTOR" AWARD

	ACTOR	FILM	YEAR
1	Daniel Day-Lewis	Gangs of New York	2002
2	Russell Crowe	A Beautiful Mind	2001
3	Jamie Bell	Billy Elliot	2000
4	Kevin Spacey	American Beauty	1999
5	Roberto Benigni	Life Is Beautiful/La Vita è bella	1998
6	Robert Carlyle	The Full Monty	1997
7	Geoffrey Rush	Shine	1996
8	Nigel Hawthorne	The Madness of King George	1995
9	Hugh Grant	Four Weddings and a Funeral	1994
10	Anthony Hopkins	The Remains of the Day	1993

THE 10 LATEST WINNERS OF THE BAFTA "BEST DIRECTOR" AWARD

	DIRECTOR	FILM	COUNTRY	YEAR
1	Roman Polanski	The Pianist	UK/France/Germany/ Netherlands/Poland	2002
2	Peter Jackson	The Lord of the Rings: The Fellowship of the Ring	USA/New Zealand	2001
3	Ang Lee	Crouching Tiger, Hidden Dragon	USA/Hong Kong/ China/Taiwan	2000
4	Pedro Almodovar	All About My Mother	Spain/France	1999
5	Peter Weir	The Truman Show	USA	1998
6	Baz Luhrmann	Romeo + Juliet	USA	1997
7	Joel Cohen	Fargo	USA	1996
8	Michael Radford	Il Postino	Italy/France Belgium	1995
9	Mike Newell	Four Weddings and a Funeral	UK	1994
10	Steven Spielberg	Schindler's List	USA	1993

Although the winner of BAFTA "Best Picture" often corresponds with the Oscar equivalent, only one recent "Best Director" coincides: Steven Spielberg for *Schindler's List*. The year Spielberg won was also the first year in which the award was named the "David Lean Award for Direction".

THE 10 LATEST WINNERS OF THE BAFTA "BEST ACTRESS" AWARD

	ACTRESS	FILM	YEAR
1	Nicole Kidman	The Hours	2002
2	Judi Dench	Iris	2001
3	Julia Roberts	Erin Brockovich	2000
4	Annette Bening	American Beauty	1999
5	Cate Blanchett	Elizabeth	1998
6	Judi Dench	Mrs. Brown	1997
7	Brenda Blethyn	Secrets and Lies	1996
8	Emma Thompson	Sense and Sensibility	1995
9	Susan Sarandon	The Client	1994
10	Holly Hunter	The Piano	1993

There were no separate acting award categories until 1968, when Katharine Hepburn won for *Guess Who's Coming to Dinner* and *The Lion in Winter*.

THE 10 LATEST LONDON FILM CRITICS CIRCLE "DIRECTOR OF THE YEAR" AWARD WINNERS

	DIRECTOR	FILM	YEAR
1	Phillip Noyce	The Quiet American/Rabbit-Proof Fence	2002
2	Alejandro González Iñárritu	Love's a Bitch	2001
3	Spike Jonze	Being John Malkovich	2000
4	Sam Mendes	American Beauty	1999
5	Peter Weir	The Truman Show	1998
6	Curtis Hanson	L.A. Confidential	1997
7	Joel Coen	Fargo	1996
8	Peter Jackson	Heavenly Creatures	1995
9	Steven Spielberg	Schindler's List	1994
10	James Ivory	The Remains of the Day	1993

Founded in 1913 and originally representing drama and music critics, the Critics Circle admitted film critics working for British publications in 1926. Its film section comprises some 80 professionals and has been presenting its awards, known as ALFS, since 1981.

THE 10 LATEST LONDON FILM CRITICS CIRCLE "ACTRESS OF THE YEAR" AWARD WINNERS

	ACTRESS	FILM	YEAR
1	Stockard Channing	The Business of Strangers	2002
2	Nicole Kidman	Moulin Rouge!	2001
3	Julia Roberts	Erin Brockovich	2000
4	Annette Bening	American Beauty	1999
5	Cate Blanchett	Elizabeth	1998
6	Claire Danes	Romeo + Juliet	1997
7	Frances McDormand	Fargo	1996
8	Nicole Kidman	To Die For	1995
9	Linda Fiorentino	The Last Seduction	1994
10	Holly Hunter	The Piano	1993

THE 10 LATEST LONDON FILM CRITICS CIRCLE "FILM OF THE YEAR" AWARD WINNERS

	FILM	YEAR
1	About Schmidt	2002
2	Moulin Rouge!	2001
3	Being John Malkovich	2000
4	American Beauty	1999
5	Saving Private Ryan	1998
6	L.A. Confidential	1997
7	Fargo	1996
8	Babe	1995
9	Schindler's List	1994
10	The Piano	1993

Among recent recipients, two (*American Beauty* and *Schindler's List*) also won the Oscar for "Best Picture".

THE 10 LATEST LONDON FILM CRITICS CIRCLE "ACTOR OF THE YEAR" AWARD WINNERS

	ACTOR	FILM	YEAR
1	Michael Caine	The Quiet American	2002
2	Billy Bob Thornton	The Man Who Wasn't There	2001
3	Russell Crowe	Gladiator	2000
4	Kevin Spacey	American Beauty	1999
5	Jack Nicholson	As Good As It Gets	1998
6	Geoffrey Rush	Shine	1997 *
7	Morgan Freeman	Se7en	1996
8	Johnny Depp	Ed Wood	1995
9	John Travolta	Pulp Fiction	1994
10	Anthony Hopkins	The Remains of the Day	1993

* Of UK release

Show Business
London Film Critics Circle "Actress of the Year" Stockard Channing as Julie Styron in *The Business of Strangers*.

TOP 10 DIRECTORS GUILD OF AMERICA

THE 10 "BEST DIRECTOR" AWARDS – 1950s

	DIRECTOR	FILM	YEAR
1	Joseph Mankiewicz	All About Eve	1950
2	George Stevens	A Place in the Sun	1951
3	John Ford	The Quiet Man	1952
4	Fred Zinnemann	From Here to Eternity	1953
5	Elia Kazan	On the Waterfront	1954
6	Delbert Mann	Marty	1955
7	George Stevens	Giant	1956
8	David Lean	The Bridge on the River Kwai	1957
9	Vincente Minnelli	Gigi	1958
10	William Wyler	Ben-Hur	1959

The Screen Directors Guild (which became the Directors Guild of America, Inc. in 1960) initiated its awards in 1948, when Joseph Mankiewicz received the first annual "Best Director" Award (officially "Outstanding Directorial Achievement in Feature Film") for *A Letter to Three Wives*. The 1949 winner was Robert Rossen for *All the King's Men*.

Did you know?

Since 1970, five nominees have been selected for each year's DGA Award. On two occasions, this has resulted in a director being nominated twice: in 1974 Francis Ford Coppola for both *The Godfather, Part II* and *The Conversation*, and in 2000 when Steven Soderbergh was nominated for *Erin Brockovich* and *Traffic*.

THE 10 "BEST DIRECTOR" AWARDS – 1960s

	DIRECTOR	FILM	YEAR
1	Billy Wilder	The Apartment	1960
2	Robert Wise and Jerome Robbins	West Side Story	1961
3	David Lean	Lawrence of Arabia	1962
4	Tony Richardson	Tom Jones	1963
5	George Cukor	My Fair Lady	1964
6	Robert Wise	The Sound of Music	1965
7	Fred Zinnemann	A Man for All Seasons	1966
8	Mike Nichols	The Graduate	1967
9	Anthony Harvey	The Lion in Winter	1968
10	John Schlesinger	Midnight Cowboy	1969

THE 10 "BEST DIRECTOR" AWARDS – 1970s

	DIRECTOR	FILM	YEAR
1	Franklin J. Schaffner	Patton	1970
2	William Friedkin	The French Connection	1971
3	Francis Ford Coppola	The Godfather	1972
4	George Roy Hill	The Sting	1973
5	Francis Ford Coppola	The Godfather, Part II	1974
6	Milos Forman	One Flew Over the Cuckoo's Nest	1975
7	John G. Avildsen	Rocky	1976
8	Woody Allen	Annie Hall	1977
9	Michael Cimino	The Deer Hunter	1978
10	Robert Benton	Kramer vs. Kramer	1979

THE 10 "BEST DIRECTOR" AWARDS – 1980s

	DIRECTOR	FILM	YEAR
1	Robert Redford	Ordinary People	1980
2	Warren Beatty	Reds	1981
3	Richard Attenborough	Gandhi	1982
4	James Brooks	Terms of Endearment	1983
5	Milos Forman	Amadeus	1984
6	Steven Spielberg	The Color Purple	1985
7	Oliver Stone	Platoon	1986
8	Bernardo Bertolucci	The Last Emperor	1987
9	Barry Levinson	Rain Man	1988
10	Oliver Stone	Born on the Fourth of July	1989

THE 10 "BEST DIRECTOR" AWARDS – 1990s

	DIRECTOR	FILM	YEAR
1	Kevin Costner	Dances With Wolves	1990
2	Jonathan Demme	The Silence of the Lambs	1991
3	Clint Eastwood	Unforgiven	1992
4	Steven Spielberg	Schindler's List	1993
5	Robert Zemeckis	Forrest Gump	1994
6	Ron Howard	Apollo 13	1995
7	Anthony Minghella	The English Patient	1996
8	James Cameron	Titanic	1997
9	Steven Spielberg	Saving Private Ryan	1998
10	Sam Mendes	American Beauty	1999

Winners for films made in the 21st century are: Ang Lee, Crouching Tiger, Hidden Dragon (2000), Ron Howard, A Beautiful Mind (2001), and Rob Marshall, Chicago (2002).

On Set
Fred Zinnemann directs Montgomery Clift in *From Here to Eternity*. The film, which took its title from a poem by Rudyard Kipling, also won eight Oscars, including "Best Picture" and "Best Director".

Lone Wolf
Kevin Costner starred in, produced, and directed *Dances With Wolves*, for which he won the DGA award. The film won seven Oscars, including "Best Director" and "Best Picture", and made over $400 million worldwide.

Runaway Success
Janet McTeer (right, with Kimberly J. Brown), in NBR-winning and Oscar-nominated *Tumbleweeds*, which is about a mother and daughter running from town to town.

THE 10 LATEST WINNERS OF THE NATIONAL BOARD OF REVIEW AWARD FOR "BEST ACTOR"

	ACTOR	FILM	YEAR
1	Campbell Scott	Roger Dodger	2002
2	Billy Bob Thornton	The Man Who Wasn't There/ Monster's Ball/ Bandits	2001
3	Javier Bardem	Before Night Falls	2000
4	Russell Crowe	The Insider	1999
5	Ian McKellen	Gods and Monsters	1998
6	Jack Nicholson	As Good As It Gets	1997
7	Tom Cruise	Jerry Maguire	1996
8	Nicolas Cage	Leaving Las Vegas	1995
9	Tom Hanks	Forrest Gump	1994
10	Anthony Hopkins	The Remains of the Day/ Shadowlands	1993

Beginning its life in New York in 1909 as the National Board of Censorship of Motion Pictures, and changing its name to the National Board of Review in 1915, NBR award-winners are selected by a panel known as the Exceptional Photoplay Committee. Its awards date back to the 1920s, but have been honouring individual actors and actresses since 1945 (when Ray Milland won for *The Lost Weekend*) and accurately predicting the Oscar-winning actor and film of that year.

THE 10 LATEST WINNERS OF THE NATIONAL BOARD OF REVIEW AWARD FOR "BEST ACTRESS"

	ACTRESS	FILM	YEAR
1	Julianne Moore	Far From Heaven	2002
2	Halle Berry	Monster's Ball	2001
3	Julia Roberts	Erin Brockovich	2000
4	Janet McTeer	Tumbleweeds	1999
5	Fernanda Montenegro	Central Station	1998
6	Helena Bonham Carter	The Wings of the Dove	1997
7	Frances McDormand	Fargo	1996
8	Emma Thompson	Sense and Sensibility/ Carrington	1995
9	Miranda Richardson	Tom and Viv	1994
10	Holly Hunter	The Piano	1993

THE 10 LATEST WINNERS OF THE SUNDANCE GRAND JURY PRIZE – DRAMATIC FILMS

	FILM	DIRECTOR	YEAR
1	American Splendor	Shari Springer Berman and Robert Pulcini	2003
2	Personal Velocity: Three Portraits	Rebecca Miller	2002
3	The Believer	Henry Bean	2001
4	Girlfight/ You Can Count on Me	Karyn Kusama/ Kenneth Luergan	2000
5	Three Seasons	Tony Bui	1999
6	Slam	Marc Levin	1998
7	Sunday	Jonathan Nossite	1997
8	Welcome to the Dollhouse	Todd Solondz	1996
9	The Brothers McMullen	Edward Burns	1995
10	What Happened Was …	Tom Noonan	1994

THE 10 LATEST WINNERS OF THE NATIONAL BOARD OF REVIEW AWARD FOR "BEST DIRECTOR"

	DIRECTOR	FILM	YEAR
1	Phillip Noyce	The Quiet American/ Rabbit-Proof Fence	2002
2	Todd Field	In the Bedroom	2001
3	Steven Soderbergh	Traffic/Erin Brockovich	2000
4	Anthony Minghella	The Talented Mr. Ripley	1999
5	Shekhar Kapur	Elizabeth	1998
6	Curtis Hanson	L.A. Confidential	1997
7	Joel Coen	Fargo	1996
8	Ang Lee	Sense and Sensibility	1995
9	Quentin Tarantino	Pulp Fiction	1994
10	Martin Scorsese	The Age of Innocence	1993

THE 10 LATEST WINNERS OF THE NATIONAL SOCIETY OF FILM CRITICS "BEST DIRECTOR" AWARD

	DIRECTOR	FILM	YEAR
1	Roman Polanski	The Pianist	2002
2	Robert Altman	Gosford Park	2001
3	Steven Soderbergh	Traffic/Erin Brockovich	2000
4	Mike Leigh	Topsy-Turvy	1999
5	Steven Soderbergh	Out of Sight	1998
6	Curtis Hanson	L.A. Confidential	1997
7	Lars von Trier	Breaking the Waves	1996
8	Mike Figgis	Leaving Las Vegas	1995
9	Quentin Tarantino	Pulp Fiction	1994
10	Steven Spielberg	Schindler's List	1993

The National Society of Film Critics was formed in 1966 by magazine writers who had been denied admittance to the New York Film Critics Circle, whose membership comprised exclusively newspaper writers. Its awards were first presented in 1967, for films of 1966, when the winner in the "Best Director" category was Michelangelo Antonioni for *Blowup*, which also won "Best Film".

THE 10 LATEST WINNERS OF THE NATIONAL SOCIETY OF FILM CRITICS "BEST ACTOR" AWARD

	ACTOR	FILM	YEAR
1	Adrien Brody	The Pianist	2002
2	Gene Hackman	The Royal Tenenbaums	2001
3	Javier Bardem	Before Night Falls	2000
4	Russell Crowe	The Insider	1999
5	Nick Nolte	Affliction	1998
6	Robert Duvall	The Apostle	1997
7	Eddie Murphy	The Nutty Professor	1996
8	Nicolas Cage	Leaving Las Vegas	1995
9	Paul Newman	Nobody's Fool	1994
10	David Thewlis	Naked	1993

Michael Caine won the first ever National Society of Film Critics "Best Actor" award for his title role in British-made *Alfie* (1966). The next, Rod Steiger for *In the Heat of the Night*, and some subsequent winners have only occasionally coincided with the Academy Awards' choice of "Best Actors".

THE 10 LATEST WINNERS OF THE NATIONAL SOCIETY OF FILM CRITICS "BEST FILM" AWARD

	FILM	YEAR
1	The Pianist	2002
2	Mulholland Drive	2001
3	Yi yi: A One and a Two ...	2000
4	Being John Malkovich/ Topsy-Turvy	1999
5	Out of Sight	1998
6	L.A. Confidential	1997
7	Breaking the Waves	1996
8	Babe	1995
9	Pulp Fiction	1994
10	Schindler's List	1993

THE 10 LATEST WINNERS OF THE NATIONAL SOCIETY OF FILM CRITICS "BEST ACTRESS" AWARD

	ACTRESS	FILM	YEAR
1	Diane Lane	Unfaithful	2002
2	Naomi Watts	Mulholland Drive	2001
3	Laura Linney	You Can Count on Me	2000
4	Reese Witherspoon	Election	1999
5	Ally Sheedy	High Art	1998
6	Julie Christie	Afterglow	1997
7	Emily Watson	Breaking the Waves	1996
8	Elisabeth Shue	Leaving Las Vegas	1995
9	Jennifer Jason Leigh	Mrs. Parker and the Vicious Circle	1994
10	Holly Hunter	The Piano	1993

Key Role
National Society of Film Critics- and Oscar-winning "Best Actor" Adrien Brody as Wladyslaw Szpilman in Roman Polanski's *The Pianist*, which was based on the true story of a Polish Holocaust survivor.

THE 10 FIRST WINNERS OF AFI'S LIFE-TIME ACHIEVEMENT AWARD

	WINNER	YEAR*
1	John Ford	1973
2	James Cagney	1974
3	Orson Welles	1975
4	William Wyler	1976
5	Bette Davis	1977
6	Henry Fonda	1978
7	Alfred Hitchcock	1979
8	James Stewart	1980
9	Fred Astaire	1981
10	Frank Capra	1982

* Of award

This award is bestowed by the American Film Institute on individuals whose "talent has in a fundamental way advanced the film art; whose accomplishment has been acknowledged by scholars, critics, professional peers and the general public; and whose work has withstood the test of time". In 1993 the criteria were extended to include individuals with active careers and work of significance yet to be accomplished.

THE 10 LATEST WINNERS OF AFI'S LIFE-TIME ACHIEVEMENT AWARD

	WINNER	YEAR*
1	Robert De Niro	2003
2	Tom Hanks	2002
3	Barbra Streisand	2001
4	Harrison Ford	2000
5	Dustin Hoffman	1999
6	Robert Wise	1998
7	Martin Scorsese	1997
8	Clint Eastwood	1996
9	Steven Spielberg	1995
10	Jack Nicholson	1994

* Of award

Award-winners are getting younger: the first winner, John Ford, died at the age of 79 in the year of his award, and Frank Capra was 85, whereas most of the more recent winners have been in their 50s or 60s – or, in the case of Tom Hanks, 40s. While the first 10 winners are all dead, the latest 10 – even Robert Wise, aged 88 – are all alive.

THE 10 LATEST WINNERS OF THE LINCOLN CENTER TRIBUTE

	WINNER	YEAR*
1	Susan Sarandon	2003
2	Francis Ford Coppola	2002
3	Jane Fonda	2001
4	Al Pacino	2000
5	Mike Nichols	1999
6	Martin Scorsese	1998
7	Sean Connery	1997
8	Clint Eastwood	1996
9	Shirley MacLaine	1995
10	Robert Altman	1994

* Of award

The Film Society of Lincoln Center in New York has been hailing a single individual – an actor, actress, or director – as the subject of its Gala Tribute each year since 1973, when the first recipient was Charles Chaplin.

Did you know?

Screen Actors Guild award winners receive a 40-cm (16-inch) bronze statuette known simply as The Actor®. Each one is numbered on its base; starting with No. 1 in 1995, a total of 283 have been presented up to 2002.

THE 10 LATEST WINNERS OF THE SCREEN ACTORS GUILD AWARD

	WINNER	YEAR†
1	Clint Eastwood	2003
2	Edward Asner	2002
3	Ossie Davis/Ruby Dee	2001
4	Sidney Poitier	2000
5	Kirk Douglas	1999
6	Elizabeth Taylor	1998
7	Angela Lansbury	1997
8	Robert Redford	1996
9	George Burns	1995
10	Ricardo Montalban	1994

* Of award

The Screen Actors Guild started awarding Lifetime Achievement Awards in 1963, when Eddie Cantor became the first recipient. The Guild did not present awards in other categories until 1995.

They Call Me *Mister* Tibbs!

Sidney Poitier – pictured here as Detective Virgil Tibbs in *In the Heat of the Night* (1967) – was the first 21st-century winner of the Screen Actors Guild Lifetime Achievement Award.

THE 10 LATEST WINNERS OF THE WRITERS GUILD OF AMERICA AWARD*

	WRITER	FILM	YEAR†
1	Michael Moore	Bowling for Columbine	2002
2	Julian Fellowes	Gosford Park	2001
3	Kenneth Lonergen	You Can Count on Me	2000
4	Alan Ball	American Beauty	1999
5	Marc Norman, Tom Stoppard	Shakespeare in Love	1998
6	Mark Andrus, James L. Brooks	As Good As It Gets	1997
7	Joel and Ethan Cohen	Fargo	1996
8	Randall Wallace	Braveheart	1995
9	Richard Curtis	Four Weddings and a Funeral	1994
10	Jane Campion	The Piano	1993

* For "Best Screenplay Written Directly for the Screen"
† Of film – awards are presented the following year

THE 10 LATEST WINNERS OF THE PRODUCERS GUILD OF AMERICA DARRYL F. ZANUCK PRODUCER OF THE YEAR AWARD

	PRODUCER	FILM	YEAR*
1	Marty Richards	Chicago	2002
2	Baz Luhrmann, Fred Baron, Martin Brown	Moulin Rouge!	2001
3	Douglas Wick, Branko Lustig	Gladiator	2000
4	Bruce Cohen, Dan Jinks	American Beauty	1999
5	Steven Spielberg, Allison Lyon Segan, Bonnie Curtis, Ian Bryce, Mark Gordon, Gary Levinsohn	Saving Private Ryan	1998
6	James Cameron, Jon Landau	Titanic	1997
7	Saul Zaentz	The English Patient	1996
8	Brian Grazer, Todd Hallowell	Apollo 13	1995
9	Wendy Finerman, Steve Tisch, Steve Starkey, Charles Newirth	Forrest Gump	1994
10	Steven Spielberg, Branko Lustig, Gerald R. Molen	Schindler's List	1993

* Of film – awards are presented the following year

THE 10 FIRST WINNERS OF THE PATSY AWARDS FOR ANIMALS IN FILM

	ANIMAL	SPECIES	FILM	YEAR*
1	Francis	Mule	Francis	1951
2	Rhubarb	Cat	Rhubarb	1952
3	Jackie	Lion	Fearless Fagan	1953
4	Sam	Dog	Hondo	1954
5	Gypsy	Horse	Gypsy Colt	1955
6	Wildfire	Dog	It's a Dog's Life	1956
7	Samantha	Goose	Friendly Persuasion	1957
8	Spike	Dog	Old Yeller	1958
9	Pyewacket	Cat	Bell, Book and Candle	1959
10	Shaggy	Dog	The Shaggy Dog	1960

* Of award
Source: American Humane Association
The American Humane Association introduced its Patsy Awards for animals in film in 1951. They were discontinued in 1986, by when the range had been extended to encompass separate awards in Wild Animal, Canine, Equine, and special categories.

Production Value

Moulin Rouge! won the Producers Guild of America Award named after legendary producer Darryl F. Zanuck (1902–79), himself the producer of 1934 comedy *Moulin Rouge*.

Sense of Achievement
Ang Lee's *Sense and Sensibility*, won the Berlin International Film Festival's Golden Bear. Held since 1951, the Festival awards this prize for the top film and its Silver Bear to actors and actresses.

THE 10 LATEST WINNERS OF THE "GOLDEN BEAR"*

	FILM	DIRECTOR	YEAR†
1	In This World	Michael Winterbottom	2003
2	Bloody Sunday	Paul Greengrass	2002
3	Intimacy	Patrice Chéreau	2001
4	Magnolia	Paul Thomas Anderson	2000
5	The Thin Red Line	Terrence Malick	1999
6	Central Station	Walter Salles	1998
7	The People vs. Larry Flynt	Milos Forman	1997
8	Sense and Sensibility	Ang Lee	1996
9	L'appât	Bertrand Tavernier	1995
10	In the Name of the Father	Jim Sheridan	1994

* Awarded by the Berlin International Film Festival
† Of award

THE 10 LATEST WINNERS OF THE SILVER BEAR, "BEST ACTOR"*

	ACTOR	FILM	YEAR†
1	Sam Rockwell	Confessions of a Dangerous Mind	2003
2	Jacques Gamblin	Safe Conduct	2002
3	Benicio Del Toro	Traffic	2001
4	Denzel Washington	The Hurricane	2000
5	Michael Gwisdek	Night Shapes	1999
6	Samuel L. Jackson	Jackie Brown	1998
7	Leonardo DiCaprio	Romeo + Juliet	1997
8	Sean Penn	Dead Man Walking	1996
9	Paul Newman	Nobody's Fool	1995
10	Tom Hanks	Philadelphia	1994

* Awarded by the Berlin International Film Festival
† Of award

THE 10 LATEST WINNERS OF THE SILVER BEAR, "BEST ACTRESS"*

	ACTRESS	FILM	YEAR†
1	Meryl Streep/ Nicole Kidman/ Julianne Moore	The Hours	2003
2	Halle Berry	Monster's Ball	2002
3	Kerry Fox	Intimacy	2001
4	Bibiana Beglau/ Nadja Uhl	Legend of Rita	2000
5	Juliane Köhler/ Maria Schrader	Aimee & Jaguar	1999
6	Fernanda Montenegro	Central Station	1998
7	Juliette Binoche	The English Patient	1997
8	Anouk Grinberg	Mon homme	1996
9	Josephine Siao	Xiatian de xue	1995
10	Crissy Rock	Ladybird Ladybird	1994

* Awarded by the Berlin International Film Festival
† Of award

THE 10 LATEST WINNERS OF THE VENICE "GOLDEN LION"

	FILM	DIRECTOR	YEAR*
1	The Magdalene Sisters	Peter Mullan	2002
2	Monsoon Wedding	Mira Nair	2001
3	The Circle	Jafar Panahi	2000
4	Yi ge dou bu neng shao	Yimou Zhang	1999
5	Così ridevano	Gianni Amelio	1998
6	Hana-bi	Takeshi Kitano	1997
7	Michael Collins	Neil Jordan	1996
8	Xich lo	Anh Hung Tran	1995
9	Vive L'Amour	Ming-liang Tsai	1994
10	Short Cuts/ Three Colors: Blue	Robert Altman/ Krzysztof Kieslowski	1993

* Of film

THE 10 LATEST WINNERS OF THE VENICE "BEST ACTOR" AWARD

	ACTOR	FILM	YEAR*
1	Stefano Accorsi	A Journey Called Love	2002
2	Luigi Lo Cascio	Light of My Eyes	2001
3	Javier Bardem	Before Night Falls	2000
4	Jim Broadbent	Topsy-Turvy	1999
5	Sean Penn	Hurlyburly	1998
6	Wesley Snipes	One Night Stand	1997
7	Liam Neeson	Michael Collins	1996
8	Götz George	Der Totmacher	1995
9	Roberto Citran	Il Toro	1994
10	Fabrizio Bentivoglio	Un'Anima divisa in due	1993

* Of film
The Venice Film Festival was inaugurated in 1932 as an adjunct to the Venice Biennale, an annual arts festival. At the first event, an audience referendum named Frederic March "Favourite Actor" for his role in *Dr. Jekyll and Mr. Hyde*.

THE 10 LATEST WINNERS OF THE VENICE "BEST ACTRESS" AWARD

	ACTRESS	FILM	YEAR*
1	Julianne Moore	Far From Heaven	2002
2	Sandra Ceccarelli	Light of My Eyes	2001
3	Rose Byrne	The Goddess of 1967	2000
4	Nathalie Baye	An Affair of Love	1999
5	Catherine Deneuve	Place Vendôme	1998
6	Robin Tunney	Niagra Niagra	1997
7	Victoire Thivisol	Ponette	1996
8	Sandrine Bonnaire/ Isabelle Huppert	La Cérémonie	1995
9	Vanessa Redgrave	Little Odessa	1994
10	Juliette Binoche	Three Colors: Blue	1993

* Of film

Did you know?

Winning films at the Venice Film Festival were originally presented with the Mussolini Cup, named after Italian dictator Benito Mussolini. Since the post-War revival of the Festival, films have won the Golden Lion, the symbol of the city; actors and actresses receive the Volpi Cup.

Lights, Cámara, Action
Javier Cámara in Pedro Almodóvar's *Talk to Her*. The film won the European Film Award as well as the Oscar for "Best Screenplay".

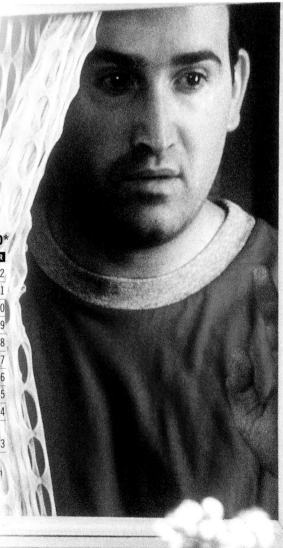

THE 10 LATEST WINNERS OF THE EFA "BEST EUROPEAN FILM"*

	FILM	COUNTRY	YEAR
1	Talk to Her	Spain	2002
2	Amélie	France	2001
3	Dancer in the Dark	Denmark	2000
4	Todo Sobre Mi Madre	Spain	1999
5	La Vita è bella	Italy	1998
6	The Full Monty	UK	1997
7	Breaking the Waves	Denmark	1996
8	Land and Freedom	UK	1995
9	Lamerica	Italy	1994
10	Urga – Territoria Liubvi	Russia	1993

* Awarded by the European Film Academy
The European Film Academy (originally European Cinema Society) was established in 1988 by director Ingmar Bergman and 40 European filmmakers. The first winning film was *A Short Film About Killing* (Poland, 1987).

THE 10 LATEST WINNERS OF THE EFA LIFETIME ACHIEVEMENT AWARD*

	WINNER	COUNTRY	YEAR
1	Tonino Guerra	Italy	2002
2	Monty Python team	UK	2001
3	Richard Harris	UK	2000
4	Ennio Morricone	Italy	1999
5	Jeremy Irons	UK	1998
6	Jeanne Moreau	France	1997
7	Sir Alec Guinness	UK	1996
8	Marcel Carne	France	1995
9	Robert Bresson	France	1994
10	Michelangelo Antonioni	Italy	1993

* The European Film Academy has been presenting Lifetime Achievement Awards since 1989, when the first winner was Italian director Federico Fellini.

EXPERT POLLS

TOP 10 GREATEST FILMS CHOSEN BY THE AMERICAN FILM INSTITUTE

	FILM	YEAR
1	Citizen Kane	1941
2	Casablanca	1942
3	The Godfather	1972
4	Gone With the Wind	1939
5	Lawrence of Arabia	1962
6	The Wizard of Oz	1939
7	The Graduate	1967
8	On the Waterfront	1954
9	Schindler's List	1993
10	Singin' in the Rain	1952

These are the Top 10 of a long list selected as the "100 Greatest" films by more than 1,500 leaders of the American movie community for a poll conducted in 2000 by the American Film Institute. They in turn were selected from an even longer list of 400 nominated films. All-time polls such as this are of interest in that they provide an indication of the staying power of many earlier films, whereas those of a particular year often contain entries that are later eclipsed. In the AFI's Top 100, the decade of the 1950s was especially well represented, with a total of 20 films, followed by the 1960s and 1970s with 18 each. The 1980s made a poor showing, with only six films, none of which was ranked higher than the 24th place for to *Raging Bull* (1980). Of the eight films from the 1990s, just one made the Top 10, the others appeared in the lower reaches of the Top 100.

TOP 10 BRITISH FILMS OF THE 20TH CENTURY*

	FILM	DIRECTOR	YEAR
1	The Third Man	Carol Reed	1949
2	Brief Encounter	David Lean	1946
3	Lawrence of Arabia	David Lean	1962
4	The 39 Steps	Alfred Hitchcock	1935
5	Great Expectations	David Lean	1946
6	Kind Hearts and Coronets	Robert Hamer	1949
7	Kes	Ken Loach	1969
8	Don't Look Now	Nicolas Roeg	1973
9	The Red Shoes	Michael Powell/ Emerich Pressburger	1948
10	Trainspotting	Danny Boyle	1996

* Derived from a poll of 1,000 film professionals – producers, directors, writers, actors, technicians, critics, and others – conducted by the British Film Institute in 1999.

TOP 10 BEST AMERICAN SOUND FILMS CHOSEN BY JEAN-LUC GODARD*

	FILM	DIRECTOR	YEAR
1	Scarface	Howard Hawks	1932
2	The Great Dictator	Charles Chaplin	1940
3	Vertigo	Alfred Hitchcock	1958
4	The Searchers	John Ford	1956
5	Singin' in the Rain	Stanley Donen/ Gene Kelly	1952
6	The Lady from Shanghai	Orson Welles	1948
7	Bigger than Life	Nicholas Ray	1956
8	Angel Face	Otto Preminger	1952
9	To Be or Not to Be	Ernst Lubitsch	1942
10	Dishonoured	Josef von Sternberg	1931

* Founded in 1951, the influential French film journal *Cahiers du Cinéma* had the distinguished French director Jean-Luc Godard (b.1930) nominate his Top 10 films each year from 1956 to 1965. This specific overview was separately done by Godard and published in the journal's December 1963–January 1964 issue.

TOP 10 SCREENPLAYS CHOSEN BY THE WRITERS GUILD OF AMERICA*

	FILM	SCREENWRITER(S)	YEAR
1	Citizen Kane	Orson Welles, Herman J. Mankiewicz, John Houseman (uncredited)	1941
2	Casablanca	Murray Burnett and Joan Alison (play); Julius J. and Philip G. Epstein, and Howard Koch	1942
3	The Godfather	Francis Ford Coppola and Mario Puzo (also novel)	1972
4	Chinatown	Robert Towne and Roman Polanski (uncredited)	1974
5	All About Eve	Joseph L. Mankiewicz and Mary Orr (story; uncredited)	1950
6	Some Like It Hot	M. Logan and Robert Thoeren (story); I.A.L. Diamond and Billy Wilder	1959
7	Sunset Boulevard	Charles Brackett (also story); Billy Wilder, and D.M. Marshman	1950
8	Annie Hall	Woody Allen and Marshall Brickman	1977
9	The Graduate	Charles Webb (novel); Calder Willingham and Buck Henry	1967
10	The Godfather, Part II	Francis Ford Coppola and Mario Puzo (also novel)	1974

* According to a 2001 survey of the members of the Writers Guild of America, conducted by the Library of America.

TOP 10 — BEST FILMS – 1952*

	FILM	DIRECTOR	YEAR
1	The Battleship Potemkin	Sergei Eisenstein	1925
2	The Gold Rush	Charles Chaplin	1925
3	Bicycle Thieves	Vittorio De Sica	1948
4 =	City Lights	Charles Chaplin	1930
=	La grande illusion	Jean Renoir	1937
=	Le Million	René Clair	1930
7	Greed	Erich von Stroheim	1924
8	Hallelujah	King Vidor	1929
9 =	Brief Encounter	David Lean	1945
=	Die Dreigroschenoper	Georg Wilhelm Pabst	1931
=	Intolerance	D.W. Griffith	1916
=	Man of Aran	Robert J. Flaherty	1934

* This all-time "10 Best" is from a survey conducted in 1952 by the committee of the Festival Mondial du Film et des Beaux-Arts de Belgique and the Cinémathèque Royale de Belgique by polling a number of leading directors and other major figures in the film industry. The replies, from 63 individuals representing nine countries, provided both this overall list and the personal Top 10s of individual directors, four of which are reproduced here.

TOP 10 — BEST FILMS CHOSEN BY LUIS BUÑUEL

	FILM	DIRECTOR	YEAR
1	Underworld	Josef von Sternberg	1927
2	The Gold Rush	Charles Chaplin	1925
3	Bicycle Thieves	Vittorio De Sica	1948
4	The Battleship Potemkin	Sergei Eisenstein	1925
5	Portrait of Jennie	William Dieterle	1948
6	Cavalcade	Frank Lloyd	1933
7	White Shadows in the South Seas	W.S. Van Dyke	1928
8	Dead of Night	Alberto Cavalcanti, et al	1945
9	L'Age d'Or	Luis Buñuel	1930
10	I Am a Fugitive from a Chain Gang	Mervyn LeRoy	1932

Spanish-born (later naturalized Mexican) director Luis Buñuel (1900–83) unselfconsciously included his own surreal film *L'Age d'or* in his Top 10. In the same poll, Cecil B. DeMille chose four of his own films.

TOP 10 — BEST FILMS CHOSEN BY ORSON WELLES

	FILM	DIRECTOR	YEAR
1	City Lights	Charles Chaplin	1930
2	Greed	Erich von Stroheim	1924
3	Intolerance	D.W. Griffith	1916
4	Nanook of the North	Robert J. Flaherty	1922
5	Sciuscia	Vittorio De Sica	1946
6	The Battleship Potemkin	Sergei Eisenstein	1925
7	La femme du boulanger	Marcel Pagnol	1938
8	La grande illusion	Jean Renoir	1937
9	Stagecoach	John Ford	1939
10	Our Daily Bread	King Vidor	1934

Orson Welles (1915–95) chose several films that had received critical plaudits – *Sciuscia* had won an Honorary Academy Award, while both *La femme du boulanger* and *La grande illusion* had won the New York Film Critics Circle Best Foreign Language Film award.

TOP 10 — BEST FILMS CHOSEN BY VITTORIO DE SICA

	FILM	DIRECTOR	YEAR
1	Man of Aran	Robert J. Flaherty	1934
2	The Kid	Charles Chaplin	1921
3	La chienne	Jean Renoir	1931
4	Le million	René Clair	1931
5	L'Atalante	Jean Vigo	1934
6	Kameradschadt	Georg Wilhelm Pabst	1931
7	Potomok Chingis-Khana	Vsevolod Pudovkin	1928
8	The Battleship Potemkin	Sergei Eisenstein	1925
9	Hallelujah	King Vidor	1929
10	La kermesse héroïque	Jacques Feyder	1935

TOP 10 — BEST FILMS CHOSEN BY DAVID LEAN

	FILM	DIRECTOR	YEAR
1	Intolerance	D.W. Griffith	1916
2	Varieté	Ewald André DuPont	1925
3	The Crowd	King Vidor	1928
4	City Lights	Charles Chaplin	1930
5	White Shadows in the South Seas	W.S. Van Dyke	1928
6	A nous la liberté!	René Clair	1931
7	La grande illusion	Jean Renoir	1937
8	Les enfants du paradis	Marcel Carné	1945
9	Le jour se lève	Marcel Carné	1939
10	Citizen Kane	Orson Welles	1941

One of the films selected by British director David Lean (1908–91) – himself later a double "Best Director" Oscar winner – was of special historical interest: *White Shadows in the South Seas* was MGM's first sound picture, and the first in which the company's trademark lion, Leo, roars in the opening credits.

A Step Ahead

The frequently-cited film *The Battleship Potemkin* relates the story of a 1905 mutiny of sailors in Odessa, Russia, culminating in a massacre of civilians on the harbour steps.

TOP 10 SIGHT & SOUND CRITICS' POLL – 1952

	FILM	DIRECTOR	YEAR
1	Bicycle Thieves	Vittorio De Sica	1949
2 =	City Lights	Charles Chaplin	1930
=	The Gold Rush	Charles Chaplin	1925
4	Battleship Potemkin	Sergei Eisenstein	1925
5 =	Intolerance	D.W. Griffith	1916
=	Louisiana Story	Robert Flaherty	1947
7 =	Greed	Erich von Stroheim	1924
=	Le jour se lève	Marcel Carné	1939
=	The Passion of Joan of Arc	Carl Theodor Dreyer	1928
10 =	Brief Encounter	David Lean	1945
=	Le Million	René Clair	1930
=	La règle du jeu	Jean Renoir	1939

The British film magazine *Sight & Sound* started polling international critics and directors for their "10 Best" lists in 1952, and has followed it with a new survey every decade ever since.

TOP 10 SIGHT & SOUND CRITICS' POLL – 1962

	FILM	DIRECTOR	YEAR
1	Citizen Kane	Orson Welles	1941
2	L'Avventura	Michelangelo Antonioni	1960
3	La règle du jeu	Jean Renoir	1939
4 =	Greed	Erich von Stroheim	1924
=	Ugetsu Monogatari	Kenji Mizoguchi	1953
6 =	Battleship Potemkin	Sergei Eisenstein	1925
=	Bicycle Thieves	Vittorio De Sica	1949
=	Ivan the Terrible	Sergei Eisenstein	1945
9	La terra trema	Luchino Visconti	1948
10	L'Atalante	Jean Vigo	1934

Citizen Kane entered the list in 1st place this year – and stayed there in every subsequent decennial poll.

TOP 10 SIGHT & SOUND CRITICS' POLL – 1972

	FILM	DIRECTOR	YEAR
1	Citizen Kane	Orson Welles	1941
2	La règle du jeu	Jean Renoir	1939
3	Battleship Potemkin	Sergei Eisenstein	1925
4	8½	Federico Fellini	1963
5 =	L'Avventura	Michelangelo Antonioni	1960
=	Persona	Ingmar Bergman	1967
7	The Passion of Joan of Arc	Carl Theodor Dreyer	1928
8 =	The General	Buster Keaton/ Clyde Bruckman	1927
=	The Magnificent Ambersons	Orson Welles	1942
10 =	Ugetsu Monogatari	Kenji Mizoguchi	1953
=	Wild Strawberries	Ingmar Bergman	1957

TOP 10 SIGHT & SOUND CRITICS' POLL – 1982

	FILM	DIRECTOR	YEAR
1	Citizen Kane	Orson Welles	1941
2	La règle du jeu	Jean Renoir	1939
3 =	Seven Samurai	Akira Kurosawa	1954
=	Singin' in the Rain	Stanley Donen/ Gene Kelly	1952
5	8½	Federico Fellini	1963
6	Battleship Potemkin	Sergei Eisenstein	1925
7 =	L'Avventura	Michelangelo Antonioni	1960
=	The Magnificent Ambersons	Orson Welles	1942
=	Vertigo	Alfred Hitchcock	1958
10 =	The General	Buster Keaton/ Clyde Bruckman	1927
=	The Searchers	John Ford	1956

For the first time, more than half the films in the list were US-made, with *Singin' in the Rain* a rare example of a "popular" film that also received critical acclaim.

The Greatest Film

Orson Welles directed and starred in *Citizen Kane*, consistently hailed by his peers as the greatest film ever made.

TOP 10 SIGHT & SOUND CRITICS' POLL – 1992

	FILM	DIRECTOR	YEAR
1	Citizen Kane	Orson Welles	1941
2	La règle du jeu	Jean Renoir	1939
3	Tokyo Story	Yasujiro Ozu	1953
4	Vertigo	Alfred Hitchcock	1958
5	The Searchers	John Ford	1956
6 =	L'Atalante	Jean Vigo	1934
=	Battleship Potemkin	Sergei Eisenstein	1925
=	The Passion of Joan of Arc	Carl Theodor Dreyer	1928
=	Pather Panchali	Satyajit Ray	1955
10	2001: A Space Odyssey	Stanley Kubrick	1968

The 1992 poll represents the cosmopolitan nature of film, with directors from the US, France, Japan, the UK, Russia, Denmark, and India finding places in it.

TOP 10 SIGHT & SOUND DIRECTORS' DIRECTORS – 1992

	DIRECTOR
1	Federico Fellini
2	Orson Welles
3	Akira Kurosawa
4	Francis Ford Coppola
5	Luis Buñuel
6	Martin Scorsese
7	Ingmar Bergman
8	Charles Chaplin
9	John Ford
10	Alfred Hitchcock

Among more than 100 directors polled by *Sight & Sound* for their votes for other directors are such luminaries as Milos Forman, Sam Mendes, Sydney Pollack, Tim Robbins, and Quentin Tarantino.

TOP 10 SIGHT & SOUND DIRECTORS' DIRECTORS – 2002

	DIRECTOR
1	Orson Welles
2	Federico Fellini
3	Akira Kurosawa
4	Francis Ford Coppola
5	Alfred Hitchcock
6	Stanley Kubrick
7	Billy Wilder
8	Ingmar Bergman
9 =	David Lean
=	Jean Renoir
=	Martin Scorsese

TOP 10 SIGHT & SOUND CRITICS' POLL – 2002

	FILM	DIRECTOR	YEAR
1	Citizen Kane	Orson Welles	1941
2	Vertigo	Alfred Hitchcock	1958
3	La règle du jeu	Jean Renoir	1939
4	The Godfather/ The Godfather, Part II *	Francis Ford Coppola/ Francis Ford Coppola	1972 1974
5	Tokyo Story	Yasujiro Ozu	1953
6	2001: A Space Odyssey	Stanley Kubrick	1968
7	Battleship Potemkin	Sergei Eisenstein	1925
=	Sunrise	Friedrich Wilhelm Murnau	1927
9	8½	Federico Fellini	1963
10	Singin' in the Rain	Stanley Donen/ Gene Kelly	1952

* The poll considered the two *Godfather* films as comprising two parts of a trilogy and ranked them as them as a single entry (referred to as "the combined *Godfather*s").

The Directors' Director
Federico Fellini directs *Fellini Satyricon* (1969). He topped the poll of fellow directors in 1992, and was narrowly overtaken by Orson Welles in 2002.

THE 10 LATEST WINNERS OF THE MTV AWARD FOR "BEST MOVIE"

	FILM	YEAR*
1	The Lord of the Rings: The Fellowship of the Ring	2001
2	Gladiator	2000
3	The Matrix	1999
4	There's Something About Mary	1998
5	Titanic	1997
6	Scream	1996
7	Se7en	1995
8	Pulp Fiction	1994
9	Menace II Society	1993
10	A Few Good Men	1992

* Of film; awards are made in late May/early June the following year

At the first-ever MTV Movie Award ceremony, held on 10 June 1992, the "Best Movie" was *Terminator 2: Judgment Day* (1991), which also received accolades in several other categories. These have been modified over the years, but usually include "Best Movie", "Best Male", "Best Female", "Best Breakthrough Performance" (now separately for male and female), "On-screen Duo" (now "On-screen Team"), "Best Villain", "Best Comedic Performance", "Best Song", "Best Kiss", and "Best Action Sequence". Occasional one-off awards have included "Best Dressed", "Best Cameo", and "Best Line". Since the 1996 Awards event, "Best Fight" (first won by Adam Sandler and Bob Barker for *Happy Gilmore*, 1995) has appeared annually, while a new category, "Virtual Performance", for computer-generated characters, was introduced for the films of 2002.

THE 10 LATEST WINNERS OF THE MTV MOVIE AWARD FOR "BEST KISS"

	FILM	KISSERS	YEAR*
1	Jason Biggs, Seann William Scott	American Pie 2	2001
2	Julia Stiles, Sean Patrick Thomas	Save the Last Dance	2000
3	Sarah Michelle Gellar, Selma Blair	Cruel Intentions	1999
4	Joseph Fiennes, Gwyneth Paltrow	Shakespeare in Love	1998
5	Adam Sandler, Drew Barrymore	The Wedding Singer	1997
6	Will Smith, Vivica A. Fox	Independence Day	1996
7	Natasha Henstridge, Anthony Guidera	Species	1995
8	Lauren Holly, Jim Carrey	Dumb and Dumber	1994
9	Demi Moore, Woody Harrelson	Indecent Proposal	1993
10	Marisa Tomei, Christian Slater	Untamed Heart	1992

* Of film

The winners of the first "Best Kiss" award were Anna Chlumsky and Macaulay Culkin for *My Girl* (1991).

Did you know?

At the 1996 MTV Movie Awards, the ham and cheese sandwich in *Smoke* (1995) won the "Best Sandwich in a Movie" award, defeating the turkey club sandwich in *Four Rooms* and the submarine sandwich with tomatoes and provolone in *GoldenEye*.

THE 10 LATEST PEOPLE'S CHOICE "FAVORITE MOTION PICTURE"

	FILM*	YEAR†
1	The Lord of the Rings: The Fellowship of the Ring/ Spider-Man	2003
2	Shrek	2002
3	The Green Mile	2001
4	The Sixth Sense	2000
5	Titanic	1999
6	Jerry Maguire	1998
7	Independence Day	1997
8	Apollo 13	1996
9	Forrest Gump	1995
10	The Firm	1994

* Dramatic Motion Picture prior to 1997
† Of award
The People's Choice Awards began in 1975. The votes, which come from members of the US public and are closely monitored by The Gallup Organization, are un-directed, thus enabling nominations for any eligible film or individual. The criteria for these is different from other awards in that films are not necessarily of the previous year.

As the Crowe Flies
Russell Crowe in the title role of Gladiator, MTV's choice as the top film of 2000.

THE 10 LATEST PEOPLE'S CHOICE "FAVORITE COMEDY"

	FILM	YEAR†
1	My Big Fat Greek Wedding	2003
2	Shrek *	2002
3	Meet the Parents	2001
4	Big Daddy	2000
5	There's Something About Mary	1999
6	Liar Liar	1998
7	The Nutty Professor	1997
8	Dumb & Dumber	1996
9	The Santa Clause	1995
10	Mrs. Doubtfire	1994

* No separate comedy category this year; however, the winner of "Favorite Motion Picture", Shrek, itself was a comedy.
† Of award

THE 10 LATEST PEOPLE'S CHOICE "FAVORITE ACTRESS"

	ACTRESS*	YEAR†
1	Julia Roberts	2003
2	Julia Roberts	2002
3	Julia Roberts	2001
4	Julia Roberts	2000
5	Sandra Bullock	1999
6	Julia Roberts	1998
7	Sandra Bullock	1997
8	Sandra Bullock	1996
9	Jodie Foster	1995
10	Julia Roberts	1994

* Dramatic Motion Picture Actress prior to 1995
† Of award

THE 10 LATEST PEOPLE'S CHOICE "FAVORITE ACTOR"

	ACTOR*	YEAR†
1	Mel Gibson	2003
2	Tom Hanks	2002
3	Mel Gibson	2001
4	Harrison Ford	2000
5	Tom Hanks	1999
6	Harrison Ford	1998
7	Mel Gibson	1997
8	Tom Hanks	1996
9	Tom Hanks	1995
10	Tom Cruise	1994

* Dramatic Motion Picture Actor prior to 1995
† Of award

TOP 10 FAVOURITE WEEPIES*

	FILM	YEAR
1	Titanic	1997
2	Bambi	1942
3	Kramer vs. Kramer	1979
4	E.T. the Extra-Terrestrial	1982
5	Brief Encounter	1946
6	Beaches	1988
7	The Champ	1979
8	The English Patient	1996
9	It's a Wonderful Life	1946
10	Kes	1969

* This list presents the results of a survey of 1,000 British adults conducted in 2000 by tissue manufacturers Kleenex.

THE 10 LATEST WINNERS OF THE MTV MOVIE AWARD FOR "BEST ACTION SEQUENCE"

	FILM	SEQUENCE	YEAR*
1	Pearl Harbor	Attack scene	2001
2	Mission: Impossible 2	Motorcycle chase	2000
3	Star Wars: Episode I – The Phantom Menace	Pod race	1999
4	Armageddon	Asteroid destroying New York City	1998
5	Face/Off	Speedboat chase	1997
6	Twister	Truck driving through farm equipment	1996
7	Braveheart	Battle when Scots first defeat English	1995
8	Speed	Bus escape and airport explosion	1994
9	The Fugitive	Train wreck	1993
10	Lethal Weapon 3	Mel Gibson's motorcycle crash	1992

* Of film
At the first MTV event, the winner in this category was Terminator 2: Judgment Day (1991), for the L.A. freeway chase. The film won a total of six of the categories for which it was nominated.

THE 10 LATEST WINNERS OF THE MTV MOVIE AWARD FOR "BEST VILLAIN"

	VILLAIN	FILM	YEAR*
1	Denzel Washington	Training Day	2001
2	Jim Carrey	Dr. Seuss's How the Grinch Stole Christmas	2000
3	Mike Myers	Austin Powers: The Spy Who Shagged Me	1999
4	Stephen Dorff/ Matt Dillon	Blade/There's Something About Mary	1998
5	Mike Myers	Austin Powers: International Man of Mystery	1997
6	Jim Carrey	The Cable Guy	1996
7	Kevin Spacey	Se7en	1995
8	Dennis Hopper	Speed	1994
9	Alicia Silverstone	The Crush	1993
10	Jennifer Jason Leigh	Single White Female	1992

* Of film
The ceremony held in 1992 saw this somewhat contradictorily titled award going to a role in a film that was released in January 1992 itself: Rebecca De Mornay in The Hand That Rocks the Cradle.

THE 10 WORST OF 1953 – HARVARD LAMPOON

FILM
1 The Robe
2 Salome
3 Beneath the 12 Mile Reef
4 Hondo
5 Torch Song
6 Call Me Madam
7 How to Marry a Millionaire
8 Easy to Love
9 I, the Jury
10 Gentlemen Prefer Blondes

Harvard Lampoon, America's oldest humour magazine, has been awarding its annual anti-accolades since 1939, when, as well as a Top 10, it identified *The Wizard of Oz* as the "Most Colossal Flop".

THE 10 WORST OF 1954 – HARVARD LAMPOON

FILM
1 Haaji Baba
2 There's No Business Like Show Business
3 The Egyptian
4 The High and the Mighty
5 Magnificent Obsession
6 Beau Brummel
7 The Student Prince
8 Knights of the Round Table
9 Demetrius and the Gladiators
10 White Christmas

THE 10 WORST OF 1955 – HARVARD LAMPOON

FILM
1 Not As a Stranger
2 Ulysses
3 The Prodigal
4 Hit the Deck
5 The Tall Men
6 The Rains of Ranchipur
7 Battle Cry
8 The Last Time I Saw Paris
9 The Long Grey Line
10 Underwater!

Underwater! is notable for its press premiere, when it was screened at the bottom of Silver Springs lake, Florida, to 150 journalists wearing aqualungs.

THE 10 WORST OF 1956 – HARVARD LAMPOON

FILM
1 The Ten Commandments
2 Alexander the Great
3 Trapeze
4 The Benny Goodman Story
5 Gaby
6 Serenade
7 Bhowani Junction
8 Miracle in the Rain
9 The Vagabond King
10 The Proud and the Profane

THE 10 WORST OF 1957 – HARVARD LAMPOON

FILM
1 Raintree County
2 The Pride and the Passion
3 Peyton Place
4 Island in the Sun
5 Jeanne Eagels
6 Funny Face
7 The Hunchback of Notre Dame
8 The Sun Also Rises
9 Pal Joey
10 April Love

THE 10 WORST OF 1958 – HARVARD LAMPOON

FILM
1 South Pacific
2 The Vikings
3 The Roots of Heaven
4 The Last Hurrah
5 Marjorie Morningstar
6 The Buccaneers
7 The Big Country
8 The Old Man and the Sea
9 A Certain Smile
10 Windjammer

THE 10 WORST OF 1959 – HARVARD LAMPOON

FILM
1 The Best of Everything
2 The Miracle
3 Career
4 Never So Few
5 Solomon and Sheba
6 The Tempest
7 A Summer Place
8 They Came to Cordura
9 Say One for Me
10 Hercules

THE 10 WORST OF 1960 – HARVARD LAMPOON

FILM
1 Butterfield 8
2 Strangers When We Meet
3 The Gazebo
4 Ice Palace
5 Exodus
6 It Started in Naples
7 Pepe
8 Pollyanna
9 Because They're Young
10 High Time

THE 10 WORST OF 1961 – HARVARD LAMPOON

FILM
1 = King of Kings
  = Parrish
3 By Love Possessed
4 The Devil at 4 O'Clock
5 The Last Sunset
6 The Young Doctors
7 Ada
8 Flower Drum Song
9 Babes in Toyland
10 Sergeants Three

Dolls' House

Valley of the Dolls was critically slated, but like Jacqueline Susann's novel – the bestselling of all time – on which it was based, it was a huge success, earning $44 million at the US box office.

THE 10 WORST OF 1962 – HARVARD LAMPOON

FILM

1 The Chapman Report
2 If a Man Answers
3 Hemingway's Adventures of a Young Man
4 Diamond Head
5 The Wonderful World of the Brothers Grimm
6 White Slave Ship
7 Mutiny on the Bounty
8 Taras Bulba
9 Barabbas
10 = The Mongols
   = The Tartars
   = The Huns

THE 10 WORST OF 1963 – HARVARD LAMPOON

FILM

1 Cleopatra
2 The V.I.P.'s
3 The Prize
4 It's a Mad, Mad, Mad, Mad World
5 How the West Was Won
6 Heavens Above!
7 55 Days at Peking
8 Act One
9 = The Birds
  = Bye Bye Birdie

Elizabeth Taylor's $1 million fee and $194,800 spent on her 65 costumes alone contributed to *Cleopatra*'s reputation as the biggest-budget film of all time. Initially a commercial flop, it ultimately recouped its massive investment.

THE 10 WORST OF 1964 – HARVARD LAMPOON

FILM

1 = The Greatest Story Ever Told
  = The Carpetbaggers
  = Sylvia
  = Cheyenne Autumn
  = Station Six-Sahara
  = Kiss Me, Stupid
7 The Outrage
8 The Fall of the Roman Empire
9 One Potato, Two Potato
10 Youngblood Hawke

The Greatest Story Ever Told miscast John Wayne as a Roman centurion. His sole line, "Truly, this man was the son of God", was delivered with his characteristic Western drawl.

THE 10 WORST OF 1965 – HARVARD LAMPOON

FILM

1 The Sandpiper
2 The Hallelujah Trail
3 Lord Jim
4 What's New, Pussycat?
5 The Agony and the Ecstasy
6 Shenandoah
7 Genghis Khan
8 Thunderball
9 The Great Race
10 The Yellow Rolls Royce

Peter O'Toole appeared in no fewer than three of this year's "Worst Films": *The Sandpiper*, *Lord Jim*, and *What's New, Pussycat?*

THE 10 WORST OF 1966 – HARVARD LAMPOON

FILM

1 Is Paris Burning?
2 Hurry Sundown
3 The Oscar
4 The Fortune Cookie
5 The Bible
6 A Countess from Hong Kong
7 The Blue Max
8 Fantastic Voyage
9 Torn Curtain
10 Penelope

Despite appearing in this list, *The Fortune Cookie* gained Walter Matthau the "Best Actor" Oscar, while *Fantastic Voyage* won awards for its sets and special effects.

THE 10 WORST OF 1967 – HARVARD LAMPOON

FILM

1 Guess Who's Coming to Dinner
2 Valley of the Dolls
3 Up the Down Staircase
4 One Million Years BC
5 The Comedians
6 Reflections of a Golden Eye
7 Thoroughly Modern Millie
8 Doctor Dolittle
9 The Fox
10 Carmen Baby

THE 10 WORST OF 1968 – HARVARD LAMPOON

FILM

1 The Lion in Winter
2 Ice Station Zebra
3 Rosemary's Baby
4 Star!
5 The Boston Strangler
6 Candy
7 Barbarella
8 You Are What You Eat
9 The Seagull
10 Boom!

THE 10 WORST OF 1969 – HARVARD LAMPOON

FILM

1 Easy Rider
2 Medium Cool
3 Putney Swope
4 Bob & Carol & Ted & Alice
5 Topaz
6 The Maltese Bippy
7 True Grit
8 John and Mary
9 Hello, Dolly!
10 Last Summer

10 TOP WORST FILMS

THE 10 WORST OF 1970 – HARVARD LAMPOON

FILM
1 Love Story
2 Airport
3 Patton
4 Joe
5 Soldier Blue
6 Getting Straight
7 The Strawberry Statement
8 Little Fauss and Big Halsey
9 Julius Caesar
10 The Statue

Every new intake of Harvard freshmen is shown *Love Story*, at the top of this year's list, and encouraged to heckle it.

THE 10 WORST OF 1971 – HARVARD LAMPOON

FILM
1 A Clockwork Orange
2 Carnal Knowledge
3 Summer of '42
4 Fiddler on the Roof
5 The Last Movie
6 T.R. Baskin
7 Kotch
8 Willard
9 The Music Lovers
10 Dealing

Along with *Midnight Cowboy* (which won), *A Clockwork Orange* was one of only two X-rated films nominated for a "Best Picture" Oscar. Its director Stanley Kubrick had it withdrawn from release until after his death.

THE 10 WORST OF 1972 – HARVARD LAMPOON

FILM
1 Last Tango in Paris
2 The Candidate
3 The Getaway
4 Sounder
5 Deliverance
6 Play It As It Lays
7 The Emigrants
8 What's Up, Doc?
9 Man of La Mancha
10 The Man

Notwithstanding the *Lampoon's* verdict, *Last Tango in Paris*, *Deliverance*, and *The Emigrants* all received "Best Director" Oscar nominations, while *Sounder* was nominated for "Best Picture".

THE 10 WORST OF 1973 – HARVARD LAMPOON

FILM
1 The Great Gatsby
2 Day of the Dolphin
3 Jonathan Livingston Seagull
4 The Seven-Ups
5 A Touch of Class
6 Blume in Love
7 The Way We Were
8 The Exorcist
9 Save the Tiger
10 American Graffiti

This year's Top (or bottom) 10 included *The Exorcist*, which was actually the highest-earning film of the year, and *Save the Tiger*, for which Jack Lemmon won the "Best Actor" Oscar.

THE 10 WORST OF 1974 – HARVARD LAMPOON

FILM
1 Lenny
2 S*P*Y*S
3 Harry and Tonto
4 Airport 1975
5 Blazing Saddles
6 The Night Porter
7 The Trial of Billy Jack
8 Murder on the Orient Express
9 Daisy Miller
10 The Front Page

Blazing Saddles, *The Trial of Billy Jack*, *Airport 1975*, and *Murder on the Orient Express* were among the 10 highest-earning films of the year.

THE 10 WORST OF 1975 – HARVARD LAMPOON

FILM
1 Barry Lyndon
2 Tommy
3 At Long Last Love
4 The Other Side of the Mountain
5 The Hindenburg
6 The Day of the Locust
7 The Story of O
8 Mahogany
9 Shampoo
10 Once Is Not Enough

Brenda Vaccaro received a "Best Supporting Actress" Oscar nomination for her role in *Once Is Not Enough*, based on Jacqueline Susann's novel.

THE 10 WORST OF 1976 – HARVARD LAMPOON

FILM
1 A Star Is Born
2 The Enforcer
3 Murder by Death
4 Slapshot
5 The Omen
6 Lipstick
7 Mikey and Nicky
8 The Missouri Breaks
9 Car Wash
10 King Kong

Following *Hello, Dolly!*, *What's Up, Doc?*, and *The Way We Were*, *A Star Is Born* became the fourth Barbra Streisand film to appear in these lists.

THE 10 WORST OF 1977 – HARVARD LAMPOON

FILM
1 Looking for Mr. Goodbar
2 It's Alive
3 The Turning Point
4 A Nightful of Rain
5 New York, New York
6 Coming Home
7 Oh, God
8 Semi-Tough
9 The Goodbye Girl
10 The Gauntlet

Cult horror film *It's Alive* had actually been released three years earlier; by the time it was included, its sequel *It Lives Again* had also been made.

THE 10 WORST OF 1978 – HARVARD LAMPOON

FILM
1 Sgt. Pepper's Lonely Hearts Club Band
2 Rabbit Test
3 Interiors
4 Superman
5 Foul Play
6 Up in Smoke
7 F.I.S.T.
8 Magic
9 Ice Castles
10 Same Time, Next Year

Joan Rivers' sole venture into directing led to *Rabbit Test*, a comedy about a pregnant man.

THE 10 WORST OF 1979 – HARVARD LAMPOON

FILM
1 Manhattan
2 The Muppet Movie
3 The Amityville Horror
4 Apocalypse Now
5 10
6 All That Jazz
7 Rocky II
8 1941
9 The Rose
10 Star Trek: The Motion Picture

Steven Spielberg's *1941* was one of his few disasters, failing to recoup its $35 million budget.

THE 10 WORST OF 1980 – HARVARD LAMPOON

FILM
1 Xanadu
2 Altered States
3 The Blue Lagoon
4 Dressed to Kill
5 The Jazz Singer
6 9 to 5
7 Yanks
8 Fame
9 Flash Gordon
10 The First Family

Musical extravaganza *Xanadu* cost $20 million to make but was a flop, whereas *9 to 5* was the second highest-earning film of the year.

THE 10 WORST OF 1981 – HARVARD LAMPOON

FILM
1 On Golden Pond
2 Tarzan, the Ape Man
3 Superman II
4 Stripes
5 History of the World, Part I
6 The Fox and the Hound
7 Arthur
8 Reds
9 The Great Muppet Caper
10 Raiders of the Lost Ark

Henry Fonda and Katharine Hepburn won "Best Actor"/"Best Actress" Oscars for *On Golden Pond*.

THE WORST OF 1982 – HARVARD LAMPOON
10

	FILM
1	Star Trek II: The Wrath of Khan
2	The Verdict
3	E.T. the Extra-Terrestrial
4	Gandhi
5	An Officer and a Gentleman
6	Missing
7	Tootsie
8	Rocky III
9	Annie
10	Conan the Barbarian

In the penultimate year of its annual list, *Harvard Lampoon* included nine of the 20 highest- earning films of the year.

THE WORST OF 1983 – HARVARD LAMPOON*
10

	FILM
1	Silkwood
2	Terms of Endearment
3	Mr. Mom
4	Sudden Impact
5	National Lampoon's Vacation
6	Broadway Danny Rose
7	Return of the Jedi
8	Twilight Zone: The Movie
9	Yentl
10	Flashdance

* This was the last year the *Harvard Lampoon* published its awards on an annual basis, although there were partial revivals for the films of 1990 and 1992, and a "10 Worst" list was issued for 1994.

Axe to grind

One Oscar-winner portrays another: Faye Dunaway as Joan Crawford in camp classic *Mommie Dearest*, winner of five Razzie Awards, and later selected as the "Worst Film of the Decade".

THE GOLDEN RASPBERRIES' WORST FILMS OF THE 1980s
10

	FILM	YEAR
1	Can't Stop the Music	1980
2	Mommie Dearest	1981
3	Inchon!	1982
4	The Lonely Lady	1983
5	Bolero	1984
6	Rambo: First Blood Part II	1985
7	Howard the Duck/Under the Cherry Moon	1986
8	Leonard: Part 6	1987
9	Cocktail	1988
10	Star Trek V	1989

Founded by film critic and writer John J.B. Wilson, the Golden Raspberry Award Foundation™ has been presenting its annual awards, popularly known as the "Razzies", since 1980. A parody of such established awards as the Oscars, it includes numerous categories, receiving special publicity for its winning worst films (or "cinematic stinkers"), actors, and actresses. In keeping with the spirit of the event, the award itself consists of a plastic raspberry atop a reel of Super-8 film, spray-painted gold.

THE GOLDEN RASPBERRIES' WORST FILMS OF THE 1990s
10

	FILM	YEAR
1	The Adventures of Ford Fairlane/ Ghosts Can't Do It	1990
2	Hudson Hawk	1991
3	Shining Through	1992
4	Indecent Proposal	1993
5	Color of Night	1994
6	Showgirls	1995
7	Striptease	1996
8	The Postman	1997
9	Burn Hollywood Burn	1998
10	Wild Wild West	1999

The winners in the 21st century have been: *Battlefield Earth* (2000), *Freddy Got Fingered* (2001), and *Swept Away* (2002).

Did you know?

The Golden Raspberries selected *Showgirls* (1995) as the worst picture of the decade. Among its record seven awards, "Worst Director" Paul Verhoeven became the first winner to accept his prize in person.

THE 10 HARVARD LAMPOON'S "WORST ACTORS" OF THE 1950S

	ACTOR	FILM	YEAR
1	Clifton Webb	Cheaper By the Dozen	1950
2	Robert Taylor	Quo Vadis?	1951
3	Jerry Lewis	Sailor Beware, Jumping Jacks, etc	1952
4	Victor Mature	The Robe	1953
5	Tony Curtis *		1954
6	Kirk Douglas	Ulysses/ Indian Fighter	1955
7	Gregory Peck	Moby Dick	1956
8	Rock Hudson	A Farewell to Arms	1957
9	Kirk Douglas	The Vikings	1958
10	Sal Mineo	Tonka	1959

* No film identified – The Roscoe Award was presented to Tony Curtis "… whose marcelled and Mobil-greased locks have titillated scores of bobby-soxers".
Winners during the early years of the *Lampoon*'s awards were: 1939 Tyrone Power for *The Rains Came*; 1945 Van Johnson for *Thrill of a Romance*; 1946 Orson Welles for *The Stranger*; 1948 Burt Lancaster for *I Walk Alone*, and 1949 Gregory Peck for *The Great Sinner*. In 1952, when Jerry Lewis received this award and his film partner Dean Martin was identified for "Worst Support Male Performance", the *National Lampoon* received a record number of complaints.

THE 10 HARVARD LAMPOON'S "WORST ACTORS" OF THE 1960s

	ACTOR	FILM	YEAR
1	Frank Sinatra	Can-Can	1960
2	Richard Beymer	West Side Story	1961
3	Charlton Heston	Diamond Head/ The Pigeon That Took Rome	1962
4	Burt Lancaster	The Leopard/ Seven Days in May	1963
5	James Franciscus	Youngblood Hawke	1964
6	No award		1965
7	George Peppard	The Blue Max	1966
8	Richard Burton	Doctor Faustus/ The Comedians	1967
9	Sidney Poitier	For Love of Ivy	1968
10	Peter Fonda	Easy Rider	1969

THE 10 HARVARD LAMPOON'S "WORST ACTORS" OF THE 1970s

	ACTOR	FILM	YEAR
1	Elliott Gould *	Getting Straight	1970
2	Jack Nicholson	Carnal Knowledge	1971
3	Robert Redford	The Candidate	1972
4	Jack Lemmon	Save the Tiger	1973
5	Burt Reynolds	The Longest Yard	1974
6	Ryan O'Neal	Barry Lyndon	1975
7	Clint Eastwood	The Enforcer	1976
8	Kris Kristofferson	Semi-Tough	1977
9	Warren Beatty	Heaven Can Wait	1978
10	Marlon Brando	Apocalypse Now	1979

* Also for dumping Barbra Streisand
"Worst Actor" awards were presented intermittently in the 1980s and 1990s as follows: 1980 Jack Nicholson for *The Shining*; 1981 Warren Beatty for *Reds*; 1982 Clint Eastwood for *Firefox* and *Honkytonk Man*; 1983 Al Pacino for *Scarface*; 1990 Patrick Swayze for *Ghost* and *Road House*; 1992 Michael Douglas for *Basic Instinct*, and 1994 Eric Stoltz for *Naked in New York*.

One in the Eye for Kirk

The *National Lampoon* picked Kirk Douglas as the "Worst Actor" of 1958 for his role as warrior Einar in Richard Fleischer's big-budget epic *The Vikings*.

THE 10 GOLDEN RASPBERRIES' "WORST ACTORS" OF THE 1980s

	ACTOR	FILM	YEAR
1	Neil Diamond	The Jazz Singer	1980
2	Klinton Spillsbury	Legend of The Lone Ranger	1981
3	Laurence Olivier	Inchon!	1982
4	Christopher Atkins	A Night in Heaven	1983
5	Sylvester Stallone	Rhinestone	1984
6	Sylvester Stallone	Rambo: First Blood Part II/ Rocky IV	1985
7	Prince	Under the Cherry Moon	1986
8	Bill Cosby	Leonard: Part 6	1987
9	Sylvester Stallone	Rambo III	1988
10	William Shatner	Star Trek V	1989

The Golden Raspberry™ Awards for individual actors were inaugurated for films of 1980. In 1990, Sylvester Stallone was singled out as the "Worst Actor of the Decade" for *Cobra*, *Lock Up*, *Meet Me Half Way*, *Rambo: First Blood Part II*, *Rambo III*, *Rocky IV*, *Rhinestone*, and *Tango & Cash*.

THE 10 GOLDEN RASPBERRIES' "WORST ACTORS" OF THE 1990s

	ACTOR	FILM	YEAR
1	Andrew Dice Clay	The Adventures of Ford Fairlane	1990
2	Kevin Costner	Robin Hood: Prince of Thieves	1991
3	Sylvester Stallone	Stop! Or My Mom Will Shoot	1992
4	Burt Reynolds	Cop and a Half	1993
5	Kevin Costner	Wyatt Earp	1994
6	Pauly Shore	Jury Duty	1995
7	Tom Arnold/	Big Bully/Carpools/ The Stupids	
	Pauly Shore	Bio-Dome	1996
8	Kevin Costner	The Postman	1997
9	Bruce Willis	Armageddon/ Mercury Rising/ The Siege	1998
10	Adam Sandler	Big Daddy	1999

Subsequent winners have been: 2000 John Travolta for *Battlefield Earth*; 2001 Tom Green for *Freddy Got Fingered*, and 2002 Roberto Benigni for *Pinocchio* (with special mention to Breckin Meyer, who dubbed his voice for the English-language release). "Worst Actor" winner Tom Green – whose *Freddy Got Fingered* picked up other Razzies, including "Worst Picture", "Worst Director", and "Worst Screenplay" – was the first ever to dare to show up in person to collect his award.

THE 10 HARVARD LAMPOON'S "WORST ACTRESSES" OF THE 1950s

	ACTRESS	FILM	YEAR
1	Elizabeth Taylor	The Conspirators	1950
2	Corinne Calvet	On the Riviera	1951
3	Marilyn Monroe	Niagara	1952
4	Terry Moore	Beneath the 12 Mile Reef	1953
5	Grace Kelly *		1954
6	Debbie Reynolds	Hit the Deck/ Susan Slept Here	1955
7	Jennifer Jones	The Man in the Grey Flannel Suit	1956
8	Kim Novak	Jeanne Eagels/ Pal Joey	1957
9	Rita Hayworth	Separate Tables	1958
10	Lana Turner	Imitation of Life	1959

* No film identified – The Roscoe Award was presented to Grace Kelly as "Ironclad Virgin of 1954"
The *Harvard Lampoon* presented the first of its "Worst Actress" awards, for films released in 1939, to Norma Shearer for *Idiot's Delight*. Awards were intermittent during the War years, but in 1941 Betty Grable received a "Worst Performer" award. They were resumed in 1945, when June Allyson won for *Her Highness and the Bellboy*. Subsequent 1940s winners were: 1946 Alexis Smith for *Night and Day*; 1948 Lana Turner for *The Three Musketeers* and Shirley Temple for *Fort Apache*; and 1949 Shirley Temple for *Mr. Belvedere Goes to College*.

THE 10 HARVARD LAMPOON'S "WORST ACTRESSES" OF THE 1960s

	ACTRESS	FILM	YEAR
1	Eva Marie Saint	Exodus	1960
2	Susan Hayward	Ada/ Back Street	1961
3	Jane Fonda	The Chapman Report	1962
4	Debbie Reynolds	How the West Was Won/Mary, Mary	1963
5	Carroll Baker	The Greatest Story Ever Told/The Carpetbaggers/ Sylvia/Cheyenne Autumn/Station Six-Sahara	1964
6	No award		1965
7	Ursula Andress	Casino Royale	1966
8	Raquel Welch	One Million Years BC/ The Biggest Bundle of Them All/ Bedazzled	1967
9	Barbra Streisand	Funny Girl	1968
10	Jane Fonda *	Spirits of the Dead	1969

* Also for marrying Roger Vadim

THE 10 HARVARD LAMPOON'S "WORST ACTRESSES" OF THE 1970s

	ACTRESS	FILM	YEAR
1	Ali MacGraw	Love Story	1970
2	Candice Bergen	T.R. Baskin	1971
3	Ali MacGraw	The Getaway	1972
4	Barbra Streisand	The Way We Were	1973
5	Julie Andrews	The Tamarind Seed	1974
6	Diana Ross	Mahogany	1975
7	Barbra Streisand	A Star Is Born	1976
8	Marthe Keller	Black Sunday	1977
9	Jane Fonda	Coming Home/ Comes a Horseman/ The China Syndrome	1978
10	Jane Fonda	The Electric Horseman	1979

The *Harvard Lampoon* continued to present its "Worst" awards into the 1980s and occasionally during the 1990s. Subsequent actress recipients of the award included: 1980 Shelley Duvall for *Popeye*; 1981 Katharine Hepburn for *On Golden Pond*; 1982 Meryl Streep for *Sophie's Choice*; 1983 Natalie Wood for *Brainstorm*; 1990 Bette Midler for *Beaches*; 1992 Lorraine Bracco for *Medicine Man*; and 1994 Moira Kelly for *With Honors* and Patricia Arquette for *True Romance*.

THE 10 GOLDEN RASPBERRIES' "WORST ACTRESSES" OF THE 1980s

	ACTRESS	FILM	YEAR
1	Brooke Shields	The Blue Lagoon	1980
2	Bo Derek/ Faye Dunaway	Tarzan, The Ape Man/ Mommie Dearest	1981
3	Pia Zadora	Butterfly	1982
4	Pia Zadora	The Lonely Lady	1983
5	Bo Derek	Bolero	1984
6	Linda Blair	Night Patrol/Savage Island/Savage Streets	1985
7	Madonna	Shanghai Surprise	1986
8	Madonna	Who's That Girl?	1987
9	Liza Minnelli	Arthur 2: On the Rocks/ Rent-A-Cop	1988
10	Heather Locklear	Return of the Swamp Thing	1989

Bo Derek was identified as the "Worst Actress of the Decade" for her performances in *Tarzan, the Ape Man* and *Bolero*, both of which were directed by her husband, John Derek.

THE 10 GOLDEN RASPBERRIES' "WORST ACTRESSES" OF THE 1990s

	ACTRESS	FILM	YEAR
1	Bo Derek	Ghosts Can't Do It	1990
2	Sean Young	A Kiss Before Dying	1991
3	Melanie Griffith	Shining Through/A Stranger Among Us	1992
4	Madonna	Body of Evidence	1993
5	Sharon Stone	Intersection/ The Specialist	1994
6	Elizabeth Berkley	Showgirls	1995
7	Demi Moore	The Juror/ Striptease	1996
8	Demi Moore	G.I. Jane	1997
9	The Spice Girls	Spice World	1998
10	Heather Donahue	The Blair Witch Project	1999

21st-century winners are: 2000 Madonna for *The Next Best Thing*; 2001 Maria Carey for *Glitter*, and 2002 Britney Spears for *Crossroads* tied with Madonna for *Swept Away*. Madonna's latest appearance came on top of previous Razzies that led to her winning the overall award as "Worst Actress of the Century". In achieving this ultimate distinction, she beat competition from nominees Elizabeth Berkley (who had also won "Worst New Star"), Bo Derek, Brooke Shields, and Pia Zadora ("Worst New Star of the Decade").

Author's Acknowledgments

The author would like to thank: Academy of Motion Picture Arts and Sciences (Academy Awards®/Oscars®), Allocine, American Film Institute, American Humane Association, Berlin International Film Festival, Box Office Guru, Box Office Mojo, Box Office Prophets, Box Office Report, British Academy of Film and Television Arts (BAFTAs), British Film Institute, Bureau of Labor Statistics, *Cahiers du Cinéma*, Cannes Film Festival, Christie's, Directors Guild of America, Dodona Research, *Empire*, European Film Academy, Exhibitor Relations Co., Inc., Film Society of Lincoln Center, *Forbes*, Kim Fuller, Golden Raspberry Award Foundation™, Brad Hackley, *Harvard Lampoon*, Hollywood Foreign Press Association (Golden Globes), Stewart Horthy, IMAX® Corporation, International Intellectual Property Alliance, International Motion Picture Alliance, Internet Movie Database, London Film Critics Circle, Lumiere Database, Motion Picture Association of America, Movie Marshal, Movie Times, MRIB, MTV, National Board of Review, National Society of Film Critics, William Nicholson, ACNielsen EDI, The Numbers, Official UK Charts, *People*, People's Choice Awards, Producers Guild of America, Quigley Publishing Company, Dafydd Rees, Patrick Robertson, SCMS, Screen Actors Guild, *Screen Digest*, *Screen International*, ShowBizData, *Sight & Sound*, The Sky is Falling, *Variety*, *Variety International Film Guide*, Venice Film Festival, VSDA VidTrac, WorldwideBoxOffice, Writers Guild of America.

Publisher's Acknowledgments

The publisher would like to thank Jenisa Patel, Simon Wilder, Dawn Young, and Anita Roy.

Picture Credits